Praise for *Pagan Holiday*

"Perrottet succeeds as entertainer. . . . Quite engaging . . . There is not a dull page in this book."
— *The Seattle Times*

"Required reading . . . A charming popular history of ancient Roman sight-seeing."
— *Forbes FYI*

"The single most unexpected revelation in [*Pagan Holiday*] is the understanding of just how little impact two millennia have had on the tourist experience. . . . The fun . . . lies in the juxtaposition of past and present. . . . Entertaining . . . a fascinating travelogue. Perrottet freely admits that this itinerary remains the most popular tourist journey in the world. He makes it easy to see why."
— *The Denver Post*

"A brilliantly researched and beautifully written travel diary and history about tourists, ancient and modern, traipsing around the Mediterranean in search of glorious pasts . . . What makes Perrottet's history so compelling is that while he colorfully re-creates the travel experience, he doesn't gloss over its ironies, economics or politics."
— *Rocky Mountain News*

"Retracing the ancients' strangely familiar steps, Perrottet finds something truly rare: a fresh, funny take on this beaten path."
— *Outside*

"A wonderful, off-beat, illuminating book written by a wonderful, off-beat, illuminating author, *Pagan Holiday* chronicles the original road trip, the ur-journey that sprung a Pandora's box of Kerouacs and wood-paneled cross-country station wagons. A great read!"
— MICHAEL PATERNITI, author of *Driving Mr. Albert*

"Delightful . . . With considerable wit, the author brings contemporary similes into his account, making an amusing and lively, as well as erudite and factually sound, account. . . . For all their misadventures, Tony and Les had a grand time . . . as will the reader."
— *The Washington Times*

"Where else does the past come alive with such play and wit as in this splendidly original book? Here you can learn that ancient Roman tourists would cancel all travel plans if they dreamed about owls or bears; that they would travel all the way to Delphi in Greece, only to ask Apollo's oracle whether or not they had been poisoned; or that the satirist Juvenal was an insomniac thanks to the evening street traffic in Rome. Just enter this volume and enjoy Tony Perrottet's Grand Tour of antiquity."

—NANCY MILFORD,
author of *Savage Beauty* and *Zelda*

"Makes the most of an inspired notion . . . A charming, evocative account . . . A rollicking Roman holiday." —*Kirkus Reviews*

"Just when it seemed certain that travel writers had exhausted the pantheon of destinations, Perrottet offers a fresh perspective—by taking the road most traveled. . . . [Perrottet's] wry personal account blends seamlessly with his historical narrative. . . . [A] real triumph."

—*Publishers Weekly*

"Roll over, Homer. Here's the ancient world as we've never seen it before: through the eyes of the original Roman sightseers, as related by a besieged travel writer. Learned, hilarious, hair-raising—and with the best last line since Joyce's *Ulysses.*"

—JOHN COLAPINTO, contributing editor,
Rolling Stone, and author of *As Nature Made Him*

"Who would've believed that today's camera-toting, fannypacked hordes could be blamed on the ancient Romans? *Pagan Holiday* regales the reader with wonderfully quirky insights about the world's oldest tourists. Perrottet succeeds where most fail—namely, in writing about travel and history in a way that's witty, smart, and fun."

—JASON WILSON, series editor of
The Best American Travel Writing

"A fascinating and often humorous look at a world long gone and the tourist culture that has grown up around it . . . Perrottet's writing sparkles." —*Library Journal*

TONY PERROTTET has written for *The New York Times, Esquire, Outside, Civilization, Islands,* and *The Sunday Times* (London), among other publications. He is Australian and lives in Manhattan with his wife and son.

PAGAN HOLIDAY

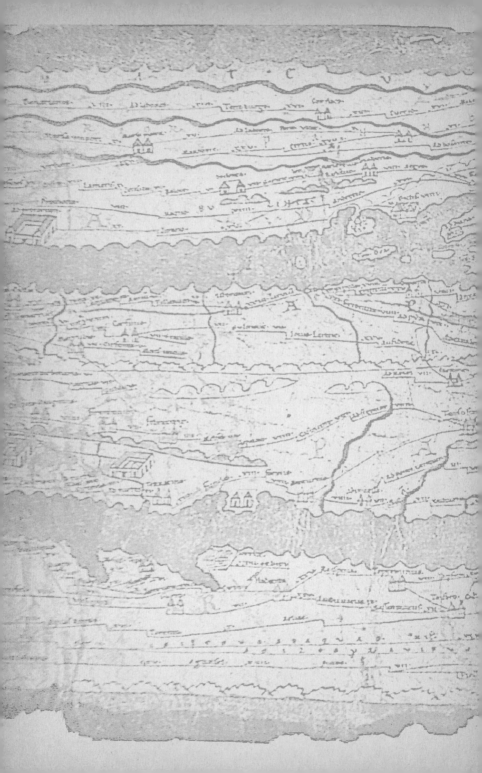

TONY PERROTTET

PAGAN HOLIDAY

On the Trail
of Ancient Roman Tourists

ORIGINALLY PUBLISHED AS *Route 66 A.D.*

RANDOM HOUSE TRADE PAPERBACKS
NEW YORK

2003 Random House Trade Paperback Edition

Copyright © 2002 by Tony Perrottet
Map copyright © 2002 by David Lindroth

This work was originally published in hardcover
by Random House, Inc., in 2002, as Route 66 A.D.

Owing to limitations of space, acknowledgments of permission to
use illustrative material will be found on page 393.

Library of Congress Cataloging-in-Publication Data

Perrottet, Tony.
Route 66 A.D.: on the trail of ancient Roman tourists / Tony Perrottet.
p.   cm.
Includes bibliographical references and index.
0-375-75639-6 (pbk.)
1. Mediterranean Region—Description and travel.   2. Mediterranean
Region—Antiquities.   3. Perrottet, Tony—Journeys—Mediterranean Region.
I. Title: Route 66 A.D.   II. Title.
D973 .P394   2002
909'.09822—dc21   2001048539

Random House website address: www.atrandom.com
Printed in the United States of America

2 4 6 8 9 7 5 3 1

Book design by Carole Lowenstein

For Lesley and Juno,
the ruling divas

Don't you swelter all day in the sun? Aren't you all jammed in with the crowds? Isn't it hard to get a bath? Aren't you soaked to the bone whenever it rains? Don't the din and the shouting and the other petty annoyances drive you completely mad?

But of course you put up with it all because it's an unforgettable spectacle.

—EPICTETUS, Stoic philosopher (c. A.D. 55–135),
querying the pleasures of a journey
to Olympia for the Games

CONTENTS

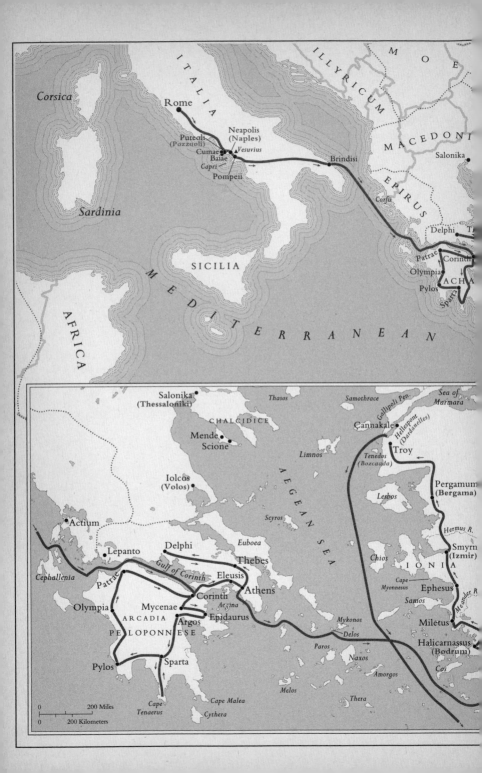

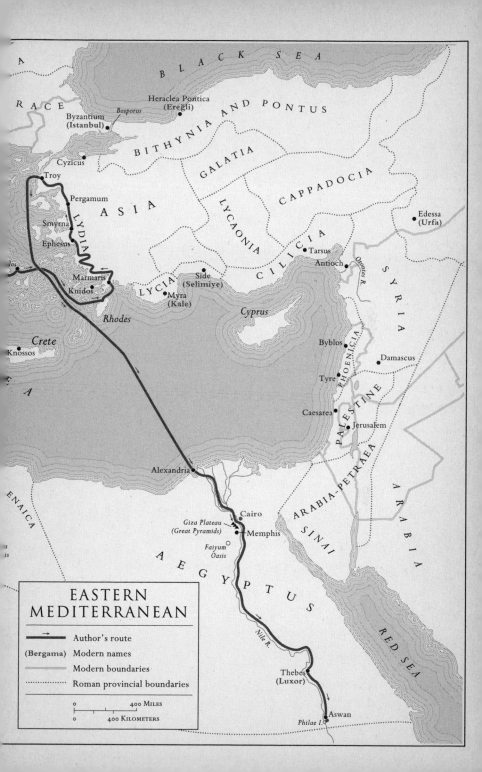

BLACK SEA

THRACE

Heraclea Pontica (Ereğli)

Byzantium (Istanbul)

Bosporus

Cyzicus

BITHYNIA AND PONTUS

GALATIA

CAPPADOCIA

Troy

Pergamum

ASIA

LYDIA

Smyrna

Ephesus

LYCAONIA

CILICIA

Tarsus

Antioch

Edessa (Urfa)

Orontes R.

SYRIA

Marmaris

Knidos

LYCIA

Side (Selimiye)

Myra (Kale)

Cyprus

Rhodes

Crete

Knossos

Byblos

PHOENICIA

Damascus

Tyre

PALESTINE

Caesarea

Jerusalem

Alexandria

ENAICA

Cairo

Giza Plateau (Great Pyramids)

Memphis

Faiyum Oasis

ARABIA-PETRAEA

SINAI

ARABIA

AEGYPTUS

RED SEA

Nile R.

EASTERN MEDITERRANEAN

→ Author's route

(Bergama) Modern names

Modern boundaries

.... Roman provincial boundaries

0   400 MILES

0   400 KILOMETERS

Thebes (Luxor)

Aswan

Philae I.

PART ONE

PAGAN HOLIDAY

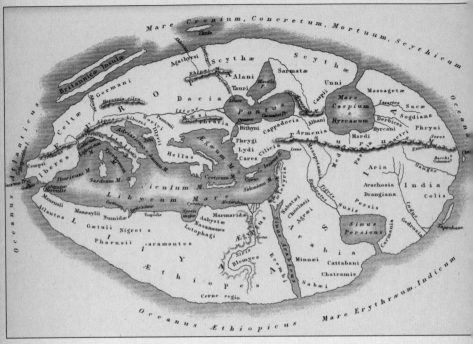

Reconstruction of an ancient Roman world map,
from the *Description* of Dionysius the Guide,
second century A.D.

Jupiter's Panorama

IT MUST HAVE BEEN LIKE a film premiere at Cannes. Throngs of excited spectators filed their way into the heart of Rome, shamelessly ogling the latest fashions and pointing out the celebrities in their midst. An impatient crowd was soon milling outside the venue—an elegant, column-lined arcade called the Vipsania Colonnade, expressly built as a sort of open-air art gallery—where a sensational new opus was about to be unveiled. White-robed priests were busy sacrificing animals to guarantee the ongoing favor of the gods. Choruses of youths sang patriotic anthems. Silver fountains burbled in nearby gardens, while food vendors and beggars noisily worked the crowd. At last, this colorful audience of ancient Romans—everyone from perfumed aristocrats in their silk gowns and brilliant togas to impoverished slum dwellers in their grimy tunics—jostled to the foreground, all trying to have their observations heard above the cacophony.

Looming above them was a dazzling spectacle—a map of the world as large as a drive-in movie screen, showing the three known continents, Europe, Africa, and Asia.

Two thousand years later, it's easy to imagine the frisson of that heady scene—especially if you happen to be, as I was, piecing it together in the fabulous halls of the New York Public Library in midtown Manhattan, a modern-day Roman temple whose interior gleams with marble and ceilings swarm with depictions of the pagan gods. I'd fled there to escape the first heat wave of summer—steam was rising from the sidewalks like the fumes from Hades—and besides, New York reality was starting to close in on me, in more ways than one. But in that silent refuge, surrounded by piles of musty, leather-bound volumes, I found myself easily transported back to that moment in Imperial Rome, circa 5 B.C., when the world's horizons suddenly opened.

Few ancient citizens had even seen a street map before that day, let alone a chart of such divine ambition. The image would have been as futuristic then as the first satellite photos from NASA.

Exhaustive research for the map had been orchestrated by a man named Marcus Agrippa—a Roman war hero who must qualify as one of the great anal retentives of history. In order to measure the world's dimensions, Agrippa had summoned the leading scientists to Rome and provided them with archives full of field coordinates accumulated by the Imperial Army. An elite corps of land surveyors was dispatched to plot every uncharted corner of Rome's domain; in addition, the captain of every ship was required to file charts of the coastlines he had navigated. This new geographical database was then applied to the accepted mythological model of the earth. (Ancient geographers knew the world was round, but believed that terra firma occupied only the northern hemisphere, and was surrounded by the uncrossable river Ocean.)

The result was, not surprisingly, a map of unprecedented accuracy.

The emperor Augustus was presented with a miniature version for his palace; it was engraved in solid gold, with the provincial capitals marked by precious gems. But it was the monolithic image erected in the public colonnade that was the true triumph of Roman ingenuity. Sadly, not a single scrap has survived, although the tantalizing remarks of Latin authors allow us to speculate that it stretched sixty feet along the arcade and rose to thirty feet in height. The details may have been applied in pigment, but quite possibly it was one of the fabulous "paintings in stone" then fashionable in Rome—an interlocking pattern of polished marble, amethyst, and alabaster, with each piece carved in topographical relief by Greek craftsmen.

To the crowd gathered in the colonnade that day, nothing could have been more enlightening.

For a start, Romans discovered that the land masses of the earth together formed an oval shape. The three continents, Europe, Africa, and Asia, all clustered around the Mediterranean—which was then a Latin lake, identified simply as Mare Nostrum (our sea). In fact, Roman hearts must have swelled with pride to see the sheer size of Caesar's domain: The imperial eagles flew all the way from the Pillars of Hercules (Gibraltar) to the seven mouths of the Nile.

Rome had been chosen by the gods to rule over all of creation. One glance at Agrippa's Map (as it was known) proved that the task was largely complete.

Despite its distortions—remote lands like India were drawn largely from hearsay, while the frontiers were roamed by legendary Amazons, Troglodytes, and Lice-Eaters—the Map marked a revolution in the Western perception of the world. Carved onto that sprawling stone canvas was every known river, every mountain range, every port, and every city (one Roman pedant consulting it in A.D. 70 was even able to identify an obscure provincial outpost named Charax, a mile and a quarter from the Persian Gulf). But what made the image strikingly *modern*—and truly compelling for that Roman audience—was its practical application. The Empire's glorious highway system—Rome's pride and joy—was chiseled across its surface, the routes spreading like hardened arteries to the farthest corners of civilization. Major sea lanes could be identified, crisscrossing the Mediterranean blue. And just for good measure, the showboating general Agrippa had written a geographical commentary to accompany his masterwork, with the entire voluminous text inscribed on marble tablets along the nearby walls of the arcade. A library of facts and figures was now placed at citizens' disposal—handy data like the lengths of important rivers (Danube: 560 Roman miles), the physical dimensions of provinces (Illyria: 325 by 530 miles), circumferences of prominent islands (Sicily: 618 miles), and the distances between cities.

For the first time in history, a population had the world laid out before it like a buffet. Not only could viewers locate a famous site—the Colossus of Rhodes, say, or the ruins of Troy—but they could determine its exact distance from Rome and the best travel route to reach it.

And with every inch of the route under Caesar's protection, the Map's message was clear: The world was the Romans' oyster. Plan your holiday now.

The first age of tourism had begun.

ROMANS ON THE ROAD

Ensconced in the library, with a mountain of arcane texts piling around me, I delved more deeply into the ancient travel bug. And in fact, for centuries after Agrippa's Map was unveiled, legions of Romans were inspired to follow its exotic allure. The most surprising thing was how familiar their journeys were: As their memoirs, plays, and letters home revealed, these trailblazing sightseers sought out many of the same attractions, enjoyed many of the same pleasures—and suffered many of the same indignities—as modern travelers do today.

Across the entire Mediterranean world, an elaborate tourist infrastructure, anticipating our contemporary version, emerged to cater to the Romans' distinctive needs. They stayed at roadside inns, complained about hard mattresses and bad service, ate at dubious restaurants, got drunk in smoke-filled taverns, and wrote poems about their hangovers. The ancient sightseers visited lavish temples—the equivalent of our modern museums, crowded with wondrous artifacts—and handed over hefty donations to shyster priests for a glimpse of a Gorgon's hair, a Cyclops's skull, or Ulysses' sword. Just like us, they sought out celebrated historic landmarks like the Parthenon and the Pyramids. But inspiring far more enthusiasm from these ancient wanderers were the sites of mythic lore—the spot where the god Jupiter had come to earth, Venus had bewitched a mortal, or the hero Achilles had killed Hector in the *Iliad*.

The parallels became even more striking within the tourist enclaves, I discovered. Clustering around these growing tourist attractions were hordes of professional tour guides—called *mystagogi* (those who show sacred places to foreigners)—and it seems that the Romans were just as exasperated by their endless prattle as we are today. ("Jupiter, protect me from your guides at Olympia!" prayed a roving academic named Varro, "and you, Athena, from yours at Athens!") The pioneering tourists bought cheesy souvenirs wherever they went, such as painted glass vials showing the Lighthouse of Alexandria or miniature statues of Apollo, and they commissioned portraits by local artists, with famous sites in the background. They pored over guidebooks written on papyrus scrolls, and even etched graffiti onto their favorite monuments. It's still there, alongside more recent efforts such as BRIG-GENERAL MAUGHAM 1820 and HARRY POTTER RULES 2001. (The erudite ancients often preferred to inscribe Homeric verse, although the most popular shorthand scrawl was the rhapsodic I WAS AMAZED.)

And the Romans gladly paid for a good floor show. Crowd-pleasing Egyptian priests kept crocodiles in a pond and at scheduled times fed them morsels of flesh, squirted wine into their mouths, and then hand-polished their sharp teeth. Spartans showed off their macho prowess, sorcerers conjured, oracles pronounced. In Aswan, Egypt, enterprising boatmen took tourists on rides along the Nile, rather as they do today—if the price was right.

As for the reviews, many of the ancient travel experiences echo down the ages—particularly one Roman traveler's comment about the locals of Alexandria: *Unus illis deus Nummus est.* "They worship only one god there—Cash!"

And just like today, the irritations of the road were forgotten on the return home. The happy voyagers would then boast about their trips at banquets, show off their art and souvenirs—and so inspire still more eager sightseers to explore a world saturated by magic and myth.

As for me, I had my own dark reasons to catch that ancient travel bug.

By the time I was on the subway back downtown that night, I was carrying a modern version of Agrippa's Map, with a thin red line scrawled from Rome to Egypt's frontier.

It was time to revive a great tradition.

The Pompeii
McDonald's

SCUSI," my girlfriend, Lesley, was asking anyone who would listen, "where are the penises?"

A valid question in many situations, no doubt, and here in the back alleys of Pompeii, it was being urgently repeated in every known language.

"*Los penes?*"

"*Die Pimmel?*"

"*Les baïonettes?*"

Soon there were dozens of us scouring the walls for ancient etchings of male genitalia, which had once directed drunken sailors to the local brothels. It's now a key ritual for visitors to this fabled Roman port, which was buried under volcanic ash in A.D. 79, and I wasn't going to miss out. Dazed by summer heat, Les and I had already inspected the famous plaster casts of petrified Pompeiians who'd died with expressions of agony and disbelief. We'd wandered the chariot-rutted avenues and admired the fresco-covered villas of gluttonous millionaires. Now we were following the phallic trail into a dark, cramped "wolf house," where above each narrow bed stall a crude painting still survived, of prostitutes graphically advertising their repertoires.

"*Sessantanove,*" explained the old Italian guard gleefully. "You understand? Sixty-nine!"

The pagan ghosts were putting on quite a show. But somehow, vivid as it all should have been, the ancient magic felt strangely elusive to me.

Pompeii, it hardly needs saying, is today's prime destination for anyone even vaguely interested in communing with the Romans, which is why we'd come here on a day trip as soon as we'd arrived in Italy. In fact, its discovery had single-handedly reshaped the modern fascination with antiquity. Before excavations began here in 1748, scholars paid attention only to the Empire's dead white-toga males—all those generals, senators, and poets who ended up as busts in dusty museums. But when Pompeii was uncovered, we were introduced to the far more compelling human details: the Romans' cuisine, décor, hairstyles, perfumes, winemaking, dentistry, sex lives (especially the last—an undying point of human empathy). Nineteenth-century painters conjured scenes from Roman life based on Pompeiian artifacts, all redolent of decadent sensuality; later, Hollywood took up the banner, in immortal epics such as *Ben-Hur, Quo Vadis,* and *Gladiator.*

With actual Romans frozen in such excruciatingly recognizable situations, Pompeii is still celebrated as that thrilling place where time dissolves—an open doorway onto the past, where one can gaze upon the classical world, unmediated and direct.

Fresco in a Pompeii brothel: A prostitute advertises her skills.

There was only one problem—and it seemed a quintessentially modern one: *the hordes.*

Tour groups from every nation on earth were storming down the cobbled streets, their guides waving yellow flags like military mascots and bellowing facts in a babel of tongues. Each time we paused at something of interest, another group would charge toward us, pointing frantically, cameras whirring. Pompeii is Italy's most popular attraction, bigger than Venice's Grand Canal, the Leaning Tower of Pisa, or Michelangelo's *David.* It receives over two million visitors a year, making it feel less like an archaeological site and more like Pompeii World.

Even the lecherous old brothel guard had to keep the human tide moving.

"Signori—out!" he crisply ordered. "Koreans—in!"

Tourism itself has come a long way since the unveiling of Agrippa's Map. It is now officially the world's biggest industry—and the Mediterranean world is still squarely on the front line. At Pompeii, I almost wanted Vesuvius to erupt again, just to freeze in time the mad vignettes— from the twenty-eight air-conditioned coaches lined up by the wire fence ("We'll beat the crowds," I'd predicted) to the virtual riot in the ticket lines (a dozen different currencies were accepted, so arguments over the exchange rates had ground progress to a standstill). Once inside the site, every nation indulged its foibles. There were the drunken Aussies playing rugby in the Roman arena. The French matrons in the amphitheater, testing the acoustics with a rondel of "Frère Jacques." The Japanese mysteriously posing for photos in front of stray dogs. The terrifying German guides bellowing *"Achtung! Raus!"* Not to mention a Pasolini-esque Italian guide, silk jacket hanging debonairly over his shoulders, somehow separated from his group. Unruffled, he was wandering the crowds singing: "Where are my children? I have lost my angels, my children."

Les was doing a sterling job at rising above the hysteria. She valiantly joined the fray, briskly leading the brothel hunt, head down, elbows out.

By the way, Les happened to be three months pregnant. I could only put this uncharacteristic Zen temperament—this newfound ability to ignore crowds—down to her new condition.

As for me, the chaos was stealing from my longed-for Pompeii all its vaunted imaginative power. I was feeling no closer to the ancients here than when I looked at their statues in museums, cold marble busts with eyes hollow and blank, and not a shred of personality.

Of course, I'd expected the Mediterranean to be *popular,* particularly in summer—but the reality was still a shock. The ancients were simply part of a production line whose gears were deafening.

For hour after hour, Pompeii-O-Rama ground on. And then, in midafternoon—just when I thought things couldn't get much worse— Les had a hunger attack.

"I want something's *flesh*!" she announced—one of her million movie lines.

This was the last straw. We were at the farthest end of a vast site, miles from any museum café. Was there some sort of conspiracy against me? I feverishly wondered. Was this whole trip a dreadful mistake? Of course, one of the few things I'd actually learned so far about being pregnant is that getting something to eat—fast—is a nonnegotiable demand.

"No, *no*," the guard warned sternly, as we stood uncertainly at the back exit, gazing at what appeared to be a modern street—if an unusually desolate one.

"If you go there"—he swept his arm like a guardian of the underworld—"you can *not* come back."

And yet, we went—onward, into the shadowy netherworld of New Pompeii.

New Pompeii is the depressed town that lurks on the fringes of its ancient namesake, referred to only in hushed whispers like some mad and unsavory relative locked in the belfry. Its populace has provided the Roman ruin with guards and laborers since the site was discovered 250 years ago, but ancient Pompeii's popularity has not rubbed off. Corrupt and crime-ridden, New Pompeii's existence is not even mentioned in most guidebooks.

To be honest, as we slunk through the sepulchral streets, I could understand why. It was 4 P.M., and the town looked like an abandoned back lot for a spaghetti Western.

Coming so recently from New York, we found the all-powerful Italian siesta still a source of minor culture shock. Needless to say, all the restaurants in town were firmly shuttered. Waiters peered out at us as if we were dangerously insane—foreign junkies, perhaps, dragging themselves out of the gutter for an angry fix. We could have espresso, by all means; gelato by the tub load; even whole baskets of gift-wrapped *biscotti*. But as for *real* food, as Lesley demanded—impossible.

We stumbled on under the merciless sun, past restaurants named Vesuvio, Amphora, Apollo—closed, closed, every place closed—until we both sighted the golden arches of the Pompeii McDonald's.

It was *open*. I hadn't passed beneath the yellow M for fifteen years, but Ronald's nose was shining like the Holy Grail.

Heat-struck but trying to maintain our dignity, we took a plastic booth beside some wax plants and stared up at the glowing menu. I felt that familiar mixture of relief and sinking gloom. Resorting to the Pompeii McDonald's symbolized my defeat as a traveler—on a par with staying at the Hilton in Katmandu. But Lesley was doing her best to convince me that the place had a certain surreal charm. For a start, this was clearly the most happening place in town. *La trattoria americana* was full of teenage Pompeiians, all in pastel designer jeans, hanging out for possibly the same reasons we were: It was cheap. It was air-conditioned. It had food.

"They even have antipasto," Les marveled.

Soon enough, in the spirit of New Pompeii, I was chomping on a delicate *filetto di pesce* and waiting for Les to return from what she would triumphantly declare "the cleanest toilets in Italy." Up on a giant video screen, a hypnotic music clip began playing. Local rockers were dressed up as Roman gladiators. One minute they were stomping across the deck of a sea galley; the next they were riding the winged horse Pegasus across the sky.

If you couldn't get some historical perspective in the Pompeii McDonald's, I thought, where could you?

It slowly began to dawn on me that the ancient world survived in strange and subtle ways.

WHEN WORLDS COLLIDE

Nobody admits to being a tourist these days; it's considered a humiliating, even shameful state (as Evelyn Waugh put it: "The tourist is always the other chap"). And admittedly, seen from up close, the mechanics of the industry can be pretty appalling.

But from a wider perspective—beneath its boisterous veneer—mass tourism today is the purest expression of the tradition that began when Agrippa's Map stood in Imperial Rome.

For those first tourists, the whole *point* of travel was to go where everyone else was going—to see what everyone else was seeing, to feel what everyone else was feeling. There was a virtual checklist of tourist attractions as well as an appropriate response to them. Sight-seeing was a form of pilgrimage.

It's a modern notion of travel to seek out unique and private visions of the world—to be the first to climb the Matterhorn, the only foreigner in Timbuktu. To have mind-blowing adventures, life-altering encounters. To drive across America on recreational drugs with Neal Cassady at the wheel. On returning home, the heroic modern traveler, like some pumped-up porn star, likes to boast of going farther, harder, deeper. Original experience is worn like a badge of honor.

But that initial, ancient impulse to share the accepted wonders of the world has never actually been abandoned, even by those of us who would rather be buried under burning ash than join a bus tour of the Mediterranean. It's an underlying point of connection between the ancient Romans and every traveler wandering the region today. The difference is that those first sightseers accepted the logic of their situation. They were never put off by being part of a crowd. In fact, a certain level of hubbub was an expected part of the project.

As the philosopher Epictetus said of the Olympic Games, the site was jam-packed, hot, noisy, and uncomfortable—but that was a small price to pay for an "unforgettable spectacle."

This had been my mistake! There, among fifty thousand other tourists, the realization hit me with a joyful delirium. Why should I let the multitudes bother me? On the contrary! I embraced them!

To paraphrase Mark Twain in *The Innocents Abroad:* I basked in the happiness of, for once in my life, drifting with the tide of a great popular movement.

Everyone was going to Europe—I too was going to Europe! Everyone was going across the Eastern Mediterranean! I too was going across the Eastern Mediterranean!

By the time Les rejoined me, I had achieved my own version of Zen calm.

I, Spectator

Tourism is a delicate flower that needs a certain degree of political and economic stability to thrive, and the halcyon days of the Pax Romana—roughly 30 B.C. to A.D. 200—is the longest unbroken period of peace that Europe has ever managed. In fact, the first two centuries A.D. form one of Western culture's rare windows of calm—an interlude, in retrospect, of ghostly serenity. Safe transit around the Mediterranean was a unique dividend, and Romans came to accept it as their birthright. In fact, around A.D. *140*, when a celebrated orator named Aelius Aristides announced with Panglossian assurance that humankind was enjoying "the best and most perfect times that ever were," he stressed that the ease of travel was one of Rome's greatest triumphs.

"Cannot every man go wherever he wishes, without fear?" he floridly mused. "Aren't all our harbors busy? Aren't the mountains just as safe as the cities? There are no rivers that have not been bridged, no ocean gulfs that cannot be crossed. Even the sandy road to Egypt presents no obstacles; no terrifying mountain pass, no torrents or savages block the way.

"Homer once prayed: 'The world should be open to all men.' That wish is now realized. To be the Emperor's subject—to be a Roman—is the only passport one needs."

Aristides happily noted that piracy had been stamped out. Highway robbery was rare; barbarian incursions unthought of; civil disturbance all but nonexistent. He went on to suggest, rather less convincingly, that life under Rome was so good that its subjects did not even mind paying taxes.

In some respects, travel has not been so easy since. With the entire Mediterranean politically united for the first—and, so far in history, only—time, citizens had no need to carry documents. The imperial currency (gold *aurei* and silver *sestertii* and *denarii*) was standard in lands the euro has yet to penetrate, from the deserts of Morocco to the border villages in Iraq. Conveniently, the Empire had two common languages: Latin prevailed in the west, Greek in the east. Educated citizens were bilingual and could discuss a dinner menu as easily in Spain as in Syria.

And the sheer volume of Roman *viatores,* or *peregrinatores* (wayfarers), would not be equaled until the modern era. The Empire's great highways, which formed a granite ring road around the entire Mediterranean coast, were in constant use, their stones worn and rutted by the ceaseless passage of iron wheels. The waves were just as busy: "Look at the sea covered with ships!" marveled one author. "There are more men afloat these days than ashore!" Students traveled to famous academies; patients journeyed to health spas; artists were in perpetual motion, seeking out commissions. Celebrity orators like Aristides went on long lecture tours, their performances as wildly popular as those of Wilde and Dickens in the nineteenth-century United States. Athletes flocked to competitions, actors to theater festivals, poets to readings.

But the most distinctive growth was in travel simply for the sake of seeing—tourism. For the first time in history, sheer pleasure became a worthy motive of travel.

THE SOPHISTICATED WAYFARER

To visit sumptuous temples full of treasures and relics, we brave the dangers of land and sea. Greedily seeking the tales of early legend, we travel through every nation . . . happily reliving ancient times, gazing at stones which moved great artists to song and string.

Aetna, *anonymous Roman poem, first century* A.D.

The quest for the marvelous was taken up by Romans as soon as they had the opportunity, and is entirely recognizable to us today.

"Many of us endure all sorts of hardships," intoned the philosopher Seneca in the middle of the first century A.D., "to behold some remote sight. For Nature made us born admirers; her jewels would be lost without an audience." Romans had become both "migratory and curious," noted the scholar Pliny the Younger, setting out en masse to explore their vast domain. And when the author Plutarch remarked with some bemusement on "globe-trotters who spend the best part of their lives in inns and on boats"—gadabouts who continuously "traverse unknown cities, sail new seas, but are at home everywhere"—I felt more than a twinge of familiarity.

Of course, modern travel is a notoriously democratic pursuit, at least within the industrialized world, first experienced most often by near-penniless backpackers. I'd taken my own initial trips during breaks from college, hitchhiking for weeks at a time with a twenty-dollar Wool-worth's tent. Those original Roman tourists were often young—in their twenties and thirties—and usually had a studious, almost pedantic bent. But they were always, by necessity, quite *rich*.

These first lucky wanderers were drawn from what historians refer to for convenience as "the imperial elite." This group, at the peak of the Empire's elaborate social pyramid, included both the traditional Roman blue bloods and aristocrats from the provinces—the well-born peers of Ephesus, Cádiz, Athens, and Marseilles, who had often studied in Rome and lived there for much of their lives. These imperial Brahmins formed a tight-knit, homogeneous caste, immediately recognizable—by their

Roman faces: the so-called Faiyum portraits, preserved for two thousand years in the deserts of Egypt.

choice of dress, their eloquence, their bearing, their hauteur and refinement—to one another and to their inferiors.

Never before had such a large class enjoyed such incredible wealth relative to the rest of society, or such extravagant personal (if not political) freedom as these ancient scions.

The *spectatores* (sightseers) came from every subset of this elite. There were refined youths combining tourism with foreign study ("It is a young man's *duty* to see the world," pronounced one pagan holy man). There were feisty Roman women—art lovers and socialites—who longed to see the Empire. Lawyers, poets, and generals taking a break from their routines. Middle-aged philosophers. Elderly antiquarians. For these ruling-class swells, running into a fellow tourist on the road was always a pleasure: They all knew one another's families, had gossiped about their peccadilloes, and may even have dined together back in Rome. As a group, they moved confidently through the cities of the provinces, taking their enormous privileges for granted.

Wealthy Romans were the first true "citizens of the world"; they were conquerors on tour.

These aristocrats had no real need to work; leisure in ancient times was cultivated as an end in itself. Many *ardeliones* happily frittered their lives away, keeping up a hectic social calendar of drunken banquets like foppish P. G. Wodehouse characters. But for the more intelligent and cultivated Romans, faced with an unprecedented amount of downtime, ennui could actually be a genuine problem.

"Idleness is wont to make men hate their lives," sighed Seneca. Even at the most debauched parties, wrote the poet Lucretius, Romans suffered attacks of melancholy—"a bitterness arose, a pang among the flowers." "Carpe diem," said the poet Horace. But for some, seizing the day meant more than a relentless regime of wine, roast flamingo, and song.

Tourism was an ideal means of using time gainfully, expanding one's education, and establishing the credentials for connoisseurship within that smart social set. Many Romans researched scholarly monographs while on their journeys—on religion, art, astronomy, or history. Some, like five Neoplatonist philosophers who signed graffiti in Egypt, traveled in study groups.

In fact, the Roman tourists were very much like the young European aristocrats of the eighteenth century who embraced the Grand Tour of France and Italy—and the children of American industrialists who continued the European touring tradition with even greater gusto in the nineteenth.

A Sculpture Gallery in Rome at the Time of Augustus *(1867)*,
by Sir Lawrence Alma-Tadema, one of the great historical genre painters
of the Victorian era.

A foreign sojourn was edifying, it was fashionable, it was prestigious. It was little short of a social imperative.

And what were the favorite destinations that satisfied these yearnings? Greece, Asia Minor, and Egypt, said Pliny, were the lands "beloved of the learned."

Much, it might be said, as they remain today.

The
Once and Future
Tourist Trail

OF ALL THE MODERN ECHOES of ancient travel habits, the most striking is that the favorite Roman tourist route remains the most popular trail on earth. In fact, when you map out that original itinerary, it looks like any Marvels of the Mediterranean package today.

It's as if, whenever the same conditions of peace and prosperity are met throughout history, the patterns of tourism reassert themselves with renewed strength, sprouting hydralike from the severed stump of the past.

The Grand Tour of Antiquity began, of course, in Italy. After an emotional farewell to their beloved Rome—travelers would, after all, be away for two to five years—they clattered on iron-wheeled wagons down the Appian Way. They paused at the Bay of Naples, the most fashionable beach resort of the time, whose carnal pleasures put modern Ibiza to shame, before reaching the port at the peninsula's heel. Here passenger boats embarked, just as they do today, toward the east. And it was on board, sails filling in the Adriatic, that the real adventure began.

The ideal Roman circuit can most easily be gathered from Germanicus, the immensely popular grandnephew of the emperor Augustus, who set off on a tour from A.D. 17 to 19. The handsome victor of many bloody campaigns against the German tribes—later idealized as the archetypal noble Roman in Robert Graves's historical novel *I,*

Claudius—Germanicus took advantage of the benefits package that came with his official post as consul, opting to take his wife, Agrippina, and five-year-old son, Gaius (the future Caligula), on an extended sight-seeing junket.

For Germanicus, like every Roman, Greece was the first stop: Those sacred valleys, their olive groves bathed in light, were the very well-springs of civilization. Here, the tourists showed that they were history lovers first and foremost, avidly seeking out all the Greek monuments, graves, temples, and relics that evoked the heroic past. "We are moved in some mysterious way by places which bear the traces of those we admire," wrote one of Cicero's friends, confessing that he found "the favorite haunts of distinguished men" more moving than their writings. The boyishly eager Germanicus found that he could, in the words of Tacitus, "reenact in his own imagination mighty triumphs and mighty tragedies."

But "history" to Romans was never limited to the deeds of mere mortals. The myths and legends born in Greece were just as real to tourists—and their relics far, far more exciting. Whether it was the bones of defeated Titans displayed in temples (probably the thighs of mammoths), the egg that hatched the beautiful Helen (probably an ostrich egg from Africa), or a shadowy grotto said to be frequented by Pan and his nymphs, the touch of the gods was irresistible.

Germanicus visits Athens for the Parthenon and to meet the great philosophers in vine-covered taverns. He goes to Delphi for its oracle; Sparta for its glorious military traditions; and even appears at the world's most illustrious sporting event, the Olympic Games, where he races a chariot around the hallowed stadium where Jupiter had once wrestled the Titan Chronos, and Hercules thrown the discus.

After Greece, Romans followed the siren call of the Aegean—island-hopping east to Rhodes, to inspect the remains of the Colossus (it had fallen in an earthquake two centuries before; today nothing remains).

After cruising the sensual coast of Asia Minor, modern-day Turkey, Germanicus weighs anchor at the site of ruined Troy—the pagan Jerusalem, setting of Homer's *Iliad,* and the most evocative of all ancient tourist sites. He inspects the relics of Trojan heroes, makes sacrifices at the war graves, and is rewarded, apparently, with a vision of Hector's ghost.

From Asia, tourists headed to the most hyped destination of the ancient world: Egypt. Romans were fascinated by this mysterious land and its silent monuments, where shaven-headed priests still worshiped crocodiles, embalmed corpses, and demonstrated sorcery.

From the port of Alexandria, Germanicus bounces on camelback to the Pyramids, then signs on for a Nile cruise to Thebes, modern-day Luxor. In the dizzying heat, he clambers by torchlight into ghoulish tombs and listens to wizened priests tell stories of the Pharaohs—all no doubt intoned in the same solemn voice as that which is used in Luxor's kitschy light-and-sound shows today. At last, he reaches the sacred waterfalls of Isis, at the Empire's frontier: Beyond lies the kingdom of the Ethiopians, whose skin has been burned black by the setting sun—not to mention the cave-dwelling Troglodytes, the blood-drinking Massagetae, and the Blemyes, men with no heads.

Germanicus would have had no reason to doubt these confused reports—after all, those mythical African kingdoms sounded scarcely less fabulous than those he had already seen. But it is unlikely that he felt any urge to investigate.

Romans happily accepted their standard attractions as definitive. They still delighted in the timeworn Seven Wonders—the original "best of" list devised by an unknown scholar in the third century B.C. (and properly known as the Seven Sights, or Things to Be Seen). The first tourists liked to keep to the beaten path. They wanted to behold the pillars of their own culture.

In fact, they created the first Heritage Trail, whose specter would haunt European culture as persistently as any other achievement of the Empire.

THE ETERNAL LODESTAR

Since the end of the Second World War, the Western world has enjoyed the longest stretch of peace since the Pax Romana. When the economic quantum leap of the 1950s and '60s combined with cheap air travel to jump-start mass tourism, its focus was entirely predictable. The Mediterranean had history. It had natural beauty. It had glamour. Its lovely coastline became a testing ground for what would become an international pattern of annual tourist migration.

In fact, the continuities of tourism verge on the monomaniacal. "The grand object of traveling," Samuel Johnson observed, "is to see the shores of the Mediterranean." Then, Rome and Naples were the twin climaxes of the Grand Tour, but the Romantics soon repopularized Greece as the focus of poetic allure. In the nineteenth century, the rediscovery of Troy launched a thousand tourist ships. And when, in 1864,

British entrepreneur Thomas Cook devised the world's first international package tour, it was to that wondrous land so loved by Roman tourists—Egypt. In fact, Mr. Cook settled on the exact itinerary our friend Germanicus had followed in A.D. 19—Alexandria, the Pyramids, a pleasant Nile cruise to the Valley of the Kings. Johnson also observed that anyone who had not been to the famous sights would be "always conscious of an inferiority, from his not having seen what is expected a man should see." The same might be said today. A sojourn in the Med is still a rite de passage, as much as it was for the pioneering Roman wayfarers—it's up there with births, weddings, honeymoons, and funerals.

The problem is, while there were once only a few thousand antiquarians drifting along those spacious ancient shores, the Mediterranean is now a giant whirlpool of a market.

The statistics are dizzying. According to the UN's World Tourism Organization in Madrid, some 700 million people now take foreign trips every year; by the year 2020, the figure will be 1.6 billion. And fully a third of the world's tourists still come to the Mediterranean. At last count, Italy clocks up around 36 million tourists a year. Greece, 12 million. Turkey, 9 million. Egypt, 10 million. And all the favorite Roman destinations—Capri, Rhodes, the pagan sites of Greece, the coast of Turkey, the Pyramids—remain the perennial sight-seeing hot spots.

Which is why, perversely enough, many of us have avoided them all our lives.

Rites of Passage

Today, there are a lot of good reasons to tackle the Mediterranean maelstrom, although your loved one's becoming pregnant probably isn't among them. At least that would be the conventional view. But I present myself as an extreme case study of the contemporary wayfarer, caught between the two opposing traditions of Western travel.

I was one of those people—a typical breed these days—who had been to just about every place on earth *except* the Mediterranean. I'd spent months in Zanzibar, Iceland, and Pago Pago but had never made it to Italy. I'd visited Tierra del Fuego five times but never seen Rome.

To some observers, this seemed vaguely pathological; to others, it made perfect sense. It was the only way to deal with the explosion of modern tourism that—as far as I could gather—had turned every sacred site of Greco-Roman lore into a multi-ring circus.

Of course, when I'd set off on my first round-the-world trip many years ago, I'd had every intention of ending among the sacred sites of antiquity—to gaze at "stones which moved great artists to song and string." I had actually spent long years studying classical history in Sydney, Australia, where I was brought up, and been among the last generation of adolescents to have Latin verbs thrashed into me by deranged Irish-Catholic priests. I'd pored over the Greek poets, even transcribed hieroglyphics. But once I hit the road, there was no chance of my getting anywhere near Rome or Athens. I made it as far as India and stayed for months. One glimpse of Old Delhi convinced me that the world was far too exciting a place to waste any time on the Med.

Those hallowed shores suddenly seemed so predictable and stale. So expensive. So overrun. So picked over. So written about. So . . . *finished*.

How could you see anything new there? Who could look at it afresh?

Instead, I ended up living in South America, wandering the back blocks of Asia, and finally moving to the capital of the Third World, New York. When I started taking trips with Lesley, I still refused to go anywhere near southern Europe. She suggested Venice. We ended up in the Colombian Amazon. Provence sounded charming . . . but Tanzania was where we went.

Like most people, I never gave up on the Mediterranean. I always assumed I'd get around to seeing the Colosseum, the Parthenon, and the Pyramids sometime. But the trip could always wait. It was a lot like the idea of having a kid, in fact. Why do something everyone else is doing? There was always a good reason not to. Always next year, or the next.

Two events shattered this blissful dithering. First, I discovered all that archival data about the ancient Roman tourists—and it occurred to me that a modern traveler could retrace their route with a sort of double vision, seeing the same historical sights and using more or less the same forms of transport. Perhaps it really *was* possible to explore the Med in a way that was vaguely original.

Second, one midsummer's night in our little East Village apartment, Les showed me with some astonishment a little plastic strip that displayed two blue dots instead of one.

Here we were, with one last chance to travel in the old style—just the two of us—before the very act of movement would resemble Napoleon's army breaking camp. And if we had only one big journey left to make, to where else could it be? The choice felt inevitable—like the outcome of that pregnancy test. The most timeworn of trails was beckoning, and it had a certain ring to it: heavy with child in the cradle of civilization.

What's more, the Mediterranean would presumably be easy traveling. After all the Third World hellholes I usually dragged her to, Italy, Greece, Turkey, even Egypt should be a breeze. (Hadn't Germanicus' wife, Agrippina, been pregnant on their journey, and even given birth en route? Hadn't Cleopatra been carrying Julius Caesar's child on their famous cruise down the Nile?)

Lesley—and her obstetrician—had only a couple of small conditions for a second-trimester tour.

"No terror," Les insisted matter-of-factly. "No squalor."

"Sure," I promised, calculating just how little money we had to spend in four months on the road. "No terror. Minimal squalor."

It did occur to me that, even for those wealthy Roman tourists, many of their archetypal travel experiences—like arriving in strange cities, looking for hotels, battling guides, getting lost—were not entirely comfortable. But that has always been part of the challenge.

The Empire
on Ten Denarii
a Day

In september of a.d. 66, coincidentally enough, the emperor Nero himself sailed off to Greece with his wife, Messallina, to savor the pleasures of the Grand Tour. The pair spent over a year to take in the various arts festivals—staying in the lap of luxury, moving around the Greek countryside with a caravan of retainers like a horde of ravening locusts. Formal banquets were prepared at every stop, and the emperor's wine was chilled with snow carried down from local mountains. The Olympic Games were even held a year late to allow Nero to compete; he added poetry reading to the athletic events and, not surprisingly, took home the laurels himself.

Sixty years later, when the restless emperor Hadrian traveled from Rome to the Nile on a six-year-long sojourn—like his peripatetic subjects, he wished "to see with his own eyes all he had read of in any part"—he received almost as lavish treatment. Even lesser VIPs like Germanicus were given royal welcomes from local governors, who personally arranged their sight-seeing tours.

The routine was rather different for the average Roman tourist. Far more typical was the affluent citizen who set off alone—or with a companion or two—and a handful of servants and slaves. These wayfarers had no special entrée to the official circles of power. They had to find inns along the way and whatever dining was available. They had to hire their own local guides and arrange their own wagons, their own berths on ships, their own Aegean cruises.

Which made those Romans on the road true pioneers—the guinea pigs of Western travel—at the mercy of the incipient tourism industry.

POSTCARDS FROM THE PAST

Where can we find the words of these unsung heroes? Before I left New York, I'd filled an extra bag with arcane Latin volumes and photocopied texts. But as any historian admits, when it comes to antiquity, we're working with the merest fragments from a once-vibrant literary culture.

Time has savaged the oeuvres of even the most prominent ancient authors. For example, only half the writings of Tacitus and Cicero survive. Dozens of lesser literary lights are known only by name. (The situation is even worse for the ancient Greek writers so dear to Roman readers: Only a tenth of the plays of Aeschylus are still with us, a mere 7 percent of the works of Sophocles.) And the cultural gap when reading what does remain is vast. The ancient literati are often mind-bendingly dull for modern tastes, their sentences rigid with eye-glazing displays of learning—which is why they often need to be paraphrased, or chopped into literary sound bites, to be digested. Worse, they rarely recorded their own personal emotions or impressions. Accounts of the most lavish scenes can seem oddly clinical—cold data, about as entertaining to read as a shopping list.

Luckily, some Romans could also be hilariously funny about their joys and misadventures on the road; they loved obscene jokes, and had a captivating sense of wonder at their strange world. The fresh observations, juicy comments, and witty asides are scattered through the archives of the world's libraries like silver coins below the shimmering waters of Rome's Fontana di Trevi.

Among the many unexpected gems, we find a travelogue in verse by the literary master Horace, recounting a misbegotten road trip in Italy ("Because of the drinking water, which was horrible, I declare my belly a public enemy and wait, not very happily, while my fellow travelers finish dinner . . ."). There were novels in Greek and Latin, including the lurid *Satyricon,* about a traveler trying to find a cure for impotence in a demimonde of thieves and prostitutes. On a more edifying plane, there was the poet Ovid remembering his youthful wanderings in the Aegean ("Whether we plowed the blue waves in a brightly painted boat, or roamed the countryside in a speeding wagon, our chatter made time pass quickly," he recalled in a letter to his old road companion. "It's a won-

A cinematic depiction of Romans relaxing and unwinding at the baths, from Federico Fellini's 1970 version of Petronius' first-century novel, Satyricon.

derful bond to have braved the sea's perils together—together to have fulfilled our vows to the Gods—to have shared great experiences, and be able to joke about them later . . ."). Among the more practical sources were a copy of the world's oldest guidebook, the *Description of Greece*, dating from the second century A.D.; an ancient highway map of the Empire, reproduced on a scroll over twenty feet long; and a Greek–Latin phrase book intended to show travelers how to behave at the baths. There were lists of graffiti scrawled in the brothels of Ephesus and edited volumes of papyrus letters that had lain for millennia in the town garbage heaps of Egypt. And just to round off the collection was the bizarre biography of a traveling pagan prophet named Apollonius of Tyana ("Even the Gods don't spend all their time in Heaven," Apollonius pompously announced, sounding like an ancient travel agent coming up with a jingle. "They take journeys to Aethiopia, to Olympia, to Mount Athos . . .").

The reports from women tourists, meanwhile, were rare and usually oblique—casual mentions of Germanicus' wife appearing at official dinners, for example, and the graffiti of a centurion in the Valley of the Kings, who signed on behalf of his wife and daughter. There was proof that some feisty Roman women did travel alone: Marcus Agrippa's wife, the spirited and bohemian Julia, went to Troy—but we know about this only because she was nearly drowned in an accident (she was being carried on a covered litter across a raging river) and there was an official furor about the lack of a bridge. There was a Greek comedy skit about two women inspecting a temple-museum, who with a change of scene sound remarkably like two New York grandes dames loudly commenting on the objets d'art in the Met ("My dear! Look at these statues! Why, that naked boy looks like he'd bleed if I scratched him!"). Some references suggest that women even clipped their hair and traveled as men, like the heroines in Shakespeare's comedies. And there may have been many more as feisty as a certain Eppia, who apparently left her husband to travel to Egypt with a rich gladiator. ("She eats dinner with the sailors," the satirist Juvenal noted gleefully, "walks the quarter-deck, and hauls rough ropes like a navvy.")

All in all, there were enough literary shards to vividly reconstruct those Roman journeys and to discern the tourist infrastructure that sprawled across the Empire.

A BED FOR THE NIGHT

The most fundamental element was accommodation—the sine qua non of leisure travel, and in Roman times, no less than today, a matter of inexhaustible variety and interest to tourists.

On the major highways, matters could not have been easier: An elaborate system of roadside inns had been built by the first emperor, Augustus, to help communications through his vast domain. These clean and comfortable hostelries—located twenty-five miles apart, the average day's journey—were designed to accommodate government officials and couriers, but if rooms were available, Roman travelers "of the better sort" were more than welcome to stay. Likewise, at major tourist attractions like Olympia, there were luxurious establishments waiting for new arrivals, with spacious rooms built around leafy courtyards. A recently excavated establishment in Murecine by the Bay of Naples—dubbed by Italian newspapers the Grand Hotel Pompeii—offered suites with colorful frescoes of the Muses, statues of fauns, decent meals from the kitchen, and special quarters for the servants and wagon drivers. The inn even had its own thermal baths.

In large provincial cities an informal old-boys' network supplemented hotels. Roman writers seemed always to be running into drinking partners from their younger days—foreign students who had returned home, or Italians who lived as expats—and hitting them up for hospitality. They presented distant friends of friends with effusive letters of introduction ("Sir, I beg you to look upon this man as if he were myself," began one papyrus). Naturally, this casual approach was hit-or-miss. The novelist Apuleius called on one such contact, but the host turned out to be a "smelly old bore" whose meals were paltry ("I dined only on conversation").

Of course, nobody could rely on friends for every step of a long journey. There were times in smaller towns, excursions along lesser roads, and nights when the comfortable hotels were full. That was when even the very wealthy Romans fell back on the more typical classical inns, insalubrious places often named after animals—the Camel, the Elephant, the Cock, the Crane—with signs accompanied by graphic illustrations and occasionally with advertisements:

> INSIDE, THE GOD MERCURY WILL BLESS YOU WITH WEALTH,
> APOLLO HEALTH, THE OWNER SEPTUANUS FOOD AND A BED.
> NOBODY WILL REGRET WALKING IN THESE DOORS.

Despite such valiant attempts at P.R., the dismal standard of lodging was the single favorite topic of complaint among ancient tourists—a litany of hard straw mattresses, leaky roofs, smoky kitchens, mosquito plagues, and demented innkeepers running informal brothels. Hotel restaurants had an even worse reputation than today's establishments. Rumors were reliably passed on about human flesh being added to stews, with unhappy gourmands finding fingers and knuckle joints in their meals. Another sign warned:

> STRANGER!
> BE CAREFUL WHERE YOU STAY!

It may seem extraordinary that wealthy Romans would tolerate these fleapits for even a single night, but necessity made the affluent flexible. Ancient inns were like the rough-and-ready Elizabethan coaching houses where nobles would often put up on journeys; even in the nineteenth century, European aristocrats accepted the reality of basic lodging when on the road.

And today—well, when you're tackling the Mediterranean on a limited budget, it's best to be prepared for anything.

Lucian Takes
a Sex Tour

Wʜᴀᴛ ᴡᴀs ʙᴇɪɴɢ ᴀɴ ᴀɴᴄɪᴇɴᴛ sɪɢʜᴛsᴇᴇʀ really like? Among so
many shattered fragments lurks an intact travel story attributed to a
Rabelaisian satirist named Lucian, who cruised the coast of Asia Minor
around A.D. 160, stopping at the cultural hot spots en route. Written in
the form of a dialogue, his account provides a sort of "Day in the Life of
an Ancient Tourist"—and happens, as an added gift to posterity, to be
quite funny.

It's set in the port of Knidos, today a lonely ruin on the Turkish coast,
whose opalescent waters are overshadowed by Miami-style summer
resorts at beaches nearby. But in ancient times Knidos was a flourishing
tourist trap. Its big draw was the original X-rated artwork—a sculpture
of Aphrodite, the winsome goddess of love. The sensational *Aphrodite of
Knidos* had been the first female nude in Western art (previously the
Greeks had depicted only male gods naked), and in Lucian's time, more
than five centuries afterward, it was still regarded as the most provocative
depiction of a woman ever made. A mere glimpse of the statue turned
men weak at the knees: Stories abounded of youths trying to grope the
goddess's limbs and smother her face with kisses. (Sadly, the original
sculpture has been lost, but Roman copies can be seen in Naples, the
Louvre, and the Vatican museums, although there is no record of their
inciting the same reaction.)

Lucian made a special point of visiting Knidos with his two unusual
travel companions, young Greeks with the tongue-twisting names of

Charicles and Callicratidas. In his account, Lucian presents his friends as intriguing case studies in contemporary sexual tastes. Most ancient men were what we would consider bisexual—it was considered quite acceptable for adult males to sleep with women or adolescent boys. But the eccentric Charicles was attracted exclusively to women, Callicratidas only to the lads (women he avoided as a "pit of doom").

The pair's debate about the romantic virtues of each sex creates the framework for Lucian's story, called *Affairs of the Heart:* For ancient tourists, every port of call was a chance for intellectual stimulation, and Knidos with its love goddess promised to be a gold mine of material.

Omens for the visit were propitious—Aphrodite herself guided the ship into port with placid winds—and at dawn the next morning, the touristic trio ventured ashore. The merchandisers of Knidos were already busy, cashing in on their city's fame by selling erotic souvenirs. Lucian and his friends "found no little amusement in the wanton products of the potters"—just like tourists in the Aegean today, where gift shops overflow with soft-porn postcards and marble dildos.

At last, the stimulated trio make their way to the splendid Temple of Aphrodite. Like all ancient precincts, this resembles less a place of worship than a pagan entertainment complex, run by sunny-faced priestesses wearing scarlet robes and garlands of fresh flowers. Its high walls protect a verdant garden sanctuary, with paved cloisters and sweet-scented groves of myrtle, a tree sacred to Aphrodite herself. Luxuriant grapevines drape the walls, homage to Dionysus, the Roman Bacchus, whose wine was a notorious "promoter of love." And at the heart of this Oz-like garden stands a gleaming marble pergola, home to the temple's raison d'être.

Lucian and his friends excitedly climb the steps, pass through bronze doors, and drink in a heavenly vision: the immortal Aphrodite, stark naked on a dais.

Like all ancient statues, she was painted from head to toe in lifelike tones: Her skin was alluringly smooth, her hair golden, her eyes glistening with a "joyous radiance"—even her arrogant smile was bewitching.

Reproductions of the image seem demure to us today, and Aphrodite's expression oddly inert; Romans would certainly have seen more brazen images every day of their lives. But the statue was an erotic classic, towering like the first *Playboy* nudes of Marilyn Monroe over the subsequent army of mass-produced *Sports Illustrated* calendars.

The heterosexual Charicles becomes so excited that, in Pavlovian fashion, he leaps up to kiss the goddess on her rosy lips.

The Knidians knew how to milk every coin from their marble sex kitten: In order to gain a rear view, one of the temple guides had to unlock a separate room, for a special fee.

Until this point, the pederast Callicratidas has been unmoved by the goddess's charms. But feasting his eyes on the posterior perspective, he lets out a gleeful cry: The divine bottom is strikingly *boyish*.

"By Hercules!" he says, quivering. "What slender hips! How delicately molded the buttocks! How sweetly they smile!"

At this point, the guide, an elderly woman, hovers back into view. Lucian has noted an unsightly dark stain on Aphrodite's milky inner thigh, and the attendant, fishing for her tip, breathlessly relates a famous anecdote about how it appeared.

Many years before, a young local nobleman had become romantically obsessed with this gorgeous incarnation of Aphrodite. He began to visit the temple daily, staring fixedly at the statue and carrying on whispered conversations with her.

> Eventually, as his passion grew more inflamed, the young man scratched love messages all over the temple walls. He brought everything he owned to the altar as offerings to the goddess. In the end, the violent pitch of his desires turned to desperation, and audacity became his pimp.
>
> At dusk one night, he slipped in behind the door and hid in the inner sanctum—keeping still, hardly even breathing. When the attendants closed the door as usual, he was locked inside alone with the statue. But what need is there for me to spell out the sordid act committed on that unmentionable night? These stains from his amorous embraces were seen the next day; the blemish on the goddess's leg proves what she's suffered.
>
> The young man concerned is said to have thrown himself off a cliff, and vanished utterly.

Marveling at this tale of carnal frenzy, Lucian and his friends retire to the shady garden and recline on the couches provided for the faithful. There, over a jug of wine and bowls of fresh berries, they consider what lessons can be drawn from this famous work of art.

The topic: Which is the finer, conjugal love or pederasty?

Surely women can arouse invincible passions even when made of stone! Not so, retorts the misogynist—the love-besotted male made love to her statue from behind, "as though to a boy."

The argument lurches on for pages, riddled with recondite references from Homer and Euripides. Finally, torn between the rhetorical calisthenics of the pair, the judge Lucian awards victory to the pederast: Sexual desire for a woman is fatally muddled by mankind's brute need to procreate, he agrees; the passion for a young boy, by contrast, is closer to friendship, focused and pure.

"Thus ended our stay in Knidos," Lucian contentedly sighs, "with its combination of gay earnestness and cultured fun." As the day's heat rises, crowds of local worshipers start arriving, so the trio of sightseers head back to their waiting boat.

In the pagan world, dense with wonder, there was always another attraction on the horizon—and another intriguing debate to exercise the mind.

ON THE VIA DEL COLOSSEO

And then, there we were, back from the Pompeii McDonald's, ricocheting in a taxi through the dark streets of Rome. I was determined to maintain my newfound perspective as I tackled the physical world of the ancient tourists—starting with the divine, unprecedented, impossible city that shaped their hearts and minds.

PART TWO

ALL ROADS LEAD FROM ROME

Farewell
to the Megalopolis

IMPERIAL ROME, as historians love to point out, was the New York of its day—a vast, gangling, bloated organism, teetering on the verge of complete logistical collapse, far and away the largest concentration of humanity the world had ever seen. With over one million inhabitants by the end of the first century A.D., it was triple the size of ancient Babylon, the former urban record holder, ten times the size of classical Athens, and immeasurably more spectacular than either had ever been. Living in this teeming city, the self-ordained Capital of the World, was hopelessly addictive. For the intrepid Roman tourists about to leave on their Grand Tours, a journey that would take them away for several years, the prospect of departure was often bittersweet.

For a sentimental farewell, citizens climbed the smooth carved steps of the Capitoline—the most sacred of the city's seven hills, crowned by the cavernous, golden-roofed Temple of Jupiter Optimus Maximus—to savor the breathtaking view for one last time. From this lofty aerie, Rome stretched to the horizon in every direction; its marble structures blanketed the countryside "like snow," as Aelius Aristides evocatively put it in his oration of A.D. 140, all brilliantly sparkling in the Italian sun. The beautification program that had begun under Augustus was long complete (I FOUND ROME A CITY OF BRICK, the first emperor boasted on his tomb. I LEAVE IT TO YOU A CITY OF MARBLE). Now a viewer's eye would skip greedily across an intricate honeycomb of streets, identifying one architectural icon after another: the Circus Maximus, where audiences of 250,000 roared over the chariot races; the bronze-covered dome

of the Pantheon, temple to all the gods; the towering ellipse of the
Colosseum. But the most astonishing thing was the city's sheer size: A
survey in the fourth century, taken when Rome was actually slightly
smaller than its second-century peak, counted 46,602 multistory tenement buildings; 1,790 palatial villas; 340 temples; 856 bathhouses; 6
Egyptian obelisks; 10 aqueducts; 4 gladiatorial schools; 28 libraries; 36 triumphal arches; 290 warehouses; 1,352 swimming pools—not to mention
the dozen famous public latrines. The largest of these complexes, Forica,
was as big as Notre-Dame Cathedral, its marble seats heated in winter
and decorated with mosaics, silver fountains, and dolphin motifs.

Visitors who saw this pageant for the first time were struck dumb with
awe: According to a Syrian named Callimachus, there were two types of
people on earth—those who had seen Rome and those who had not.
Heaven could show nothing fairer, raved the poet Claudian. It was the
greatest man-made creation in the ancient world, referred to simply as
Urbs (the city).

But as any departing Roman also knew, to truly appreciate this inspiring vista, it was wise to climb the Capitoline hill on a breezy day. Otherwise, a noisome brown haze would be hanging low over the city's
streets, capable of dulling their majestic polish and sparkle. Charcoal
smoke from household kitchens, bakers' ovens, blacksmiths' furnaces,
funeral pyres, and clouds of dust kicked up by shuffling pedestrians all
combined to create a preindustrial version of air pollution. And even at
those lofty heights, a steady roar would be rising from the streets, invading the hallowed precincts of Jupiter, occasionally interrupting the
priests' pagan liturgies, and threatening to overwhelm any delicate poetic
musings on Rome's divine Destiny.

In fact, Romans descended from the hill with a twinge of trepidation.
For beneath all of those glittering temples and golden monuments, the
Eternal City was utter pandemonium.

The Romans' talent for urban planning was never expressed in their
own city. Its maze of alleys, never more than ten feet wide, was less like
a system of public thoroughfares than a diabolical obstacle course. By
government decree, wheeled traffic had been banned during the daylight
hours, so even patricians had to pick their way through the city by foot,
their sandaled feet skidding along a nauseating bouillabaisse of Tiberine
mud, rotting vegetables, broken bricks, pebbles, mule dung, and the
occasional dead cat. In this claustrophobic labyrinth, every passageway
was clogged by tradesmen—fish vendors, carpenters, wine merchants,
booksellers, milkmaids, apothecaries, and butchers, whose hanging

sheeps' heads made the paving even more slippery with blood. Barbers went to work shaving men in the middle of the street; blinding clouds of smoke escaped from ovens; jugs of wine swung precariously above tavern doorways.

People made their way in cramped conga lines through these sunless alleys, gathering filth on the hemlines of their finest togas, their toes stomped by the heels of soldiers, and always enduring the thick-skinned brusqueness of fellow Romans as they jostled one another. "Where's your head—in the clouds?" bellowed an enraged citizen at the poet Horace when he accidentally stumbled. "One man digs an elbow into my side, another a hard pole," lamented the satirist Juvenal after a bruising stroll; "one bangs a beam, another a wine cask, against my skull." But the most serious dangers when traversing Rome came from above. The city was a vast, unsecured construction site. Wooden beams and loose tiles and bricks would regularly plunge into the crowded streets, braining the unlucky. A more common threat was to one's dignity, since an intermittent rain of slops from chamber pots poured down from tenement windows. The great lawyer Ulpian is said to have argued many court cases to redress such messy urban insults.

No wonder Romans had a love-hate relationship with their city. In those intense, exhausting streets, they were reminded every day that an overseas jaunt might not be such a bad thing.

SÉANCE AT DAWN

Four o'clock in the morning, fresh from Pompeii, and I was realizing with satisfaction that modern Rome had refined at least one great ancient tradition: world-class noise.

All night, the steady stream of muffler-free Vespas along the Via del Colosseo had sounded like they were running across our bed; everything from the brain-piercing sirens of ambulances to the expectorations of local *vagabondi* were amplified by the narrow street below. And this was merely the overture: At dawn, a parade of Roman garbage trucks, street cleaners, and delivery vans began grinding down the lane, vibrating the hotel walls and triggering an operatic chorus of car alarms and howling dogs. Eventually the morning peak hour, with its permanent gridlock of drivers leaning on their horns, drowned everything else out in a shrill symphony. Lesley had managed to sleep through the entire acoustic extravaganza, but I was in danger of becoming a gibbering wreck.

So, in the pale morning light, I consulted my Latin volumes and exulted in ancient complaints about noise pollution.

"Insomnia is the main cause of death in Rome," wailed Juvenal in A.D. 100. "Show me the bedroom that lets you sleep!" The main culprit was traffic, even then. For the very reason that wheeled vehicles were banned during the day, Rome's cumbersome delivery carts were forced to do their rounds after dark. And since axle grease was rarely used in ancient times—olive oil and animal fat were prohibitively expensive—every lurch of the transports let out a piercing squeal that penetrated even the remotest apartment.

"The thunder of wagons in those narrow twisting streets," Juvenal groaned, "the oaths of the draymen caught in a jam, would shatter the sleep of a deaf man—or a lazy walrus."

Hangovers were apparently hell in Imperial Rome. Vehicles might have been forced off the streets an hour before dawn, but they were immediately replaced by a rising crescendo of bakers hawking their bread, blacksmiths pounding their anvils, priests shrieking their morning rituals, shepherds bringing milk from the countryside, and shrill children chanting their alphabets.

"All Rome is at my bed head!" moaned the poet Martial, writhing on his mattress one morning after a wine-soaked night on the town.

In modern Rome, technology had merely raised the pitch a few hundred decibels. For Les, being able to sleep through noise was the only pleasant side effect of pregnancy so far. She finally rolled over and looked at my sunken, bloodshot eyes.

"This will get you in training for fatherhood," she chirped, and bounded out of bed.

A couple of cappuccinos later, we were happily immersed in the Queen of Cities, trying to imagine the world the first tourists left behind. Of course, ancient Rome was all around, in a manner of speaking. In front of the Colosseum, Italian actors were dressed in Roman centurion uniforms—antiques from the days when sword-and-sandal hits such as *Spartacus, Cleopatra,* and *Caligula* were shot in situ at the film studio Cinecittà. The new centurions posed for tourist photos, charged a small fortune, and casually groped the ladies whenever they had the chance. In the Forum Romanum, the summer sun ricocheted around the broken columns mercilessly, making you wonder how the ancients survived without sunglasses. Water was still pouring from first-century drinking fountains; little boys dashed among the statues waving plastic swords instead of toy guns. We staggered around the ruins like the wide-

Centurions pose for tourists in front of the Colosseum.

eyed provincials of ancient times: Around the corner was Trajan's Forum; up the hill, the emperors' palaces on the Palatine. There's the Pantheon! The Circus! Temple of Vesta!

"Rome in her greatness!" intoned the poet Propertius. "Stranger, look your fill!"

There was only one small problem with *modern* Rome, as far as I could tell: It was just too beautiful.

I caught myself taking photographs of *everything*. Rubble. Plazas. Doorways. Rooftops. All those timeworn facades oozing pinks and ochers and tangerines. Gelato stands. Fruit stalls. Shopwindows. Even the gutters appeared painterly, when the light was right. The layers of art history—Classical, Gothic, Baroque, Rococo, Neoclassical, and beyond—were all jostling for attention. Italian artists complain about being oppressed by the weight of so many styles, and you can see why. It's impossible to concentrate on any one epoch.

Modern Rome is simply a magnificent blur—a gorgeous smear.

Surrounded by all this fragmented beauty, the inhabitants take refuge in a charming uniformity. They take pride in their anarchist streak, their ungovernable chaos, but on a day-to-day basis they may be the world's most amiable conformists. The clothing boutiques are full of outrageous creations, but nobody actually wears them: In fact, modern Romans look like they've all been decked out from the same Benetton outlet. They zip back and forth on their Vespas, all exquisitely groomed as if they're rushing off for an interview with the pope; extended families in color-coordinated outfits arrange themselves at the outdoor cafés like medieval *tableaux vivants*. There are no tasteless notes in Rome, no failed experiments, no extravagant gestures, no reeling public drunks, and almost no foreign restaurants—Italian cuisine is pleasingly monolithic, with almost every menu offering subtle variations on the time-honored themes. A wild night out for Roman kids is sipping soft drinks in the Campo de' Fiori, or hanging out on the Spanish Steps playing Eagles' songs on the guitar. All of Romans' creativity goes into the art of living well.

As a result, there must be no more seductive place on earth to while away summer days, sipping wine and eating pasta in the outdoor cafés. But when you're trying to picture the explosive world of Ancient Rome, it all seems too . . . *controlled.*

What made Ancient Rome unique as a city—what defined it to its inhabitants and the world—was its exhilarating extremes, its giddy combination of grandeur and squalor. It was exuberant, energetic, confronting, cosmopolitan, a volatile cocktail of wealth, penury, lust, and degradation.

Modern Rome, by comparison, is like a soothing watercolor hanging in a dentist's waiting room.

At some point I had to admit that on an *imaginative* level, Ancient Rome had less in common with modern Rome than with the more overpowering, rough-edged, and crass metropolis we'd just left behind: New York.

The Urban Monster

It had always seemed to me a little unsavory, the pleasure that historians—usually European—appeared to derive from comparing Ancient Rome to New York. (As the French academic Jerome Carcopino fulminates in his magisterial opus, *Daily Life in Ancient Rome:* "If Rome was as enormous for her day as New York is for ours; if Rome . . . was a colossal devouring town, which stupefied the stranger and the provincial as the American metropolis astonishes the Europe of today, she paid even more dearly for the dimensions which her dominating position had inflicted upon her.") But a couple of days away from Manhattan, the idea was becoming more fetching.

After all, Ancient Rome's 1.25 million inhabitants shared an undying conviction that they were living in the ultimate city, a universal capital upon whose activities "the eyes of Gods and Mortals were fixed." Its shocking extremes existed cheek by jowl: Beggars clustered around golden monuments; fabulous mansions "comparable to the mad schemes of kings" stood next to downright slums. In fact, most Roman citizens crowded on top of one another in high-rise tenements called *insulae* (islands), comprising a population density that would not be equaled until New York's Lower East Side in the nineteenth century. Rome was the first great city of immigrants, a melting pot of the Mediterranean where 90 percent of its inhabitants could trace their lineage back to a new arrival within the past three generations. All this produced a rough street democracy: Patricians and plebeians, millionaires and tradesmen rubbed shoulders every day.

The comparison is not as whimsical, or as anachronistic, as it might at first seem. Imperial Rome was, in many ways, the first modern city: Sir Peter Hall, for example, in his exhaustive study of urban history, introduces Ancient Rome five hundred pages late, at the beginning of the industrial age. (Ancient Rome, he notes, "served as a kind of rehearsal trailer for all the cities that would come much later.") As the world's first true megalopolis, Rome had to deal with problems that are today the grist of daily life—housing shortages, unemployment, waste management, garbage disposal. Romans devised the first traffic laws, building codes, fire brigades, and police forces. They organized massive international importation of food (135,000 tons of grain a year, carried by purpose-built fleets from Egypt); erected enormous aqueducts to bring water from hundreds of miles around; created public latrines and a magnificent system of underground sewers that some patriots insisted were engineering marvels on a par with the Pyramids.

Despite all this, Ancient Rome remained a logistical nightmare, an unwieldy juggernaut lurching from fiasco to fiasco, a city that objectively speaking was unworkable—just like home.

In fact, Imperial Rome and New York are matching bookends to the last two thousand years of Western urban history, the two behemoths that have defined our conception of what a city can be. On a metaphorical level, the cities are described by both contemporaries and historians in the same hyperbolic terms. All the familiar images of Heroic New York—that mythic metropolis, at the height of its power in the early to mid-twentieth century, when its pretensions to being the "world capital" had genuine weight—were first trotted out in Latin two thousand years ago about Rome. You can even take quotes about the pair and interchange them at will. H. G. Wells, when he saw New York in 1906, raved about "the unprecedented multitudinousness, the inhuman force of the thing." Classical observers felt the same mix of wonder and horror at Rome. To Juvenal—the dyspeptic satirist admired by Céline and George Orwell—it was simply "a monstrous city."

During my predawn reading sessions, I started keeping a notebook of the more striking parallels.

"Ever-rising rent is a subject of eternal lamentation in ancient literature," sums up Monsieur Carcopino. According to Juvenal, a year's rent for a "shabby, ill-lit attic" in Rome could buy a first-class villa in the country. In this savage real estate market, extortionate subleases were common, as were sub-subleases. "All low-income citizens should have marched out of Rome, in a body, years ago," Juvenal sniffs. These overpriced Roman tenement houses, adds Carcopino, "suffered from the fragility of their construction, the scantiness of their furniture, insufficient light and heat, and an absence of sanitation." (*Egad! It's our apartment on Tenth Street!*) Many were six floors high, towering seventy feet above street level. Martial had to climb two hundred steps to his dismal garret; the tenement of Felicula, next to the Pantheon, broke all building codes and rose like a mini-skyscraper, becoming one of Rome's tourist attractions. Perhaps not surprisingly, Rome also spawned the first evil landlords: According to the German historian Ludwig Friedländer, writing in 1904, "the most urgent repairs were neglected; the agent propped up a tottering wall, or painted a huge rift over, and assured the occupants that they could sleep at their ease, all the time that their home was crumbling over their heads." Whole buildings did regularly collapse (a staple of New York's evening news—although today the tenants are usually saved). The sound of cracking plaster induced panic among Romans, driving dinner-party guests out into the street as if an earthquake were hitting.

The connections become even more compelling once the ancient moralists get going. Rome was constantly denounced for its decadence, luxury, wastefulness, and permissiveness. When the historian Tacitus describes the city as "a meeting place of all that is horrible and shameful," he sounds like a fundamentalist politician from Georgia denouncing New York's S&M bars—although, in a neat historical reversal, he is actually expressing his disgust at the new cult of Christianity, which was regarded by pagans as decadent and perverse.

And the list goes on.

Imperial Rome had an unshakable reputation for crime. Lurking among the delivery wagons after dark was a menacing cast of thieves, desperadoes, and prostitutes. The Subura, a district south of the Aventine hill, by the Tiber, was notoriously seedy, the South Bronx of the city, but danger was felt everywhere. Romans liked to terrify out-of-towners with exaggerated tales: "Only a fool accepts a dinner invitation without first making out his will," mourns Juvenal.

Blood sports? Any New York writer would be fascinated to learn that our word *editor* can be traced back to the Colosseum. The Latin *editor* was the head of a gladiatorial school, whose job it was to decide whether a wounded fighter should live or die. Lurking in the sidelines of the arena, the *editor* gave thumbs-up or -down on purely financial grounds—whether it was worth it to nurse the man back to health in the gladiatorial hospital, or to let him perish like a dog. (*Just like Manhattan publishing!*) But the role was too popular to leave to a minor figure. The life-and-death power was later given to the emperor—who, to curry favor, deferred to the masses.

Lifestyle? Ancient Romans were obsessed by money and fashion; avarice and conspicuous consumption ruled all levels of society. "When has the purse of greed yawned wider?" asks Juvenal, wondering when Romans would open a temple to their real god, Cash. He continues: "In Rome we slavishly obey the latest fashion fad, spending beyond our means—and often on borrowed credit." Lucian derides one young victim: "Your only interests are resplendent clothes that drip luxury right down to your feet, and seeing that your hair is nicely cut."

Jerome Carcopino sums up the general opinion of the high-minded ancients on Rome when he rails against the city's "fever for riches, the mantle of luxury which cloaks her wretchedness, the prodigality of [the] spectacles . . . the inanity of the intellectual gymnastics . . . and the frenzy of carnal indulgence in which [the inhabitants] stupefy themselves."

It was almost making me homesick.

THE ACCIDENTAL TOURISTS

Here was another potential parallel: According to Pliny the Younger, Romans were forerunners of the proverbial New Yorkers who have never seen the Statue of Liberty. Pliny thought his fellow citizens would happily set off on a Grand Tour, traveling long distances to see the wonders of Greece, Asia, and Egypt, but were indifferent to the marvels of their own city. "We rush after what is remote and remain indifferent to what is nearby," he complains in a letter, deciding that this reflects the perversity of human nature. (Is it because "any desire loses its intensity if it can be easily satisfied," he muses, "or because we postpone visiting something we can see whenever we want, convinced that we will one day get around to it?")

But Pliny was exaggerating his case for rhetorical effect—just as the insular Manhattanite is no more than a stock figure of modern lore, a provocative half-truth.

The reality was quite the opposite. Romans were indefatigable sightseers, lapping up the lures of their own city with as much enthusiasm as any bumpkin fresh from the Sabine Hills.

It could hardly be otherwise: Lacking the modern distractions of tele-

Chariot race in the Circus Maximus, from the 1926 silent film Ben-Hur.

vision, radio, and cinema, Romans found their stimulation in the streets. They lived outdoors from dawn until dusk, thronging the city's sumptuous forums, which were forerunners of modern Italian piazzas. Every new monument provoked genuine fascination; palace renovations were inspected, temples admired. On afternoon promenades, citizens explored the cul-de-sacs of history: They climbed the Palatine hill to inspect the humble straw hut of Romulus, Rome's founding father—the fact that the edifice had burned down and been rebuilt several times with Disney-esque polish over the centuries bothered nobody—then visited the Lupercal cave, where the babes Romulus and Remus had supposedly been suckled by a hypermaternal she-wolf. Romans could even admire the wooden crib the pair slept in after their rescue by the thoughtful herdsman Faustulus. Finally, there were the incessant games: Chariot races and gladiator shows were the *Cats* and *Les Miz* of the era. Crowds lined up the night before to compete for stadium seats; when one excited mob disturbed Caligula's sleep, he ordered them cudgeled into silence. Impromptu spectacles added to the entertainment. After the Great Fire of A.D. 64, night races in Nero's imperial gardens were illuminated by human candles: Screaming Christian martyrs were rolled in resin, tied to stakes, then set ablaze (Nero quipped that it was the first time Christianity had shed light on anything).

Thrilling as all this might have been, it wasn't what made Imperial Rome such a stimulating place to live. Its inhabitants were the true spectacle. Street life in any ancient city was far more intense and interactive than any modern one could hope for. Ancient Rome took this principle to extremes: It was a giant stage, its citizens actors and observers of the drama.

There was no place on earth that could match its riotous diversity: The streets were thick with foreigners, an infinitely renewable supply of new arrivals from around the world, making people-watching a standard Roman entertainment. Ambitious young men and women—the sharpest legal minds, best-looking actors, most talented musicians—were lured to this city where professional competition was keenest, the rewards highest, the price of failure greatest. To coin a phrase, if you could make it in Imperial Rome, you could make it anywhere. The most illustrious Roman writers harked from the provinces, as by the second century A.D. did most of the emperors. At the bottom of the social scale, foreign slaves were regularly freed by their masters. Many became fabulously wealthy. Rome bubbled over with rags-to-riches stories.

This fluid, cosmopolitan society gave Roman streets their celebrated energy. On a single afternoon in the Forum, you might encounter courtesans from Parthia, Dacian slaves carrying a Greek professor's books, the German guards of the emperor drilling near the palace, Ethiopian boxers and elephant trainers, and bearded Sarmatians (from modern-day Georgia), who drank horse blood. Outlandish costumes caught the eye: There were Oriental ambassadors in brilliant silks, tattooed barbarians from Britain, even men wearing trousers. Priests of the Egyptian goddess Isis conducted their processions, heads shaved, limbs swathed in white linen robes, jangling their wooden rattles and chanting. The daily pageant included palm readers, astrologers, and international performers—Andalusian dancing girls, flute players from Morocco, child acrobats from Rhodes. Juvenal records seeing a trained monkey riding a goat's back and waving a spear, as well as "snake-eaters" from central Italy. In the crowded forums, Greek actors declaimed their lines and professional storytellers begged for an audience: "Give me a copper coin," was the standard refrain, "and I'll tell you a golden story."

Naturally, the world's most beautiful people also found their way to Rome. Many a poet noted that *Roma* was only an anagram for *amor*.

Ovid in his *Art of Love* argues that, although many Romans traveled overseas in search of carnal adventure, the "hunting" was just as good at home, especially during festivals. "Why, youths and maidens come here from either sea," he gloats. "The mighty world is in our city. Who could not find in that crowd an object for his passion?" Gorgeous women were more numerous in Rome, Ovid notes, than fish in the sea or stars in the sky. As the prime pickup spots, Ovid recommends Pompey's theater, which had a shrine to Venus, and the Colosseum, where fashionable women gather "like bees on blossoms":

> They come to see, they come to be seen;
> The place is fatal to chastity.

Juvenal suggests hanging around any of Rome's temples at night. "Easy women haunt shrines," he reminds a friend in one satire. "You fucked them by the dozens there, and . . . more often than not, you had their husbands too."

Every moment in this tumultuous city provided a new social vignette—every hour in the Forum a new rumor or piece of gossip. No wonder Romans ceaselessly wandered around the streets with their eyes permanently agog. In the imperial capital, everything was bigger, brighter, brasher.

They were, in fact, natural-born tourists, whose skills were honed every day of their lives.

BLUEPRINT OF THE GODS

And here we were today, treating modern Rome in much the same way, like ancient travelers saying farewell to the city.

This belief only deepened when I discovered that our modest little hotel was built near the site of a first-century A.D. Roman boarding-house, excavated by Mussolini's archaeologists. I'd chosen it because it had the cheapest rooms in Rome—if not all of Italy. But our boisterous attic room, inexplicably, had a balcony. Across a few terra-cotta roofs, the Colosseum rose like a magnificently rotting cake.

"O Rome!" rhapsodized Martial. "Goddess of people and continents, whom nothing can equal or even approach!"

Up on the Capitoline hill, the Temple of Jupiter is today long gone, as is that famous view; thirty feet of debris have overlaid the ancient streets, altering the city's topography so that even the original seven hills are unrecognizable. That's why, instead of looking up at Rome's grand monuments, we gaze down into their graves. The Pantheon, for example, was built on a hill so that its burnished dome would be visible across the city. Today it's hidden at the bottom of an urban valley, surrounded by café tables.

To recapture that wondrous panorama of ancient Rome, you need to take the subway out to a decrepit Museum of Roman Civilization in the EUR—a suburb created for Fascist bureaucrats, whose brutalist landscapes were used to good effect by Bertolucci in *The Conformist*. Amid the museum's dust-filled reliquaries lies an extraordinary object: a three-dimensional model of Ancient Rome, sixty feet long by sixty feet wide, built in the 1930s by obsessive curators. The creation, which was based on awesome research, stretches beneath a viewing mezzanine like a vast crystal created in a laboratory. You can mentally run past its palaces, up and down the seven hills, across the bridges—speeding through its stone canyons like Luke Skywalker across the Death Star.

With a picture of that model firmly embedded in my mind—I'd studied it for two hours, treating it as a great 3-D blueprint—modern Rome

Giant model of Ancient Rome in the Museum of Roman Civilization.

took on a new shape. Now, as we wandered the frenetic, fragmented city, I could picture the ancient roadways buried far beneath my feet. They were shimmering and slightly distorted like the ocean floor seen through a glass-bottomed boat.

And the imperial relics took on a fresh sheen. The Mausoleum of Augustus may today look like a vast eroded beehive surrounded by ragged office buildings, but I could envision it in its original glory, looming above a minimalist plaza laid out as a giant sundial with an Egyptian obelisk as the gnomon. The Field of Mars reemerged as a virtual theme park of Roman propaganda monuments, including the Colonnade of the Nations, which contained dozens of statues representing each of the Empire's conquered peoples. And finally, amongst the confusing debris of the Roman Forum, I found a broken stump, all that remains of the Golden Milestone. I could envision it again as a tall gleaming pillar (actually sheathed in bronze rather than gold), which marked the starting point of Rome's extraordinary highway system. It was here that the de facto tourist offices of the Empire set up shop. All the important provincial cities maintained representatives in the Forum—they were called *stationes municipiorum*—who behaved like the honorary consuls of the British Victorian era. Their main purpose was to assist their compatriots with trade or legal problems. But they would also, informally, give out advice about their homelands.

Restless Romans could while away afternoons chatting about the weather in Athens or shipping to Corinth. And plans might begin to take shape.

Sometime after the twelfth monument, I realized it was time for a minor correction in my approach to Rome.

We'd been spinning around the city in a frenzy, following an obsessive regime of ruin visiting, inscription reading, and statue gazing. Les had struggled gamely along at first, but eventually she began to drag her heels. She seemed increasingly suspicious that I was displaying the first signs of madness. Looking wistfully at all the Romans lounging in the sun, she said, "Why don't we just spend an afternoon in a café? Look at this place. How about a gelato?" But I was too distracted.

Now, after the fourth ancient site of the day, she sat down and refused to move. I'd pushed her too far—she was going on strike.

I glanced at our growing concern—three and a half months—and felt my usual vague disbelief. It occurred to me that she had her own private

Vesuvius to consider. Every day she talked about some new sensation or emotion. I'd felt the little visitor squirm—even heard a heartbeat—but at some profound level I didn't believe anything had changed. Les was walking a little more slowly, wasn't drinking, and had gained some weight.

But at heart I suspected she'd just been eating too much tiramisù.

At the start of our odyssey, we hadn't quite figured out how much she could and couldn't handle. Sudden waves of exhaustion rolled out of the blue; promenades came to unexpected halts. There were those hunger attacks, sending us scurrying for fresh food. Les had taken to carrying around a packet of dry biscuits, devouring them quietly in museum corners. And every step we took, there was a secret map in our minds of where the next bathroom lay . . .

It was a little difficult for me to adjust to all this, being, as I was, in a profound state of denial. Les had always been a good sport about our other so-called holidays. She'd barely complained when she'd gotten food poisoning in Sumatra, or nearly drowned on a yacht trip in the Coral Sea. It hadn't even bothered her too much when we'd gotten lost in a diamond miners' camp in Venezuela, or caught in that Argentine military rebellion, or chased by thugs in Belize City . . .

Here in Rome, I'd been bumbling along blithely, no major changes in outlook. We'd exchanged our backpacks for suitcases with little wheels attached—that was the biggest concession.

But now, on a sidewalk by the Tiber, I was beginning to see that Les's condition might make this trip a little different.

"Tone, it's not just me that's pregnant! You're pregnant too!"

I nodded sagely, not entirely sure what this meant.

We agreed to stage-manage our days a little more carefully. No more endless walks. Less-ambitious schedules. A few more taxis. Even some lounging about in cafés, Italian style, pondering the journey ahead.

It would be like traveling in slow motion. Not a bad thing, I supposed. It would force me to pause and absorb what I'd seen so far of Ancient Rome—and to grasp how almost everything in that whirlwind of a city had helped to advertise the Empire and its attractions.

On a day-to-day basis, Ancient Rome worked like a giant revolving door, luring the exotic from all over the world and subliminally planting the seeds of wanderlust in its inhabitants.

Every new religious cult found ready converts, every new delicacy an eager buyer, every foreign novelty an audience. (As the author Apuleius admitted, "I have an almost morbid interest in anything queer or out of the way.") Rich Romans paid small fortunes for imported *miracula* (human curiosities). Hermaphrodites, cretins, and dwarves were purchased as conversation pieces; when they died, they were sometimes preserved in myrrh and honey, then put on permanent display in villas, like hunting trophies. Those with more eclectic tastes headed for the city's Monstrosity Market, a heartless Sotheby's of the Grotesque. There, one could bid for Pygmies from the Nile, giants from Scythia, "androgynous beings," an Indian with no arms, a "wild man" from Africa, or a two-foot-tall adolescent with a stentorian voice. Nero was once delivered a child with four heads, which he put on exhibit alongside the "Glutton from Alexandria"—who, to delight the audiences, would devour at one sitting a whole pig, a live hen, one hundred eggs, dozens of nails, broken glass, the twigs of a broom, and a bale of hay.

Fabulous animals aroused just as much interest. The first tiger seen in Europe was presented to Augustus by envoys from India and put on public display in a gilded cage; thousands of Romans filed past every day to admire the gorgeously striped beast as it prowled back and forth behind the bars, growling at its captors. Impromptu zoos were set up for giant tortoises, crocodiles, and rhinoceroses, as well as magical creatures— "animals with human limbs," a giant bird believed to be a phoenix, a satyr preserved in salt. In the reign of Claudius, an embalmed centaur— half man, half horse—arrived from Africa, while "monster skeletons" were regularly displayed in the arenas. Some were the fossilized remains of dinosaurs exposed by earthquakes, others the bones of whales that had strayed into the Mediterranean. Roman audiences gasped at the skin of a 120-foot-long snake and dead Gorgons—sheeplike animals whose gaze was lethal to man.

A whole new literary genre—paradoxography, or "books of wonders"—catered to this Roman passion for the extraordinary, listing oddities of botany, geography, zoology, and anthropology. It was complemented by a flurry of adventure travel books—"eyewitness accounts" of Scythian cannibals, one-eyed Africans, and islands inhabited by men whose feet pointed backward. In learned circles, erudite trivia fueled the art of conversation: Youngsters studied books on how to inject fascinating facts into party banter, while banquet hostesses, like the grandes dames of Russian salons, would skillfully steer guests to debate specific matters. Recommended topics included: Where do new diseases come from? Why is *A* the first letter of the alphabet? In which hand was

Aphrodite wounded by Diomedes? Why did Homer call salt divine, but not oil? Why did Pythagoras ban the eating of fish? How does one ward off the evil eye?

These debates sometimes sank into pedantic rants that went on all night; there are reports of bored dinner guests hiding under their couches in a drunken stupor, or singing to themselves to drown out the drivel. But on the whole, Romans took them seriously, and the well-traveled found themselves at a great advantage. The guest who had personally spoken with the priests of the Nile, or seen famous art on display in Greece, had an authority that could hardly be questioned. As Dionysius Periegetes (Dionysius the Guide) says in his geographical poem: "As a result of [reading] this, you will be held in honor, and be highly regarded, as you relate particulars to someone unqualified." So much better for those who had actually gazed upon the sacred sites. Romans understood the importance of seeing wonders in situ, where they could enjoy the genius loci.

And who could spend an evening discussing the heroes of Troy or the rites of Egypt—who could sit by while lithe Asian acrobats performed, or, for that matter, who could taste imported dates, Greek olives, or rare Aegean wines—without yearning to feel the Mediterranean's warm breezes in their hair? No wonder so many decided to pack their bags. Or at least check the auspices.

Omens 101:
How to Start a Journey

On the morning we were to leave for Naples, I awoke before dawn with a stab of anxiety.

The night before, in a narrow lane, a speeding Vespa had run over a pigeon; the decapitated body, wings flapping madly, had leaped onto my foot. Wincing, I'd washed off the blood, but I couldn't get the grisly image out of my head.

Now, while Lesley was still asleep, I took one last stroll around central Rome. The Forum was deserted, its broken columns soaking in a veil of mist. The traffic hum was strangely remote; the summer heat was gathering force, ready to pounce. I climbed the steps to the Capitoline hill and peered down at the ghostly ruins.

I wondered if this trip was entirely wise in our delicate condition. Were we testing the Fates?

It was a question the Romans, at least, would have understood.

Don't start a voyage on a Tuesday; Tuesdays are bad luck. Also October 5 and August 24—better to stay at home. Don't go anywhere at the end of a month; those are evil days to travel. Dream about owls, bears, or bulls? Cancel all travel plans, disaster is certain. Never sneeze as you enter a sailing vessel. No dancing en route! And definitely, definitely don't cut your fingernails in the open water. Unless you're caught in bad weather. Then by all means, trim both hair and nails; put the cuttings in a sack, and toss them overboard as offerings to Neptune.

It might help—and certainly can't hurt.

Romans lived their lives trapped in a web of superstitions, at the mercy of their capricious gods, and the prospect of departing on a long journey always heightened this obsession. The Julian calendar was a terrifying minefield of unlucky days; the entrails of sacrificed animals regularly needed to be examined, dreams interpreted, and the natural world constantly scanned for omens.

Some divine signals were fairly straightforward: A hailstorm on your day of departure was a clear message to cancel the journey. News of fish being found in plowed fields; bees clustering in a temple roof; the birth of a boy with two penises; a statue being hit by lightning; a river running with blood—all were poor omens. The emperor Nero canceled a major trip when his limbs began inexplicably to tremble in a temple. Other omens were more subtle: Augustus abandoned a voyage to Egypt when he accidentally tripped and tore his toga (then again, the first emperor was particularly sensitive to all divine messages; he also spent one day a year begging in the streets of Rome, because he'd been instructed to do so in a dream).

The trouble with omens was that a wide spectrum of events, including apparently minor ones, could be warnings from the gods, and the divine repercussions were often ambiguous. What, for example, did you make of a flock of birds passing overhead as you stepped out the door, or if you misplaced a favorite cloak on the morning of departure, or found a fly embedded in your breakfast bread? The interpretation of such events was a delicate art, requiring a soothsayer, a numerologist, a priest, or an astrologer—or all four. Maddeningly, good omens could even turn out to be tricks from the gods, luring hapless mortals on to disaster with false confidence.

As a result, the ancients lived from day to day in an agony of anticipation, trying to decipher every stray occurrence. An upcoming journey only raised the stakes.

Travel may have been safer than ever before, but one still had to worry about disease, shipwreck, earthquakes, horseback accidents, and all the myriad decrees of the Fates. The illustrious were far from immune. Rome's greatest poet, Virgil, caught fever on tour in Greece and died on his return to Italy; the tourist-emperor Hadrian lost his young lover swimming in the Nile, which broke his heart. And in A.D. 19, the beloved prince Germanicus himself fell sick and died on his return from Egypt, never to see Rome again.

If all ancient travelers felt a mixture of excitement and dread, Romans departing on the Grand Tour had their emotions pushed to neurotic extremes. The Appian Way made quite sure of that.

A milepost announces the start of the Appian Way.

It's easy to picture the giddy moment. At dawn, their iron-wheeled wagons slowly creaked through the Capena gate, were sprinkled with water from a leaking aqueduct above, and lurched onto the Queen of Highways. Rome's oldest artery, the Appian Way was also its most spectacular—"one of the sights of the world," according to the poet Propertius. Wide and smooth, its thousands of basalt polygons fitted together without cement, all under the shade of pine and cypress trees. It was always busy, and the traffic pleasingly entertaining—women driving chariots, rural peasants on foot, bejeweled horse riders. (Juvenal describes seeing a praetor trailed by five slaves on foot carrying cases of wine and a commode.) But there were few travelers who did not peer warily at the large shapes looming from the mist by the side of the road. Mausoleums and sarcophagi lurked on every side.

Perversely enough, the grand exit from Rome was also the Abode of the Dead.

Burials were not permitted within the city limits, so the Appian Way was lined with elaborate family vaults. All manner of *funeralia* was on show: There were towering altars, faux-Egyptian pyramids, great circular vaults that contained the remains of whole dynasties, as well as shrines that doubled as rest shelters for travelers. In all, some three thousand tombs have been identified in the first eight miles beyond Rome's gates, turning the Appian Way into a drive-through necropolis. What's more, most tombs bore philosophical inscriptions that would have provoked more thought than the advertising billboards of today.

Some were quite upbeat: READ, PASSING FRIEND, WHAT ROLE I ONCE PLAYED IN THIS WORLD . . . AND NOW THAT YOU HAVE READ, HAVE A PLEASANT JOURNEY. Others were bluntly hectoring: I ADVISE YOU TO ENJOY LIFE MORE THAN I DID! Another had a bas-relief of the buried man eating at a lavish table with his family and friends. WHAT GOOD IS IT FOR THE DEAD TO BE SEEN FEASTING? the inscription asked. THEY WOULD HAVE DONE BETTER TO HAVE LIVED THIS WAY. BEWARE OF DOCTORS! advised another. THEY WERE THE ONES WHO KILLED ME. The unsubtle display served to remind wayfarers that they, too, were mortal—as if Romans needed reminding.

Of course, the signs on the Appian Way simply codified the mixed feelings that travelers have always felt embarking on a journey—hope, regret, fear, wonder, the desire to live life to the full, coupled with the fear of something going terribly wrong. It's the same delirious concoction of human possibilities that has made the journey itself such a useful metaphor for life. After all, Homer's *Odyssey,* one of Western civilization's oldest extant pieces of literature, is fundamentally a travel story.

Although I wasn't sure if our Grand Tour would reach the heights of epic, sitting there on the steps of the Capitoline did give me pause.

DICKERING WITH DEITIES

To their credit, Roman tourists did try to take matters into their own hands. As Aristides remarked: "It is customary for those traveling by land or sea to make resolutions." Romans took a bluntly legalistic attitude to the caprices of the gods.

It was basically: "Let's make a deal."

A departing traveler would make sure to visit a temple—of Mercury the traveler, the popular, wing-footed god of wayfarers; or Rediculus, god of the return journey; or, in the East, Hercules, symbol of extraordinary courage and strength—and strike a private bargain for their safe journey. But the best place in Rome to do it was up on Capitoline hill, at the temple of Jupiter Optimus Maximus. This was the real motive for

Roman tourists to climb those marble steps. Jupiter was not only the king of all the gods, he was the divine protector of strangers. And just for good measure, he was flanked in the temple by his wife, Juno, and the goddess Minerva, both patrons of Rome.

It was a moment of high drama, entering the splendid chamber whose ceiling and walls were covered in gold leaf, then gazing upon the statue of Jupiter presiding on a giant throne, with all of Rome before him. Travelers had to press through the crowds of suppliants who were arguing their cases out loud to the statue, and dodge busy sacristans. Like all pagan images, the enormous figure was treated as if it were actually alive: Jupiter had his own priestly servants—some to tell him the hours of the day, others to anoint his hair with oil, and others to dress him in robes on state occasions when he was given official duties to fulfill.

Despite the pomp, the bargaining procedure was surprisingly bureaucratic. Temple priests would inscribe a *votum* (pledge) on a piece of papyrus, which said: "In return for a safe journey, I will perform [a certain act] when I reach my destination." Rich men swore to make expensive sacrifices or to donate money to the temple; the poor offered terra-cotta statues. The act could also be symbolic: The famous orator Aristides once promised to dedicate a speech to the gods in exchange for a trouble-free voyage across the Mediterranean. The handwritten contract would then be sealed and affixed by wax to the statue itself; by all accounts, Jupiter's muscular thighs were thick with these tiny shreds, creating an effect like a skin disorder.

One day, the traveler hoped, he or she would return to the temple and celebrate a successful transaction by inscribing another parchment, which read *Julius VSLM*—shorthand for *Julius Votum Soluit Libens Merito* (Julius has paid his vow with pleasure and merit). The priests would then store the scrap in the temple's vast archives for posterity. Every temple's floor was cluttered with the offerings of those who had fulfilled these sacred promises—everything from ears of corn to silver tripods and golden horns of plenty were piled in the hundreds.

If anything went wrong with these divine deals—assuming travelers made it back—the disgruntled worshipers would be within their rights to abuse the god, kicking the statue or worse.

As the sun pierced the mist on the Capitoline hill, I decided to make a small deal myself—with Juno, queen of Mount Olympus and the goddess of childbirth.

If we made it intact through Greece and Turkey—if we arrived safely at our destination on the desert frontier of Egypt—if Lesley didn't fall victim to Islamic kidnappers, Aegean ferry disasters, ague, or hepatitis— then I would, like Aristides, perform a "certain act."

Which was, like the ancient contracts, a secret to be kept until our return.

And so we headed south, to the land where ancient tourists went to ease themselves, voluptuously, into travel mode.

PART THREE

THE HEDONISM COAST

Dolce Vita
by the Bay of Naples

IF ROME WAS THE NEW YORK of antiquity, the Bay of Naples was the Hamptons. Every summer, the Mediterranean heat (with its attendant banes of typhoid and malaria) emptied the imperial capital of its *bella gente,* and the entire fashionable world sallied forth to re-create itself one hundred miles south, by the craggy, sun-drenched shores of Campania. There, within sight of the smoking funnel of Mount Vesuvius, surrounded by a hypnotic sea of blue, the emperors had built their luxury palaces, the millionaires their most sumptuous villas. Most patrician families owned two or three slices of local real estate, and many boasted half a dozen. According to the Greek geographer Strabo, who visited around A.D. 10, the whole gorgeous beachfront south to the Sirens' Point (now Sorrento) presented a continuous glistening wall of marble-colonnaded mansions—each one lavishly frescoed with images of Neptune, arching porpoises, and gangly octupuses. The Romans loved to swim in these warm, protected shores, far from the sea monsters and evil sprites that prowled deeper waters, and the sculpted courtyards of their retreats, engraved with the patterns of waves, had direct pathways leading down to sandy coves. Even more fabulous developments crept up and down the jagged cliff sides, crowding out one another for the most commanding sea views. Some had five tiers, with manicured gardens that stretched for acres. One particularly ostentatious villa was built by a status-crazed retired army general named Lucullus, who had a private tunnel carved through a mountain to fill his fishpond, an engineering eyesore that earned him the withering nickname "Xerxes in a toga."

In this glamorous enclave, the many meanings of *holiday* were first explored. The bay's popularity dated back to the first century B.C., when high-profile residents like Julius Caesar, Pompey, and Mark Antony—the CEOs of the Roman Republic—had taken time out from their hectic schedules for "active vacations," reading poetry in the sun, writing philosophy, debating with fellow aesthetes, and working out on the beach. But by the time of the emperors of the first century A.D., the pleasures of the flesh took precedence over those of the spirit. Soon enough, on hot summer nights, the hills of the bay were echoing with the sounds of drunken carousing, as revelers jaunted from one cove to the next, quaffing fresh oysters at nude swimming parties.

The town of Baiae (pronounced *Bay*-eye) became the world's first great seaside resort, with a reputation for truly Herculean debauchery—a free-for-all atmosphere that resembled less a Martha Stewart soirée in the Hamptons than spring break at Daytona Beach. By these steamy shores, the mythic connection between sexual abandon and the seaside, which is such a staple of tourism advertising today, was first forged. The scholar Varro complained that in Baiae, "unmarried women are common property, old men behave like young boys, and lots of young boys

A modern interpretation of party time by the Bay of Naples, from the 1980 film Caligula.

like young girls." It was "as if the location itself demanded vice," mourned the moralist Seneca, noting that otherwise respectable citizens took to inviting prostitutes out on barges, garlanding the waves with rose petals, and competing with one another in drunken singing competitions.

Egged on by the excesses of Tiberius, Caligula, and Nero, the rest of the Bay of Naples followed Baiae's lead, becoming the ancient world's ultimate theater of the senses—a Crater of Luxury, where Romans could truly let down their hair. Concealed among jagged cliffs, caressed by cool sea breezes, they indulged in prodigious bouts of eating, drinking, and fornication; on trophy yachts, whole weeks were blissfully whiled away sailing in sun-drenched circles. The bay's once-exclusive social scene was spiced up by nouveaux riches, whose shameless extravagance pushed the bounds of taste to new extremes, and by raunchy pockets of ancient lowlife. The port of Puteoli was a repository of rough trade: Aristocratic revelers often went slumming along the waterfront with assorted sailors, footpads, actors, pimps, thugs, and sleazeballs. Noblewomen went incognito as prostitutes. Nero himself liked to cruise the seediest taverns in disguise.

This notorious round-the-clock bacchanal lured tourists in droves. Travelers could rent rooms in the many boardinghouses that were clustered near the shore; they could lounge in beachside restaurants and *popinae* (bars); and when they wearied of self-indulgence, they could select from a cohort of multilingual guides to show them the sights. As in any seaside resort today, from Copacabana to Kauai, the sybaritic decadence was leavened by more-respectable acts of sight-seeing. This arc of southern Italy had actually been settled by Greeks back in the eighth century B.C., and a smorgasbord of key locales on the grand cultural trail could be visited either on foot, in a litter, or, when possible, by luxury boat. Silk-canopied ferries, rowed by teams of slaves, went out to the islands of Capri and Procida, whose magically steep shores rose on the horizon like monstrous shark fins; day trips ran to weather-beaten Doric temples, overgrown shrines, and the Vineyards of Bacchus, where sea nymphs were said to climb from the waves to nibble on grapes each night. In one corner of the bay, the quiet cultivation of poetry and the intellect was not dead: the idyllic little city of Neapolis—Naples— became the world's first artist colony, where Romans could meet world-famous writers or attend literary readings.

Yet, in the dizzying round of high fashion, conspicuous consumption, and self-gratification, nobody could quite forget that this was also the domain of Vesuvius. The earth regularly shuddered and trembled, plumes of gas steamed from volcanic vents, and the sulfuric scent of potential disaster hung over the hot baths where oiled lovers slipped off for secret trysts. Partygoers seemed not to worry much; in fact, the ominous proximity of the underworld was appropriate, since for the ancient Romans, like many other peoples, death and pleasure were inextricably linked. The great eruption of Vesuvius in A.D. 79 was only a momentary interruption to the bay's annual routine. A fraction of this sensual coastline was petrified for posterity—along with some fifteen thousand luckless Pompeiians—but the fiesta went on the next season with added determination. As one cheery song goes in the *Satyricon,* the ancient novel set by these shores:

> O woe, woe, man is only a dot:
>   Hell drags us off and that is the lot;
> So let us have a little space,
>   At least while we can feed our face.

A PARADISE INHABITED BY DEVILS

Two thousand years later, the Bay of Naples survives as one of Italy's sunniest pleasure gardens. Glamorous resort towns like Sorrento, along with the vertiginous islands of Capri and Procida, are regarded as pearls of the Mediterranean, backdrops for Grace Kelly and *The Talented Mr. Ripley,* where the voluptuous delights of summer can be enjoyed to the full.

The city of Naples—geographically, the most logical base for a visit—has not fared quite so well. It has bloated into the largest and most troubled corner of southern Italy, while once-thriving towns like Puteoli and Baiae have withered or disappeared. It's as if history has been on a vendetta against Naples for antiquity's sins: For century after century, it has attracted the A-list of rapacious world conquerors, leaving it today the poorest city in western Europe, the most backward, the most crime-ridden. It even managed a cholera epidemic in the 1970s. It is also deliriously beautiful. Seen from the water, the baroque waterfront shimmers like a color-saturated mirage, its exuberant tutti-frutti framed by medieval fortresses. Of all the world's great cities, only Rio de Janeiro looks so alluring from a distance, and so wounded up close.

This baffling contradiction was already proverbial in the eighteenth century, when Naples was described as a paradise inhabited by devils—

especially by northern Italians. The stereotype of Neapolitans, one local noble complained, was of "ignoramuses, assassins, traitors, pederasts . . . charlatans and buffoons," whose criminal tendencies were innate. Today, the local reputation has hardly improved: The men of Naples are said to be lazy, spoiled *machistas* (an old Italian joke: Christ must have been *napolitano*: He lived at home until he was thirty, thought his mother was a virgin, and was convinced he was God). The women are supposedly enslaved by ancient superstitions, addicted to lotteries, obsessed with death. Everyone is under the thumb of the brutish local mafia. Drugs, extortion, and *miseria* are the grist of news reports from the city.

Goethe famously gushed, "See Naples and die." Northern Italians have changed that to *Vedi Napoli e scappa* (See Naples and run away).

And anyone whose first glimpse of the city is the central railway station—as it is for almost all modern travelers coming from Rome— might be tempted to agree.

Initiation Rites

W E STOOD on the crowded Naples train platform and stared, open-mouthed.

With its shattered floor tiles and nebulous gloom, Napoli Termini looked less like a gateway to the legendary Crater of Luxury than a prison detention center in Panama City, circa 1935. In the shadows, an army of pickpockets was circling around arriving passengers like overfed vultures taking their pick of abandoned lambs. We had no idea where to even find a hotel in Naples, so we made a quick dash toward the railway tourist office.

While Les was minding the bags by the door, a character with dried blood on his face came up and stood two feet away, peering at her with a cheerily predatory expression. His left hand kept working furiously below his trousers, until a policeman shooed him off.

When I came out to check what was going on, Les had a look of puzzled shock that I was familiar with from other travel debacles, landing in Third World hellholes without a clue.

"I thought traveling in Europe was going to be easy," she said. "You know: no terror."

I watched a trio of Dickensian cutpurses licking their lips at the sight of us.

"They say Europe ends at Rome city limits."

It was some consolation, I supposed, to realize that we were still at one with the wandering ancients: Arriving in a strange town has always been the most delicate moment of travel, and it wouldn't have been any easier for those Romans who didn't have their own mansions lined up by the bay, or friends to stay with. Worn out by the hot four-day journey on the Appian Way, caught in the world's first summer traffic jams, they had to confront the most urgent order of business: to go wandering the unfamiliar streets—none of which had numbers or even names—in search of a *hospitium* (house of hospitality). At night, the confusion was even worse, since only the main crossroads were lit. The torches were often mounted behind masks, like rows of jack-o'-lanterns—creating a rather spectral ambience, one imagines, for someone coming home from a dinner party with a belly full of Falernian wine.

Those first few hours in an unfamiliar city were a vulnerable time then too, when travelers were forced to rely on the dubious charity of locals.

"There are shysters," one Greek guidebook writer warned darkly, "who wander the city and swindle the well-to-do strangers who come to town."

Today, in almost every city on earth, the tourist industry has spawned grassroots organizations to save the fresh-faced traveler from being torn apart by wolves. Here in Naples, with its gruesome crime rate, a mysterious local "business association" had set up a special booth to direct new arrivals to the humble hostelries of the city.

We were a little unnerved by the railway station, and exhausted—my excuse was the aftereffects of a bottle of red wine called Tears of Christ I'd drunk the night before, recommended for its "sulphurous and gunpowdery tang"—so, against my better judgment, I went inside.

A woman in a low-cut frock smiled knowingly—did I even detect a leer?—pocketed my cash deposit, and scribbled the address of the Hotel Casanova on a piece of paper.

"Solid Italian name," I said, shrugging.

Rocketing away from the station in a taxi, peering through a miasma of pollution, my initial impression that Naples was just like a frayed Latin American capital was confirmed. The shadowy streets stretched out in an endless span of fume-blackened buildings dating from some regrettable architectural cul-de-sac of the nineteenth century; row after row of shops sold machine parts, paper, old clothes, pretty much anything that people couldn't use. Among its many claims to fame, Naples also has the highest population density of any city in Europe, and every single inhabitant seemed to be out there on the streets, riding a Vespa at maximum velocity. The traffic was truly a wonder to behold: In Rome, the river of motorbikes speeding down narrow streets had seemed insane enough, but here in Naples, chaos was elevated to a weird and compelling art. Red lights were ignored—they were mere decoration, to brighten up the streets. The aim was to keep the flow going, to press on, to fill the surging veins of this vast, unwashed animal of a city. Pedestrians stepped out blindly from the curb and were carried along, vessels in the urban blood.

"There are shysters!" The words were ringing in my ears as I noticed the taxi driver take a peek at us in his mirror and then turn off his meter. Here we go, I thought, the traditional welcome.

In fact, Italian-language books should include the Italian for the following highly useful phrases under the heading Arrivals:

- Signore, your meter appears not to be working.
- Oh, the Albanian-made piece of rubbish!
- In which case, signore, might I note your taxi license number?
- Ah, I have left my documents at home.
- Damnable luck . . . but do I spy a carabiniere, so that we might discuss this matter in more detail?
- Unnecessary! The machine is working again just fine.

Watching the taxi driver speed off—flinging choice epithets from his window—I began to see why contemporary guidebook writers, trying to be positive, refer to Naples so cautiously, as the "black sheep in the family of Italian cities," the "ugly duckling of the Med," a city of "hidden treasures," "a diamond in the rough."

Maybe Naples really *was* populated entirely by thieves, derelicts, drunks, and desperadoes.

If we'd wanted that, we could have stayed at home in the East Village.

THE DARKEST *CELLA*

In the chthonic gloom of the Hotel Casanova's foyer, a crone hidden behind a metal grille looked suspicious at our arrival.

"You want the room for the *whole* night?"

A bald, elderly businessman in a three-piece suit, with a twenty-year-old secretary on his arm, brushed past, tossing his room keys on the desk and giving us a cavalier wink. At the top of the dark stairs, our room looked out at a well-made brick wall; the air was heavy with a sweet chemical odor, presumably aimed at deterring roaches, yet the bath hadn't been scrubbed in years.

As it happened, the rooms of the Hotel Casanova were uncannily like the *cellae* of the ancient Roman boardinghouses that have been excavated in Pompeii: small, airless boxes, with a couple of straw-covered pallets for beds and an intricate mosaic of graffiti all over the walls (one choice example: INNKEEPEER, I PISSED IN THE BED. YES, I ADMIT IT. WANT TO KNOW WHY? YOU FORGOT THE CHAMBER-POT). These were the standard, third-rate lodgings that Roman tourists regularly had to accept. Although spa towns like Baiae had far more comfortable hotels, with dozens of porters, cleaning staff, and cooks, it was common to end up in a more modest inn for several nights (overbooking during peak periods was not restricted to Bethlehem).

Rudimentary décor wasn't all the Hotel Casanova had in common with the ancient *hospitia*. Most of the cheaper Roman hotels were run by women who doubled as madams. One buxom hotelier was reported dancing drunkenly outside her hotel with castanets, offering passersby the fruits of Amor with the staff. ("Rest your body here beneath the vines," she coos. "Garland your head with vines, and snatch sweet kisses from a young maiden's lips.") Cheap inns were usually more perfunctory: As in the backpacker hostelries of Bangkok today, a lone male traveler would get a late-night knock on the door from one of the slave-maids, and every Roman bedstead boasted an engorged figure of Priapus to watch over the proceedings. Any woman working in a hotel was regarded as a prostitute by the authorities; barmaids, waitresses, and cleaning girls were forbidden to bring charges for rape under Roman law, since it was considered that their lifestyles made it inevitable.

On special occasions, a traveler might be treated to the services of the innkeeper herself—a sobering thought, as I recalled the crone down below.

In the Hotel Casanova, I checked the bed—no used condoms, at least. Somewhere down the dank hall, a couple were in the middle of a blood-curdling screaming match (on the other hand, being Italians, maybe they were just discussing the weather). From Les's expression, I could see she wasn't thrilled with the accommodations. But the Tears of Christ was seeping through my brain like acid. Why not crash here one night? I thought. We'd certainly stayed in far worse places. Then again, she hadn't been in *la condizione de maternità,* as some Italians coyly put it, in those days.

When the hot-water tap let out a brown spurt, gurgled, and ran dry, Les drew the line.

"It's a rat hole!" (Her favorite Anne Bancroft quote from *To Be or Not to Be*.) "We're going to get our deposit back."

"Are you sure?" I lay down exhausted on the sagging bed. "They might put some mafia hit men onto us . . . toe cutters . . . knee cappers . . ."

"Tone, we talked about this: no squalor."

"None?"

"Not if we can avoid it. Minimal squalor."

Two hours later, we were going through the unnerving ritual of arrival again, picking a new *pensione* out of the telephone book. This time, we went for a place on the top floor of an old apartment building, reached by an antique mahogany-paneled elevator. By dumb luck, we hit pay dirt.

With a theatrical flourish, the aged *padrona* revealed a room with a huge window that looked out between two other tall buildings, across the docks, to Naples harbor. The shimmering water was a piercing shade of blue I'd never seen before in nature. In the far distance sat Vesuvius itself—ever since the last eruption, in the 1940s, broken into two camel humps. Active or not, there was something about that remote eroded form that was improbably calming.

This was the view travelers had been coming to see for over two thousand years. The warm sun was streaming in, lighting up Classic Southern Italian Hotel Room number 2, the sort of place people stayed in old Lena Wertmuller movies and Merchant Ivory period pieces, with "O mio babbino caro" playing over and over in the background. Silk curtains flapping in the sea breeze. Light ricocheting off the white tile floor. Compared to everything else in Naples, it was indeed the earthly paradise.

The fact that the short old signora who ran the place was clearly insane hardly bothered us at all.

THE HOTEL HADES

What is it about finding a decent hotel in Europe? Why should it be so difficult? It's an age-old question, especially in the Mediterranean, where rooms, since darkest antiquity, have been inevitably small and quirky, their ambience shaped by the disordered personalities of their owners— and a building block of comedy long before *Fawlty Towers* was conceived.

Even back in the fifth century B.C., the Greek playwright Aristophanes took a bleak view of travelers' inns.

In his play *The Frogs,* the central character, Dionysius, is planning a visit to Hades, so he asks the demigod Hercules, who went there on one of his Twelve Labors, for some travel tips. Most important: On the highway to the underworld, which is the inn "with the fewest bedbugs"? Down by the gloomy river Styx, Charon—Hell's ferryman—recommends a hotel inauspiciously called the Last Resting Place. After staying at this infernal lodge, the protagonist is chased by its two terrifying landladies, who think he's skipped out on them without paying the bill. They threaten to knock his teeth in, throw him off a cliff, and slit his throat with a billhook.

The truth is, the Landlady from Hades is alive and well and working in Naples—running our Classic Southern Italian Hotel Room number 2.

Signora Crispi was a stocky old doorstop of a woman, who spoke in a deep, half-muffled rasp, disturbingly like Marlon Brando in *The Godfather.*

"Where are you from?" The words would come out slowly, with a vaguely menacing lilt. "*Nuova York* . . . Oh . . . *Che bella* . . . I had a cousin . . . He went to America . . . Never heard from him again . . . Boy with no manners . . . *Capisce?*"

She ran her eight-room hotel with an iron fist, aided by her middle-aged son and two skull-faced cleaning women who always wore white lab coats and looked like they should be swabbing a mental hospital in Siberia. It was a little disconcerting to stumble out of our sun-filled room early in the morning and confront this spectral bunch, cigarettes hanging from their pale lips, all staring blankly at our door.

It turned out La Signora was a hands-on landlady. She wanted to know your business. Where you were going that day. What you'd done. Whom you'd spoken to. At first it seemed like a quaint and amiable Neapolitan trait, the grandmotherly affection of a career *padrona* for lost and wandering souls. Just the sort of heartwarming, intimate feature you'd expect in an Italian *pensione* (and we'd be able to tell people when we got back home, "Oh, we found this charming little place in Naples . . ."). Soon enough, things got out of hand. The Signora started bustling into our room at every opportunity. Offering extra towels. Bits of advice. Did we have soap? she'd wheeze. Oh, she thought she'd forgotten the soap. Back again: Did we need a fresh bath mat? Another lightbulb? She was insatiably curious, eyes darting at our belongings under the pretense of solicitude. We had the distinct sensation that we might return one afternoon to find the Signora and all her crew in our room, trying on our underwear.

If Les stayed in the room to draw, it would drive the Signora into a claustrophobic frenzy, knocking on the door every fifteen minutes. "Oh, signorina . . . *cara mia* . . . when are you going to go out? We have to clean the floor . . . *Capisce?*"

Les tried to explain that she wasn't going anywhere, that it didn't matter about the cleaning, we'd do without it for a day.

"Non importa!" Les exclaimed on the fifth attempt.

"Doesn't *matter?*" the Signora bellowed in her tobacco-raw voice. "It matters to *me!*"

Trying to distance ourselves from La Signora's prying eyes only made things worse. We started to transgress. Every day, it seemed, we did something wrong. "Antonio . . . *caro mio* . . . would you remember to turn off the lights? Yesterday you left the bathroom switch on . . . you wouldn't believe the price of electricity in Napoli." "Antonio . . . *amore mio* . . . you forgot to close the window . . . you know if it rains, that can be a disaster . . . *Capisce?*" The shriveled little woman would grate this out, hands clasped as if in prayer, apparently so sorry to disturb us, yet it would take twenty minutes to disengage from her clutches. There was something about her—maybe it was her rasping *"capisce?"*—that chilled the blood and struck terror into the stoutest heart. Each day, we'd try to creep into our room unnoticed, only to be caught in our tracks by the ghastly wheeze from some shadowy corner.

It was driving us batty, but we weren't going anywhere, and the sinister little Signora knew it. Where else in Naples could we find a room with a view of the harbor at an even vaguely modest price?

Nowhere. Nowhere but the Hotel Hades.

THE FIRST ARTS COLONY

As we hit the streets every morning, dodging motorbikes careening onto the sidewalk, it was a struggle to remember that under the Roman emperors, Naples was considered the most sedate of the bay's seaside settlements—"the city of idle repose," conducive to meditation and the composition of poetry. "Peace untroubled reigns here," raved the poet Statius to his wife in A.D. 93, "and life is leisurely and calm, with quiet undisturbed and rest unbroken." In contrast to its depraved neighbors, Naples was then a low-key resort, with only one famous temple—of Parthenope, one of the Sirens who lived on the rocky cape of Sorrentum nearby. Women with the wings and claws of birds, the Sirens sang the lovely songs that lured sailors to their deaths.

By Statius' time, the artsy ambience had turned Naples into a thriving writers' retreat every summer, with budding authors descending on the town to read their works in public auditoriums. The most illustrious full-time resident had been Virgil, who composed most of his mammoth *Aeneid*—the Latin answer to Homer's *Iliad* and *Odyssey*—there during the reign of Augustus. Virgil, the world's first literary celebrity, was publicity shy. He was famous for slipping out of his crowded poetry readings to avoid his admirers; he even ran from fans in the street, ducking into friends' villas or strangers' houses, like a rock star after a concert. But his popularity put Naples on the literary map. Soon, all the literary heavies of Rome chose it for their seasonal visits—bringing with them all the machinery of the writer's life that we recognize today.

There was a grueling schedule of *recitationes* (poetry readings), most of which lasted for a full night, and some for three days. There were local publishing houses employing slaves to transcribe manuscripts; a system of grants (via gifts from wealthy patrons); critics who savaged authors and one another. There were vast private libraries—one, with three hundred thousand scrolls, had once belonged to Aristotle in Athens. Wealthy aristocrats threw banquets for their favorite writers, while impecunious poets enjoyed more bohemian, potluck meals. One invitation survives:

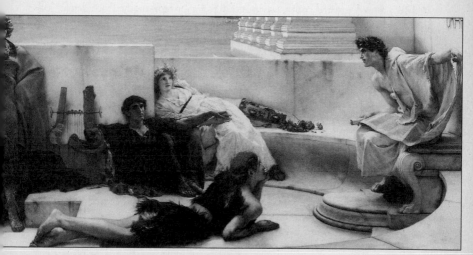

A Reading from Homer *(1885), by Sir Lawrence Alma-Tadena,*
depicts the edifying vacation.

Artemidorus provides cabbage, Aristarchus salted fish,
Philodemos one small liver, Apollophanes some pork.
Let's dine at four sharp! I wish
For garlands, slippers, scent and talk.

Martial describes a less picturesque version of the literary life, as he is pursued by an aspiring young poet:

You read to me as I stand, you read to me as I sit,
You read to me as I run, you read to me as I shit.
I flee to the baths; you boom in my ear.
I head for the pool, you won't let me swim.
I hurry to dinner, you stop me in my tracks.
I arrive at the meal, your words make me gag.

Poetry competitions were immensely popular, and every four years Neapolis hosted the prestigious Sebasta in the city's largest amphitheater. Readers stood on a dais and orated; those with poor voices sometimes hired actors to read their work, but stood alongside to make the appropriate hand gestures themselves. The riotous crowd atmosphere resembled a modern American poetry slam—every mot juste was greeted with exclamations of delight and approval; choice metaphors provoked eager roars; rhetorical flights demanded standing ovations—although, instead of financial reward, poets competed for a crown made from leaves of corn.

The Sebasta's status was such that Nero chose Neapolis for his artistic debut, reciting his epic poem on Troy to the accompaniment of the lyre. Despite his "weak and husky" voice, he granted encore after encore, urged on by his trained teams of applauders. These professionals were soon standard at Roman readings: They were briefed in advance on the text, so that they could erupt into fits of ecstasy at the most evocative literary flights. The audience was forbidden to leave while the emperor Nero was on stage, even though his concerts went for thirteen hours. It's said that a laboring woman was forced to give birth in the auditorium; one old man supposedly feigned death to get to the bathroom during a marathon show.

These lofty literary pleasures seem unusually distant in modern Naples, where not a single stone of Neapolis remains standing. In particular, its last two centuries as a gritty industrial port have erased all hints of the quaint Roman city, although like most impoverished, traditional out-posts, the mean streets of Naples could also be calendar-book pictur-esque. Every morning from the Signora's window, we could see the women across the street lower buckets on ropes, to be filled with fruit; old men in singlets sat with grandchildren on their balconies, singing snatches of opera. The Hotel Hades was on the fringe of the Spanish Quarter, famous for its lines of laundry poetically hung across streets so narrow that the occupants on opposite sides could chat; it's also the place where teams of enterprising pickpockets shadow visitors' every move, ready to relieve them of burdensome belongings.

In fact, this modern waterfront area of Naples felt less like the literary colony of old than the reincarnation of antiquity's rough-and-ready port, Puteoli—where one short-term resident, the seedy narrator of the *Satyricon,* expressed the timeless philosophy of economic redistribution: "We understood amongst ourselves that, whenever opportunity came, we would pilfer whatever we could lay our hands on, for the improve-ment of the common treasury."

Puteoli was full of sleazy all-night bars, whose names were inscribed on awnings, and Roman tourists knew that they drank there at their own risk. Juvenal describes a typically desperate clientele of contract killers, fugitives, hangmen, coffin makers, "and one castrated priest who's passed out on the job, still clutching his drums." Jostling for cheap cups of wine were officers from the naval station of Misenum, who behaved with all the modesty and restraint of GIs on R and R in South Korea. Wealthy Roman tourists sometimes brought teams of bodyguards to protect them—or to push them home blind drunk in wheelbarrows—but usually, leaving Puteoli's nightspots was an unnerving prospect. Gangs were known to roam the back alleys. These were comprised of young men from rich families who were looking for a thrill after a late-night party—the club kids of antiquity—beating up pedestrians, hurling abuse, smashing storefronts, groping women. But in the wee hours, gen-uine ruffians also held up stray wanderers at knifepoint. Newcomers were particularly vulnerable to such mishaps. As the third-century nov-elist Heliodorus observed: "Ignorance in a foreign country makes the traveler blind."

The wisdom of this dictum was brought home to me every day in mod-ern Naples—and not just because a stroll down the wrong alleyway might lead to the social redistribution of the contents of one's wallet. Neapolitans in general seemed decidedly unforgiving of the missteps of strangers.

A taxi driver in New York once told me that exactly 20 percent of his passengers were "problem people"; they'd either be crazy, try to welch out on the fare, be sick, or just give him a hard time in some way. One out of five, that was New York's asshole quotient. Here in Naples, it became a parlor game to go over the events of any given day and assess the local competition. In Naples, it was more like one out of two. Shopkeepers who'd scream if your Italian pronunciation was off or you used a northern Italian dialect. Fruit vendors who'd throw change in your face if you questioned their creative pricing. Waiters who gagged at the prospect of serving you. Even a millennium or so of wretched southern Italian poverty couldn't fully explain the city's edge.

In Roman times, this brittle relationship between visitors and locals was actually codified in something called the Festival of Laughter at an obscure town called Hypata (at least according to a story by Apuleius). This centered on a practical joke perpetrated, hilariously, on an unsuspecting foreigner. The unlucky mark would be accused by locals of a heinous crime, immediately put on trial in the marketplace, found guilty, and then shown the torture implements. Just as the victim was reduced to a blubbering heap, the whole thing was revealed to be a prank. For the rest of the day, he would be laughed at through town—although, as a consolation prize, he was given a bronze statue, a battered hero of the first recorded comedy festival.

I had some idea how he felt, when we made the foolish mistake of trying to catch a bus in Naples.

In the middle of the morning, at the Piazza Garibaldi, a uniformed ticket inspector swung through the doors like a potbellied commando, howling *biglietti, biglietti, biglietti*. As soon as this rotund official saw our bus tickets, his furious expression was transformed into pure glee.

"Invalido!" he crowed triumphantly. "You have to pay a fine."

"What do you mean?"

"INVALIDO!"

Apparently we hadn't stamped our tickets in the machine at the back of the bus. That's the Italian system: You buy a blank ticket, and mark it in this orange box with the time and date. Nowhere, of course, is this actually explained; nobody else, as far as I could tell, ever actually did it.

"You have to pay a fine!"

We stared at the inspector incredulously, so he started elaborating at the top of his lungs. "Fine! *Fine!* Fine! Pay me! Or we go to the carabinieri!"

Sweat was pouring down his bright pink face, saturating his tight collar. His eyes were bulging. I was worried he was having an apoplectic fit.

Les politely refused to cough up, arguing our ignorance of the system. Everyone else on the bus was having the time of their lives, laughing away—at us, of course. One old lady almost fell out of her seat with pleasure, cackling, "You have to pay! You have to pay a fine!"

When I inquired about the sum, the inspector pondered for a moment, then decided on a figure in lire, about sixty dollars. The other passengers nodded in approval.

Les folded her arms. "Inconceivable."

"Then jail for you!" The harpy laughed.

After five minutes of exchanging these local pleasantries, the bus lurched toward our stop. The inspector had by now reduced the fine to about ten dollars, so I decided to cut our losses and hand it over. He clutched the bill and turned around to the passengers with a flourish, as if he were a magician and they his audience.

"Hey, are you just pocketing the money?" Les asked.

He bellowed to the bus: "What does she mean, I'm just keeping it? She thinks I'm just keeping it!" Everyone roared with laughter.

Asshole quotient that morning: Eight out of ten.

But then, in travel, ignorance can also have its upside. After every abrasive encounter, as if it wanted to restore some cosmic balance, Naples would give us a lucky break—allowing us to stumble into a hole-in-the-wall restaurant like some heartwarming outtake from *Nights of Cabiria,* run by a brother and sister, where the menu was fixed and for five dollars a head we feasted on home-cooked rigatoni, fried anchovies, and salad, and for a dollar extra the sister would grab us a beaker filled with wine from an eight-gallon drum, squirted out through a gas pump, and the brother would ply us with his mother's *limoncello* liqueur on the house, just because we were foreign and vaguely lost, then regale us with tales about the nefarious characters lurking outside.

And as we would stagger, slightly drunk, mildly bewildered, through the shadowy streets of the port, we'd catch another glimpse of the sparkling harbor, and the hydrofoils zipping back and forth beneath Vesuvio. And we'd be reminded that the poet Statius was not exaggerating, back in A.D. 93, when he told his wife that Neapolis was home to "a thousand beauties."

Above all, Statius stressed, the city was the perfect jumping-off point for touring the many other sights of the bay—Cumae, Sirens' Point, the isle of Capri—thus "providing all the amusements that a varied life affords."

And so, despite it all, Naples remains today.

The
Pleasure Trail

Thanks to some improbable archaeological finds, we have a fair idea of how Romans spent their leisure time by the bay: the first mass-produced souvenirs, in the form of cheap glass vials, have turned up in digs all over the Mediterranean. These chintzy relics—the ancient versions of water-filled snowscapes—were engraved with drawings of local must-sees, to be taken back home to Rome, Ephesus, or Marseilles and put on the family mantelpiece.

Sightseers flocked to the harbor of Puteoli, which was quite safe and respectable by day. Along its mammoth piers, each crowned with giant marble statues of sea horses, they could while away a sunny morning watching the maritime traffic in one of the world's busiest ports— marveling at the huge grain ships from Egypt and the maneuvers of triremes from the naval base of Misenum, their three banks of oars slapping the waves. Tourists visited the vast *stagnum Neronis* (fish pool of Nero). Then there was Virgil's tomb—the maestro's ashes were buried in a grotto by the road from Naples, which became a literary pilgrimage site much like James Joyce's grave in Paris today (or, given Virgil's cult status and untimely death, Jim Morrison's).

Romans often took these short excursions while reclining in private litters, their slaves jogging along the sandy beaches at low tide. Sometimes they sailed or rode on horseback. The most athletic young men would struggle up the slopes of Vesuvius, sweating in their cotton tunics along the route that is lined with tour buses today, to gaze down at the infernal crater.

Afterward, back at their resorts, Romans indulged in less demanding activities. Wearing bathing costumes of fine cotton or soft goatskin, they swam from the beachfronts, or took a late lunch in waterside restaurants—calamari and bouillabaisse were favorite local dishes, enjoyed alfresco and washed down with local wine, which was laced with perfume and drunk from foaming conch shells. But the greatest regional delicacies were oysters. These were artificially cultivated on farms in Lake Lucrinus, where special saltwater tanks were heated by under-floor ducts to maintain production in winter. Roman epicures could tell by taste whether their oysters had been raised in Lucrinus, Circeii, or Rutupiae, while the scientific wonder of the *balnea pensilia* (heated oyster beds) became famous tourist attractions in themselves.

Every afternoon, our sated visitors unwound at the luxurious *thermae* (volcanic hot baths). These enormous complexes—"as big as entire provinces," raved the soldier-historian Ammianus Marcellinus—dotted the whole bay, each with soaring vaults, sweat rooms, exercise yards, and swimming pools of all temperatures. Romans spent hours here—oiling their sculpted physiques, strutting through the domed buildings, and working out with weights in an ambience as competitive and lascivious as any modern gym. The sermonizing philosopher Seneca made the mistake of renting rooms above one bathhouse in the area, and wrote a scathing letter about the operatic cacophony emanating from the open dome: Between the endless grunting of the ballplayers, the noisy brawls between louts, the drunkards singing in the hot tubs, the screeches of women having their armpits plucked, and the bellows of the sausage vendors and cake merchants, he wasn't getting a lot of philosophizing done.

The baths were the ideal place for a traveler to land a dinner invitation—and the banquets of the bay were legendary for their single-minded gluttony. In the *Satyricon,* a feast given by the social climber Trimalchio—perhaps the most famous meal in literature after the Last Supper—contains a stomach-turning parade of theatrical delicacies: Dormice basted in honey, rabbits baked with wings to look like Pegasus, fruit arranged as genitalia, and the roasted heart of a lion that had devoured three gladiators. The pièce de résistance was a sewn-up roast boar; when its belly was slit, out flew a flock of thrushes, which the waiters ran about catching with nets. At the meal, the guests were even more astonished by the antics of their host, Trimalchio. Farting relentlessly as he ate, wiping his hands on a slave boy's hair, spouting garbled verse to his guests, he was one of a class of former slaves who had made fortunes in trade—the arrivistes that many patricians felt were sullying the blue-blooded standard of the bay.

The author of the *Satyricon,* Petronius—snob, bon vivant, drinking buddy of Nero—apparently modeled Trimalchio on such real-life figures as Vedius Pollio, a millionaire freedman whose enormous villa was a scene of Olympian excess. The pools were packed with eels, regarded by Romans as a great delicacy, and it was rumored that Vedius fed them with the flesh of his slaves. On one occasion, when the emperor Augustus was a guest, a servant accidentally broke a crystal goblet. Like some James Bond villain, Vedius was about to have the quivering minion tossed to the sharp teeth of his pets, until Augustus intervened: The emperor ordered the slave to be freed, and had every piece of crystal in the house broken and thrown into the pools instead.

He should be the patron saint of waiters today.

Many of the Romans' formal attractions still exist near Naples, although in fragmentary form. So while Les used her watercolors to paint the view from La Signora's light-filled madhouse, I hopped the Vesuviano train headed west, and one by one I checked them off my list.

Virgil's tomb lies in a park by a roaring highway, although when I dropped by, the grotto had been closed up by police because of too many muggings (in fact, nobody is sure if the grave is even Virgil's—the site was identified as such in the Middle Ages, when the poet was idolized as a wizard). The ancient port of Puteoli, now called Pozzuoli, is a jovial if scrappy seaside suburb that curls around the remains of a huge amphitheater. The rotten-egg smell from its volcanic vents, which once heated the Roman hot baths, still hangs over the town. All along that volatile coast—known, evocatively, as the Burning Fields—that sulfuric odor creeps out of nowhere; it escapes from the earth like hot breaths from hell.

This connection was not lost on the death-fixated Romans. One of their favorite day trips was to a cave in Cumae, where, according to Virgil, a seven-hundred-year-old prophetess—the first sibyl—told the hero Aeneas of a nearby route to the underworld.

Today the site is part of a remote and rarely visited archaeological park—and murder to get to by public transportation. I arrived in the middle of a downpour and followed a trail through gloomy forests brushed with mist. The cave was announced by a series of trapezoidal doors carved into sheer rock. It was definitely an unsettling place. Inside its dark underground tunnels, peals of thunder echoed back and forth; icy water dripped onto my head from the ceiling. The memory of a thousand mysterious rituals seemed to ooze with the moisture from moldy walls—as did the words of Virgil, who imagined the sibyl's utterances being whispered by a hundred mouths in the darkness, while leaves inscribed with men's fates blew about the tunnel. By the first century A.D., when Roman tourism was taking off, the cave was little more than a sideshow curiosity. Priests showed off a stone water jug that supposedly contained the first sibyl's bones, while a few shabby soothsayers offered to read fortunes on the steps of a nearby temple. A half-drunk tourist might well have asked about the romantic prospects of his or her Grand Tour—and received an answer as specific as a daily horoscope in the *Post*.

For genuine Apollonian prophecy, Romans knew, they would have to wait for Greece.

CUPID'S BEACH RESORT

But what about Baiae? I wondered. What had happened to the greatest of the ancient spas, worshiped by hedonists, denounced by moralists? In the modern village, called Baia, I'd seen some unassuming fish restaurants and a desolate concrete waterfront where pages of newspaper blew in the breeze; a few ruins from the baths sat in the hills, their domes and vaults barely recognizable. But it didn't even hint at Baiae's reputation as the Roman tourist playground par excellence, whose reputation for debauchery was unsurpassed.

The more I read about the ancient resort, the more alluring it became. It was said that Cupid had bathed by its turquoise shores and dropped a spark from his torch into the warm waves; ever since, anyone who swam at Baiae fell hopelessly in love. For Roman tourists, the mating rituals began every day at dusk: This was where the southern European tradition of the summer promenade was invented and refined. In the cool of the late afternoon, vacationers from around the world strolled an expansive seaside arcade—prototype for the modern boardwalk—past shellfish vendors, flute players, storytellers, and jugglers. They admired a giant lighthouse, one of the largest in the Mediterranean, and inspected the *villae maritimae* (water palaces) of the superrich, with their onyx floors, private canals, and artificial islands; early in the first century, a local schoolboy would ride a dolphin across the bay for the amusement of the crowds. But the main purpose of the arcade was social—to see and

Roman beach culture: nymphets sport prototype bikinis in a fresco from a villa in Sicily.

Foundation of Roman luxury villas in Baiae.

be seen. Strollers would meet, admire jewelry, rubberneck, flirt, and ogle. The salt air was electrified with scandal and gossip: Robin Leach would have felt quite at home in its fashion-obsessed grip.

The climax of the promenade was a romantic sunset. "The shadows of the wooded hills fall across the sea," said Statius, "and the palaces seem to swim on the water's crystal surface." But this serene moment was merely the calm before the storm: After dark, as the waves of Baiae gently steamed from volcanic heat—referred to as Cupid's erotic flame—the Roman social spectacle really hit its stride, with partygoers hopping by torchlight from moored yachts to beachside canvas tents to banquets in their villas. Most visitors liked to stay up all night for the revelries.

Who knew? Maybe you would spot a famous celeb—someone related to the emperor, a disreputable senator—dashing by with a toga around his knees.

But where were the remains of this factory of hedonism? An academic at Naples's National Museum of Archaeology explained Baiae's ghostly absence:

Appropriately enough for the erstwhile Roman Gomorrah, the resort area of Baiae was now completely underwater. It was thanks to a volcanic phenomenon called bradyseism, apparently, which makes parts of this unstable coastline gradually crumble like a cake dipped in coffee, and sink to the ocean floor. Sometime in the Middle Ages, Baiae had begun to flake away; now it was gone.

But that didn't mean all was lost, the museum academic assured me: Underwater archaeology is in vogue in Italy, and an enterprising Neapolitan diving club had started up a scuba operation, with permission of the local authorities, allowing the more adventurous visitors to savor the ancient ruins.

No matter that the waters near Naples harbor were among the filthiest in the Mediterranean. I signed up, without a second thought.

THE COMMEDIA DELLA SCUBA

One would never wish to confirm the tired clichés about Italians' shaky organizational skills—or make any cruel comparisons with the ancient Romans, who built their empire on order and efficiency—but this is how a diving operation at Baiae is run:

A motley crew gathers in the dive shop at 10 A.M. sharp—myself, a tubercular Frenchman, and a gaunt trio of South Africans who are staying in Naples on a cruise ship. We all furiously don brightly colored wetsuits, none of which even remotely fits. About an hour later, the dive master arrives in a silver sports car, looks out at the sky, and decides the weather is too poor to go.

We clients stare in disbelief at the sea, which is entirely placid and calm. We complain and harass the dapper, chisel-featured young dive master, whose name is Emilio, at the top of our voices. He relents, saying we'll head out in twenty minutes.

Another hour later, everyone is still milling around aimlessly. The dive master is discovered in front of a mirror, brushing his shoulder-length hair lovingly while sipping an espresso.

Diving in the rain, of course, is not everyone's idea of the sporting life: Although we all know it will be perfectly still under the water, Emilio would rather we amuse ourselves by examining the different styles of dive gear the store has for sale. To an Italian sportsman, maintaining your fashion sense is far more important than actual physical activity; there's nothing more humiliating than breaking a sweat or, in the case of a diver, getting wet.

"It's really not so nice out there," Emilio confides, with a world-weary sigh. After much fuming and gnashing of teeth, a mutiny ensues. The clients insist they'll go out diving anyway, without him. The dive master panics, and agrees to go—in another twenty minutes, say.

It probably didn't help that three of the clients were South Africans, accustomed to diving in some of the world's most turbulent waters. They virtually carried Emilio out to the boat (actually a barely seaworthy old fishing skiff) that would take us to the dive site. After repairs on the engine, we finally chugged off into the Romans' Mare Nostrum.

Despite the confusion, dark skies, and drizzle, I couldn't help feeling secretly triumphant. This was it—after so many years, I was actually *on* the Mediterranean.

But like Naples itself, the water that had looked so glorious from a distance was less alluring up close. Plastic bags, Coca-Cola cans, bottles, mulched pages of magazines drifted by, along with fluttering teams of daisy-sized pink jellyfish known as medusae. If they could survive, I figured, the water couldn't be pure sewage. Still, I was beginning to see why Emilio was so lacking in enthusiasm for the dive.

"Ooh look, Dennis," said the lead South African, doing a poor Monty Python impersonation as we leaped over the side. "Look at all the lovely filth down here."

After discovering that my regulator leaked, and swallowing great gulps of glutinous Neapolitan water, I realized that it wouldn't kill me—at least not immediately—so I dutifully followed the others down into the cloudy green murk.

The eerie silence of the underwater world closed in as I sank to the bottom. What I could make out, sixty feet down, wasn't exactly the Caymans: the sea floor was strewn with rusted metal barrels, sunken old dinghies, broken iron chains. Then Emilio was suddenly grabbing my arm, excitedly pointing to a big algae-covered block. It looked like a standard-issue concrete water break, the sort of anonymous cubes dumped on shorelines around the world. But he ran his fingers over some markings on its side—row after row of regular diamonds.

It dawned on me that this wasn't concrete but the base of the great lighthouse of Baiae, past which Romans once strolled on summer nights. Square holes, now covered in verdant slime, allowed the tides to ebb and flow through the foundations.

All at once, the murk and darkness of the water was no longer nauseating—it was evocative and haunting, like stumbling across a lost city in a rain forest. We drifted across the Porto Giulio, where a grand causeway once led to a naval harbor. I'd seen a few of the things archaeologists have raised from this site, a statue of Ulysses, piles of coins, the base of a fountain. Soon we were in shallow water, the residential area of Baiae, where the Romans' most sumptuous pleasure domes were carved into the shore. It was possible to make out pieces of columns beneath their film of green. And then—I could hardly believe my eyes—a whole courtyard was exposed. The mosaics were vivid, white with black wave patterns.

I'd seen floors a hundred times more elaborate in museums, but this sent a shiver up my spine. It was like the opening credits of *I, Claudius.*

· This must have been one of the magical, multitiered villas of Baiae, whose dining rooms jutted into the sea so that drunken luncheon guests could lower themselves down alabaster steps for an afternoon swim. According to vividly painted scenes, Roman nymphets effectively invented the bikini here, flitting about in two-piece garments as they swam, driving the old men to fits of lechery. This was where a thousand Roman marriages went on the rocks, as otherwise conservative couples were transformed into antiquity's swingers. (Martial wrote about a chaste Roman wife who spent too long in Baiae's famous hot baths, lost her inhibitions, and ran off with a handsome slave boy: "She came to town Penelope/And left it Helen of Troy.") Here, again, Seneca railed: "Why must I look at drunks staggering along the shore or noisy boating parties?" Why, he wondered, did he have to have his sleep broken by the shrieks of naked prostitutes being chased into the sea, or "the squabbles of nocturnal serenaders"? And this was where Caligula stunned even his most ardent supporters by building a three-mile-long bridge of boats, so that he could lead an army legion back and forth, festooned at night by torches and colored lights—all to disprove an astrologer's prediction that he had no more chance of becoming emperor than of riding a chariot across the bay. The display soon degenerated into an enormous public rave party: So many drunken revelers crowded onto the bridge that boats overturned, drowning dozens.

A plastic bag floated across my goggles, wrapping itself around my head. I didn't care in the slightest. Up on the surface, spitting out a laboratoryful of bacteria, I felt like—*at last!*—I'd beheld the Roman past directly. It was more exciting than Atlantis.

Even going back to the Hotel Hades that night didn't take the blush off my sense of triumph.

"Antonio . . . *caro mio* . . . the taps . . . I found your hot-water tap was dripping . . . it's so expensive, the hot water, in Napoli . . ."

Capri:
The Emperor's
New Hideaway

THERE WAS ONE MORE EXCURSION I had to take before leaving Naples, and that involved the purer seas offshore.

Of the many fairy-tale islands rising from the bay like titanic pillars, Capri has always featured most prominently in Roman carnal legend. Captivated by its vertiginous beauty and sapphire waters, the emperor Augustus had claimed the "Isle of Goats" as his own private resort, ordering twelve sumptuous villas to be built on its sheer cliffs, each named after one of the gods. By all accounts, he spent the summers there quite innocently, watching village boys work out at gymnastics. But then his successor, the decidedly more libertine Tiberius, withdrew his court to the island in A.D. 27—issuing his government edicts by flashing semaphore from a lighthouse—and the imperial sex life suddenly became a subject of intense speculation.

Dour and introverted, Tiberius spent fifteen years in the loneliest aerie, the Villa of Jupiter, surrounded by cacti, Sirens, and, it was whispered, teams of exotic *spintriae* (adepts at unnatural practices). The emperor was a satyr, island residents reported, wallowing in depravity, taking out his lusts on captive children of both sexes. Nobody will ever know the exact truth. But decades after Tiberius' death, the biographer Suetonius gathered the most malicious rumors into his *Lives of the Caesars,* creating one of the great hatchet jobs of history.

Ever since, Capri has been associated with sexual license—"a pagan paradise in a Catholic sea," as Bruce Chatwin enthusiastically put it in his essay "Self-Love Among the Ruins," "where the wine was excellent, the sun always shone, and the boys and girls were pretty and available." Europe's aristocratic free spirits descended on the island to build fantastic mansions reminiscent of the Romans' architectural excesses. The Casa Malaparte, with its sleek brush strokes of design against the raw island rock, became a climactic backdrop for Brigitte Bardot in Godard's erotically charged 1960s classic *Contempt*. By then, Capri was blazing more brilliantly than ever, luring stars from Hollywood and Cannes, Brando and Stanwyck, Greene and Onassis, playboy yachtsmen, gamblers, and socialites, whose carnal antics the world press breathlessly pursued . . .

And all this lay only three miles off the shore of Sorrento, a simple boat ride away from the busy docks of Naples—or so the theory went.

THE CURSE OF SAN GENNARO

"You can't go to Capri today!" the Signora bellowed. "Today is the fiesta of San Gennaro . . . right here in Napoli . . . you can see the miracle . . . *è bello! bello! bello!*"

I tried to explain that one of the great joys of being away from New York in September was *avoiding* the Festival of San Gennaro. I'd already observed the prefiesta setup in Naples, and the genuine Italian version, with its rows of sausage vendors and cheap carnival games outside Il Duomo, looked very much like its bastard spawn on Mulberry Street, Little Italy. Admittedly, in Naples there was a little more Catholic tradition to back up the event, as thousands gathered to watch a vial of Saint Gennaro's blood liquefy and flow—*il miracolo*. But the prospect of waiting twelve hours on a hard church pew somehow didn't seem appetizing.

"No, *no!*" the Signora's son chimed in, tears welling in his eyes. "I saw the miracle once. It made the hair on my arms stand on end! Even talking to you now, my hairs are standing on end!"

It was no use. Over in Capri, there were those pagan pleasures to be had—and tonight they were going to be on a potentially Roman scale.

It was a flawlessly sunny Saturday morning, and I'd heard that the island would be hosting one of the stellar events of the Italian social calendar—a concert celebrating the twentieth anniversary of Italy's most successful soap opera. The extravaganza would be televised live around the country, and the *bella gente* were descending on Capri in droves. It sounded like a throwback to the great fiestas of the ancients, the sort of patrician gathering that lured leading lights from around the Empire, to be discussed and dissected for years afterward. Every hotel room on the island had been sold out three months in advance, but I figured we could zip over on the hydrofoil, take in the ambience, and get the last hydrofoil back to Naples at 11 P.M. sharp.

"Eleven P.M.?" The Signora nearly choked. "They close the harbor at six! *Capisce?* I don't care what your timetable says. You can't come back at eleven! Believe me, Antonio . . . I've lived in Napoli all my life . . ."

I hurried Les into the elevator. As we rattled down, we could still hear that voice: "But the miracle! The miracle of San Gennaro . . . *è bello . . . bello!*"

That afternoon, we were enjoying one of the subtler pleasures of Capri. On the cliffs of the Villa of Jupiter, where the emperor Tiberius pushed people who offended him to their deaths, you could sit and listen to all the Italians, breathless from the ascent, who would gaze out at the five-hundred-foot drop into a blue so deep it was almost black and wheeze, "Oh, mamma mia!"

"Listen," Les said, nudging me every few minutes. "They really say it!" It was endlessly entertaining.

Certainly, not many views are more deserving of the accolade as the one from Tiberius' retreat. As seen from the water a few hours before, it had appeared to be physically impossible to land on Capri at all, let alone build a palace on its highest point. The cliffs rose in sheer stone curtains from the waves, blocking every approach. But then the rocks opened, and the hydrofoil slipped like a dart into the hidden port. We gorged on fresh mozzarella and olives by the beach, amazed that anywhere should look so clean and bright and pure. It seemed like the gods had come down and given the earth a good wax polish.

The security of this single landing point, combined with the stupendous scenery, was what made Capri the perfect vacation hideaway for the emperors. But up at the Villa of Jupiter—or the outline of its excavated remains—the fragrant air was heavy with the depiction of Tiberius by that father of all muckraking biographers, Suetonius. The emperor emerges from that scandalous account as an aging ghoul whose face was covered with boils and pustules. He would dress little boys up as minnows so they could "nibble at his parts" when he swam in his private pool, and maimed any who complained about his lecherous advances. When he wasn't debauching himself, Tiberius apparently amused himself with mock trials of political enemies—tormenting his victims like wingless flies before personally ejecting them off his private precipice (Suetonius adds almost in passing that a favorite imperial send-off was to tie a man's penis with cord and then force him to drink enough wine to burst his bladder). Local fishermen were horrified to find the bodies of illustrious senators washing up at the doorsteps of their huts.

Every once in a while, a historian pipes up that Tiberius was a shy man, a hermit, who preferred debating philosophy with his Greek friends to sodomizing innocents. Not that it matters. The truth behind the stories passed into irrelevancy long ago. The legend has a life of its own, a dark undercurrent to Capri's otherwise harmless reputation for beauty and sensual abandon. It follows a direct line from Suetonius to the Marquis de Sade (a famous early visitor to Capri) and finally to the indelible image of Peter O'Toole as Tiberius in the film *Caligula*—face running with sores, dashing from orgy to orgy in a shower of bodily fluids.

Of course, the ancient Romans themselves were quite taken with the idea of Tiberius as satyr; without their ongoing fascination, Suetonius' calumnies would never have survived. From the moment of the emperor's death, the Villa of Jupiter became a top tourist attraction, a titillating must-see for any visitor to the bay who wanted a fresh mise-en-scène for his or her own excess.

Roman boating parties regularly drifted across from the mainland. Slightly hungover from a picnic on their private yacht, the sightseers sweated their way up the sun-scorched stone path. They would rest for a moment in the shade, then wander about the abandoned palace, alternately gasping at the views and recounting with relish the most salacious tales.

Here were the "nooks of lechery," where Tiberius would conduct unspeakable acts: This was his actual bedroom, whose walls were lined with obscene manuals penned by the most depraved experts of Egypt, and hung with a vast sordid painting of the huntress Atalanta fellating the hero Meleager; here was the tower that flashed his sinister orders to the mainland, including the execution of young girls, who, being virgins, had first to be violated by their captors . . .

And then, having revived their own flagging passions, the tourists might repair to one of the holiday villas to get the party going once again.

Back down the steep, cobbled paths of modern Capri—heavy with bougainvillea, intoxicatingly free of Vespas—a few black-shrouded harridans were waving their canes angrily at the dozens of girls in miniskirts. A steady stream of Italian socialites was arriving for the evening's festivities; liveried bellhops were lugging mountains of leather luggage up the narrow pathways like teams of Egyptian slaves. The hotels of the Rich and Famous looked no less palatial than the mansions of their Roman forebears. Their swimming pools jutted out over sheer cliffs, and staggeringly expensive restaurants commanded sweeping sea views. On the rocks below, sunbathers were splayed about like oily white starfish. The most privileged guests were paying twenty dollars an hour to rent a sliver of black sand, where they could squeeze onto a plastic banana chair. Ten dollars more would obtain an umbrella. No sign of how much extra to actually swim.

Out of curiosity, we checked a few hotels to see if there was any space. The receptionists coolly confirmed what we'd already been told: Every room in Capri had been booked for months. We went ahead and bought our tickets back to Naples on the last hydrofoil.

Eleven P.M.—summer Saturday special.

Les was wary about cutting it so tight—she had one of her ominous premonitions. But I had to witness the full drama of the evening. I looked up at the sky, a perfect gleaming dome of Capri blue. *What could go wrong?*

THE NEW SATURNALIA

As dusk settled over Capri, the air crackled with excitement, as intoxicating as anything on the ancient boardwalk of Baiae. Within the blink of an eye, the intimate village plaza had been cordoned off, rows of seats laid across it, and the walls festooned with thousands of fresh red roses. Invited guests began arriving in twos and threes, to the firefly sparkle of paparazzi bulbs. It was an event of high Italian fashion—a blur of supergolden coifs, taut brown cheeks, and dazzling sequins. One jaw-dropping gown after another swept by, a parade of radical color combinations usually reserved for the curtains of Holiday Inns by the Jersey Shore. Cleft-chinned playboys paused by the windows of Hermès, Armani, and Prada boutiques to adjust their cuff links and smooth their hair. Sitting next to us in the café, a trio of elderly Italian women excitedly identified soap stars for us from the celestial parade. They even had a photograph of one star in a magazine, having a drink with Roberto Benigni. Now *this* was celebrity.

By 8 P.M., the cobblestone streets were packed to capacity; it was tighter than a people jam in a Beijing railway station. Up on the glitter-spangled stage, musicians struck up with George Michael arrangements from the 1980s. Actresses crooned to old love songs; slapstick comics took the stage. Television cameras panned the audience.

It was, as they say, bigger than *Ben-Hur*.

But there was only so much fabulousness that we could physically take. Squeezed ever farther onto the sidelines, Les even griped that it was no more a Gatsby-esque extravaganza than a *Wheel of Fortune* taping in a San Diego mall. *De gustibus non est disputandum*. Soon we were in full retreat. We dodged and swerved our way through the crowded back alleys, then ducked at random into a shabby doorway. It took us a few seconds to realize that, miraculously, we'd wandered straight into a relic of Capri's last golden age. Tucked away from all the Cartier and Chanel stores, paint peeling in sheets from its ceiling, the trattoria was all but empty; in fact, it had the desperate air of a dining room on a sinking cruise ship. But covering an entire wall were faded photos from the 1950s: Grace, Orson, Barbara, Marlon—all had dined here, when Capri, for one last time, was internationally peerless, the social empyrean of the Med.

This was glamour we could relate to more easily. There were Jean-Luc, Brigitte, and Sophia at play . . . and you could picture the elderly Graham Greene poised at a table in the corner. It was the perfect place to sit out the rest of the evening.

Sipping an aperitif by the cracked window, I watched the lights of Capri harbor twinkling far below. There didn't seem to be any boat movement, but I wasn't worried: I'd called up at 8 P.M. and confirmed that the late hydrofoil would be coming from Naples.

When I mentioned this to some islanders at the next table, they looked at one another and smirked.

"In Capri, you have to do more than call!"

"Oh, I don't believe it," Les sighed.

At 10:45 P.M., at the docks, a crowd of twenty people was gathered around the harbormaster, gesticulating and jabbering. The last hydrofoil had been canceled; it wasn't coming from Naples to pick us up. The captain had decided there was "too much turbulence," but we all knew better, looking around at the few paying passengers and dead-calm sea.

Bad luck for those of us stuck on Capri.

Several of the more dignified passengers couldn't stomach this affront.

Cell phones were whipped out, calls placed to the hydrofoil company in Naples, the weather station, local hotels. Then we all stared around abjectly in the dark.

After such a sumptuous evening's entertainment, nobody could quite accept that we were trapped on this bare island without a bed: Capri had seemed so delicious, fragrant, and welcoming; suddenly it was bleak and inhospitable. Mangy dogs appeared out of nowhere, prowling around our feet; drunken teenagers lurched from dark doorways, shouting garbled war cries. It may have been late summer, but the wind whipping off the sea was numbingly cold.

That was when Les turned her accusing eyes on me and said: "Tone, *do* something!"

I made two dozen calls from a pay phone, trying to find a room. Nobody was the slightest bit sympathetic. Tonight of all nights, the hoteliers could not have cared less.

"Of course we have no beds!" one old bat muttered, disgusted.

"Are you completely crazy?" another one yelled at me.

"Mia ragazza è incinta," I trotted out, in ritual fashion, having looked up the word for *pregnant*. As a last resort, I thought the Mary and Joseph routine might appeal to the Italian sense of family, which I understood was a big deal.

"Can you perhaps suggest a place—"

"You won't find a room in Capri!" she snarled, before slamming down the phone. "Not tonight!"

Les looked at me expectantly, ready for some all-encompassing solution. In the old days, we would have just curled up in a cold doorway with a bottle of Chianti and waited for dawn, putting it all down to experience. But things had changed. Even I had to accept that now.

TRAPPED ON THE ISLE OF GOATS

"Okay. We could always go to a bar," I suggested to Les in a hopeful tone. "Get warm. Gather our thoughts. Create a plan."

We took the funicular back up to the main town and wove through the people jam, Les trying to protect her abdomen from drunken elbows. I spotted the five-star lounge bar of the Grand Hotel Quisisana—the Waldorf of Capri—which had some lavishly comfortable sofas. Soon we'd grabbed one in the corner, staking out our pathetic turf, and nursing twenty-five-dollar cocktails, too expensive to actually drink. It wasn't much in the way of home, but blinking at the languidly decadent scene around us, I quickly realized we'd arrived *somewhere:* This was the equivalent of crashing an ancient Roman free-for-all, I imagined—or the modern shadow of it. It was 2 A.M., and the in crowd of young Italian socialites had taken over the bar, disporting themselves in all their reconstructed glory. The faces of the girls looked taut and leonine—framed by artificially colored manes—and a bit frightening, like Greek tragedy masks garlanded by clouds of smoke.

Still hoping for a solution, I sought out our own kind, hoping for a lucky break.

"Hey, this beer just cost eighteen bucks!" an American voice boomed across the bar. "What the fuck is this?"

The waiter shrugged, and suggested that the first drink was always expensive on Capri. The others would be half that price.

"Oh, man." His girlfriend giggled. "We must have *sucker* written right across our foreheads."

The couple from New York were on their honeymoon. They planned to party all night. I guess in the back of my mind I was dreaming they'd say: *Hey, look, use our hotel room tonight. Here's the key.*

But they didn't.

Things were getting desperate. Les was feeling sick, talking about cramps. I was racking my brain to think what else I could do, although in a somewhat irrational, delirious fashion. She could sleep on the banquette, I figured, but the cigarette fumes were getting toxic.

At the other end of the bar, I recognized two paragons of Italy's gilded youth from the hydrofoil incident—rich kids who'd turned up at the last minute. When they'd heard that the boat was canceled, one girl had burst out laughing and turned away. Now she was still laughing, stretching her perfect Venus de Milo figure across a leather lounge. She was wearing a translucent shred of silver gauze, held on by spaghetti strings; it clung to her body like Saran wrap. I had to ask what they were doing for the night; maybe her father owned a twenty-five-room villa and there was plenty of space just waiting to be used . . .

"You know, you really can't come to Capri without a reservation." She smiled gaily. "Not on a Saturday. Not in summer."

"I'll keep that in mind." I shuffled back to our corner.

Les was no longer asking me what the results were of these abject social forays. I imagined her ending up in a hospital in Capri. What I'd have to say to her folks. I wished I could teleport us back to the Hotel Hades. It was as if we were being punished for ignoring the weird rites of San Gennaro.

By 4 A.M., the bar was closing up. The waiter wanted to go home, and no, they wouldn't let Les sleep on the couch. Outside, the cold wind was whistling down the cobbled narrow alleys; Capri's quaint little souvenir shops were dark and menacing; the stars looked down like brilliant shards of ice.

We were standing forlorn beneath the steps of the Hotel Las Palmas, the first hotel on Capri. This was where the glitterati used to stay, back in the 1950s. It was glowing with bright lime-green lights, looking down on us like some renovated Roman temple.

"We could sit in the foyer," Les suggested. I wasn't too keen. The Las Palmas was one of the first places I'd called, and the receptionist had been unusually rude. But Les had a feeling about it. She didn't know why.

"Why don't you ask again at the desk?" she said with sudden animation.

Reluctantly, I asked the oafish desk clerk if there was a room. He knitted his brows and said: "Give me ten minutes."

It was like magic; I couldn't believe my ears. A guest had been expected from Naples on our canceled hydrofoil, and his room—*the last hotel room in Capri*—was empty. It was 4 A.M., so the management decided to double its money.

"Is a very nice room," the clerk said, grinning a bit malevolently as he led us up in the elevator. "One of our *very* best!"

And it was true; it was a five-star luxury suite, with private balconies overlooking the plaza itself, royal beds, a Jacuzzi, flower arrangements, and garden furniture. The wardrobe alone was the size of our apartment in New York.

"Ah . . . how much does it cost?" I delicately inquired; not that I could turn it down. Les was already curled up on the bed in a fetal position.

The clerk rattled off some astronomical figure in lire, all the time dangling the keys in front of my eyes.

"In American dollars—around four hundred fifty."

As Petronius so aptly put it in the *Satyricon*:

> *Ye gods and goddesses! O what a night!*
> *How soft the bed! We clung so warm and tight,*
> *Our lips exchanged our souls in mingled breath.*
> *Farewell all worldly cares! O welcome, death!*

The Call of
Aurora

AFTER A SPELL by the Bay of Naples, Romans tourists were ready to confront the Lands of the Dawn. And despite the Capri fiasco, we were ready to head east as well—although not everyone saw the logic of following the Roman route so closely.

"You want to go to Benevento? . . . Why? . . . *Why*, Antonio?"

"Well, the old Appian Way used to run through there."

"No, you take it from me . . . there's nothing there! *Niente, niente.* You go to Bari! You go to Sicily. *Che bella!* Like a dream . . ."

"No, it's Benevento tomorrow."

The Signora seemed about to tear out her hair. "Antonio, listen to me . . . I beg you. I am Italian. All my life I have lived here—"

"After Benevento, we'll go to Brindisi."

"Oh, my God! What for? . . . What *for*?"

"To catch the ferry to Greece. The via Appia ended there."

"Oh, no, Antonio, no. There's nothing! Nothing!"

This Cassandra-like prophecy, of course, was not entirely accurate.

The overgrown remains of the Appian Way could still be seen in the green farmland of the south, surrounded by flocks of staring sheep and swaying fields of corn. In the provincial outpost of Benevento, Trajan's great triumphal arch marked the Roman highway to the eastern provinces; by the Adriatic Sea, the stump of a marble column announced the end of the road.

Admittedly, making the trip by second-class Italian train was not what you'd call high style. At pit stops en route, hoteliers blasted soccer results through their foyers. Taxi drivers grasped, waiters scammed. And the port of Brindisi was colonized by fast-food stores, devoted to extorting the unlucky ferry passengers who were trapped in their town for a night.

But all along the way, whenever things grew tawdry or difficult, I tried to remember Horace. The poet made the same journey along the Appian Way at the very beginning of the imperial era, and things continually went awry. It's all recounted in one of his verse *Satires:*

Early in the trip, he declares his bowels "a public enemy" after their explosive reaction to the local water. Inns en route provide a succession of "nasty tavern keepers" and ugly meals—anorexic chickens and granite bread being high on the list. Staying overnight in Benevento, Horace is nearly choked to death by smoke when a spark from a kitchen sets a wooden ceiling on fire. Then he comes down with conjunctivitis. A few days later, he arranges a date with a "lying young wench," then awaits her in vain until midnight (he turns to the traditional panacea of the lone male traveler, ritual self-abuse: *somnia . . . nocturnam vestem maculant ventremque supinum* [dreams . . . stained my nightclothes and stomach as I lay on my back]). The low point of the journey comes in the Pontine Marshes, where Horace is kept up all night by mosquitoes, croaking frogs, and sailors, blind drunk on cheap wine, who keep up an off-key sing-along until dawn.

By the time the poet gets to Brindisi, you get the impression that he's pulverized, physically and spiritually, by the whole experience of travel. Everything that could go wrong, did.

After our shaky start to the trip in Rome, Naples, and Capri, I found this strangely comforting.

I was really following the Romans' footsteps now.

PART FOUR

HERMES' HIGHWAYS

A Road Trip
Through Greece—
Papyrus Guidebook
in Hand

For CULTIVATED ROMANS, Greece was the emotional core of the Grand Tour. Landing on its shores sparked the same giddy excitement as Henry James's Bostonians would feel many centuries later on their pilgrimages to Europe: It was a true rite of passage, a once-in-a-lifetime experience of the Old World, a respectful homage to the wellsprings of civilization, the enviable and proper finish of any citizen's education. Every inch of Hellenic soil was saturated with history and myth, every city jam-packed with monuments and artworks that Romans had learned about since childhood. On that craggy coastline, framed by natural stone arches and weathered fingers of granite, temples from the dawn of antiquity stood like sacred treasuries, repositories of the most marvelous pagan artifacts and relics of the heroes. The mountains above were riddled with holy grottoes, the playgrounds of nymphs and sprites; in moist forest groves, each oak, hillock, stream, and rock had somehow been touched by the gods themselves.

Greece—then the Roman province of Achaia—was a small, barren, and politically irrelevant corner of the Empire, but it was, as they say today, the ultimate culture trip.

It was also easily accessible from Italy, just a short hop by Liburnian galley across the Adriatic. Even in the first century B.C., Greece had been popular with Roman sophisticates like Cicero and Ovid; but it was in the first and second centuries A.D., with the Pax Romana making travel secure, that Latin tourists began arriving in legions. They wanted to see for themselves the sites of legend, where the gods had once romped, where Hercules had fought and Penelope pined. This steady flow of affluent visitors soon turned Greece into the busiest leg of the ancient sight-seeing circuit, and thus the great laboratory of Western tourism itself.

It was here that Romans established their first clear-cut sight-seeing itinerary—the Hellenic "greatest hits," whose contours we have inherited today. Every modern Wonders of Greece bus tour includes Athens, Delphi, Olympia, Sparta, and Epidaurus—the highlights beloved by the ancients. At these eternal tourist venues the first nostalgia industry flowered, with Greeks selling packaged visions of the country's distant past along with the standard services like inns, meals, and guides: the country was "learning to be a museum" (in one historian's caustic phrase) at a tidy profit, while promoting Hellenic pride along the way. And it was in Greece that locals first suffered tourist burnout, becoming jaded in their dealings with the eager foreign visitors.

Roman tourists tackled the Greek sight-seeing decathlon with determination and inventiveness. The region's compact size lent itself to the first road trips. Travelers would hire a wagon on the outskirts of Athens (choosing from a range of vehicular options), then enjoy one of the excellent Roman highways that had been built in the reign of Augustus. En route, they would refer to graphic itineraries—stylized maps, with symbols to indicate the quality of roadside inns (one, two, or three towers, like stars on Michelin maps today). Even the most modest Greek sites had souvenir stalls, fast-food vendors, and tavernas—although the quality of meals was not always top-notch. Unlike today, however, dissatisfied customers in Greece could pay to have a curse put on a second-rate facility. (A lead plaque would be engraved with a spell to bind or paralyze a victim, and then buried in a cemetery. A typical example found in Athens reads: I BIND BY SPELL KALLIAS THE TAVERN-KEEPER AND HIS WIFE THRAITTA . . . AND THE TAVERN OF THE BALD MAN AND THE TAVERN OF ANTHEMION NEARBY . . . ALL THESE I BIND BY SPELL THEIR SOUL, THEIR TRADE, THEIR HANDS, THEIR FEET. A certain "Mania the bar-girl" is singled out on the same plaque, for unspecified misdemeanors.)

The high-profile sites like Delphi and Olympia, dense with cultural significance, attracted the first teams of professional guides or "explainers"—the *mystagogi* who skulked around the entrances of the sites and badgered visitors until they were hired. Classical writers continually complain about these ubiquitous characters, who seemed to be more persistent in Greece than anywhere else. (Which is why the Roman antiquarian Varro so memorably prayed: *Et me Iuppiter Olympiae, Minerva Athenis suis mystagogis vindicassent*—"Jupiter, protect me from your guides at Olympia, and you, Athena, from yours at Athens!") Any traveler today can sympathize with the trials of the author Plutarch, who depicted a pair of guides at Delphi prattling away parrot-fashion with their prepared spiel, not letting anyone get a word in edgewise, then loudly reading the inscriptions from the statues verbatim. When asked a question that strayed beyond their rote, the learned guides were completely lost. Lucian, mobbed with guides in Rhodes, became convinced that they invented their sensational "facts" entirely for a gullible audience ("Abolish lies from Greece," he suggested, "and the guides there would all die of starvation, since no tourist wants to hear the truth—even for free"). Today's *mystagogi,* who sprint around Greek sites waving spurious credentials and scribbled testimonials from "contented" clients, have hardly updated their methods.

After taking in the must-sees of Greece, those Romans with plenty of time on their hands wandered into the countryside, using one of the many learned *periegeseis* (guidebooks), that had become popular by the first century; across this harsh and mountainous peninsula, every minor byway led to some legendary attraction. The vales of Arcadia, the tomb of King Agamemnon in Mycenae, the gateway to the underworld at Cape Taenarus—all had their hypnotic mythic allure.

Thrilling and splendid it all undoubtedly was. And yet, to some Romans, the cultural legacy of the Greeks could be a little intimidating. Just as Henry James's Americans found in Europe nearly two millennia later, the Romans found undercurrents of snobbishness—and subtle hints of local resentment—that sometimes gave the travel experience an unsettling edge.

The mentor-pupil relationship between the Greeks and the Romans can be traced back into the mists of time. Long before the first conquering legions marched across Aegean shores, cultivated Romans had stood in awe of Greece and its heroic past. From Rome's earliest days, its citizens had taken to worshiping the Greek gods—warm, humorous, vain characters who wandered the earth in human form and carried on like soap-opera stars of antiquity, seducing and betraying one another with relentless abandon (the austere and shadowy Latin pantheon was unspeakably dull by comparison; Romans simply appropriated the Greek legends entirely, like a publisher buying up a backlist, giving the gods new titles like Jupiter, Venus, and Mars). The Greek heroes Jason, Achilles, Theseus, and Ulysses; powerful women like Medea, Electra, and Circe; monsters like Medusa the Gorgon, the Cyclops, and Cerberus— all were household names in Rome.

Every Roman schoolboy could recount in detail how, back in the fifth century B.C., when the Latin capital was not much more than a scrappy settlement by the Tiber, the feisty Greeks had twice stopped the Persian Empire dead in its tracks—a dazzling David and Goliath act of defiance, recounted over and over like the *Star Wars* of its day, that changed the course of history by saving the Mediterranean from Oriental domination. (In fact, in the fields of Marathon, not far north of Athens, it was whispered that ghosts of the warriors refought their epoch-marking battle every night—the perfect enticement for Roman war buffs.) During the golden age that followed the final defeat of the Persians in 480 B.C., the Greeks had hammered out Western Civilization 101—the foundations of European philosophy, drama, sculpture, science, medicine, law, political science, lyric poetry, and written history, not to mention the creation of the world's most perfectly proportioned architecture. This astonishing cultural legacy was conveyed to Rome via Sicily and southern Italy by ancient Greek colonists, masterful sailors and explorers who scattered themselves around the known world in a dizzying diaspora.

By the time of the Empire, the rivulet of Greek influence in Rome had become a flood—provoked, paradoxically enough, by the city's conquest of Greece. The same generals who had "liberated" Greece from Macedonia in 196 B.C. became passionate Hellenophiles, bringing home shiploads of Greek sculpture and paintings to adorn the rude and rustic streets of Rome. A multitude of clever, subtle, opportunistic Greeks followed, infiltrating the artistic world of Rome as thoroughly as the British in New York today. As a result, the mind of every educated Roman became steeped in Hellenic culture. He or she would have studied with a Greek teacher, learned the Greek tongue, read more Greek literature than Latin (Homer and Aesop, over and again), debated with Greek philosophers, and admired Greek plays performed by Greek actors. Greek wine was thought finer than Italian, Greek cuisine more robust, Greek fashions more appealing, "Greek love" (of a man for a boy) more elevated and poetic.

Horace's verdict has become one of the clichés of antiquity: "Conquered Greece took captive her barbarous conqueror."

It was this convoluted history of admiration for the Hellenic way that Roman tourists brought with them as they crossed the Adriatic. The philosopher Epictetus summed up the prevailing attitude: Any educated person, he wrote, would consider it a tragedy to die without having seen the wonders of Greece. Yet despite all this cultural adulation, the blunt reality was that Greece was now a subject province of Rome, a political fact that complicated even the warmest encounter between tourist and local. Sensitive visitors tried to be diplomatic about Greece's fallen state, and hoped the ravages of the Roman conquest had been forgiven, if not forgotten. "Show your respect for Greeks' antiquity, their heroic deeds and the legends of the past," Pliny the Younger advised a traveling friend, to avoid friction. "Do not detract from anyone's dignity, independence or pride. Remember what each Greek city once was, but without looking down on it for being so no longer."

Others were impatient with Greek pretensions. As the Roman general Aemilius Paulus cautiously noted when he set out on his own tour of Greece, it was a civilized man's obligation to take in "things rumored great—perhaps too great."

THE DAWN OF THE WEST

Today, the overnight ferry from Italy to Greece plies exactly the same route as the ancient Roman galleys did: Departing from Brindisi (the ancient Roman port Brundisium), crossing the Adriatic, then heading east into the deep natural inlet of the Gulf of Corinth.

On my own humble voyage across the wine-dark sea, I woke with a start at 5 A.M. Les was huddled in the bunk below—the shudders of the boat had brought vivid flashbacks of first-trimester morning sickness. Upstairs, the ship was silent and deserted. In the desolate lounge, which was still oozing cigarette smoke and cheap beer from its vinyl pores, a hungover bartender in a crimson vest apologetically prepared me the ferry-standard cappuccino—toxic creek water in a Styrofoam cup.

Out on deck, however, it was a textbook Greek summer morning, cool and still, not a single wisp of cloud crossing the glowing sky. The last veils of purple night were receding into the gulf; one by one, the stars were going out. And there it was. The coastline of Greece emerged, relaxed and powerful, like a manta ray drowsing on the ocean floor. Bare hillsides, dust brown and spotted with white goats, seemed airbrushed by a protective gauze of salt mist. Somewhere on the raw headland, I vaguely recalled, a temple to Poseidon had once stood: Priests kept braziers burning at night for passing sailors, and they sacrificed giant tuna to the Lord of the Sea, pouring their black blood on the altar. I imagined I could make out a few broken pillars still standing by the rocky cove, but they might have just been gas pipes or the remains of a wrecked tanker.

Another passenger staggered out on deck, to take all this in—a scrawny, monkish-looking Japanese backpacker, who'd passed the night on a plastic bench. Wearing a Walkman, he cautiously climbed up on the front railing, arms outstretched, pretending to be Leonardo DiCaprio, it seemed.

"I the king o' the worl'!" he yelped at the top of his lungs, craning forward, suicidally, to the sea.

And then, like an atomic blast, the sun came over the mountains, setting fire to the sleep-addled recesses of my brain. It exposed every detail of the coastline, every polished copper stone, the veins in my eyelids, all at once. The sea was a mirror, every sparkling wave magnifying the beams to a painful intensity. So this was it—the legendary Greek light. Roman tourists were the first to babble about its brilliance, the clarity of the air itself—Cicero attributed the sharpness of the Attic mind to it, when he first sailed along these shores. Poets have been raving about it ever since.

A ferry in the Gulf of Corinth.

The approaching landscape began to feel oddly familiar and welcoming, as if this were a homecoming.

That misspent youth studying the Peloponnesian Wars. *Jason and the Argonauts.* The Clashing Rocks, the Harpies, and the multiheaded Hydra. Kirk Douglas in *Ulysses. The 300 Spartans.* ("Die, you Persian dogs"—dubbed from the Italian.) It was all up there somewhere, a lurid mélange of classical texts and low-budget movies. The ancient Greek characters were rising up in my memory like skeleton warriors out of the earth.

The truth is, a journey to Greece remains as significant a rite of passage for us as it was for the ancients. By the nineteenth century, Romantic poets led by Byron and Shelley revitalized the Roman fascination with Hellas and passed it on to us virtually intact. Today, the archaic heroes are still rushing about in a raucous menagerie, pouring wine, chasing boar—Perseus and Achilles, Electra and Medea, still feasting at the long table of history. And the words of a thousand expatriate writers, from Lawrence Durrell to Patrick Leigh Fermor, have proclaimed the sun-drenched Greek landscape the most idyllic on earth. Even the sardonic Henry Miller, fresh from the sewers of Paris, raved inchoately about pagan gods in his *Colossus of Maroussi,* declaring Greece a land where the boundaries between myth and reality, poetry and fact, past and present blurred. "Greece is what everybody knows," he wrote in 1939. "Even as a child or as an idiot or as a not-yet-born . . . it breathes, it beckons, it answers."

Admittedly, it's been a few years since anyone has rhapsodized about the pagan glory of Greece, or the Zorba-esque depth of village life. I was under no illusions about what to expect. Since the 1960s, Greece has become one of the most heavily visited countries on earth, inundated by armies of pallid northerners every summer. It is now commonplace to deride it as an example of all that can go wrong when tourism is unregulated.

And yet the legendary image is still there, coiled, waiting to spring to life.

Another ferry was overtaking us, its wake parting the regular waves into a mathematical graph; caught by the blinding sun, the ship appeared as a silhouette on a sea of molten silver, the barest outline, like an etched daguerrotype. In Roman times, this journey was made by merchant galleys, the oarsmen (who were free laborers rather than slaves) working under the sun . . . a painted mainsail billowing in the trade winds . . .

Venus or Minerva presiding on the stern. The passengers would be awake and excited, waiting for a slave to warm the honeyed morning cakes on a coal stove. Filling their lungs with the same briny air. Listening to the creaking of the timber and rigging. Keeping one eye out for sea monsters, another on the land.

I took another sip of creek water from my Styrofoam cup. "He come all'a way fom Ame'ica!" the Japanese kid wailed maniacally.

The sky was lightening to an ever-thinner shade of blue. Just me and a tripping karaoke singer, drooling at the spectacle.

Athens:
The Altar of
High Culture

THE ANCIENT TRAVEL WRITER Dicaearchus of Messana warns:

> On first arriving in Athens, a stranger will hardly believe that this is
> the city he has heard so much about. The streets are nothing but mis-
> erable old lanes, the houses mean. . . . But the stranger will quickly
> realize that this is Athens indeed.

It seems that first impressions have long been a problem in Athens.
For Roman tourists, expectations were unusually high: Of all the Greek
city-states, it had produced the most original minds, the finest artists, the
noblest statesmen, leading the incandescent creative ferment of the
golden age in the fifth century B.C. Athens was the epitome of Hellenism—Greekness—and thus of civilization itself, making it the first
and most anticipated attraction in the entire land.

But as a visitor traipsed the hot roadway from the port of Piraeus—
along the once-noble Long Walls, which were by the first century A.D.
derelict and ruined; past untended fields of olive groves baking in the
intense Aegean heat; listening to the lonely lullaby of cicadas humming
in the crisp dry air; finally reaching the dusty Dipylon gates at the urban
outskirts—it was hard not to be shocked at the city's sorry decay. The
citadel of high culture appeared more squalid even than Rome's rank
Subura district. There were mounds of fish spines and rotten vegetable
peelings, gutters running with nameless slops, houses barely superior to

shepherds' huts. More than four centuries had passed since the golden age of Pericles and Socrates. Now the Athenians' clothes were torn and dirty, children ran naked, flocks of sheep wandered the alleys.

It was only on the Panathenian Way that visitors' eyes were drawn irresistibly upward—and their initial disappointment was replaced by a relieved shock of recognition: the Acropolis.

Towering above the disordered streets, that monstrous limestone crag seemed to scrape the sky, its bulk as imposing as one of the Pillars of Hercules. Marble stairways zigzagged up its sheer cliffs, where worshipers filed like ants. The Acropolis was fortress, sacred sanctuary, and sculpture court rolled into one. Even from far below, it was easy to spy the bronze helmet of the enormous Athena, the virgin warrior goddess, glinting in the crystal sunlight, and her spear raised against all enemies. Crowning it all was the Parthenon, Greece's signature icon—an architectural masterwork as symbolic in antiquity as the Eiffel Tower in fin de siècle Paris.

Nature had blessed Athens with a peerless setting, surrounded by hills of "soft-breathing grace" and vistas that stretched down to the sparkling sea. But the Greeks had improved on Nature with Art. As Roman visitors tore their eyes away from the Acropolis and proceeded along the Panathenian Way into the city center, they came across, one after another, the most uplifting public places in the world, the most inspiring houses of worship, the most graceful sculptures. To the orator Aristides, the first glimpse of Athens was "as if the goddess Athena has removed a veil from a traveler's weary eyes." The city fulfilled every ancient ideal of harmony. Imperial Rome was grandiose and overwhelming to the eye; Athens was more beautiful by far—an organic, subtle, melodious creation. To visit such a city was a spiritual experience:

"Every glimpse," Aristides rhapsodized, "purifies the mortal soul."

There was no denying that the halcyon days of Athens were long past, as remote in time to ancient tourists as Michelangelo's Florence is to us today. The city's population was only a fraction of what it had once been; the opulence of its maritime empire only memory. And yet, Athens was still the undisputed world capital of art and higher learning—a compact college town, like Oxford or Cambridge, still brimming over with intellectual excitement. Apuleius wrote that the lucky inhabitants of Athens were "permanently drunk" on "the imaginative draught of poetry, the clear draught of geometry, the sweet draught of music, the austere draught of dialectic, and—the most delicious nectar of all—philosophy."

Newly arrived travelers, strolling to the Athenian agora (marketplace), were delighted to find that the place really *did* have more philosophers than cobblers or fruit vendors. Pythagoreans could be identified by their long hair, capes, and sandals; the iconoclastic Cynics by their matted, unkempt beards. Among them were talented students from the city's four famous universities, which included the Academy, founded by Plato—and what's more, they could all be found arguing about the Immortality of the Soul in the vine-covered courtyards of tavernas, just as in the old days of Socrates. Members of the Stoic school took on Peripatetics (followers of Aristotle); Epicureans locked horns with Orphics. At neighboring tables, professional scribes composed devastating political lampoons, while gamblers tossed dice for books of Greek rhetoric. By nightfall, the trees above were full of owls, the ancient birds of wisdom. (Oddly, they were considered ill-omened creatures: If an owl flew into your house, the only recourse was to capture it and nail it alive, wings outspread, to the front door.)

The presence of so many *epheboi* (young students) meant that the pursuit of philosophy was not always a grimly serious business in Athens. Some of the more conservative Romans were shocked to see that youths lounged about entirely naked in the warm sun, disputing some obscure point, or rehearsed speeches while inebriating themselves on local wine. Others diverted themselves by inscribing obscene poems on barroom walls. (A good example of ancient sophomoric humor, accompanied by drawings of bearded philosophers, has been found elsewhere in the Empire: TO SHIT WELL, SOLON USED TO RUB HIS BELLY. / THALES ADVISED THE CONSTIPATED TO PUSH HARD. / THE SUBTLE CHILON TAUGHT THE SECRET OF FARTING SILENTLY.)

Next to philosophy, art was the great business in Athens. "Every artist is sure of being welcomed here with open arms," enthuses the travel writer Dicaearchus, "which is why the city is crowded with statues." On street corners, sculptors could be seen assessing blocks of marble recently arrived from the Aegean quarries and even the cemeteries were thick with masterpieces. Portrait painters were minor celebrities. According to one papyrus bill, the going rate for a portrait was a bushel of wheat and two jars of Knidian wine—a bargain for rich Romans. Then there were the famous drama festivals, when even the poorest Athenians would forget their hunger and crowd into free shows, grappling for the best seats at the amphitheater of Dionysus, which had been built on the very site where Thespis in 534 B.C. invented the art of theater itself (one imagines him introducing it: "Ah, this is a little experimental piece I've been working on . . ."). As at Shakespeare's Globe, audiences would be reduced to tears by the tragedies, while actors playing the Furies could cause mass panic: Clad in black with bloodless cheeks, their haunting hymns "rose and swelled, drowning out the musical instruments, palsying the heart, curdling the blood." When the spoken word was exhausted, the written word was ever present. Tourists could visit the Athenian bookshops—far older and more prestigious than those of Rome and Naples—whose inviting doorways were engraved with the names of the great poets whose works were stocked inside. Their locally produced editions were objects of beauty in themselves: Texts on the finest papyri were rolled onto superbly carved wooden scrolls, then placed in tasteful red linen wrappers. Some stores specialized in fantastic literature; others, criticism; sellers of rare books charged the public a fee just to browse their shelves. At the more highbrow literary outlets, one could meet local authors and discuss weighty matters in the native idiom.

Sensitive Romans could hardly fail to be intoxicated by this heady intellectual atmosphere. Hellenophiles often compared Rome's superficial, grasping, status-obsessed climate to the Athenian moderation, decency, and love of art. The distinction was wearing a little thin by the second century—rich Athenians, like the rest of the Greek elite, were just as materialistic, showy, and wasteful as the Romans they regarded as their friends and equals—but there was still a kernel of truth. Greeks could never completely subscribe to the Roman greed-is-good philosophy of conspicuous consumption. At heart, they still believed that there was more to life than fashion, self-adornment, and filling a villa with expensive trinkets.

This helps explain why the residential streets of Athens were ruled by vermin and wandering sheep; why the Athenians' houses were so basic, their clothes torn and dirty, their meals usually so simple ("one kind of porridge followed by another," according to one historian's appetizing description); and yet they would still pay voluntary taxes to beautify their public spaces with new sculptures. Art, theater, poetry, good conversation—these were the stuff of daily life in Athens.

As Dicaearchus of Messana opined:

> *If you've never seen Athens, your brain's a morass;*
> *if you've seen it and weren't entranced, you're an ass;*
> *if you left without regrets, your head's solid brass!*

THE BLESSED WINDS

Today, no city on a European tour has a less enviable reputation than Athens. The crucible of civilization is now regarded as a cancerous blight on the landscape, a festering wound, largely thanks to that curse on

Mediterranean air quality, the automobile. Since the 1920s, the Greek capital has multiplied exponentially, exploding from a hamlet barely larger than the original ancient city to an overburdened madhouse of ten million people. The same encircling crown of hills whose "soft-breathing grace" once enchanted Romans is now a natural prison that allows barely a whisper of exhaust fumes to escape. As a result, Athens nearly always wallows in a stagnant pool of rust. Athenian air stings the eyes, clogs the lungs, blots out the views, exhausts the spirit, and erodes the beloved monuments of the golden age like an acid bath. Travelers seem universally to despise the city, staying only one night before escaping out to the islands. Even in Naples, people warned us to avoid Athens. Judging from the verdict of the Greeks themselves, the city was entirely unlovable, on a par with Bogotá, Jakarta, and Mogadishu.

Expectations could hardly have been lower. Which might be why, of course, I quite liked the place.

It just so happens that there is a rare meteorological condition that can transform this sad shrinking violet of a city into a vision of earthly paradise, and it hit the day we arrived—an Olympian blast of the Etesian winds. I'd chosen a dirt-cheap hotel called the Pella Inn because it was located directly on the site of the ancient Panathenian Way (and, well,

Rooftop view of the Acropolis.

because it was dirt cheap). First impressions were not encouraging—it had the air of a condemned youth hostel—but then we stepped out onto our precarious balcony, and did a vaudeville double take.

Directly across the traffic-clogged road, the Parthenon hovered like a serene white space station. The fierce gale had swept the air of Athens to a hallucinogenic clarity; the temple's pearlescent marble surfaces seemed alive, flaring with diamonds of light in the dazzling sun. Sure, the streets *were* still miserable old lanes, the houses mean; but the city could not have been more alluring if we'd arrived on Cicero's galley.

Even Les was ready to accept our seedy lodgings. "It's worth it this time," she admitted, as we stared out at the copper fist of the Acropolis. "A rat hole with a view."

Making the most of the modern parallel, I quoted from a volume on ancient Athenian housing, which, even for the well-off, was monastic: " 'We must imagine houses without drains, beds without sheets or springs, rooms as cold, or as hot, as the open air, only draftier.' Just like here," I gloated.

What's more, the Panathenian Way, where our hotel was deposited, was once the main avenue of Athens—and much more than that. It was also a sacred thoroughfare, the holiest procession route of the city, along which citizens would file bearing olive branches and singing hymns. Modern urban planners still drool over the design of classical Athens, whose arrangement of temples hinged on this route. They talk lovingly—with a reverence bordering on the mystical—about the ancient city's architectural "rhythm," how its buildings "influenced space with spirit and texture."

We tried to keep all this in mind as we dashed across the murderous modern highway and into the Plaka—the district now planted on top of the ancient city. But once we were within that cobbled precinct, the ages seemed to blur, or at least peacefully coexist. The whole area is now blocked off to traffic, making it a blissful refuge from the hurly-burly outside. According to Aristides, strolling through Athens in the second century A.D. was a "dance of joy," "a happy dream." Today, the simple absence of cars in the Plaka induces a similar euphoria.

In that labyrinth of café tables and shady alleyways, the pale relics of the ancient world were emerging from their excavation sites like the tips of icebergs in a twenty-first-century sea. Once again, modern visitors to Athens were unconsciously following the exact footsteps of Roman sightseers, who would weave from the Temple of Hephaestus (today the best preserved ancient structure in Greece) to the ancient agora, cooing in pleasure at the artworks on every corner. Many of the most famous relics in the Plaka today were actually erected by the Romans in the second century A.D., when the emperor Hadrian and a local millionaire named Herodes Atticus decided to give the city a face-lift. A new "Roman Athens" was created to parallel the original Greek version, with its own Roman agora, Roman gymnasium, Roman amphitheater, and Roman library—all in the Greek style, which the Romans had adapted wholesale.

Historians today regard the copies as inferior, lacking refinement, and Roman tourists were actually inclined to agree. They preferred the landmarks of "old Athens": the prison where Socrates drank his cup of hemlock; the villa of the orator Demosthenes, where he locked himself up for months at a time to practice his brilliant speeches; the birthplace of Pericles. Honest Romans readily admitted that they were more history buffs than art lovers at heart; they agreed with Cicero's expatriate friend Atticus: "My darling Athens attracts me not so much for her Greek monuments and ancient art, but for her great men—the places where they sat, talked and lie buried." Unfortunately, none of these evocative house-museums survives today, but the echoes of ancient life in the Plaka are as inescapable as the summer heat.

Every street corner had its souvlaki stand, where regal cooks with long knives were hacking at carcasses of meat like Homeric hunters carving up roast boar. At the flea market, throngs of Greek families were browsing through mounds of antique bric-a-brac, from Byzantine icons to broken old clocks—just as in the old agora, the poet Eubulus found a jumble sale of "figs, court papers, turnips, roses, blood sausages, honey, puddings, berries, abacuses, lambs, water clocks, law books and indictments." And the plazas may now be full of Parisian-style cafés, where hip young couples sip iced Nescafé frappes and idly nibble each other's ears—but a stone's throw away lie the traditional tavernas, the exclusive preserve of bearded men who all look like Ringo Starr, chain-smoking, playing backgammon, and arguing at the tops of their voices (about shopping prices, it seems). The concentration of bars on specific Athenian streets is a relic of the ancient "drinking shops"—*kapeleiai*—where thirty saloons would be lined up on the ground floor of a building, with hotel and gaming rooms above. Jugs of wine were chilled in underwater springs; clients drank from cups that bore optimistic messages like STOP THE HANGOVER! And the all-male rule has a long tradition: Roman tourists were surprised to find that free Greek women were always cloistered away, far from sight. Romans would happily take their wives along to a dinner party, for example, but Athenians invited prostitutes, flute girls, and comely young boys.

The remain of an ancient popina, *or bar, with vats used to store food and wine.*
Popular throughout the Roman Empire, this one was unearthed in Herculaneum.

And I was relieved to discover that Art is not dead in modern Athens.
Street portraitists and bouzouki-wielding performers try their luck with
passersby; one after another, the stores of the Plaka peddle tiny model
temples, along with T-shirts emblazoned with Aphrodite's midriff and
Apollo's chiseled features. Even the chintziest stalls recall the time of the
Roman tourists: They sought out Athenian sculptors to make souvenir
reproductions of great artworks to take back home to the villa in Rome
(a second-century A.D. shipwreck found off Piraeus has even yielded life-
sized copies of enormous temple friezes). Tourists loved to sit for quick
portraits by Athenian artistes, as keepsakes of the visit—no doubt with
the iconic Parthenon placed in the background.

ACROPOLIS NOW

In Roman times, as today, that illustrious edifice lured visitors like a
magnet; it was the central element of the great limestone mesa at the
heart of Athens, where Greek history and myth collided.

Ancient tourists' excitement reached fever pitch as they hiked the processional path along the sheer cliffs of the Acropolis, with their servants leading the sacrificial animals—a pair of groomed heifers, perhaps, or a full-grown steer garlanded with flowers. The entrance to the Acropolis, called the Propylaea, which is still in use today, was a towering, column-lined hallway whose roof of translucent marble tiles was "incomparable for the size and beauty of the stone," according to one breathless visitor. Attendant priests took charge of the animals, and ushered visitors with all due ceremony onto the illustrious high plateau, where the Parthenon was only a single element in a somewhat jumbled field of wonders.

The surface of the Acropolis as it stands today is a bald pate compared to that of Roman times. The whole precinct was then crowded with temples, shrines, sacred springs, and the graves of heroes; the spilled blood of innumerable warriors had been absorbed into its cracked soil. The great statue of Athena that could be seen from down below was only the most monumental of its artworks: There was a dense forest of statuary, so that some visitors joked that Athens had a second population in marble, all gaily painted, with ivory eyes and detailed irises to give the faces expression. Their silver teeth, copper nipples, and golden fingernails sparkled in the sun.

Gazing around the famous precinct, Romans felt a panic familiar to any modern visitor who first walks into the Met or the Tate. Where to turn first? Should one rush to the Erechtheum, where the captured trophies of the Persian Wars were on display, or go straight to the pit of writhing snakes, dedicated to the god of healing? Should one pause at the Temple of Nike, the winged Victory, or seek out the tiny idol of Athena Polias, an image that had fallen from heaven itself (and profoundly sacred, even though it was a small runt idol—"a shapeless bit of wood" as Christians sneered)? Most Roman sightseers chose to savor Greek legend first: They rushed past the Parthenon to the cactus-lined cliff edge that looked out to the sparkling blue sea. It was on this very spot that King Aegeus had waited for his son Theseus to return from his duel with the Minotaur. Theseus forgot to change the boat's black sail— the signal agreed on to announce that the hero had been killed—and in grief, Aegeus flung himself to his death. To the ancients, being able to stand on such a hallowed site of legend was the most sublime highlight of travel.

At last—in the company of a professional guide—it was time to approach the Parthenon.

Visitors first paused at the steps, identifying the frieze details on the

Model of the interior of the Parthenon.

pediment above, which were painted in bright, almost garish colors. Then, with bated breath, they entered the temple itself, drinking in its heavenly proportions. At the farthest end of the polished marble interior, her face suffused with mysterious light and reflected in a still pool of water, towered the most exquisite of the Acropolis's three statues of Athena, sculpted by the incomparable Phidias. The warrior goddess stood forty feet tall, her robes made of gold, her flesh ivory; she held a jewel-encrusted spear in one hand, along with an intricately carved shield. As ever, the statue was well attended. Teams of priestesses were attending to Athena's every need—treating her, in fact, like a giant Barbie doll. Some draped her in saffron robes, others changed her earrings, still others, from elevated positions, moved their hands around her head as if they were styling the goddess's hair. Afterward, assistants held up mirrors in front of her to ensure that she approved.

Today, the Acropolis remains one of the great pilgrimage sites of the Western world.

For my first visit, I considered walking the sacred pathway in ancient Greek dress, but Lesley seemed to think that this might be interpreted as frivolous. Frankly, I doubt anyone would have noticed: The outfit would have seemed sober compared to the uniforms of the Athenian soldiers, who were frog-marching up the smooth trail in their pom-pom shoes, miniskirts, ballerina tights, and floppy hats, heroically ignoring the snickers of the international tourist parade.

Entering the site is still like a cinematic montage sequence (as the Russian director Sergei Eisenstein once observed), with one spectacle after another bursting into view. Inside, of course, pandemonium reigned. We took a seat in the sun, watching the guards blowing their whistles at the crowds, frantically trying to stop people from stealing souvenir fragments of stone off the ground. Suppliants were angrily waving their fists at the heavens, furious that the Parthenon was still covered with construction poles, part of a Sisyphean restoration project that has been going since the 1970s. French kids were chasing one another like crazed cats. Hundreds of miles of Kodak film was being exposed every hour, the modern sacrifice to Athena.

I tried to remember my Zen mantra from Pompeii: *Crowds are ancient, crowds are good.*

This chaotic, free-for-all atmosphere was hardly alien to the ancient Acropolis. Far from a solemn enclave, the sacred plateau was filled with people—not just Roman tourists, worshipers, and their guides, but officials and religious functionaries, astrologers, priestesses, maintenance workers, porters, and even police to protect the valuable temple artifacts. There was no respectful silence, inside the temples or without. At outdoor altars all over the site, sacrifices were in progress: One heard the bleating of terrified animals, the tinkle of flutes made from the shinbones of stags, and the ululation of priestesses as the knife sunk home. One smelled the scent of singed hair as a lock from an animal's mane was tossed into the fire, followed by billowing clouds of smoke carrying the odor of roasted flesh. Pagan temple attendants were skilled butchers: They divided up the carcass of every sacrificial animal, choosing one portion for the gods—usually a thigh—and examined the entrails for omens (a detailed list was posted at every temple gate to explain the cost of every such service). The remains were grilled on skewers and divided among the participants and priests. Not a scrap of the animal was wasted: If there was any excess meat, it was sold to the butchers of Athens.

In fact, there was nothing ethereal about the ancient Acropolis—even its physical arrangement was hardly the harmonious garden of modern imagination. The current layout, with its wide open spaces between important structures, was designed by nineteenth-century archaeologists, who religiously cleared and stripped its surface to match their Romantic ideal of classical purity. In their zeal to eliminate all memory of the Turkish occupation of Greece (the Parthenon, for example, had been used as a mosque), they pared it down to a tidy arrangement of temples. The truth is that the original Acropolis was a rather confusing place. But just as the ancients' painted friezes would seem gaudy to modern tastes—so different from the white marble statues we see in museums—a cluttered Acropolis would seem counterintuitive, even rather irritating. At every turn, visitors had to step over piles of offerings to the gods, from terra-cotta idols to gold wreaths, cups, and plaques. The interior of the Parthenon was bristling with inscriptions. Even the sacred olive tree was surrounded by bric-a-brac and weighed down with holy baubles.

The ancient world might have been full of wonder, but it was rarely austere and tasteful in the modern sense.

Over at the suicide spot of King Aegeus—unmarked now—a cluster of Athenians was witnessing another Greek legend come to life.

"It's a miracle," one of them said reverentially.

"It is?"

"I have lived in Athens for fifteen years"—he pointed to the sparkling blue sea in the distance—"and I have never seen Piraeus from here."

His girlfriend gazed off with an expression of divine awe.

"Come back here tomorrow—and the sky will be like a wall of brown."

PARTYING WITH THE PROFESSORS

At the base of the Acropolis, the Plaka's unearthly serenity was upset: the streets were being blocked off by a demonstration. Hundreds of college students were marching against the latest NATO action, chanting slogans, waving fists, and kicking storefronts. Athenian students are the most energetic since the Paris Commune: Every afternoon they seemed to be demonstrating somewhere, against something. Newspapers the next day showed pictures of cars burning, riot police shooting plastic bullets, clouds of tear gas.

In Ancient Athens, students also had a high profile—though one that was rather less political.

Many of the younger Roman tourists regarded a year or two's postgrad education in Athens to be a key component of their Grand Tours. The city was a high-class finishing school for every young man of breeding— a place to polish one's Greek, absorb the higher culture, network with other young scions of the Empire. It's much the same attitude rich Americans have for, say, the Sorbonne today. The poet Propertius, in the first century B.C., was inspired to study here for another reason—to ease a lovelorn heart. Distressed by his lover's coldness ("Her invitations are few now, refusals frequent,/And when she condescends to lie with me/She sleeps on the far edge of the bed/Fully clothed . . ."), he decided to immerse himself in "erudite Athens." His ostensible plan was to study philosophy and "take in the famous paintings/And feast my eyes on the bronze-work and ivory." But as Propertius certainly knew, the scholarly life involved no monastic self-denial in Athens.

Greek university dons, far from being cobwebbed fuddy-duddies, led their students on a merry round of extracurricular activities—as the title of a work by Athenaeus, the *Deipnosophistai* (partying professors), suggests. Cicero's son, Marcus, found that his professors invited him to more banquets than lectures; his oratory tutor became such a bosom drinking buddy that Marcus rented him expensive rooms on a nearby street. One imagines the rich young Roman gent gadding about town with a gaggle of teachers and golden-haired youths in tow, like an ancient version of *Brideshead Revisited*.

Nor was this experience unusual. Roman tourists invariably wanted to meet learned Greek thinkers, and they eagerly allowed themselves to be drawn into this whirlpool of alcohol-fueled wit—even if they did usually have to pick up the tab for the evening.

Like the roundtable at the Algonquin, the famous Greek symposia had basically been glorified drinking parties; even in the days of Plato and Aristotle, lofty debate was lubricated with hefty jugs of Samian wine. Alcohol, sadly, did not always encourage the rule of Reason: As the poet Eubulus reported of a typical evening, the first few drinks would inspire scintillating conversation, but "the fourth [libation] . . . belongs to Hubris; the fifth to Shouting; the sixth to Revel; the seventh to Black Eyes; the eighth to Summonses; the ninth to Bile; and the tenth to Madness." After dark, professors and students cavorted in the dark streets, playing practical jokes on one another, scribbling graffiti on the walls under juvenile pseudonyms like Sacred Erection, and squandering their incomes on the hetairai (skilled courtesans, or "companions") who infiltrated Athens by the boatload from other Greek cities.

As accomplished as Japanese geisha, these bewitching ladies of the night were excellent musicians, light-footed dancers, and skilled conversationalists. They often regarded themselves as better educators than the university tutors: As the satirist Alciphron relates it, one hetaira recommended a jug of wine for breakfast, "then we will discourse one to another on the purpose of life—which is pleasure—and you will find that I am philosopher enough to convince you."

By the first century A.D., many courtesans were catering specifically to Roman travelers—a sort of high-class escort service—and they expected extravagant gifts from their admirers. Often they would negotiate exclusive contracts with men who would cover their every need, including rent in a decent villa, fine clothes, emerald necklaces—no matter if the client was fifty years old, toothless, balding, and had a complexion the color of boiled lobster. Even ugly Romans were popular, as the local sugar daddies could offer only onions, smoked cheese, and cheap shoes.

Dealing with courtesans was not without its dangers, since rejected Athenian lovers were known to go on the rampage. And the ladies had a casual attitude to private property, stripping unwary patrons who had overimbibed. ("They set traps for everyone," Dicaearchus warned darkly.) Other Roman clients found themselves more subtly deceived: One disappointed visitor complained that courtesans enhanced their natural beauties with cork shoes for height, false breasts, and white lead for their complexions. But for many Greek women, becoming a hetaira was a lucrative career path: They owned some of the finest real estate in the city, and destitute widows regularly pushed their attractive teenage daughters into the trade.

More economical pleasures could be had in the state-run brothels, where *pornai* (buyable women) paraded naked behind thin veils, as in the Parisian bordellos of the 1920s. Male travelers on a budget frequented the Athenian cemeteries by night, where prostitutes of both sexes turned tricks among the same graves of Greek heroes as the tourists had solemnly visited by day.

While free Greek women were usually absent at the student debauches, there were some exceptions. One female philosopher, Hipparchia, is remembered as one of the bohemians of antiquity: She would turn up with her husband and then, after making several flawless logical points, make love to him behind the couches, scandalizing other guests. In another instance, Lucian describes—in what was probably a personal fantasy—meeting a "rich Lesbian" at an Athenian symposium who broke every ancient sexual taboo. She was dressed like a man, he eagerly narrates, and offered the dancing girls necklaces and gowns in exchange for carnal favors. (As one of the dancers elaborates: "I took her in my arms just as I would a man, and she kissed me and breathed hard and went through the act and seemed to enjoy herself no end.")

In Athens at the cusp of the third millennium A.D., life was decidedly more sedate. Once the student demonstrations had moved on, the Plaka felt once again like Lotus-Eaters land, where you could spend weeks sitting beneath the grapevines of sunny tavernas, sipping iced retsina.

"We should stay here awhile," Les announced. "In Athens, I mean." She wanted to hole up, take stock of our impending parenthood situation. She'd even bought me a set of Greek worry beads to calm me down. They were strung on a silver chain like a secular rosary; the idea was to flick them around in one hand, thus soothing my various neurotic compulsions—for example, avoiding our impending parenthood situation. "You're going to need them," she said.

And so I did—whenever the sun went down.

THE NIGHT STALKERS OF ATHENS

One of the lesser-known enemies of the mythological hero Theseus was a superhuman innkeeper named Procrustes—the Stretcher. This terrifying villain had an iron bed—more like a rack—onto which he tied all hapless travelers who fell into his hands. If they were shorter than the bed, he stretched their bodies to fit. If longer, he lopped off a portion.

At our hotel in Athens, it felt like the Stretcher was still at large. In fact, I was surprised that such short beds were commercially available.

In ancient times, Greek innkeepers had an even worse reputation than the Italians. Female hoteliers were often said to be witches, accused of putting Circean drugs into their cheeses; they could turn men into frogs, or hypnotize them as sex slaves. Some guests woke to find they had

grown ram's horns; women could be cursed with "perpetual pregnancy."
Perhaps because most Greek hotel rooms were such fetid and dark little
boxes, their owners were popularly associated with disease: The Athenian dream interpreter Artemidorus wrote that if a sick person dreamed
of a hotelier, then he or she would soon die. Christian fathers refused to
let their flocks stay at inns: "Where the eye and ear are polluted," one
early cleric warned, "so too is the heart."

But to be fair, the problem with many inns wasn't the management
but the clientele; one Roman inn excavated in Spain had put up a plaque
by the door:

> IF YOU'RE CLEAN AND NEAT, THEN HERE'S A HOUSE
> READY AND WAITING FOR YOU.
> IF YOU'RE DIRTY—WELL, I'M ASHAMED TO SAY
> IT, BUT YOU'RE WELCOME TOO.

Our own hotel, the Pella Inn, had the same policy; every night it seemed
more like a zoo.

One of the drawbacks of our Acropolis-view room was that, like most
European pensions, it relied on shared bathrooms—a harsh concession
for Les, who seemed to be out of the bed more than in it during the
night. The next morning, I would be given a running commentary of
her strange encounters with our fellow guests, who harked from every
lost corner of the globe. There was the Irish girl who stole all the toilet
paper. Her brutish French boyfriend, who regularly elbowed past everyone in line. The aging South American hipsters, who worked the late-
night crowd in the hallways. Then there were the two giant crew-cut
Texans, ex–Navy SEALs, who staggered home every night at 2 A.M.,
roaring drunk. Inevitably, by 4 A.M. they had monopolized the facilities:
It was a shock to one's delicate sensibilities to open the bathroom doors
and be greeted by the vast haunches of a Texan kneeling before the
porcelain altar of Bacchus. Each morning, when I went out on the balcony, a huge tattooed arm the width of a telegraph pole would be hanging limply through a hole in our partition; one of the SEALs had
collapsed into a coma.

Although I didn't much like the owner of the Pella—a gaunt, scare-
crowlike figure, he fancied himself a smooth operator, and spent his days
serving coffee to lone female guests while the one housekeeper worked
her elderly fingers to the bone—I began to feel sorry for him. In his
shady, cut-rate way, this modern Procrustes/Stretcher was at least pro-

viding semirespectable accommodation for his twenty-five dollars a night. But his clientele did not always make things easy.

One night, two Israeli women stormed the foyer with the same air of entitlement as Greek police officers on a drug bust, tossed down their monstrous packs, and barked at the owner: "We want very cheap and very clean. You must have hot water *twenty-four hours a day.* How much?"

Soon afterward, I heard they were thrown out for cooking on a gas burner in their room, setting the bedsheets on fire and nearly burning down the hotel.

It was time to move on, I realized.

Timeless Rituals
of the Road

THE GREEK TOURISM OFFICE on Syntagma Place had apparently been modeled on Mount Olympus in the movie *Clash of the Titans*. The floor, walls, and ceilings were lined with gleaming white marble, while in the center, elevated high on a circular dais, was the Goddess of Tourism, idly filing her fingernails, looking like Anita Ekberg in an ice palace. She had large blond hair, a powder-blue uniform, pink lipstick, and immortal proportions. There wasn't a single piece of travel literature to distract us from her unearthly presence.

Humbly, we stood below the dais, waiting for the priestess to give us her celestial attention. The office was the quietest place in Athens, silent except for that relentless filing of fingernails, *scrape*-scratch, *scrape*-scratch.

"Where's the fog machine?" Les whispered. "I think we need a few clouds drifting around our ankles."

The woman suddenly looked down at us with her exquisitely penciled eyes.

"*Si? Oui? Da? Ja? Yes?*"

"We were after some information," I began.

She sighed wearily and pushed forward a map of Greece.

"That's all I have," she said. "Would you like one in French?"

"Not really."

I asked a few halfhearted questions about places we wanted to visit, but she only looked bored.

"I don't know about any of that."

"How about where to rent a car?"

"There are many places in Athens."

"No recommendations?"

She stared for a moment and then went back to filing her nails, indicating that the celestial communion was over.

"Anything for *travelers* at all?" Les tried brazenly.

She put her nail file down and glared at us with Dietrich-like disdain. "Why don't you go and buy a guidebook? There is a bookstore around the corner."

Which was more or less the next stop for a Roman tourist, two thousand years ago.

IN PRAISE OF THE PAPYRUS GUIDEBOOK

No Roman sightseer, confronted with the sheer density of cultural reference in Greece, could hope to get around without some decent literature.

Since every mountain, every stream, every stone had its tale to tell—and even remote rural temples were mini-Louvres of artworks from Greece's epic and convoluted past—a visitor, much like today, ran the risk of missing a crucial insight by tackling things alone. To make sense of it all, the first guidebooks—the ancient *periegeseis*—flowered as a genre.

The founding fathers of this distinctive literary form include men who have been all but forgotten in the mists of time: writers like Diodorus, Heliodorus, our friend Dicaearchus, Heracleides of Crete. The most prolific of all was a certain Polemo of Ilium—nicknamed Monument Lover or Inscription Swallower for his slavishly detailed treatises. Tragically, all but a few fragments of those groundbreaking tomes have been lost—but the one work that has survived intact almost makes up for that vanished wealth of information. Referred to constantly by archaeologists, it is probably the most widely read tour book in history: the magisterial *Description of Greece,* written by Pausanias, a charmingly dotty scholar from Asia Minor, between A.D. 130 and 180.

The *Description* is an encyclopedic work that comprised ten papyrus scrolls, a guide to the whole of mainland Greece—city by city, river by river, statue by statue. Its unwieldy volumes, which were copied into books by scholars in the Renaissance, would have been stored in a *capsa* (literary traveling container), a round leather case like a large hatbox. One imagines an extra packhorse may have been needed to lug this up and down the Greek mountain passes; the long scrolls might have been a little awkward to refer to in situ. But such inconveniences were more than compensated for by the sheer breadth of Pausanias' erudition. This was no practical guide: Nuts-and-bolts travel data about Greece, like finding respectable accommodation in Sparta or decent stables in Arcadia, are ignored. Instead, Pausanias caters to the ancient tourist's obsessive fascination with the past. Greek monuments, artworks of their Old Masters, architecture, and history all receive lavish attention (of course, "history" includes the most fantastic incidents from mythology, since the presence of the gods in great events was an accepted reality—one of the most entertaining aspects of reading Pausanias). Any site that relates to heroic legend is lovingly detailed. While one has to look hard in Pausanias to find local color—such as references to Greek customs, landscapes, atmosphere, all those burbling human details we expect of a modern guide—it certainly does exist. In fact, haunting images of daily life in ancient Greece are woven through the text like an invisible thread.

It's the work of a true obsessive-compulsive—the editors at *Lonely Planet* would kill to have Pausanias on their team today. Unlike the average modern hack, Pausanias actually *went* to every one of the obscure places he describes—which is why it took him somewhere between twenty and thirty years to research and write his book. He never just pillages factoids from local Greeks hanging out in bars. The style may be a little dry. But modern archaeologists have long followed Pausanias' steps through the crumbling ruins of Greece, conjuring visions of when the ancient streets were still seething with activity, the temples still towering, the brightly painted sculptures of Apollo and Aphrodite still glistening in the sun. The French team relied on the *Description* while excavating Delphi in the 1890s, the Germans in Olympia; Heinrich Schliemann used Pausanias to unearth the gold of Mycenae. And the magical visions of the ancient world are still there between the lines, floating in the shadows of every page.

The question was: Why not use Pausanias as a travel guide today?

Alongside the *Rough Guide* and *Insight* and *Lonely Planet,* why not follow the ancient text as a way of peeling back the veils of history—to create an opening into the distant past, an imaginative passage, the most direct way of interpreting the fragmented clues of that fantastic world?

THE PORTABLE EMPIRE

The second indispensable travel aid a Roman needed was an accurate road map.

History has been just as cruel to ancient cartographers as to guide-book authors. Of the myriad Roman *itineraria picta* (graphic itineraries, made for the benefit of wayfarers), again, only a single example has survived intact: the so-called Peutinger Table. But posterity has also been lucky with the quality and scope of the relic. The famous Table compresses the entire Roman Empire onto a single papyrus scroll, twenty-two feet long by only thirteen inches high.

Before leaving home, I was able to examine a copy in the Map Room of the New York Public Library. Stretching across an entire row of reading desks, it was a miraculous sliver of data from the Roman world. (In fact, it survived only by being copied and recopied throughout the Middle Ages; it was lost for three centuries, then turned up in the 1700s, in the estate of the German nobleman after whom it is named.) The original now resides in Vienna, but a limited-edition reproduction of the map was issued in the original scroll form. Housed in a sumptuous calf-leather box with gold leaf embossing, it is scarcely less pleasing to the eye than a version presented to an ancient connoisseur, made by the finest publishers of Athens.

Section of the Peutinger Table, one of the Roman "pictorial itineraries,"
a road map to the Empire.

The Table is still perfectly legible, once you fathom the cartographer's conventions. Contrived to fit onto the elongated format, its sense of physical reality is as stylized as a subway map: There is no uniform scale, Italy runs alongside the coast of Africa, and the provinces deemed more important are oversized. The *itinerarium* was designed not as an atlas but as a practical traveler's aid, to provide basic information at a glance. Across its delicate surface scramble all the main Roman highways from Egypt to Scotland. Along the way, there are 555 standardized symbols representing harbors, mountain ranges, towns, spas, temples, governors' residences, tunnels, and lighthouses. The distances between cities are provided; inns are listed. There is even a ratings system for accommodations: A single tower indicates a basic lodge, not much better than a stable; double towers, a decent guest house; while a large four-sided building with a courtyard indicates a top-notch inn.

Although the only other extant highway map is a fragment found pasted inside a legionnaire's shield in Syria, we know from literary references that more specific versions were available, covering smaller areas in full detail. And there were still other Roman travel aids. Written itineraries were available—sequential lists of what to expect along highways, cataloging every village, bridge, and inn from one city to the next. Illiterate wagon drivers would learn these by heart, even though they could be extraordinarily complex. In the second century, it became fashionable to compose itineraries to the Greek highways in rhyming hexameter.

In this incipient industry, some writers became minor celebrities. In 25 B.C., a certain Crinagoras of Mytilene wrote to the guidebook author Menippus of Pergamum:

> I am preparing a sea voyage to Italy to see friends I have not visited for a very long time. I need information to guide me to the Cyclades islands and ancient Scheria. Dear Menippus, you who know all geography and have written a learned tour, please help me from your book. . . .

There is no record of Menippus' response to his fan mail.

COMPACT, MIDSIZE, OR LUXURY?

With maps and guidebooks purchased, it was time for Romans to arrange for a vehicle. Standards of wheeled transport have never been particularly democratic—money equals comfort—and in antiquity, the social elite of Rome set up their own cocoons of luxury on the road.

There was no limit to their extravagance. The richest aristocrats would ship their private wagons across the Adriatic, then travel through Greece in a slow, sumptuous convoy that included a retinue of chefs, secretaries, and slaves, who would race ahead of their masters in order to set up silk-curtained tents as dining halls and bedrooms en route. These lucky Romans were able to re-create all the luxuries of their villas in the middle of the Greek countryside, even laying out marble floor mosaics beneath their feet. They would dine on plates of beaten gold, drink their vintage wine from crystal goblets, and be surrounded by their favorite works of art, which had to be packed and unpacked every day. Some nobles invested in *carrucae dormitoriae*—sleeping carriages strewn with goose-down pillows—thus eliminating the need for overnight stops. Others had their coaches equipped with dice tables, or revolving seats in the rear to better appreciate the views en route. Certainly the most famous visit was that of Mark Antony and Cleopatra in 44 B.C.: They paraded through the Greek countryside in a gold carriage drawn by lions, dressed as the gods Dionysus and Aphrodite, like a modern traveling circus.

But the Greek populace would never see anything that even remotely compared with the fabulous retinue of Emperor Nero in A.D. 66-67. No less than a thousand carriages were made available for his fifteen-month-long procession across the province. The high-stepping horses were shod with silver and bridled with gold; his route was swept clean by outriders gaily clad as Africans; Greek love-boys were engaged to dance about the emperor's carriages, their faces painted white, for added diversion. Nero's banquets were even more sumptuous than back home in Rome: Guests were served on silver plates embedded with diamonds; goblets were carved from great chunks of lapis lazuli; the wine was chilled by snow transported on mule trains from the peak of Mount Parnassus. His wife brought five hundred asses with her on the trip, so that she could bathe in their milk every morning, thus preserving her creamy complexion; hundreds of maiden slave girls attended to her needs, all dressed in transparent slips of candy blue, yellow, green, and pink. Supplying this dazzling imperial parade brought many a Greek city to the brink of ruin, as it ground its way across the countryside like a swarm of locusts. But the visit was a great success, at least from Nero's point of view: The emperor won a modest 1,808 prizes at Greek art festivals and took five hundred statues home from Delphi as souvenirs.

Of course, the great majority of tourists traveled in conditions far beneath these extravagant heights. Rather than shipping their own vehicles, they rented them in Athens—a process that was no less convenient than it is today. Just like modern car-rental garages, the ancient stables were located in the seamier quarters of town, just outside the city walls (as in Rome, wheeled traffic was forbidden in major urban centers during daylight hours). A tourist would drop by the livery, meet with drivers from the local guilds, and arrange to rent the draft animals, the supply of feed, and two carriages—one for themselves, one for the slaves, who followed with the baggage.

Just as today, there were various grades of service, to suit all pocketbooks.

What we might call first class—the Lincoln Town Car of the day—was a covered wagon called a *carruca,* pulled by a team of mules. This prototype of the Wild West wagons had four iron-reinforced wheels and a canopy of leather to protect up to six passengers from the elements. One step down—standard class—was an open wagon, where four people could sit on pillows behind the driver. Economy class was the *covinnus,* a predecessor of the buggy, with two wheels and two mules— suitable for travelers who didn't mind handling the reins themselves (the driver led the animals by the bridle). The choices may sound straightforward, but, just like today, Roman travelers could find themselves at the mercy of unscrupulous vendors. Selecting a good mule driver was almost as important as choosing the right vehicle. The best were local celebrities, with nicknames like Podagrosus (Gout Victim). All were deeply superstitious: Every stable had an elaborate shrine to the goddess Epona, the Mare-Headed Mother.

Some flamboyant travelers spurned the cumbersome wagons: Apuleius describes riding through Greece on a white thoroughbred horse, with his two slaves following on foot. A wealthy tourist might prefer to travel in a covered litter, which could be carried by eight slaves or even strung between four pack animals—a comfortable option, but excruciatingly slow. Cash-strapped merchants, actors, and athletes often made their journeys on muleback. The second-century physician Galen shocked his well-bred contemporaries by recommending *walking* as a way of keeping healthy—just like the wretched peasants, who had no choice.

For the vast majority of tourists, economizing was unthinkable: The sheer amount of luggage they liked to travel with made a pair of covered wagons essential. Even the most austere Romans were not famous for packing light. The philosopher Seneca once tried to travel with a single carriage and modest baggage, as an experiment in "the simple life." He gave up after two days.

There were clothes to pack—valise after valise of them, smelling of the finest macerated leather. Men took a wide range of togas in lush purples and scarlets, although the unwieldy traditional outfit was usually worn only on special occasions; for everyday use, most preferred short-sleeved tunics in the Greek style. (The *synthesis* was a popular compromise at banquets: It looked like a tunic from the waist up and a toga below—which conveyed a certain formality, but left the arms free.) The fashion burden for women was far greater: It was common for a lady to change several times in the course of a single dinner party, so most Roman women would not dream of leaving home without a wardrobe of fine gowns in extravagant colors—Oriental silk was the height of fashion—plus crates of hair ornaments and sandals, and several strong-boxes filled with jewelry (pearls from the Indian Ocean were the ultimate accessory). One needed a variety of capes for the rain and cold. The fastidious carried their own plates, as well as amphoras filled with their favorite olive oil for bathing (it took the place of soap); perfumes of myrrh, balsam, and cinnamon for anointing; gifts for the friends one might visit en route . . .

Then there were less essential items. Dilettante Roman scientists might have tested the primitive form of odometer invented by Vitruvius, whose delicate metal filaments recorded the rotations of a wheel, and so logged the number of miles a wagon had covered. Others brought prototype travel alarm clocks: Portable sundials were fashionable for long journeys. One was found intact in Britain. A traveler could unpack it, set it up on a tripod, and adjust the gnomon according to the latitude and the month of the year.

All this made our own voluminous luggage—including my thirty-pound sack of ancient texts—start to seem decidedly modest.

Why is it that today, renting a car is still one of the more subtle maneuvers in any travel itinerary? It offers us immense convenience but remains fraught with potential disaster.

In Greece, the stakes are raised. Not only are rental cars inexplicably expensive, but the vehicles themselves are a motley range of exotic specimens from eastern Europe, manual, minuscule, with thousands of miles under their hoods, mysterious features, and frustrating eccentricities.

In Athens, I chose an agency from the English-language newspaper—
and discovered, after traipsing out to their suburban garage, that it rented
battered Russian cars called Donkos.

This was truly at the bottom end of *covinnus* class, I had to admit. But
the price was right.

"We'll get what we pay for," Les warned.

She wanted to go to a reputable company—a generic Avis or Hertz.
But I argued that a car is a car—even if it *is* a Donko.

Traffic Jam
on the Sacred Way

THE ROAD WEST from Athens is one of the most celebrated in history. It follows the Sacred Way to Eleusis, an ancient cave sanctuary dedicated to the fertility goddess Demeter, whose daughter Persephone's annual sojourn in the underworld created winter, and as a result the four seasons. Pausanias became an initiate of its core ritual—known as the Eleusinian Mysteries—as did many visiting Romans, including strings of illustrious poets and a half-dozen different emperors. Details are hazy—mysterious, even—but it's believed that those who swore to secrecy and participated in the emotionally demanding, weeklong event lost their fear of death. Not a bad deal, all in all.

For us, driving out of Athens in our cranky Donko, the polar opposite applied: Fear of death was unusually high on our agenda. The Sacred Way now lies somewhere beneath Greece's busiest six-lane highway—itself lined by rubbish-strewn lots, cigarette billboards, factories belching smoke. The trouble was, Athenian drivers seemed to regard this stretch as the start of the Paris-Dakar rally. Cars passed on the blind side, tailgated, blared horns; trucks stopped short in the middle of lanes. Les, battling nausea from the stop-start driving, curled up into her usual defensive huddle.

I would have turned around and gone back to our hotel if I could have found an exit from the highway. It even made me think fondly of Naples. Italians may be maniacs on the road, but they're actually good drivers. These Greeks apparently lost their minds when they got behind the wheel, trusting in divine providence to carry them along. Travelers tell stories of speeding bus drivers who, when their vehicles spin out of control, throw their hands in the air and begin praying to the Virgin Mary. I've flown the Andes in derelict prop planes and skied an Icelandic glacier in a blizzard, but nothing quite compares to the sheer white-knuckle terror of driving a Donko out of Athens.

The Greek driver's indifference to life and logic may be an atavistic throwback to the ancient road system, when *hermeia* (shrines to Hermes, wing-footed messenger of the gods, protector of travelers) were scattered along the highways at regular intervals, a spurious guarantee of divine protection. Some were merely piles of stones (the passerby would add a rock for good luck); others had four slender pillars crowned with bronze busts of Hermes, which travelers could anoint with oil as they composed a vow, or they could leave a piece of fruit as an offering. At many cross-roads, larger sanctuaries would be operated by priests. Travelers would often stop and sit for a moment with Hermes, who was regarded as the most amiable and reasonable of the gods; at the very least, they would touch their lips as a sign of veneration while passing. These days, Hermes must be taking a long vacation; Greece now boasts the second-highest road-fatality rate in Europe, after Portugal.

And the truth is, bad driving has a long pedigree on this road: In the age of Greek heroes, the most famous incident of road rage in history occurred here, en route to Thebes. At a famous crossroads—Pausanias calls it the Split—the pedestrian Oedipus was nearly run over by a stranger in a speeding chariot. Infuriated, Oedipus killed the driver, unaware that the man was his father (thus setting off all sorts of family dysfunction and cataclysms). The historian Lionel Casson suggests a pos-sible cause for the accident: Since the few traffic-worthy highways of archaic Greece were often built with double grooves for chariot and car-riage wheels, the old king might not have been trying to humiliate Oedipus but simply couldn't swerve to miss him.

By the Roman era, the main highways of Greece were put into a more orderly and standardized condition than they ever would be again. Straight, superbly paved, and fitted with gutters and drains, they were apparently a joy to use; many even had footpaths, thus avoiding Oedipus-style scrapes. Bridges spanned the rivers that Greeks had previously crossed on foot; Roman officials guaranteed regular repairs; even tolls were forbidden. The old shrines to Hermes were still maintained—although Romans called the god of travelers Mercury—but they were supplemented by a practical system of *miliaria* (milestones). These six-foot-high carved pillars showed the distance to the nearest city in both directions and were, as the name suggests, placed at every Roman mile (that's one thousand five-foot paces—ninety-five feet less than an American mile). It's a frequency that compares favorably to today's halfhearted road-sign system in Greece. In fact, the Roman orator Quintilian's praise of the user-friendly system should be faxed to every modern Greek department of roads: "It is a pleasure to measure the weary way one has come, and to know how far one has to go makes one travel more courageously. . . ."

But even in ancient times, not much could be done to improve driving in the Mediterranean, it seemed. Traffic accidents were the source of endless litigation. There was no agreement on left- or right-side driving; conical stones were placed along many roads to stop chariots from veering onto the sidewalks. Mule drivers were notorious for dangerously racing one another in the country.

Today, as the hundredth truck roared up behind us, the driver blasting his horn, I remembered one small snippet of Roman law:

"If a driver, while trying to overtake, turns over the carriage and crushes or kills [a citizen or slave] . . . he is liable, since it was his obligation to maintain a moderate speed. . . ."

It could make a catchy bumper sticker—or epitaph on a roadside marker.

FREEDOMS OF THE HIGHWAY

Roman tourists in a wagon could cover forty to fifty miles a day, although twenty-five was average; in summer, they often preferred to travel at night, by torchlight, and rest in the heat of noon. An individual on foot could muster about fifteen miles.

As for our road trip—Delphi was to be the first stop—even this sounded quite optimistic. I'd noticed a few harmless eccentricities of our Donko back on the Sacred Way—little things like the odometer being stuck, the dashboard lights not working, the left-turn signal giving out— the classic mechanical crankiness of almost any rental car these days. Occasionally, my door would pop open when I stopped at a red light. But then, in Thebes, Les made the mistake of lowering her passenger-side window. The automatic mechanism—perhaps the modern car's most unnecessary invention—gave a troubled whine and died, leaving the window wide open. At first, this seemed truly trivial, espe-

cially for a jaunt around the sunny Greek coast. But as we climbed into
the highlands, it became apparent that a permanently open window
might actually be inconvenient. The wind was blasting in, damp and
frozen. Les retreated under piles of pullovers, with gloves and a woolen
hat on. Then flecks of icy rain started spitting on her.

"What if it really pours tonight?" she began. "It's going to be like a
swamp in here. There's frost. I'll get pneumonia. And how are we going
to lock the car? We can't get out and look at things. People will just steal
our stuff."

What was really ever wrong with manual window openers? We spent
hours trying to get the automatic marvel to start working again. When
we stopped at gas stations, drunken mechanics lamely pressed the same
buttons we had. When we called the rental agency, an attendant advised helpfully, "You must seek an electrician." "On a Sunday in rural
Greece?" I gurgled. And no, there were no other cars available. "We are
under no obligation to assist," the fellow informed me.

"Piece of Russian crap," I fumed, trying to pull up the glass with my
fingertips.

"Calm down, Tone," Les sighed. "We got what we paid for."

That was a low blow.

And yet—what would a road trip be without mechanical problems?
For the ancient Romans, road travel never managed to be actually *comfortable.* Even the more expensive wagons had no springs—wheels were
bound with iron—and axles didn't pivot, so every crack or stone on the
road sent jolts through a passenger's spine. There was the teeth-jarring
creak of wheels, familiar to insomniacs like Juvenal back in Rome. Con-
di ons in the shoddy, cheaper vehicles were particularly grueling once
off the main Roman highways.

What's more, tourists had to worry about personality clashes with
their drivers, who were as hard-nosed about money then as any rental
agent today. Plato offers the following moral lesson: *A dispute breaks out in
a treeless desert between a traveler on a mule and the driver from whom he hired
it. The traveler wants to take a siesta in the mule's shadow, but the driver refuses
on the grounds that the mule had been hired, but not its shadow. Both are found
dying of injuries given to one another; the mule had fled.*

The traveler should have read the fine print on the contract.

Stairway to Apollo

DELPHI WAS THE ANCIENT WORLD'S ultimate oracle—a stunning mountain sanctuary chosen by Apollo, one legend said, because it was so inaccessible. From its divine heights, priestesses would breathe "magical gases" from a crack in the earth and gibber out prophecies passed directly from the god. The fame of these ecstatic ravings soon turned Delphi into a thriving miniature city, a Greek Machu Picchu with views that swept a hundred miles across ever-receding valleys to the molten sapphire of the sea. In Roman times, Pausanias warned his tourist readership, the approach was still "precipitous" and "difficult, even for an active man." For the last few miles, it was only a rough mule trail, deterring all but the most serious admirers.

The twenty-first century has remedied that particular failing. Now even the most indifferent visitor to Greece can be bused right up to the sanctuary's gates. But the setting still takes your breath away. The surrounding peaks also make it a natural amphitheater—the ancients would remark on how the songs of mountain birds were amplified into a crystal chorus. On our arrival, captured in that same acoustic bowl was a stream of cosmopolitan chatter:

"So I said, you touch me again and I'll scream . . ."

"The GIs were basically fucked over in Beirut . . ."

"Moi, je préfère les fromages du nord . . ."

"It's the lymph glands that carry the poison . . ."

"¿No sabes como bailar el tango . . . ?"

The random remarks of a thousand visitors were carried through the air, mingling together like the babbled Apollonic prophecies of the past.

By the heyday of ancient tourism, Delphi was in many ways past its spiritual prime. In the classical era, when the fractious Greek cities had been free to squabble among themselves, the Delphic oracle decided wars and peace treaties; the fate of empires often hung in the balance ("Rely on walls of wood!" the oracle had enigmatically directed the Athenians in the fifth century B.C., inspiring them to use the fleet that would defeat the invading Persians at Salamis). But the Roman conquest of Greece ended the sparring; the emperors had their own sources of political divination, the Sibylline books, so Delphi was no longer consulted on major issues of state. Competing oracles sprang up all over the Empire, including some who were cynical frauds (one charlatan by the Black Sea made himself fabulously wealthy by talking to a "snake god" called Glycon, who replied through an artificial reptile head whose jaws were moved by hidden attendants). In Delphi, the number of priestesses was reduced to a single one, and the incoherent prophecies were no longer translated into Greek hexameter by professional poets, as in the good old days of Homer and Herodotus, but were belted out in stolid prose.

Even so, Delphi maintained its prestige into the Roman era, and not due purely to nostalgia. The magnificence of the treasures gathered during its salad days made it easily the richest site in Greece—prompting modern historians to dub it the Fort Knox of antiquity.

Gazing up from the site's entrance, at the base of the complex, Roman visitors were confronted by a labyrinth of filigreed marble and precious metals encrusting the steep flanks of Mount Parnassus. As they climbed the steps, the sumptuous curtain parted to reveal one dazzling artwork after another. It must have seemed like an open-air Aladdin's cave: For twenty generations, offerings to the Delphic Oracle had flooded in from every corner of the known world and occasionally beyond. By the pathway stood bronze bison and gilded wolves, pearl-encrusted breastplates from Britain, Indian idols, golden bracelets from Hyperborean lands that nobody had ever visited. Every Greek city maintained its own treasury house in Delphi—a pavilion crowded with war booty dedicated to Apollo, from captured ships' figureheads to gold bullion. Towering over the glittering scene was a seventy-foot-high statue of the divine archer himself.

As we slowly forced our way up the stairway, dodging tour groups, freelance guides, and vendors, it was comforting—once again—to recall that for ancient tourists, Delphi was far from a quiet museum to be inspected at leisure. The pushiness of its *mystagogi* was axiomatic. "The

Ethereal Delphi: The classical Greek amphitheater blends with the natural arena.

guides were going through their prepared spiels, reading every inscription," complains a sightseer in a dialogue by Plutarch, "ignoring our desperate pleas that they cut short their harangues." Armies of soothsayers offered cut-rate versions of oracular prophecy, while souvenir vendors capitalized on Delphi's magical aura: Just as modern Greek stalls are laden with charms against the evil eye, their predecessors offered enchanted baubles, potions, and "curse tablets," which were buried in graveyards for the dead to take to Hades. Delphic love philters were sought throughout the Empire, despite the nauseating ingredients, which included horse sweat (a favored erotic stimulant) and minced lizard's flesh: Stories abound of *inamorati* being poisoned, or going raving mad. Vendors also offered small wax figurines, similar to voodoo dolls, which would be pierced with thirteen needles; the aim was to force a victim's actions rather than to inflict physical pain (live cats were sometimes used as a substitute).

Only after losing all these limpetlike professionals could our erudite ancient visitors relax into recondite discussions inspired by the art—on the qualities of bronze, the biographies of long-dead heroes, the meaning of coincidence and significance of portents.

As for me, I was thankful I had Pausanias in my pocket. His long and detailed description of the sacred maze of art can still be followed today—step by step, plinth by plinth, stoa by stoa—to bring the scattered stones of Roman-era Delphi back to life.

The trail wound upward, past an unassuming circular stone by the side of the path—the Navel of the World, epicenter of all ancient maps—to the steps of Apollo's temple. Its columns are today little more than stumps, but in Pausanias they tower over the countryside, emblazoned in gilt letters with the key precepts of Greek philosophy: KNOW THYSELF and MODERATION IN ALL THINGS (not a principle that won many Roman converts). Inside, the guidebook reports, was one of Delphi's most valued artifacts—a chair that once belonged to Helen of Troy. But Pausanias subtly directs his readers to a pavilion called the Lesche, a long, covered colonnade that served as a painting gallery. The entire inner wall was devoted to a single monumental mural, and ancient tourists would wander its length, savoring each portion.

Only a single blue scrap of Delphi's many paintings survives today. But the diligent Pausanias has saved us this one in words—a depiction of Ulysses' visit to the underworld, by the Old Master Polygnotos. He devotes over twenty pages to this sprawling masterpiece, which often sounds less like a painting than a cinematic storyboard of the *Odyssey,* with different episodes from the journey arranged in chronological order and extracts of text included. Curiously, Pausanias goes into enormous detail about the image's content, but apart from noting that it has "extraordinary beauty" offers little in the way of aesthetic appreciation. He's not alone in this. Ancient paintings were expected to "delight the eyes," but they were above all narratives about gods and heroes, with tidbits of information thrown in.

And what of the Delphic Oracle?

Its prophecies may not have been as earth-shatteringly important as in bygone ages, but in Roman times they were still being regularly produced in the "sacred fissure" below Apollo's temple. Because of their sentimental appeal, many tourists gladly agreed to the expensive and complicated sacrifices, including the emperor Hadrian in A.D. 120, whose question involved a vexing detail of literary biography: "Where was Homer born and who were his parents?" Onlookers stood mesmerized as the Pythian priestess descended into the gaping wound in the flanks of Mount Parnassus (I scanned the brittle earth for its outline, but landslides closed it long ago). Inside, she breathed in the ice-cold gas seeping from the earth, then succumbed to the convulsive frenzy that produced a torrent of deliriously lyrical babble. Reemerging, the priestess would stand on a silver tripod and pronounce her cryptic words, which would be chanted over and over by the viewing public down below and subject to more sober interpretation by Apollo's minions.

A good idea of the sorts of personal questions Apollo generally received is given by a fragment of papyrus, which helpfully lists a hundred easy-to-answer "Questions to an Oracle."

77. Am I to be reconciled with my offspring?
79. Will I get the money?
80. Is the one who left home alive?
81. Am I to profit by the transaction?
85. Am I to become a beggar?
88. Am I to become a Senator?
90. Am I to be divorced from my wife/husband?
91. Have I been poisoned?

Visitors who could not arrange a consultation with the oracle, which was possible only on six days of the year, need have not worried. There were dozens of user-friendly alternatives—astrologers, numerologists, palm readers, and dream interpreters—whose rates were low and responses instant. Visitors to Delphi could get advice on even the most trivial decision by throwing five dice, called *astragaloi*—the Greek version of a fortune cookie.

Naturally, our tour guide Pausanias has a better suggestion. For tourists who want an up-to-the-minute taste of the divine, he recommends the nearby village of Lebadea, where a secretive oracle called Trophonius was considered by the cognoscenti to offer Greece's ultimate brush with the future. Not every reader would have the nerve to follow Pausanias' hot travel tip: A visit was time-consuming, uncomfortable, and, frankly, terrifying—the ancient equivalent of bungee jumping.

The process—which Pausanias stresses he describes from personal experience—begins with several days of purification in an isolated mountain temple, bathing only in cold water, and going through rituals with the sacristans. At last, late at night, the initiate is taken to a moonlit stream, ceremonially dressed in a white tunic tied with colored ribbons, and told to drink from two sacred springs (tantalizingly, Greek archaeologists have been guessing at the sites in today's spa village of Lebadea, tracing them to a steep, narrow gorge).

What follows is the most famous eyewitness account of a pagan religious ritual:

One sees a round hole in the earth—man-made, and dug out with consummate artistic skill. It is shaped like a kiln, about ten feet wide, I would say, and a little over twenty feet deep. There are no steps down, so the priests provide a light, narrow ladder. When you get down into this dark pit, you can see a narrow opening between the wall and floor. It is only two feet wide, and one foot high. This is where you enter the oracle.

You lie on your back, with sacrificial honey cakes in your hands, and ease your feet into the gap. Then you put the knees inside. Immediately, your whole body is sucked into the orifice, as if some incredibly deep and fast river had caught you in its current and was sucking you down. This is where you are granted knowledge of the future, but no two people learn it in the same way: One man might see the future, another hear of it.

Afterwards, you are spat back through the same mouth.

When a man comes back from Trophonius, the priests immediately put him on the throne of Memory, and ask him what he saw and discovered. He is still shaking with terror, and hardly knows himself or anything around him. Afterwards, the priests turn him over to his friends, who pick him up and carry him back to the temple of Good Fortune.

Eventually, he comes to his senses, and can laugh again, just as before.

It was an ordeal that the pious wore as a badge of honor. And like any self-respecting extreme-sports aficionado today, Pausanias can't resist casually dropping in a note of danger:

They say nobody has been killed by going down this chasm—except for one man. Apparently he refused to perform any of the religious ceremonies, and did not come here for the purpose of consulting Apollo but to try and steal gold and silver from the holy place. His corpse was not spat out from the sacred mouth; it was discovered far away. . . .

You can just imagine a reader thinking, *How very encouraging* . . .

HOT LINE TO JUNO

In modern Delphi, we sat in the shade of a cypress tree, watching the mountains below dissolve into the salt haze of the sea, while the echoes flowed over us, every broken tongue blending into an endless cryptic crossword.

The talk of divination was getting to me; after all, a longing to know the future is hardly alien to the modern mind. We had our own oracular query, one we'd been putting off for weeks: Calling the obstetrician in New York to get the results of Lesley's amnio test. Somehow it seemed as unnerving as plunging down the orifice of Trophonius.

Les refused to do it; she thought it would somehow jinx her physical condition. The nurses had promised to call us before we left if there'd been any problems. They hadn't called.

But there was always that nagging doubt.

We shuffled back to our strange little pension in the alpine village of Arachova. It looked like a Tudor tavern, with oak paneling and faux-medieval fittings. In the small foyer were photos of the hotel's most famous guests—the Beatles. They'd stayed here during their Sergeant Pepper phase in the late 1960s, hiding out with the Muses on Mount Parnassus. The Greek hotel owner was in every picture, arms around the hirsute John and Paul, giggling with stoned Ringo, jamming on guitar with George. Our host was the image of rustic health, perpetually dragging on a cigarette. It was always a little sobering to see the poor guy at his desk now. He was one of Greece's many smoking casualties. Plastic tubes emerged from his throat. His face had the iridescence of week-old fish. Every time we collected the room key, he gave us a rueful smile.

"The results was f-i-i-i-n-e," I made out from the cheery nurse over the crackling telephone line from New York, straining to hear above the baying of dogs in the street below.

"Fine?"

"F-i-i-i-n-e, I'm saying."

Then she turned coy.

"So—do you have any *other* questions?"

"Ah?"

"Do you wanna know what sex it is?"

Les shook her head, then got up and started pacing around the room. Originally, we'd wanted it to be a surprise. But now—well, it didn't seem right that some anonymous nurse on the other side of the world should possess such intimate knowledge of the future, and we didn't.

"It's a little *boy!*" she squealed, like a game-show host.

I slowly hung up the phone. The whole baby business had just become one step more real.

Spartan Pleasures

From delphi, Roman tourists would head to the Peloponnesus—a virtual island, shaped like an arthritic claw, connected only by a narrow isthmus to the rest of Greece. The Roman highway along this umbilical cord was cut into precarious cliffs, with endless views across the Aegean. Today, the route is still a humbling introduction: You can see why Henry Miller compared his first view of this rugged peninsula to "a short, sharp stab to the heart."

As the ancient travel map, the Peutinger Table, shows, the Roman highway hung like a noose around the entire Peloponnesus, linking the towns where many of the tourist attractions lay. The modern Greek highway was built above the ancient, so we were following the same basic route (in fact, the Peutinger sometimes seemed easier to use than contemporary road maps, which are dense with Greek lettering that bears no correspondence to any road signs).

As I ground the Donko's rusty gears up and down the bare mountainsides—we'd taped a sheet of plastic over the broken window, and tied coat-hanger wire around my door so it wouldn't pop open whenever the car stopped—it was easy to picture those roving Roman tourists clattering along in their squeaky wagons, trying to read their papyrus guidebooks as they reclined on their down pillows, or idly watching the countryside roll by. In between the urban centers, Roman Greece was beautiful but impoverished: The relative prosperity of the "Indian summer" that the Empire had brought to the province did not extend to the countryside. Visitors were surprised to find a hand-to-mouth peasant world, roamed by shepherds and goatherds. Just off the roadway lay towns that had fallen into destitution; the orator Dio the Golden-Tongued described plazas that had been turned into plowed fields, while just beyond their broken gates, the land was completely overgrown—"as though this were the depths of a wilderness and not the outskirts of a city."

Not surprisingly, the tourist facilities between major attractions could be quite basic. A certain Apollinarius Sidonius was appalled by a "greasy tavern" in rural Greece, whose halls were black with smoke from all the thyme-herbed sausages forever burning on the kitchen grill. His hard-reed bed was hopping with lice; all night, lizards and spiders fell from the ceiling. Aristides preferred to sit up all night covered in dust from the road rather than climb between a country inn's filthy sheets; hotel rooms leaked during winter storms, in summer they were full of insects. (He notes dryly of one rustic establishment: "It became clear through the multitude of mosquitoes that I would have to forego sleep.") Apuleius was given a "worm-eaten old army bunk" with a broken leg—although this rather pales beside the testimony of one character in his novel, *The Golden Ass,* who woke up to see his roommate being attacked by the innkeeper-witch: She breaks down the door with a magical spell, tears out the man's heart, and then strings his corpse to the rafters by the genitals. Rural hotel porters were notoriously surly characters, perched in the courtyards, always watching out for any suspicious activity from guests after dark.

The backwoods clientele was also more rough-and-ready than in the cities: Plutarch advises travelers not to be intimidated by the taunts of sailors or muleteers at dinner. Instead, he says, one should chant loudly to oneself, to block out the noise. Drunks would play music and demand money. Apollonius of Tyana was accosted by one musician who sang Nero's poetry—"drawling out the verses which the Emperor was in the habit of murdering by his miserable modulations." When the guests said they were bored, the drunk accused them of treason.

But it was best to keep an open mind in these humble inns. Guests could meet fellow travelers and stay awake into the small hours, exchanging arcane travel stories and drinking honeyed wine by the fire. Apuleius mentions being challenged by a roomful of friendly locals to an eating race one night—although he swallowed too large a piece of polenta and nearly choked to death.

As ever, the discomforts of the journey were worth it: the Peloponnesus contained Greece's greatest sites. Like those roving Romans, we slipped into Corinth, official capital of the ancient province, famous for its sacred prostitutes of Aphrodite; tested the acoustics in the amphitheater at Epidaurus; paused at the mountain citadel of Mycenae, where, behind the Lion Gate, ancient tourists would pay their respects at the grave of King Agamemnon, leader of the Greeks in Troy.

But the true goal lay south, in a city whose very lifestyle was the stuff of violent legend.

THE ALTAR TO MACHISMO

Navigating down the hairpin bends to Sparta inspired a certain trepidation—and not just because of the grinding Russian brakes. Maybe it was the news that we were going to have a son, but the image of that warlike city seemed even less palatable than usual.

The Spartans have been awarded the prize as the testosterone-fueled fascists of ancient history. Mortal enemies of the artsy, philosophy-loving Athenians, they ran a sadistic, totalitarian regime throughout the classical age, whose heartless social code was geared exclusively to creating invincible armies. Newborn babies were inspected by an all-male council, and the physically inferior tossed into a ravine. Boys were taken from their families at age seven, raised by the state in thuggish boot camps, and toughened up by being forced to sleep in the fields and steal their food to survive. As adults, males could look forward to a jolly lifetime of bullying, bludgeoning, sparring, and silently eating gruel in crowded communal barracks. Spartan girls, meanwhile, were born only to breed: Their education consisted of running, wrestling naked, and learning domestic chores, while celibacy was a crime punishable by exile. This inhuman system, where mindless discipline was elevated to a religious principle, was much admired by European thinkers in the eighteenth century, but ever since the Romantic era the Spartans have been disdained as philistine lowlifes—antiquity's sullen skinheads. It's not surprising to learn that the Nazis adored them, celebrating Sparta as the most "Nordic" state in Greece. Hitler entertained fantasies about the superclass of male hunters and fighters, who through their inherent superiority exercised raw power over a vast population of Helots. He saw the staunch, fight-to-the-death spirit of the battle of Thermopylae in Stalingrad, and even declared that the peasant soup of the German province Schleswig-Holstein was descended from Spartan broth.

An audience admires the martial skill of the Greeks in A Pyrrhic Dance *(1869),*
by Sir Lawrence Alma-Tadena.

The Roman tourists who converged on the city in the first and second centuries A.D. were also inveterate Sparta fans: They were fascinated with the grim "Lycurgan code," which reminded them of the tough, simple, disciplined Romans of earliest antiquity, the men and women who had built the Empire. They eagerly inspected the military trophies on display in the city center, but the real attraction was Sparta's austere lifestyle options. Special local guides called "interpreters of the Lycurgan customs" proudly showed visitors around local institutions, explained the brutal system of education, and arranged introductions to charming Spartan officials like the "Controllers of the Women." Many tourists dined on grisly black broth with the men in the communal barracks, noting with approval how they still wore their hair long over traditional vermilion cloaks. The more valiant liked to spar with them. There is a record of one Roman tourist by the name of Palfurius Sura—a senator no less—electing to wrestle a muscular Spartan girl in the ring. The sex-starved poet Propertius, meanwhile, preferred to watch, going into paroxysms of delight at the naked grapplings.

Above all, there were the sadistic rituals: Every tourist tried to have his visit coincide with the annual scourging of the youths at the festival of Artemis. That was when the adolescent boys of Sparta were forced to run a merciless gauntlet through the streets, while the city's grown men flogged them savagely with sticks and whips. At the end of the ordeal, the boys prostrated themselves at the altar of the goddess, the savage huntress Artemis, whose primitive wooden idol ran crimson with splattered blood. In this prototype boarding-school ritual, it was crucial that youngsters never wince or cry out in pain. Pausanias, who attended one year, notes that the priestesses of Artemis eagerly urged Spartan men to whip the boys harder, abusing them roundly if they held back their strokes "because of a boy's good looks or social rank." Several of the frailer urchins inevitably died from their wounds; the survivors had their backs scarred for life. As a consolation, the bravest victims were honored with the title Conquerors of the Altar.

The scourging was as popular among voyeuristic Romans as the running of the bulls at Pamplona is for tourists today; raised on a diet of gladiatorial fights, they were hardly squeamish about the bloodshed. Even otherwise humane figures like Cicero reveled in the Old World tradition. The pagan holy man Apollonius was less impressed: "[Crowds] flock to see the spectacle with unbridled enthusiasm, as if it was the annual hyacinth festival." But the majority lapped up the agonies of the young, and made sure to patronize other violent Spartan events like the *sphaireis*—a bone-crunching ball game between five teams, which one historian likened to a no-holds-barred version of American football, played without helmets or padding.

All very macho, no doubt. But the secret—and rather embarrassing—truth is that these Spartan rituals only survived thanks to the ancient tourist industry. In fact, modern semiotic theorists could have a field day with Sparta: Their most famous habits were examples of what today's anthropologists call "staged authenticity"—a tradition kept alive self-consciously for profit.

Actually, the city's toughest laws and customs had lapsed long before the Roman conquest of Greece. Although the old code was given lip service, it seemed the Spartans had gone soft. But after the occupation, the Romans encouraged the revival of the harsh way of life they admired so much. In the first century A.D., the emperors began giving Spartans special treatment for their noble traditions. Increasing numbers of tourists from around the Empire arrived in search of "the real Sparta" they had read about back home, creating a lucrative trade.

It's tempting to be cynical about Sparta, putting its rituals on a par with modern tourist shows like the "native dances" held every night in Caribbean hotels. But cultural revivals are rarely so simple. Spartan families eagerly sent their sons forward every year to their thrashing for reasons that were far from mercenary. Keeping up tradition won Sparta respect throughout the Empire—ensuring that an otherwise tiny and not particularly remarkable provincial city could maintain its status in the world. To be a Spartan was to be unique, the inheritor of prestige that ran back to King Leonidas. You can almost feel sorry for the Spartans: Like old gunslingers in Wild West movies who, because of their reputations, are forever challenged by young bucks to shoot-outs, the Spartans were trapped by their past, doomed to repeat the bloodstained rites of their code. If ever they failed to live up to their image, Greeks and Romans were furious: Aristides devoted a whole oration to denouncing the Spartans for taking a fancy to pantomime.

I ♥ SPARTA

Descending through that ring of mountain peaks around Sparta—which pressed so tightly that the ancient city never needed defensive walls—I hardly expected its modern citizens to wear their badge of severity today. But somehow I couldn't hold out much hope for the city itself. It would be an industrial wasteland at best, full of sullen shadows of its unpleasant forebears.

This image slowly withered as we passed through the luscious groves of orange trees, past the flourishing flower gardens, and took a seat in the main plaza, filled with fresh-faced young families, to discover that once-fearsome Sparta has become one of the most docile towns in Greece. And because its historical ruins are notoriously thin, it sees hardly any visitors.

"Hey, where ya from?" boomed the owner of a pizza parlor we walked into. "New York? No kidding! I lived there, twenny years. Brooklyn. Ran an ice cream parlor."

His name was Kosta. He had thick black-framed glasses and a Trotsky goatee. Like so many Greeks, he'd done a tour of duty overseas to make his money without ever forgetting his plans to come home to the impoverished plot of land where he grew up. After pumping our hands, he yelled out to his waitress daughter, "Hey, Alexia! C'mere. These guys are from New York!"

"Oh, yeah? Manhattan?" She was in her twenties, with heavily made-up almond eyes, like a princess in a Minoan painting. "I liked growing up there in America, sure I did. But you can't beat Sparta."

"Best little town in Greece," her pop agreed.

I asked this Spartan Chamber of Commerce what was so great about it.

"You've been to Athens, right?" Alexia said. "Everyone's just in a bad mood. They're rude and pushy, they want to take your money, then they want you out. You try to live in the countryside, it's full of sad old people. Young people, they just have to leave."

I thought of the last six villages we'd driven through, and took her point. Sparta was a boomtown by comparison. The kinder, gentler Sparta. And then, to eradicate any doubt, Alexia insisted on taking us to something called the Hellas Cultural Association.

It was a Saturday afternoon—party time in the Peloponnesus—and from an unassuming back street we caught the semihysterical strains of bouzouki music wafting from a window. For once, it wasn't the ubiquitous "Zorba" on a perpetual loop—but actual live music, boisterous and loud.

Dark stairs led up to a bar, where an impromptu jam session was in progress. Littered throughout the tightly packed tables, a half-dozen customers, faces sweating out pure alcohol, were beating on battered guitars and tambourines, while the rest of the patrons—the most bohemian Greeks I'd ever seen—were quaffing vials of ouzo, sucking cigarettes to the stump, and absently picking at plates of olives, all the while hypnotized by the music. The place felt private and intimidatingly insular, like some mystical cabal, but the owner saw Alexia and waved us over. When he saw the silver worry beads in my hand, he mistook us for Greeks, too: With great enthusiasm, he grabbed our arms and dragged us over to the only empty table.

"Retsina," I mumbled to the waitress, in my thickest accent.

And then the whole room erupted into song, shifting easily from a mournful ballad to full-throated anthem. One by one, ouzo-addled guests stood up and clapped or sang, tears in their eyes, to signify their approval. An enormous gypsy lady suddenly swayed to her feet to dance. She spun slowly on her heels, gliding easily from one table to the next, like a great soft pinball, leaving a trail of admirers in her wake. The audience guided her around the room with their open palms, slipping hundred-drachma notes into her belt as tokens of appreciation; several threw their glasses onto the floor in musical punctuation. Through the window, the fortress hills of Sparta turned golden in the dusk.

"You see!" Alexia announced jubilantly. "This is when Greeks are really themselves! The rest is just an act."

That night, as we wandered back to our hotel through the empty provincial plaza, I was more than ready to sign on to the new Spartan code. The physical remains of ancient Sparta didn't add up to much—in fact, as the historian Thucydides once wrote, future generations would find it difficult to believe the great power Sparta had once wielded. But I looked at it this way: In the last two thousand years, Spartans had certainly learned to chill out.

And yet . . . I couldn't help wondering, a little illogically, I admit, what had happened to those feral Spartans and all those savage warriors in their brilliant vermilion cloaks and hair hanging down to their shoulders, the men who would fight to the death or commit hara-kiri in shame. Could the cultural DNA of Sparta have so completely dissolved?

I was as bad as an ancient Roman: I wanted a sign from the past.

HIGHWAY TO THE UNDERWORLD

It was only a couple of days later when I understood: the austere military code had migrated about one hundred miles south of the city, to a remote finger of harsh (and, yes, *Spartan*) desert known simply as the Mani. It's a scorched, inhuman domain of rocks and thorns—and a logical setting, at its farthest tip, for Cape Taenarus, the entrance to the underworld that Hercules used when he went to capture the three-headed dog of Hades, Cerberus. (Pausanias made the journey there to pay his respects, but was disappointed to find that the cave actually led nowhere; today, even the cave has disappeared, although the windswept, uninhabited promontory, surrounded by sheer cliffs and patrolled by the occasional quail hunter, feels like the remotest and loneliest place in the Mediterranean.) The inhospitable wasteland of the Mani was where the bravest Spartan warriors were said to have retreated after the Roman invasion of Greece. In the Middle Ages, it was the last holdout of die-hard pagans against Christians; later, of Byzantine knights against Turks.

Even today, the Maniots try to uphold the military ethic of Sparta—especially in the fortress-hotels of Aeropolis, a town named after the ancient god of war, Ares.

"I am partisan! *Boom boom!*" our elderly host, George Versakos, announced at the breakfast table on the first morning, waving a bayonet with a derringer attached to it. He gestured to a tinted photograph of himself as a partisan soldier, taken fifty-five years ago.

"Germans afraid! *Boom boom!*"

"Nescafé?" his wife asked, ignoring the man completely as she offered a lone sachet of instant on a saucer like an after-dinner mint.

Mr. Versakos snorted in disgust at this domestic interruption, and continued to show off his private war museum, a rusty collection of Turkish scabbards, cowboy Colt pistols, and antique machine guns. Now in his seventies, he was spiffily dressed, with a trimmed white mustache and a buffed Greek naval cap. His house, a three-hundred-year-old family heirloom, was actually a stone defensive tower with slits for windows. Mr. Versakos and his wife kept their paying guests in the two spare rooms—or at least tried to, when they weren't throwing things at each other or screaming abuse at the top of their voices, for their mutual hatred was implacable.

It turns out that the Spartan traditions have never quite died in the Mani. As late as the early 1900s, its scowling, illiterate peasants lived completely isolated from the rest of Greece in a primitive feudal society that was consumed by rabid blood feuds. According to one Greek poem recorded by the travel writer Patrick Leigh Fermor, Maniots went about "armed to the teeth, wilder than vampires," slaughtering one another gleefully. Women's work was to breed large families; male children were called, literally, "guns," and tutored in brutality. To further their endless and meaningless wars, the Maniots built hundreds of these stolid stone towers, so that enemy families could pick one another off with rusty antique muskets and cannons. Recently, some of these box relics have been turned into small and uneconomical bed-and-breakfasts.

In Aeropolis, Mr. Versakos continues to upset his guests' digestion every morning by leaping up from the breakfast table, waving a scimitar, and denouncing all Turks as barnyard animals.

"Greek soldier? Bravo! Turkish soldier? *Baa-baa.*"

Not sure what to say to George, I tried a little light conversation with Mrs. Versakos. "Ah . . . so your husband was a partisan in the war?"

She just rolled her eyes and pushed forward a plate of dried olives, the inexplicable core of any Greek breakfast.

"Boom boom!" Mr. Versakos repeated more loudly.

Portraits of Greek independence heroes with huge mustaches covered the walls—Mr. Versakos claimed they had all slept here in the fortress, back in the 1800s—as well as a framed photo of the Versakoses' son Nick in military uniform. Nick was carrying on the great tradition of King Leonidas as a Greek air force pilot. From behind enormous mirrored glasses, he stared back at the camera with a confident military sneer. He looked strikingly like the young Colonel Gadhafi.

"My hero son," Mrs. Versakos said enigmatically. "You will meet him."

The next morning, we did have the pleasure, when we came across Nick sprawled out on the living room floor. Compared to the photograph, he was looking somewhat the worse for wear. He was wearing a sweat-stained undershirt and was disheveled and unshaven, with a burned-out cigarette hanging from one lip. Mr. Versakos, whose outfit was as crisp as Bertie Wooster's, gazed on appalled as his offspring stretched himself, rearranged his inside trouser leg, and lit up another rancid cigarette. The son, for his part, groaned every time George went "boom boom," and muttered curses under his breath. Mrs. Versakos looked at them both with open contempt, then limped off to the laundry to do the actual work of running a guest house.

Later I asked the locals about the Versakos clan and their military fables. They were decidedly exaggerated, apparently. There were no records of independence heroes staying in the house. Even the Greek navy cap was an affectation, they opined, since Mr. Versakos had certainly never been to sea—not even on a ferry to the islands.

But, I asked, he must have been with the partisans in the war: The portrait of him proved it. Or was that all an elaborate fantasy as well?

"Oh, I'm sure he joined the partisans," a neighbor snorted. "But only to wear the uniform."

Sacred Frenzy:
The Olympic Games

From sparta, the next stop for ancient tourists was inescapable. Their wagons trundled along the basalt highway up the sunny west coast of the Peloponnesus—past the headlands of "sandy Pylos," where Homer's wise King Nestor once ruled, and where today are some of the last undeveloped beaches in all of Greece—to the hillside sanctuary of Olympia.

For forty-seven months out of every forty-eight, this religious compound set in lovely green fields was the idyllic haunt of priests, pilgrims, and sightseers: Our tour guide Pausanias devotes fully two of his ten books to its artistic splendors. But Roman tourists tried to have their visits coincide with that moment when the first full moon shone after the quadrennial summer solstice. For it was then that Olympia was transformed, and they could take part in the ultimate pagan festival: the Olympic Games. And they were prepared to put up with almost any discomfort to do so.

At the height of the Mediterranean summer, Roman tourists found themselves joining an estimated forty thousand spectators converging on tiny Olympia, many of whom had traveled from as far away as Africa and the Black Sea to attend. This "endless mass of people," as the sports fan Lucian complained, utterly swamped the modest local facilities, creating conditions reminiscent of a badly planned rock festival. The few inns were booked up for months in advance, especially the luxury hotels built for VIPs. (Two have been excavated on the site, with charming colonnades and rooms with leafy patios; athletes were sequestered together in their own hostels, creating a modest Olympic Village, along with their trainers and masseurs.) All others had to pitch their own tents—turning the Sacred Precinct of Zeus, holiest of pagan shrines, into the center-piece of a vast, anarchic campground. Even the wealthy had to arrive early to stake out their turf on a prime site on the manicured grove, alongside hundreds sleeping head to toe in temporary shelters. The poorer attendees huddled under porches, along colonnades, beneath the statues of famous discus throwers. Plato himself once had to take refuge in a makeshift barracks with snoring, drunken strangers. Local aristocrats were given whips to keep order.

Surviving as a spectator in the Stadium deserved a laurel wreath in itself. For the five days of competition, crowds sat on the bare hillside from dawn until dusk, without benefit of seats, blistered by the fierce summer sun and lashed by rain. Unscrupulous vendors made a killing as the captive audiences gorged on cut-rate sausages of dubious quality, nuts and pears, and amphoras of gut-wrenching resinated wine. Until an aqueduct was built to the site in the mid-second century A.D., there was no regular drinking-water supply in Olympia—the shady river Alpheus dried up in summer—so spectators regularly collapsed from dehydration. The lack of sanitation meant that fevers and bouts of diarrhea ripped through the crowd. Adding insult to injury, Olympia was plagued by bugs: Before the Games, priests sacrificed at a special shrine to Zeus Apomyios—Zeus the Averter of Flies—in a vain attempt to keep the infestations at bay. At the end of the festivities, Lucian complained, spec-tators could be stranded for days bargaining with wagon drivers for a ride. In fact, Lucian added, the experience was so famously uncomfort-able that a master once threatened a disobedient slave with a visit to the Olympics as punishment.

None of this deterred spectators in the least: Lucian, despite his whin-ing, attended at least four times. One Athenian baker boasted on his gravestone of having seen twelve Olympiads. Obviously, he agreed with the philosopher Epictetus that the difficulties were a small price to pay for an "unforgettable spectacle." After all, as Pausanias enticingly assured his readers, the Olympiad was when "the divine aura is the most tangi-ble on earth."

THE SPORTING LIFE

In a sense, the ancient Games were a victim of their own success.

They had been held every four years without fail since Hercules founded them in 776 B.C.; for educated Romans, history itself was dated by Olympiads. The Greeks were the first to make competitive athletics central to their daily life—the gymnasium was the most important building in any city, after the temple—and by the classical era of the fifth century B.C., some three hundred sporting competitions had sprung up around the Eastern Mediterranean. But none compared in prestige to the Olympics. Each event was sacred, dedicated to Zeus, and to win at Olympia was the closest a mortal could come to deification. The Games were so important that they were held under a Sacred Truce: When the dozens of Olympic heralds set off around Greece to announce the event, all wars between the perennially feuding city-states ceased, in order to allow the competitors and spectators safe transit. This truce, the terms of which were engraved on a golden discus, allowed diplomats to negotiate peace treaties at Olympia; their texts would be inscribed on tablets and hung in temples as offerings to the gods. In fact, religion permeated every moment of the festival: Over the five days of the competition, pagan processions, rituals, and sacrifices—including one hundred bulls—took up as much time as athletics. A visit to Olympia became as profound for pagans as a pilgrimage to Varanasi for Hindus, or the hajj for Muslims, today.

Under Roman rule, the Games reached new heights of popularity: They were without doubt the greatest recurring event in the entire Empire. At no other time were so many people traveling in the Mediterranean at once as when the heralds set out from Olympia every four years (although the Pax Romana made the Sacred Truce unnecessary). Gladiatorial combats may have gripped the crowds back in Rome, but every sophisticated Roman dreamed of visiting Olympia—and since the events were open to any free man who spoke Greek, many a Hellenophile saw fit to compete. The young Tiberius—future satyr-emperor—raced a chariot in the 195th Olympiad (A.D. 1), as did Germanicus in the 199th. Not every Roman was so unassuming. In A.D. 67, Nero added tragic poetry and harp playing to the traditional roster of sporting competitions, and handily won both (one observer remembered that the sight of the emperor singing in the Olympic Stadium provoked "whole Iliads of woe"). Admirably impartial, Olympia's judges also awarded Nero first prize in the chariot race, even though he actually fell out of his vehicle and crossed the line last. At the victory banquet, he sighed: "The Greeks alone know how to appreciate me."

Despite such lapses, nothing could match the spectacle of the Olympics: It was an all-consuming event, meeting place of heaven and earth, where every contour of ancient society was reflected on and off the field. To imagine a modern equivalent, today's Olympics would have to be combined with Carnival in Rio, Easter Mass at the Vatican, and a U.S. presidential election.

The spectators' grubby tent city was the scene for the *panegyris* (profane festival)—a round-the-clock bacchanal where prostitutes could make a year's wages in five days. There were beauty contests, drinking competitions, eating races; expert masseurs offering rubdowns to the weary; young boys in white makeup and veils performing erotic dances. The sweaty crowds were harangued by soapbox orators, theatrical troupes, jugglers, palm readers, fire eaters, and (according to the orator Dio the Golden-Tongued) "countless lawyers perverting justice." Famous philosophers came to debate, sometimes sending an advance guard to whip up interest. Poets debuted works-in-progress. Herodotus had publicly recited his history at the Olympics, Thucydides his great war chronicle. Painters and sculptors shamelessly sought out patrons. But in this carnival of self-promotion, perhaps the most notorious scene stealer was a Cynic philosopher named Peregrinus, who in A.D. 165 chose the Games as the best place to publicly immolate himself. A vast mob gathered as the old man approached the bonfire, some awestruck, others derisive of the grandstanding, still others drunkenly chanting, "Get on with it!"

We have to imagine a carnival atmosphere, where Apuleius, visiting as a student from Athens, could squander his entire inheritance in a few days. It was a common tale. Self-restraint, austerity, modest behavior—these were not qualities associated with the ancient Olympics.

THE OLYMPIAN MONEY MACHINE

The profane festival is still alive and well in modern Olympia. Since the 1960s, a little "service village" has spontaneously sprouted in this otherwise remote fringe of the Peloponnesus to cater to tour groups visiting the ruins. While generating a faux ambience of rustic Greek style, the outpost has deftly managed to re-create the time-honored Olympic traditions of overcrowding, commercialism, and gleeful exploitation. It's the modern incarnation of the old tent city.

We navigated the creaking Donko past makeshift storefronts decorated with plaster columns and Aphrodite statues, hotels called the Acropolis and Apollo and Parnassus—tavernas with plastic grapevines and menus in seven languages, all serving up "special tourist meals" of the same moussaka, Greek salad, and baklava—bars with battered blond Russian women on the lookout for lonely male travelers. Rooms in this new Olympia were surprisingly hard to come by; we found one in the sixth hotel we tried. It contained eight very narrow beds, all consumed by rising damp. At the front desk, the young Greek-Australian owner had the distant, vacant expression of one who has become resigned to a rapid turnover. We had no more reality to her than did the flitting spirits of Hades.

But after this shaky start, Olympia's promise of "unforgettable spectacle" leaped to the fore; over in the ancient Greek sanctum sanctorum, Pausanias' divine aura was still aglow.

Today, the Sacred Precinct of Zeus is still nestled within succulent hills of a brilliant Irish green; the river Alpheus wends its way nearby, hung with willows and poplars, although its course has changed since classical times. Incredibly, the site of Olympia, this greatest of all pagan shrines, was completely lost in the Middle Ages, buried beneath the shifting silt of another flooding river; it was only discovered by a visiting British antiquarian in 1766, when he noticed that local farmers were plowing up fragments of statues in their fields. Resurrected from its muddy grave, the ancient Stadium had been revealed in its original shape, sleek and narrow, but many of the other buildings are merely knee-high shards. When the Christian emperor Theodosius finally banned the Games in A.D. 391, ending their spectacular and unbroken thousand-year run, the pagan temples were vandalized. And yet, the sheer fertility of Olympia's landscape—the gentle grass and low-hanging trees such a contrast after the endless stark mountainsides of Greece—make the remains seem majestic. Even the smallest fragments look like crown jewels laid out on a green velvet cushion. And like all ancient Greek sites, the place had impeccable feng shui.

Inside the Stadium, dozens of excitable Spaniards were taking turns to kneel at Olympia's original stone starting line, then running—well, more like waddling, limping, gasping, and wheezing—up the 210-yard track. Crowds of international visitors were caught in the bottleneck of the athletes' entrance, squeezing through the vaulted arches in a maelstrom of sweat and body odor. Curses in a dozen languages echoed around the arena. Anticipation and anxiety were thick in the air.

And it has never been any other way.

On the first morning of the ancient Games, Roman tourists would be there among the rowdy throng pushing into the Stadium.

Servants carried the padded cushions and picnic lunch—a time-honored repast of bread, olives, and cheese—as they elbowed their way forward to seize a good position. Spectators knew they were sitting on the very hill where Zeus had once wrestled his father, the Titan Kronos, for control of the world, and the heady atmosphere of myth added an extra thrill to every moment. It was well known that the gods themselves took as much interest in the results as did mortals.

The tourists rubbed shoulders with Greeks from all social classes—attendance was free—although, as usual, this touching democratic principle did not extend to slaves or women. Females were forbidden to compete—instead, they were given a separate, second-string Games in Olympia dedicated to Hera, Zeus' consort (they included sprints between virgin girls, who raced in tunics with the right breast exposed). Romans would have been disappointed that women could not even enter the Stadium as spectators: Back home, women were allowed to sit in the Circus alongside men and had a separate tier in the Colosseum. Still, there are stories of women slipping into events in disguise. Once, a matron from Rhodes cropped her hair and wore a trainer's tunic to watch her son compete. Unfortunately, in her excitement at the boy's victory, she leaped over the trainer's barrier, catching the tunic's fringe and exposing her deception.

The Olympics always commenced with a bang: the famous chariot race in the Hippodrome. For days beforehand, spectators had discussed the event, debating the relative merits of drivers, the form of the horses; true aficionados frequented the stables, inspecting the fodder and even sniffing the dung to establish the animals' health. Around the horse track, foreigners and Greeks noted the conditions of the turf and began to lay bets with their neighbors. There was a buzz of excitement as spectators witnessed the forty colorful chariots proceeding to the starting gate, each led by four horses. Ten Olympic judges in purple robes took their positions in a booth halfway down the course.

At last, the starting gate opened with a string of thuds—it was shaped like a ship's prow, with an ingenious crank system to open the forty gates in reverse order, so that no driver had an unfair advantage—and the crowd let out a deafening roar as the chariots charged down the turf, careening in a mass around the turning post. The accidents alone were spectacular: Audience members in the front rows were sprayed with mud and splinters. Spectators shrieked, swore, wept, tore their hair, waved handkerchiefs, hid their faces, their cries drowning out the thundering of hooves. The full course was twelve laps, about six miles, and every turn produced new disasters and triumphs of skill. A cheer erupted like a thunderbolt as the winning chariot crossed the line, startling the live-stock in their fields miles away. The Hippodrome was littered with debris: On one occasion, only one vehicle made it safely to the finish.

And so the Games began. The enthusiasm of the crowd never flagged over the eighteen time-honored events, as the stark naked, oiled athletes competed under the stern gazes of priests and judges. Some competitions remain in the modern Olympic iconography—racing, wrestling, boxing, javelin, discus. Others, like the sprints in full body armor, have been abandoned. One of the crowd's favorite events was an all-in brawl called the *pankration,* where everything from finger breaking to strangling was permitted. Spartans excelled at this jolly sport: It was an unusual year when several casualties were not cremated by the Alpheus.

And every night, after the sports, the spectators continued the excitement off the field—taking advantage not just of the partying but of the unbeatable sight-seeing.

Olympia probably had more works of art per square foot than anywhere else in Greece, proudly shown off by feisty sacred guides. But tourists made a beeline for the Temple of Zeus—a rather stolid, squat building compared to anything in Athens, but containing the ultimate glimpse of divinity. The statue of Olympian Zeus, sculpted by Phidias, was one of the Seven Wonders of the World; beholding it was an unforgettable experience, a great moment in any Roman's life.

Today, segments of the temple's Doric columns lie tumbled in the grass like limestone cogs. No doubt pagan devotees ran their fingers curiously along the same fluted flanks: the local stone was a conglomerate of fossilized shells—an inferior material for architectural detail but an evocative fabric to honor the god of nature. Ushered through the giant bronze doors, they stopped in their tracks, awestruck: the bearded figure of Zeus was glowering back at them in the flickering torchlight. He loomed forty feet high, presiding on a throne of cedar; his muscular flesh was made of ivory, his robes from gold, and in his outstretched palm stood a winged statue of Victory. The god's head almost touched the ceiling; in fact, noted the geographer Strabo, "it looks as if Zeus were to stand up, he would unroof the temple."

The statue's sheer size was intimidating enough. But it was the god's expression that truly humbled the viewer: It conveyed both the invincible power of Zeus and his sympathetic humanity. His gaze was said to terrify stray dogs that came into the temple; men and women found that

Olympia's sanctum sanctorum: the remains of the Temple of Zeus.

it made them forget all the sorrows of their lives. Most Romans shared the deep emotion of the general-tourist Aemilius Paulus, who felt that he had "beheld the god in person." Pausanias, on being told that the statue was only forty feet high, at first could not believe it: the sheer force of Zeus' presence made it seem immeasurably larger. Many tourists had to fight the urge to prostrate themselves—for the gods demanded dignity of mortals, not groveling.

"Father and King, Protector of Cities, God of Friendship, God of Hospitality, Giver of Increase . . ."

Zeus had a busy schedule during the Games. He was dressed in the robes of a judge, and attendants came in after each event to tell him the results. Great crowds of pagan suppliants would stand around his knees, arguing their cases out loud; others climbed to the temple's specially built mezzanine, where they could admire the sculpture at head level, and whisper their more private requests into Zeus' ear. Outside on the temple steps, women who had been told in dreams that they were favored by the god awaited sexual congress—mythology is full of mortal women impregnated by the divine being, and bearing wonderful children. Nobody doubted that Zeus was personified here: When the mad Caligula ordered the god's head to be replaced with a sculpture of his own, the statue let out a deafening peal of laughter, making the work-men flee.

The Olympian Zeus was only the tip of the iceberg for ancient art lovers: Pausanias was truly in pedant's heaven here, glutting himself on images from one riverside museum-temple to the next. The open fields were a glittering parade of sleek bronze torsos, since every champion received a statue. Among the celebrity sportsmen were Milo of Kroton, who was so strong that nobody could even bend his little finger, and the boxer Theagenes, whose statue, Pausanias notes, was actually enchanted: When one of the boxer's former opponents started whipping and insult-ing it, it fell and crushed the man to death. Despite the obvious provo-cation, the statue was tried for murder, and sentenced to be thrown into the sea. Subsequently, the fields around Olympia bore no fruit for several seasons, so the statue was fished up again and put back in place.

After taking in such wonderful sights—spiritually fulfilling, histori-cally intriguing—the happy spectators would all charge back into the Stadium, ready for the next event.

INVENTING THE OLYMPIC SPIRIT

Today, it requires a serious leap of imagination to recall the cultural coherence that buoyed the ancient Olympics, when our own Games seem to promote only conflict and cynicism.

Nothing could dull the ancient passion for the Olympics extrava-ganza—certainly not scandal. Ever since 388 B.C., when a certain Eubu-lus of Thessaly bribed three Olympian boxers to throw their fights against him, corruption charges were a regular feature of the Games. Judges used the fines to erect statues of Zeus, which were inscribed with moral poems "to show that you win at Olympia with the speed of your feet and the strength of your body, not with money."

Nor was commercialism offensive. Athletes were professionals, living on stipends from civic bodies and private patrons (the modern obsession with amateurism was begun by the father of the modern Olympics, the Frenchman Pierre de Coubertin, who was keen to keep the riffraff out of competition after its revival in 1896). They traveled in troupes from one sporting event to the next, picking up cash prizes as they went. Of the hundreds of regular games held across the Eastern Mediterranean, Olympia was unique for not handing out money—champions were crowned with wreaths of wild olive, fashioned from the branches of Zeus' sacred tree—but as the poet Pindar said, a champion won "sweet smooth-sailing" for the rest of his life. They were regarded as heroes, little short of demigods, and paraded triumphantly through their home cities in four-horse chariots; an adoring populace awarded them lifetime pensions, free food, villas, tax immunity, front-row seats at the amphitheater. In this age before TV endorsements, they made fortunes from cameo appearances at lesser games—one obscure town in Asia Minor paid a boxer thirty thousand drachmas, around one hundred times a Roman army soldier's annual pay—or entered politics. The wrestler Marcus Aurelius Asclepiades became a senator in Athens, anticipating Jesse Ventura by twenty centuries. Other victors were invited to Rome as masseurs in the imperial palace or even as personal trainers to the emperor.

Good sportsmanship, meanwhile, was thin on the ground. In the intensely competitive ancient world, defeated athletes were openly mocked. Publicly humiliated, says Pindar, they went "skulking down back roads, hiding from their enemies, bitten by their calamity." There were no second prizes at Olympia. The ultimate sore loser was a certain Kleomedes, who, according to Pausanius, was disqualified and "went out of his mind with grief." On his return home, he attacked a school, pulling down a pillar and collapsing the roof on sixty young boys inside.

As the centuries wore on, few voices were ever raised against this feverish sporting cult. The occasional philosopher thought the obsession philistine, emphasizing the body at the expense of the spirit and mind: Diogenes once denigrated a sprinter who was boasting about his pace, acidly noting that the fastest animals, the rabbit and deer, also happened to be the most cowardly. But the voices of such spoilsports were faint—drowned out by the multitudinous chorus of fans who defended athletics on the grounds that they promoted endurance, physical beauty, and moral fiber.

Every four years, when the sacred heralds ran out from Olympia's gates announcing the next Games, the athletes readied for business, and the sports fans drew up their travel plans.

We loaded up the Donko, ready to slip out of our own version of an Olympian barracks. But as I went to check out, a time-honored encounter was being reenacted at the front desk.

According to Lucian, at the end of the ancient Games, the crowds trying to leave the rubbish-strewn site always seemed to be full of Cynic philosophers. These classical hippies—who usually infested the streets of Athens like lice in a rotten mattress—were in their element among the motley stragglers, wandering about in filthy tunics, their hair matted and unwashed, berating the pious, mocking the gods, mooching meals from the gullible. Lucian was both amused and appalled by the antics of the Cynics, convinced that they were little better than con artists.

At our budget hotel in Olympia, the vacant-eyed owner liked to judge guests by their appearance; dressed like Ivana Trump herself, she could barely disguise her disdain at any guest wearing blue jeans. But she was soon to discover that modern Cynics work their magic in suit and tie.

"There is a karma that governs all our financial dealings," a dapper old Englishman was saying at the front desk. "A friend in need is a friend indeed . . ."

He had all the trappings of a country gentleman—silver hair, well-groomed mustache, frayed tweed coat—and had obviously been staying at the hotel for some time.

"Of course, I do feel awful to impose on you like this," he went on, in the smooth, offhand manner of an oft-repeated spiel. "I really don't know how to repay you for your kindness . . ."

"Obviously you can't," the woman said tersely, rapidly neatening her very neat desk.

"I find myself in sticky circumstances, and I must simply throw myself at your mercy."

"Yes, yes."

The cultured voice droned on: "Completely unexpected . . . your generosity is wonderful . . . terrible inconvenience . . ." It appeared that this yellow-toothed shark had been scamming his way around Greece, staying for a few weeks at each location, casually insinuating himself into the favors of Greek hoteliers—who were always delighted to have such a respectable guest, and one who actually wanted to savor the ruins for *week after week*—then at the last moment revealing his sadly penniless situation. A gentleman cad, with a winning smile, old-school tie, and battered suitcase—the sort that turns up in New York art galleries looking for the free wine and canapes.

"Needless to say, I shall wire you the funds the very instant they're available."

"Needless to say."

And the hotelier's eyes glazed over as the patter droned endlessly on.

One of the most surprising things about traveling in modern Greece is how eggshell thin the mass tourist empire really is. All you have to do is

take a small step sideways—drive half a mile away from the most con-
gested sites or beaches—and suddenly you're in a different world.

After the swarming fields of Olympia, we turned inland—creeping
along a mountain highway in a logjam of tour buses until, out of des-
peration, I followed a Greek sign to a side road at random. The stifling
atmosphere lifted like a curtain. Barren ocher mountains soared to a sky
so pale it was almost white. The road was a single winding lane that led
through tiny heat-baked villages where old men with heavy mustaches
sat like mushrooms in the shade, sipping thimbles of coffee and playing
dominoes. There were broken Orthodox chapels, trimmed with dead
flowers, where black-clad widows swept the floors and tended roadside
icons.

To my mind, this was most encouraging. We'd sampled all the civilized pleasures of Greece's greatest hits. It was time to savor some fresh
air, some foliage, some gentle open spaces. After all, the Romans may
not have shared the modern hunger for pure wilderness, but they were
not immune to the power of nature, which they saw as a manifestation
of the divine.

"You encounter a grove," Seneca explains in one almost Thoreau-like
rave. "The ancient trees are thickly clustered; their interlacing foliage
shut out the sky; a huge darkness encloses the open fields. And a bewil-
derment seizes you, revealing that you are in the presence of a god. Or
you behold some deep grotto that has been hollowed out by Nature
alone. The soul feels something higher. It is right to place altars at these
places, to worship the sources of great streams . . . or where hot springs
bubble up, or by lakes unfathomable or mysteriously somber."

Yes, it was time for our souls to soar among the peaks.

Et in Arcadia Ego . . .

AND THEN THERE WE WERE, hiking the very vales of Arcadia—mythic blueprint for earthly paradise, ancient Greece's Shangri-la, time-honored image of nature at its most idyllic and serene.

Unfortunately, paradise wasn't behaving quite as advertised.

The intermittent fog was so thick you could barely make out the trail ten feet ahead, let alone the spectacular Lousios gorge, which supposedly yawned to the horizon like the Grand Canyon. There were tantalizing glimpses of sheer granite cliffs through the layers of mist—inexplicable shafts of sunlight—candy-bright rainbows floating for a few moments above the dark treetops. But it was hard to appreciate these heavenly visions because a steady cold rain had soaked us to the bone. The mule track beneath our sodden feet—a favored walking route for travelers, hermits, and pilgrims since the Romans' day—had turned into the gray, gluelike paste usually seen only in photos of trench warfare. As peals of thunder rolled ominously, Arcadia didn't seem such an advisable place to be lost.

Disconcerting though it all was, the province was just living up to its reputation, at least according to the most archaic legends. The historian Simon Schama makes the point in his book *Landscape and Memory:* Our modern image of Arcadia as a placid and bountiful garden was actually a late reworking of the original myth. To the earliest Greeks, the place was a more menacing vision of nature, a brutal, untamed forest filled with bestial inhabitants. This ancient Arcadia was ruled by the anarchic, sex-crazed god Pan, a manic half-goat who went about sodomizing livestock

Haunted paradise: a chapel in the Lousios gorge, Arcadia.

and incessantly masturbating as he played his pipes. Pan's subjects—the original Arcadians—were lusty primitives, dressed in skins and subsisting on milk and corn; far from a sun-dappled idyll, their home in "paradise" was racked alternately by droughts and floods. It was the Romans who most effectively tamed the image, tearing up its mythic roots. They were unnerved by raw landscapes, desolate mountain ranges, or any wilderness untouched by the hand of man; instead, writers like Virgil and Pliny the Younger conjured Arcadia as a controlled and manicured garden, a pagan Eden where shepherds lolled by charming lakes and crops grew without effort. This new Arcadia was a *locus amoenus* (place of delight), and the dewy-eyed painters of the Renaissance passed the tamer romance on to the present day. (Although the old, libidinous vision of raw nature can still be found in modern Arcadias; Central Park's sinuous maze, the Ramble, lures no shortage of latter-day satyrs, perched like gargoyles in the bushes.)

The village of Stemnitsa, where we'd put up the night before, had the vaguely macabre mien of a Transylvanian village. Even at noon, clouds of mist drifted through the medieval streets, past slate-gray buildings and abandoned churches; the doughy white faces of peasants peered at us fearfully from behind shuttered windows, which were adorned with cru-

cifixes and garlands of garlic hanging out to dry, as if Nosferatu were on
the prowl. We pushed open one doorway marked KAFE to reveal a tiny,
dark room thick with pipe smoke and crowded elbow-to-elbow with
mud-splattered shepherds who stared at us in bovine silence, like a set
piece from Breughel. In the village's only store, where every surface was
thick with grease, a black-hooded crone was buying what appeared to be
a pound of cat's vomit (it turned out to be an oily form of lard, a Greek
schmaltz). When we did find a restaurant, the waitress snapped: "What
will you eat?"

"What do you have?" Les asked cautiously, in the absence of a menu.
She rolled her eyes. *"Food!"*

"Oh, man," Les muttered, as we retreated gingerly to the car. "These
Arcadians have a lot of attitude."

Thankfully, the only hotel in town, the Trikolonion, was a more hospitable refuge; it resembled a wooden alpine chalet, and was run by a
jovial, blimp-shaped Greek matron who juggled three unwashed babies
on her bosom as she prepared an improbable feast of smoked trout for
our dinner in front of the blazing wood fire ("Oh, yes, we Arcadians are
a despicable people!" she giggled). As I drowned my sorrows in rose
retsina, served in small metal buckets, I scanned the pages of Pausanias
for tips on where to turn.

Having wandered the real Arcadia valley by valley, Pausanias can be
counted on for an objective description. Arcadia was in Roman times—
as now—the most inaccessible corner of the Peloponnesus, a mountainous heartland riddled with precipitous pathways. These connected
ancient cities whose names dissolved from maps many centuries
ago—places like Stymphalus, Orchomenus, Mantinea, and Cheimerion
(although one small Arcadian polis, Kleitor, does live on in our anatomi-
cal parlance, thanks to its "conspicuous conical hill"). Many of these out-
posts were already falling into decay in Pausanias' time, leaving poetic
ruins in every glade. But it was in the inhabited margins of Arcadia that
the magical allure existed for tourists, who would tramp methodically
from one cliffside aerie to the next, paying homage at remote sanctuaries.
They could visit moss-covered temples where priests guarded the most
exotic Greek artifacts—giants' teeth, Medusa's hair—and gaze upon the
near-secret grottoes or holy springs where Pan and his sprites once
pranced. On the way, they might encounter dazzling scenes of rural piety:
Fine horses, carefully bitted and bridled, were flung from Arcadian cliffs
into river gorges, as sacrifices to Poseidon; women still lay charms at the
grave of Penelope, Odysseus' long-suffering wife; ritual parades of white-
robed boys went by on mountain passes, hyacinths garlanding their hair.

In short, Arcadia was where tourists could sense the primordial flavor of old Greece.

I had all this in mind when, somewhere around the fourth bucket of retsina, it seemed like an excellent idea to walk down the mountainside from Stemnitsa, following the steep mule trail to the magnificently obscure ruins of Gortys ("a village in my time," writes Pausanias, "which in the old days was a city")—going via the medieval monastery of Prodromou. This latter, isolated but still filled with monks, would be an equivalent of Pausanias' sacred sanctuaries, I hoped.

They both sounded like places that hardly anyone in his right mind would want to visit today—allowing me to test my theory that, in modern Greece, where the most sacred sites had become the most profane, ancient enchantment must still lie in its remotest corners.

Les—who was stone cold sober—just walked over to the window and, watching the rain already coming down in the darkness, said: "You're joking, right?"

THE WILD MEN OF THE MOUNTAINS

And so the next morning found us blundering through impenetrable fog, dodging sharp branches that protruded like tortured skeletons into the trail, wondering how long it would take for someone to find us if we were, say, struck by one of the bolts of lightning that seemed to be crashing ever closer. Les's self-preservation instinct, which was increasingly fine-tuned as the pregnancy advanced, had been lulled by a relatively clear morning sky; the hotelier's husband had gleefully assured us that the weather would remain fine. Now the thunder was rolling in Wagnerian peals overhead, cold drops of rain were slithering down our necks like snakes, and flecks of hail were starting to pelt. Les's expression was a stoic, inscrutable mask. She was taking it all in surprisingly good stead, I thought, only occasionally murmuring, "The gods were angry that day, my friends . . ." We staggered on, already too far to turn back.

To be fair, Pausanias does give some warning about the terrible weather in these mountains. Arcadians, he says, believed that cataclysmic storms constantly racked their homes because this was where the Greek gods once battled the Titans; proof was found in the enormous bones that were found in local caves, assumed to be the thighs of defeated giants (actually mammoths' bones, they were displayed on the altar of a nearby temple; travelers still reported seeing them in the village of Dimitsana's museum in the late nineteenth century). Apparently the peasants would often "sacrifice here to the lightning and the storms and the thunder." Judging from the skies so far, it looked like they'd had plenty of opportunity. It wasn't much comfort to recall that anyone killed by a bolt of lightning was revered; their bodies were solemnly buried, having been blessed by Zeus himself.

We slowly descended the stone steps, which by now had turned into sculpted waterfalls around our ankles. For superstitious ancient wayfarers, the deluge would have been the least disturbing part of being lost in the fog. Werewolves stalked these mountains, Pausanias notes: The members of secret cults would sacrifice humans and then eat their flesh, but those who accidentally consumed part of a victim's entrails would be forced to "herd with wolves." This story also appears in sober accounts by Plato and Pliny the Elder. The learned authorities agreed: Wolf-men could regain human form only if they abstained from human flesh for a full nine years. Even more unsettling, the river Styx itself ran through northern Arcadia; it still thunders down a cliffside in a majestic waterfall, near the modern village of Solos. Pausanias solemnly reports that the river's dark waters are deadly poisonous; they shatter crystal and stone, and corrode all metals, even gold. According to Seneca, the Styx's water had no smell, but one sip would instantly "bind the bowels." (Which could work well for modern travelers, if marketed correctly.)

By midmorning, the lightning had eased, but the rain was still heavy. Les was about to go to sleep under a cypress tree when the mists parted to reveal a prefabricated cottage.

In Pausanias' time, there would have been a priestly custodian here, to offer a bracing drink. In fact, Apicius, author of the only surviving Roman cookbook, provides a recipe for a brew "with which travelers are refreshed by the wayside":

Conditum Melizomum Viatorium—
Honey Refresher for Travelers

The Wayfarer's Honey Refresher (so called because it gives endurance and strength to travelers) . . . is made in this manner: Flavor honey with ground pepper. In the moment of serving put honey in a cup, as much as is desired to obtain the right degree of sweetness, and mix with spiced wine . . . to facilitate its flow and the mixing.

I decided we should throw ourselves on the mercy of whoever lurked inside.

"No way!" Les yelled. "They'll murder us and take all our stuff!"

This self-preservation thing was getting way out of hand. "What else are we supposed to do? You'll get pneumonia out here."

"But we have no idea who they are!"

She'd been living in New York way too long. After about fifteen minutes of cajoling, I persuaded her to let me knock on the door, as she hung back suspiciously.

Two pairs of goggle eyes bobbed up at the window—belonging to a couple of crusty Arcadian farmers. Their frayed handlebar mustaches twitched beneath rosy red cheeks; both wore mud-caked galoshes and suspenders like characters from the Brothers Grimm. I could barely understand a word they said, but gathered that they harvested olives somewhere in these virtually impenetrable hills. They could tell we were half dead, so they dragged us in from the rain, and boiled water for instant coffee on the potbellied woodstove, about the only piece of furniture in their splintery little house. As always, the grains of Nescafé were portioned out as if they were gold dust. Not quite as gourmet as peppered honey and spiced wine, perhaps, but sipped Greek style, with six spoonfuls of sugar in each cup, it did provide the same short-term energy kick. This goofy pair made pretty good custodians of the trail, we thought—like the Spartans, they were obeying the ancient laws of hospitality. According to Homer, you should always be kind to travelers in case they were gods wandering the earth in disguise.

"Baby?" One of the farmers grinned insanely at Les, but since no knives could be seen in the vicinity, she was slowly relaxing. "Boy? Girl?"

"Ah . . . boy."

They threw up their arms in obvious relief, and shook my hand.

"Thanks to God! Thanks to God!" Maybe they thought I'd have tossed it into a ravine, Spartan style, had it been a girl.

That was when we discovered why their eyes were so pink and glassy. Mustaches twitching furiously, they pulled out an industrial-size bottle of ouzo from a drawer and pushed it slowly across the table toward us.

"Not for me," Les said, looking significantly at me. But it seemed churlish to refuse.

"Ah . . . to Pan," I said, raising the toast.

"Yusas!" they crowed.

The scalding liquor burned through my veins like acid; I hadn't touched any aniseed brews since my university days, when I unwisely guzzled an entire bottle of Pernod, and woke up at dawn in the locked courtyard of an empty restaurant with no idea how I'd arrived there. But the ouzo wasn't so bad; it brought my legs back to life. I should reconsider Arcadians, I decided. They weren't such a bleak bunch after all.

"Again," the farmers said, nodding as they passed me the bottle. The laws of hospitality worked both ways, so I took a few more swigs of the gum-scorching concoction. Les just rolled her eyes.

"Maybe we better get going," she finally declared. Just when we were having a bit of a laugh.

The storm had eased, so I asked the wild men about the *monastiri Prodromou.*

"Slow, slow," they insisted, as they ceremoniously shook our hands and pointed us on the right path. I wasn't sure if this was their only English, or if they were genuinely worried that I'd drunkenly lead Les off some mist-shrouded precipice.

An hour later, the sun exploded through the clouds, and I nearly went down on my knees in thanks. The Lousios gorge gaped in the distance, and beams of light lit up the monastery as if directed by Cecil B. DeMille. Its few decrepit buildings clung precariously to a cliffside like an eagle's nest. Maybe this would be my ancient Greek sanctuary, I dreamed, a little maniacally, with Orthodox monks instead of priests of Demeter or Apollo or Zeus . . .

BROTHER YIANNI, THE HOLY HERMIT

Sparkling rainwater cascaded from ivy-covered gutters; a tangle of chicken coops and vegetable gardens extended along the pathway; two enormous goats glared menacingly as we passed. At the oak doorway to the inner sanctum, a wizened, hollow-eyed monk appeared on cue, with a suitably Tolkien-esque flourish. In the brilliant sunshine, his beard, stiff with decades of grease, glimmered like steel wool against his long black robe and tall, cylindrical hat.

Without a word, the patriarch pointed to Les's pants, and then to what looked like a row of burlap bags hanging on a wall. They were evidently skirts, which visiting women had to wear out of respect for the holy place.

"I have to put on one of those?" She winced. "It's hard enough to look good when you're pregnant."

"Oh, you're only going to meet a few senile old monks."

She pulled the billowing brown skirt straight up over her jeans. "Look at this. Like a sack of potatoes."

With a satisfied nod, the monk ushered us up a narrow stone stairwell into Stygian darkness. Cats slunk past our ankles; buckets full of food scraps were moldering in odd corners, giving off a moist, fruity perfume. This wing of the monastery had been built directly into the raw granite wall of the mountains here in the fourteenth century, for the purpose of housing a pair of Byzantine religious icons. We entered the gray stone parlor. Like a medieval torture chamber recently renovated by Ikea, the furniture was upholstered with a summery flower pattern. But the monk gestured to the central wall—the original cliff face, which had become a rutted gray canvas.

The gold-leaf halos of the saints glowed with supernatural brightness. The most imposing was a half-naked figure with a white beard hanging down to his knees, which barely hid his hollow, pallid chest—the patron saint of hermits, perhaps. Greek script flowed by his side, like secret runic spells.

As Pausanias has shown again and again, ancient Greek sanctuaries were far more than places of worship; their complementary role as museums allowed the pious to gaze upon sacred relics and evidence of the divine. His pages are dense with examples. There were man-made artifacts dating from primordial times—barbaric wooden statues of Zeus with three eyes, crimson idols of Dionysus piled high with laurel and ivy, a statue of Aphrodite ringed with clippings of women's hair. Some temples boasted Cyclops skulls or the hides of slaughtered monsters. But the most valued exhibits bore the ineffable touch of the gods themselves. In Chaeronea, the pious tourist could gaze upon the scepter of King Agamemnon, sculpted by Hephaestus, the clubfooted blacksmith of Mount Olympus. Priests kept offerings of cakes and meat before this divine relic (prompting Pausanias' first English translator, Sir James Frazer, author of *The Golden Bough,* to assert: "A ruder conception of religion than is revealed by this practice of adoring and feeding a [scepter] it might be hard to discover amongst the lowest fetish-worshippers of East Africa"). Elsewhere, a temple displayed the stump of the strawberry tree under which the god Hermes had reputedly been suckled as a baby. Tourists could seek out the actual boat oars supposedly used by the Argonauts on their famous voyage with Jason, or the shackles used to chain the princess Andromeda before her rescue from a sea monster by Perseus. There were perpetual fires, altars made of blood and ashes, a gold peacock dedicated to Hera—all lovingly exhibited between marble columns, burnished by torchlight, and framed by curtains of royal purple and gold.

Today, the monks of Prodromou are keeping up this time-honored Greek tradition, happily interrupting their schedules to show off mystical keepsakes.

The old warlock-monk was watching us like a hawk, and I wondered if I was supposed to fall to my knees on the lime-green shag. I asked a few questions about the icons, trying to make a little conversation. My patience for Byzantine art is sadly limited—the saints seem indistinguishable, as do their cardboard outfits. But the quality of the painting itself, floating on the time-weathered wall, did have a luminescence that the afterglow from the ouzo could only partly account for.

"*Wait,*" the patriarch commanded, handing me a huge bowl of pink Turkish Delights. "English-speaker will come."

"Oh, *no,*" Les whispered. It was probably going to be some amateur monk-guide, about to trap us into a three-hour diatribe on Byzantine art history. "I can't stand wearing this thing any longer," she said, waving her musty sack dress. "I'll see you outside."

Seconds later, a much younger monk bounded into the room, almost breathless with excitement.

Brother Yianni, the official monastery Anglophone, was short and jaundiced, as if he'd long been gnawing on roots for sustenance; his limp black hair was tied back in a ponytail like a Hollywood film agent (Orthodox clergy are forbidden to shave or cut their locks). He couldn't have been happier to see me if I'd been the prophet Isaiah come down to earth for a chat ("Greetings! Yes! My friend!"). I quickly extracted the icon lore from Brother Yianni—they were painted around A.D. 1100, then hidden from the Turks for centuries—before steering the conversation around to him. I couldn't quite grasp why someone so evidently sociable had signed up in a cloister.

Luckily, Brother Yianni was comfortable in the confessional mode; in fact, I could barely shut him up.

"I did not join the monastery until I was thirty," he began, arranging himself on a snappy tartan settee. "Before, in my twenties, I led a very shameful life. I was living in sin . . ."

"Where's that?" I asked. "Sounds interesting."

He let out a high-pitched gurgle at this feeble humor, like a chicken being strangled.

"My family was always very religious, but I turned to drinking and the company of women. This was not the correct path for me. I was terribly unhappy, always thinking about philosophical questions: Why am I here on earth? What am I doing? And so I decided to make some journeys.

"I went as a pilgrim to Israel, trying to find the inner peace. In Egypt, I sought out the desert near Alexandria, where the Greek prophets once lived in caves. And India . . . there were many wonderful places. I spent some months in an ashram, studying with holy men. I was always interested in meditation, in yoga, in the Buddhist way of thought. But it did not work."

He peered at me significantly.

"I wearied of so much searching. Moving about the world like a . . . ghost. The Chinese philosophers say: When you are restless, stand still; when you are at peace, then move."

"I know the theory." I flinched, a little suspicious that this was a prepared spiel to convert wayward travelers. "Personally, I'm quite a fan of senseless movement. I find it therapeutic."

Brother Yianni smiled indulgently. "One who travels is running away from something. As much as any drunkard."

There was something appealingly surreal about debating the value of travel with a monk in the mountains of Arcadia. It's an age-old argument, and one that certainly went on among ancient Romans. At the birth of cultural tourism, there was no shortage of world wanderers who, after their journeys, discovered that they had found no inner contentment or wisdom.

The killjoy moralist Seneca cast doubts on the peripatetic frenzy that seized his countrymen: "Traveling," he notes dryly in one of his letters, "will bless you with knowledge of strange peoples, shapes of mountains, plains extending to unknown lengths, valleys with eternal waters trickling through . . . but you will not become a better person, or more sensible." Two centuries later, the philosopher-emperor Marcus Aurelius put the same view in his painfully long-winded *Meditations:* "Let it be clear to you that the peace of green fields can always be yours in this, that, or any other spot; and that nothing is any different here from what it would be either up in the hills, or down by the sea, or wherever else you will." Needless to say, on this trip, I'd had occasion to wonder if my own years of perpetual motion didn't have some unseemly neurotic implications—choosing to be a permanent outsider, drifting on the sidelines, collecting experiences like colorful postage stamps, a genuine inhabitant of no particular place. Living in New York hardly counts as finding a home—it's a city frantically rebuilding and distracting itself, caught in endless motion, where you can skip across the surface of life forever. On the other hand, how can you trust people who stay put in one spot? Their lack of curiosity seems pathological, a morbid sickness. By blocking out all those potential experiences, they seem even more evasive, and afraid, than anyone . . .

I shrugged. "Maybe it's not running away from anything. Maybe it's running *toward* life." A suitable comeback aphorism suddenly occurred to me. "As Saint Augustine said: The world is a book; he who stays at home reads only one page."

"Oh, I do not believe that." Brother Yianni chortled, fixing me with another knowing look. "After my time in India, I came back home, here to Greece. Right at this spot, at Prodromou, the great journey ended for me. I found this monastery one day, and have not left."

"Not once? Not outside the gates?"

"Never. In eight years."

I tried to keep the incredulity from my face: We really were two pretty extreme case studies. To Yianni I must have seemed frivolous and self-deluded. And he looked to me furtive and trapped—a naturally social animal who had made a rash decision at a low point in his life.

But Brother Yianni changed his tone to a conspiratorial whisper:

"I will be honest: I am not one hundred percent sure if I will not change my monastery. There are more than twenty holy places in Arcadia, and all of them have different rules. Some allow more meeting with . . . the outside world. Of course, you can't get married in any of them. Only priests can marry, if they do it before they are ordained." (This reminded me of a newspaper item I'd seen a few days earlier: A synod of Orthodox priests officially complained that the compulsory long beards and ankle-length robes were making it difficult to find wives; apparently, young Greek women just weren't going for the Byzantine look anymore.)

"But if you decided to become a priest . . . ?"

Yianni drew back with a cautious and world-weary sigh.

"Oh, you know, it's problematic, the woman aspect," he said cautiously. "If you find the right woman, it is the ideal life. But if it is not the good relation, then everything is bad. Life is a big hill, every day a struggle. I will never marry. But I think a more . . . *open* monastery . . . might be best for me."

"Maybe one close to a nightclub?"

Yianni gurgled.

"Quite often the women come here to visit. Really, quite often."

It was time to leave—if we didn't get down to Gortys and back to Stemnitsa by dark, life would indeed become a big hill. But I could hardly stem the torrent of words.

On the way out, I saw Brother Yianni standing at the monolithic oak door, looking about frantically, as if to ask: What now? Where's the next visitor?

And then this Arcadian slunk off, to pore over some ecclesiastical vellum. Or maybe to pursue Pan's favorite pastime.

DETRITUS OF THE GODS

Outside in the courtyard—where Les had been backed into a corner by two donkeys—the trail to Gortys resumed.

Whole cloud systems were now gathering in the Lousios gorge; they would emerge out of nowhere, crackle with electricity, then disappear without a trace. More titanic battles, I supposed, as we trudged ever farther down the slippery rubble pathway—through translucent curtains of rain—and into the ghostly heartland of what was, in classical times, a thriving rural world.

Then the Greek countryside was steeped with folklore. A Roman traveler would have witnessed spiritual scenes that today can be imagined only in remotest Tibet or Bhutan. One day, you might have passed a trio of holy men carrying uprooted saplings on their backs as part of a fertility rite; the next, crowds of women wailing and tearing their flesh in mourning for the hero Achilles, killed in battle twelve hundred years before. There were enchanted springs where lepers swam to cleanse themselves of disease; roadside apothecaries who made enchanted balms of roses and lilies. In muddy villages, families might be garlanding bronze goats to protect their crops from disease. Clusters of old men gathered in cemeteries, pouring the blood of slaughtered lambs onto graves so that their ancestors in Hades could drink. Forests were decorated with pagan piety: Tree stumps were carved into rough statues of the gods, oaks adorned with the horns of sacrificial animals, beeches hung with skins, stones moistened with perfume libations. Travelers were especially respectful of local cults, and kissed their hands in reverence when passing shrines.

Two hours later, at a sodden crossroads, we were amazed to see an actual sign—in Greek script. I took out my little dictionary, trying to identify the letters. Definitely a *G* . . . in the middle a *T* . . . ending in an *S*. This was encouraging news. Maybe the place really did exist after all.

Finally, at the bottom of the ravine, we crossed a small stone bridge. A stream of sky-blue water rushed noisily past, known to the Greeks as a place where Zeus himself was washed at birth ("the coldest water of any river in the world," Pausanias proposes). And there it was—the stone outline of Gortys, its ancient foundations overgrown by wildflowers,

bristling carpets of yellow, pink, and purple, all patrolled by fat buzzing
bees.

The core of the remains stretched across a lush wet glen, next to an
empty farmhouse. The sweet perfume of thyme hung in the air. And the
sun chose this moment to burst directly from the clouds—making the
entire moistened landscape sparkle with powdered silver. This was Arcadia the benign, a blessed moment, a world in its own secret life, cut off
by the towering cliffs.

We scampered about like sugar-frenzied five-year-olds, lapping up the
warmth among the glowing fragments of columns and mosaics. "Here's
a temple! This was the agora!"

My pages of Pausanias, soaked through with rainwater, were never
more vivid—the ancient eyes they provided were now crystal clear,
allowing us to follow the guidebook writer's steps past all the overgrown
walls, along a bathhouse reclaimed by tree roots, down into the great
Sanctuary of Asclepius, the god of healing, whose marble statue "as a
beardless youth" presided. This shrine was Gortys's pride and joy: It even
exhibited a breastplate and spear tip left by none other than Alexander
the Great as an offering to the deity (his visit must have been the high
point of the city's civic history, like George Washington's pit stop in
Poughkeepsie).

I sat in one of the round-backed stone chairs. Any Roman traveler
would have paused here to unwind for a day or two and make a prophy-
lactic offering to Asclepius for his health. A fountain had been excavated,
where the faithful once bathed their feet and read the bronze plaques
embedded in the temple walls, testaments to the wondrous cures the sick
had received here for centuries. They were surrounded by tiny replica
limbs, hands, legs, and penises, offered up as thanks for particular cures
(a pagan practice that survives in many Christian churches).

Drowsing away the afternoon in that idyllic vale, it did occur to me
that the Roman tourists' search for significance in rocks, springs, and
saplings was not so different from how we modern travelers often go
about things. The ancients drew their sense of wonder from what were,
to the uninformed observer, nothing more than bits of wood, fragments
of hide, or the stumps of trees. But these simple objects had enormous
historical backgrounds. Roman *spectatores* expended enormous energy to
visit the giant boulders that were said to be leftovers of the actual clay
that Prometheus had used to shape mankind; or the shreds of myrtle said
to have been touched by Aphrodite; or the glade where Zeus had
descended in the form of a swan to have his way with the lovely Leda.

Like the Australian Aborigines who sing the landscape into being, poetic Greek stories gave the world its meaning, its shape, its context. Every stone had a tale, every rock a saga.

And here we were going to absurd lengths to stand among what were, actually, some fairly scrappy ruins. Even in its heyday, Gortys had been a profoundly minor Greek city-state—home to a few thousand provincials—an outpost whose rise and fall could hardly be more irrelevant to the currents of world history as we judge them today. To the naked eye, what remains of Gortys might be the merest rubble, a scattering of giblets; but in the imagination, it was an empire. For once, it was a relief to forget that ancient tradition of travel (*Crowds are good!*) and slip back into Romantic mode, witnessing a site alone, away from the hubbub and the paraphernalia of civilization. It was the remote, luscious setting, and the ruins' utter dereliction—uncluttered with interpretive signs or protective walkways or security guards or tour guides or ticket vendors or bookstore-cafés—that made Gortys come to life. This odd little place seemed more potent than Olympia, Delphi, the Acropolis of Athens— all the high-profile Greek sites—rolled up together.

There wasn't a soul to see us—our visit left no trace—so it felt like we'd slipped between the sheets of time.

PART FIVE

THE TRANSIT OF VENUS

Island-hopping
the Aegean

From mainland greece, ancient tourists set their sights on the splendors of the East: The perfumed shores of Asia Minor lay only a week's sail away, across the Aegean Sea.

The dozens of islands that lay en route may today be considered the very definition of sun-drenched Nirvana, invaded as they are every summer by pale northern Europeans, but the Romans were quite uninterested in their natural beauty. They regarded them as barren rocks, best left to illiterate goatherds. The emperors blithely used the remoter islands as natural prisons for exiles, with many a disgraced aristocrat preferring to open his veins rather than face banishment to Seriphos, Folegandros, or Gyaros. It was never an idea of leisure to seek out empty beaches where one could muse alone on golden sands. In fact, a lonely stretch of beach, without all the supporting pleasures of civilization, made the Romans' skin crawl; the silence was like a reminder of the grave. When it came to exploiting the sybaritic potential of the seaside, they preferred resorts like Baiae, full of noise, bustle, partying, waterfront dining.

As a result, Romans selected an itinerary via the Aegean islands that were shrouded in myth and arcane lore. They aimed to visit Delos, the sacred birthplace of the god Apollo, and Rhodes, where the remains of the mighty Colossus had crashed spectacularly to earth.

Like any sea voyage in antiquity, this mini-odyssey took a modicum of planning. While the Roman seas were thick with shipping—as Juvenal remarked, there seemed to be more men afloat than on shore—there were no scheduled passenger services from Greece: Travelers had to make private arrangements. The wealthiest wanderers simply chartered their own vessels, commandeering whole merchant ships for their personal use. Most tourists, however, had to spend some time in Athens's thriving port, Piraeus. Here they lingered in the Forum of Corporations, a boisterous column-lined arcade where all shipping companies had their offices. Lists of departures were posted—every week, a dozen vessels loaded with Greek exports would be sailing to the great eastern hubs of Ephesus, Knidos, Pergamum, Smyrna. Noting the names of departing vessels, they would then proceed to the waterfront and negotiate directly with the *magister navis* (shipmaster), who was responsible for the commercial aspect of the voyage.

Naturally, this sounds easier than it was—like most ancient harbors, Piraeus existed in an atmosphere of barely contained hysteria. Out on the water, the scene was deceptively idyllic: Square-rigged Liburnian galleys tacked past graceful skiffs whose triangular sails hung low on their masts like Arab dhows; tall merchant ships were escorted to their berths by pairs of long-oared dories. But back on shore, confusion reigned. From all accounts, travelers had to weave through a virtual maritime circus: The port was awash with transients and traders. Mule carts laden with Aegean marble lumbered from the cavernous portside warehouses; vendors hawked the latest arrivals of olive oil and hides at wholesale prices; fishermen put enormous tuna up for auction. Jostling for space along the docks were shipwrights and riggers repairing damaged ships; caulkers heating foul-smelling pots of pitch over open fires; sand men filling sacks for ballast; slaves unloading grain under the glare of their overseers. The summer heat—ancient sailors took to the waves only from May to October—did not make a visit any easier.

At the wharves, rows of galleys were squeezed into their berths. Roman-era vessels were as intricately carved, gilded, and decorated as any in Renaissance Venice, and could be identified by the brilliantly painted statues on their sternposts. Many were named after gods— Apollo, Mars, and Neptune; others after rivers like the Nile and the Danube; some after abstract qualities—Victoria, Pax, Concordia, who were represented as women. The poet Ovid in A.D. 8 sailed in the *Helmet,* whose figurehead was the warlike goddess Minerva, clad in armor and waving a spear. But regardless of these specific invocations, every ship gave pride of place on deck to a rose-garlanded altar to Aphrodite, winsome goddess of beauty and love, and—most important—protector of sailors. Her image transported even callus-palmed oarsmen to flights of poetic fancy: It was said that the goddess herself could often be seen skipping along the waves beside boats, a ravishing young woman surrounded by water nymphs and muscular mermen, all singing and blowing on conch shells. As one last decorative precaution, every ship had eyes painted on the bow, so that it could see where it was going—a tradition still common on Mediterranean fishing boats.

Tourists knew that shipmasters were more than happy to take paying passengers on an ad hoc basis, boosting their profits with a few silver coins (these trans-Aegean boats took anywhere from a few to fifty on their open decks). Having left their luggage in a Piraeus inn, travelers strolled up and down the dock with their servants, trying to assess which boat was most sound, most comfortable, and most favorably omened. The compact, maneuverable Liburnians, with two banks of oars, were popular with merchants on the Aegean runs, as were the far lighter *cercuri* from Cyprus—their crescent-shaped hulls, high in the prow and stern, used the same basic design, in fact, as Mediterranean vessels since earliest antiquity. For heavier cargoes, there were the *corbitae* (merchant freighters)—slow but steady on the water. Usually a berth could be arranged in one visit to the docks, but negotiations could sometimes drag on. Apollonius of Tyana got into an argument with one captain who refused to take him because his ship was already dangerously overloaded with souvenir statues of the gods—even then a lucrative Greek export. Apollonius later instigated a walkout of passengers from a ship because he had a premonition that it would be wrecked. Sure enough, his vision came to pass.

Ships' captains—the *gubernatores,* who commanded the nautical rather than commercial side of voyages—were highly sensitive to premonitions, and they were notorious for delaying departures at the slightest ill omen. The more superstitious were known to wait in port for weeks until the auspices allowed—making the departures list a theoretical guide only. The roster of bad omens was extensive. A passenger sneezing on the gangplank was considered disastrous, as was any dream a sailor had that involved a black goat, a bull, or an owl. A crow settling on the rigging caused panic. And sailors never left port without first sacrificing a bull to Neptune, pleading for a safe journey.

"May your sailing be auspicious," goes one maritime blessing recorded by Heliodorus. "May Poseidon lord of Safety and Hermes god of Profit join in your voyaging and foster it. May they make every sea smooth and every wind fair. May they render every harbor a haven, and every city hospitable."

It was best for a traveler not to be in a hurry. Delays were common and inexplicable.

Even today, Greek departure schedules are not exactly watertight.

Modern Piraeus is essentially a giant sea terminal, a vast gridlike system of wharves where gleaming white ferries tower like chalk cliffs over narrow concrete berths. The ships now head to every sunny island in the Aegean. But to follow the ancient itinerary, we had to head for Mykonos—jumping-off point for Apollo's sacred island of Delos.

Les eagerly agreed to this plan, assuming that Mykonos would fit the *Captain Corelli's Mandolin* fantasy of a Greek island, full of whitewashed buildings with blue doors, aged peasants driving donkeys, and convivial tavernas. I thought it best not to mention that it had become the party capital of the entire Mediterranean—a crowded open-air venue for ecstasy-fueled raves.

We arrived in Piraeus by subway and were rapidly funneled along with hundreds of others into a cavernous ticketing hall. Elderly Greek women elbowed past with sides of bloodied lamb under their arms; men staggered under the weight of new TVs and microwaves; agents for the ferry lines waved flyers from their tiny booths, singing out the names of distant islands. On every wall, bright neon lights announced imminent departures to Naxos, Paxos, and Sifnos, which the wits of the Pella Inn back in Athens called Syphilos.

"Don't take this one," an elderly woman muttered to me as I waited in a line to buy our tickets. "It is the bad boat to Mykonos."

I moved to the next line.

She nodded shrewdly at me. "Much better. It has an *escalator* between decks."

And so it did, although the escalator wasn't actually working. After finally locating the right ferry among the fifty other identical ships in port, we discovered it also had a swimming pool, which was empty, and a "Scandinavian discothèque," which was thankfully without electricity. As the vessel lumbered out of port, Les staked out a spare corner of a plastic orange bench on the uppermost deck so we could watch the petroleum refineries around Piraeus slowly recede into salt mist. The Scandinavian backpackers, denied their discothèque, were already stripping off, basting themselves like sausages on a grill. The Greeks on board descended en masse into the three bars to play cards and smoke in the dark.

Unfurling ahead was Homer's "dark-gleaming sea," which we could regard, as the ancients did, as seductive and terrifying in equal measure.

At Poseidon's Mercy

ON ANCIENT MERCHANT SHIPS, the standard of accommodation was casual. There were no private cabins. From the available accounts, it seems that even wealthy travelers rolled out their own bedding and feather pillows each night on deck, or had their servants do so. If women of economic means were on board, their maids erected small tents for the evening—temporary cabins that would be removed each morning. Drinking water was provided, but passengers brought their own food from Piraeus, along with a few jugs of vintage wine; their servants would then be given access to the ship's galley.

For the Roman tourists who journeyed beyond mainland Greece each year—they would have made up only a fraction of the fifty or so passengers on each ship—this was hardly a luxury cruise. But since this was the accepted standard of the day, a core part of the travel experience, it was tolerated with much the same cheery bravura as today's affluent adventure travelers might display when sharing hammocks on the deck of an Amazon River boat, or taking a slow train through rural India. And for our erudite ancients, shipboard life was not without its pleasures. By day, they would play dice, sing, read, or drowse to the lapping of the waves. After dinner, like-minded travelers pontificated over a glass of decent Chian wine and observed the brilliant night sky, picking out the polestar, used by sailors for navigation, and the constellations of the zodiac burning in the Milky Way, which poets said was the highway to heaven, lined with palaces of the gods. From time to time they tended the altar to Aphrodite, arranging its garlands of roses and myrtle, hoping her gentle feminine hand would calm the rages of blue-bearded Poseidon.

And yet, the Romans were always nervous on open water. They would have reasoned to themselves, cautiously: Only two days' sail to Delos . . . and two more to Rhodes . . .

If the omens were good, surely—*surely*—nothing could go wrong.

It's one of the many appealing paradoxes of the ancient world that the Romans, the only people in history to rule the entire Mediterranean Sea, were such terrible sailors. Having purged the seas of pirates,

The sea god Poseidon in a benign mood, protecting a ship from the Clashing Rocks in the 1963 film Jason and the Argonauts.

Romans were content to leave the thriving business of merchant shipping to Greeks, Syrians, Egyptians, and Phoenicians—peoples who instinctively loved the wide open waters. While most sailing vessels were owned by Italians, the captains and crews were invariably drawn from the great seafaring nations of the East.

Even mild sea swells brought out the landlubber in ancient Romans. In one epistle grimly titled "The Trials of Travel," Seneca describes his experience taking a small sailboat across the mild Bay of Naples. The weather turns rough, Seneca turns green, but the pilot refuses to land. At one point, near shore, poor Seneca, by now doubled over with mal de mer, throws himself overboard, then has to clamber up over rough rocks to dry land. He wryly notes that now he knows why the great Ulysses spent twenty years lost and getting shipwrecked at every corner: It wasn't because Poseidon was angry with him, as Homer reports in the *Odyssey*, but because he suffered from incessant seasickness.

When it came to the Aegean, whose deep waters can be unexpectedly turbulent, Romans grew suicidal. Ovid experienced one moderate blow in A.D. 8:

> *Look how the billows huge as mountains move:*
> *Each one, you think, will touch the stars above.*
> *Look how the valleys deep between them sink:*
> *Each one might reach to Hell's profoundest brink.*

He concludes:

> *My hour has come: no hope of life remains:*
> *Down I shall sink, and escape from all my pains.*

And it wasn't just rough seas that Romans found to fret about. Pillars of stone known as the Clashing Rocks moved randomly across the high seas, grinding unlucky ships to splinters between them. Scylla and Charybdis, the monster and the whirlpool, were also still at large; not to mention the giant fish and sea monsters that would swallow ships whole. Tourists knew this was no mere fantasy: The petrified bones of the "monster of Joppa"—which the hero Perseus had turned to stone using Medusa's head—had been brought from Syria and displayed in a Roman arena (its backbone was forty feet long and eighteen inches thick; it was either fossilized whale bones or the remains of a prehistoric proboscidean). In A.D. 70, Pliny the Elder confidently reported that a Triton was sinking ships off the Gulf of Cádiz. Many travelers had actually seen examples of these vicious mermen pickled in the temple-museums of Rome and Greece. According to Pausanias, they had the lower bodies of a dolphin and rough skin like a shark's—plus long green hair, gills behind their ears, and mouths full of fangs.

But of all these horrific threats, shipwreck was most genuinely feared, claiming untold lives every sailing season and ruining even the finest captains. Sailors regarded rocks as the barbs of Poseidon's trident that would rake the waves. Travelers could hardly fail to remember that back in Rome, former sailors made up more than half the beggars in the streets, proffering the shattered timber from their ships' hulls as they wailed for alms.

It's hardly surprising that when finally sighting their home harbor, passengers would heartily join the captain on the stern as he offered a sacrifice of thanks.

At least there was one seafaring danger that Romans no longer had to worry about.

Before the Empire, the coast of Asia Minor had been a hornet's nest of freelance cutthroats who preyed on the shipping lanes of the Aegean. Augustus had ended that. By the time of Roman tourism, pirates were as much folkloric figures as they are today, appearing only as lurid characters in steamy romance novels. Still, stories of their former cruelty lingered as favorite topics of shipboard conversation. It was said that if passengers on a captured vessel indignantly declared themselves Roman citizens, the pirates would feign terror and beg forgiveness—before prodding them down the ship's ladder into the open sea, the simplest version of walking the plank.

The most famous victim of piracy on the trans-Aegean route was the young Julius Caesar. He was a little-known figure in his early twenties when his ship was seized on the way to Rhodes, where he was traveling to study rhetoric. But even as a prisoner, Caesar demonstrated the breathtaking chutzpah that would distinguish the rest of his career. He insisted the pirates quintuple the ransom they were asking for him, saying that any less was unworthy of his noble rank, then proceeded to behave as if the pirates were his personal servants. He demanded that they listen while he practiced his oratory, insulted them for not appreciating his finer metaphors, and ordered them to be silent during his siesta. The cutthroats apparently found Caesar amusing; they even laughed when, as the ransom arrived, he promised to return and execute the lot of them. Of course, Caesar went straight to the port of Miletus, raised a fleet, and hunted the pirates down. Not only did he retrieve the ransom, he saw every one them nailed to a cross.

As they passed the shipboard hours, Roman tourists also took an academic interest in the paraphernalia of nautical life.

They enjoyed examining the sailing maps, which were marked with latitude (longtitude would not be reckoned until the eighteenth century), and the Maritime Itineraries—written lists of harbors and landmarks that ship captains preferred to use on unfamiliar coastlines. Often called by their Greek name *periploi* (voyages around), they lacked the instant visual impact of charts but included minute navigational details—river mouths, hidden sandbanks, water sources, and shelters from storms, as well as handy mythological crib notes. (I was carrying one called the Antonine Itinerary from the second century A.D.: "Delos to Mykonos is 500 stadia . . . Mykonos to Icasia is 300 stadia . . . here is the island Ortyx, named by the goddess Asteria, sister of the goddess Latone, who was carried here on the back of a giant quail when she fled from the force of Jupiter.") There were also ancient wind maps, which described the twelve winds: the Zephyr came from the west, while the Boreas, a "male" wind from the north, apparently had the power to impregnate mares on shipboard. These unreliable elements were thought of as minor gods, the bratty sons and daughters of the great wind god, Aeolus.

With the heightened emotions of a sea voyage, stories of magic and legend took on a new reality. One of the most famous nautical tales in history (and inspiration for a powerful Emily Dickinson poem) dates from the early first century A.D., when a scholar named Epitherses found his comfortable cruise interrupted by haunted voices.

Plutarch transmits a report that he heard firsthand:

It was already evening when the winds dropped, and the ship drifted towards Paxos (near Corfu). Almost everybody was awake, and a good many had not finished their after-dinner wine.

Suddenly from the island of Paxos was heard the voice of someone loudly calling out—asking for Thamus—so that everyone was amazed.

Thamus was the ship's Egyptian pilot, a man whose name even many people on board did not know. Twice he was called and twice he made no reply, but the third time he answered. And the caller, raising his voice, said, "When you come opposite to Palodes, announce that the great god Pan is dead."

On hearing this, everyone was shocked and argued over whether it was better to carry out the order or not to become involved. Thamus made up his mind that if there was a loud wind, he would sail past and keep quiet, but if there was no wind and a smooth sea, he would announce what he had heard. So, when he came opposite Palodes, and there was neither wind or waves, Thamus, from the stern, looking towards the land, shouted the words as he had heard them: "Great Pan is dead."

Even before he had finished, there was a loud cry of lamentation, not of one person, but of many, mingled with exclamations of amazement.

Other reports from the sea were far more fanciful: A subgenre of Roman travel literature provided eyewitness accounts from sailors who were blown off course to the domains of the Amazons and the Indians, or who weighed anchor at uncharted specks of land that turned out to be enormous sleeping sea monsters. Mariners related their horror as the creatures awoke and dived to the bottom of the sea, dragging shore parties to the proverbial watery graves.

Lucian gleefully parodied the Roman passion for tall sea tales and fantastic travel literature in general. In *A True Story*—a direct inspiration for the adventures of Baron Munchausen—the narrator discovers a land that is made of delicious cheese, another that is ruled by witches with asses' legs; then he sails to the moon, where he takes part in a battle with inhabitants of the sun. To round off the trip, he takes a tack to visit the underworld.

The inner circle of pain—it turns out—is reserved for lying travel writers.

PARADISUS OPTIMUS MAXIMUS

Today, despite all our travel-brochure dreams of private and empty island beaches, the Roman ideal of safety in numbers has squarely triumphed in the Aegean—a fact that was obvious the moment our ferry disgorged its human cargo onto the docks of Mykonos.

Again I turned to my travel mantra (*Crowds are good, crowds are ancient*) as we plowed through dozens of desperate local women waving hand-written signs, whose unenviable lot it was to entice bewildered travelers to stay in their spare rooms. Mykonos may be the starting point for Delos, but its new role as the Aegean's party central was squarely in the forefront, luring not only ferries full of backpackers but enormous cruise ships and express charter flights from every major city in Europe.

Crowds are ancient, crowds are good . . .

From the balcony of our hotel, Penelope's Rooms, I had a clear view of the whitewashed maze that was Mykonos, just waking up from last night's debauch. If only I could maintain my Zen-like state, accept the Roman attitude to the seaside, I should be happy in the throngs.

Which meant going directly to the most famous beach on Mykonos—called Super-Paradise.

In the blistering midafternoon heat, a veteran commuter bus bounced us along an arid goat trail, past one beach named Paradise—as the name suggested, a second-rate place—and finally what was billed as the ulti-mate Aegean getaway, Super-Paradise.

Super-Paradise was certainly something to behold. Every inch of the rapidly eroding shoreline was covered with blue plastic chairs; on top of these were hundreds of bronzed nightclubbers trying to sleep off their hangovers. This must have been difficult, given the cacophonous activity in the water. There were water-skiers, hang gliders, and plastic bananas, all being dragged around by speedboats; Jet Skis roared, outboards whined. But more impressive, right behind the beach were six disco bars, each with its own DJ, each competing to blast techno rhythms into our sun-addled brains.

Disco employees—gym-toned girls in chartreuse bikinis—shimmied along the beach, trying to pull sunbathers up to join them on the dance floors. As we watched, a motley crowd accepted the offer. The lissome paid dancers could be easily identified, bumping and grinding, MTV style, with some decidedly unaerobicized vacationers, including two elderly Danes whose skin was scorched as pink as newborn baby's.

My Zen-like equanimity was taking a beating.

It was early October, and the season was winding down. Soon the Aegean would turn—shifting gears to winter. Already, despite the hot sun, the afternoon wind had a chill to it. Here at Super-Paradise, there was a hysterical edge to the air—everyone was glancing nervously from person to person, as if to reassure one another that they were having the time of their lives.

One by one, the dancers became self-conscious and slunk back to their beach chairs. Soon only the professionals in their lime-green bikinis were on the dance floors, gyrating absently.

"You done Super-Paradise all wrong," advised a guy outside Penelope's Rooms. He was Greek, but he had a thick Cockney accent, and he always seemed to be loitering in our courtyard, keen for conversation.

"The time to go to the beach is eight A.M. Then you leave by eleven, you know what I mean? That's when the party people hit the beach. They're coming down off their highs, so they just lie there all day. Then by one o'clock, the cruise-boat people turn up, and it's a bloody nightmare. Know what I mean?"

Theo kept hopping from one foot to the other, adjusting his fluorescent shorts, telling me about his year-round commuting between Britain and Mykonos.

I asked him the secret of his leisured lifestyle.

"Oh, I'm self-employed," he confided in a low voice. "Best decision I ever made."

"A writer?" I tried innocently.

"Oh, no, mate. Business, you know?"

"I think we've got the local ecstasy dealer living next door," I told Les.

Our balcony looked across Mykonos harbor. Windmills perched poetically on the headlands, although their arms no longer turned since they'd been renovated into condominiums. Lining the steep flanks of the bay, the maze of stucco buildings glowed like white-hot coals. The Aegean habit of whitewashing homes seemed a bit perverse at noon, when they redoubled the sun's brilliance into a retina-scorching blur; but at dusk, it was hard to imagine anywhere more enticing.

That night, while Les crashed out with minor heatstroke, I paid a quick social call to Theo, then headed down into the labyrinthine streets. Party fever was in the air. Down dark cobbled alleyways, house music boomed from the doors of clubs with forthright names like the Skandinavian Bar and Drink! At the gay boîtes (Banana Bar, Klyt Klub), ravers were gathered at strategic points, beaming beatifically into space. The outdoor tables of expensive fish restaurants clustered by lapping waves; the waiters were serving four-inch-long sardines and emaciated calamari as if they had just been plucked from the sea. Sadly, the Aegean has been ruthlessly overfished in recent years, and the whole seafood smorgasbord was flown in from the North Atlantic every day.

Outside one of the more animated bar-cafés, three robustly drunk, identical blond women were saying something to me in Swedish, then switched effortlessly to English.

"But everyone here is from Stockholm!" scoffed the most violently sunburned, whose name was Frida, looking me up and down. "You are the only one who is not."

The trio had been on Mykonos for two weeks, they announced, and came to this same bar every night for the live music and a ready supply of alcohol unimaginable back in Sweden. I ordered retsina—it came in a screw-top bottle—as a woolly guitarist slouched out to the courtyard and started strumming folksy versions of U2 songs.

"Even *he* is from Stockholm," Frida advised. "He comes to Mykonos every summer."

The crowd of modern Vikings was becoming frenzied by the warm air and the alcohol. Soon enough, they were swaying back and forth in their chairs and singing along:

But I still haven't found what I'm looking for . . .

The Greek owner kept the acrid wine flowing. She had been running this place for twenty years, she said, and had bought four houses and two cars; both her kids were doctors.

Then I got the check and found out how. I stared at all the zeroes in mild disbelief: The price was double what you'd pay in a New York bar.

"Are these Swedish prices?" I asked Frida.

She snorted in disgust. "In Stockholm, you would not even get one sip for that!"

I reminded myself that the Aegean islanders have always been diligent entrepreneurs.

In the ancient Cyclades, shipwrecked foreigners were captured, branded, and sold as slaves. It was even said that Greek islanders would set up fake lighthouses on the wrong side of dangerous channels, driving passing ships onto the rocks. Sponge divers would then retrieve the valuable cargo.

I emptied my pockets, feeling the hangover already coming on.

No, I still haven't found what I'm looking for . . .

THE FLOATING ISLAND OF APOLLO

For our boat trip to Delos the next day, much to Les's dismay, the wind was fierce, cold, and strangely erratic. Even under perfect weather conditions, the deep passage is one of the trickier stretches of water in the Mediterranean; today it was fizzing like Alka-Seltzer.

This rough sea has always been one of the considerations in visiting Delos. Aristides left a detailed account of his experience there on September 30, A.D. 144. As a young man he had been ordered in a dream to compose lyric poems to Apollo, the god of song, so he made sure to call in there on a trans-Aegean journey.

Unfortunately, the crossing from the mainland was terrifying.

> When I disembarked at Delos I was furious at the helmsman, who had behaved like a lunatic, sailing against the winds and plowing through the waves. Immediately I swore that I would not set foot back in the ship for two days.

Aristides stormed off in a huff, to sacrifice at the Temple of Apollo, and sing his poem to the god (which he admits was not really very good). He then retired to his room in a harborside inn, telling his slaves to admit no visitors.

Around dusk, the sailors from his ship turned up, hammering on his door and insisting they sail immediately. The seas were calm and the breeze steady, they said. Aristides' slaves told the sailors to go away, and they left in a fury, muttering oaths. Then, at around 4 A.M.:

> an extraordinary hurricane broke out, and the sea was stirred up by a fierce whirlwind, and everything was deluged. Some of the small ships in the harbor were cast up on land, and others collided and were crushed. The merchant ship that was carrying us had its cables broken, and was tossed up and down, and was only barely saved with much shouting and confusion from the sailors. . . .
>
> At dawn, my friends, whom I happened to have taken along on the voyage at my own expense, hurried up to me, calling me their "Benefactor and Savior." The sailors were also grateful to me, and marveled at the evils from which they had just been saved.

Aristides' stubbornness in refusing to sail suddenly seemed to everyone present divinely inspired—a reward from Apollo for his tribute in verse.

On the plus side, the rough crossing has always been enough to preserve a unique atmosphere in Apollo's birthplace, as if it exists in a separate dimension.

At the beginning of time, Delos had been one of the many floating islands of the Aegean, wandering the seas as unfixed as the stars, until Zeus himself secured it to the ocean floor with an adamantine chain. Its sacred status spilled over into the world of mortals. Since Apollo protected all traders who came to his island, for several hundred years in the classical Greek heyday Delos became a commercial phenomenon—the first great duty-free port in history, where ten thousand slaves could change hands in a single day. But the island's blessings ended in the first century B.C., when waves of pirates left it in ruins. By the time Roman tourists were visiting, the once-prosperous port had become a ghost town.

This did not deter visitors in the least. Although only a few Athenian priests lived on Delos year-round, the stream of pilgrims to the sacred island was continuous.

Like Aristides, they strode from the harbor, along an avenue lined with statues of crouching jaguars, to admire the Altar of Horns that had been crafted by Apollo as a boy (it was probably a simple rough-hewn block of stone, but Martial considered it a worthy contender for one of the Seven Wonders because of its sacred aura). They beheld the very palm tree that the goddess Leto had clutched while giving birth to the god. The eerie abandonment of Delos only heightened the sense of the divine. Apart from a few waterfront inns, the city itself remained in dereliction, with the Aegean winds blasting eerily through all the salt-encrusted warehouses, marketplaces, and long pillared halls.

This elegaic mood persists today, since nobody is permitted to live on Delos because of its archaeological importance. And yet, for one of the Aegean's major sites, there is a surprising absence of guards, rules, and regulations. The gravel road from the dock still passes the famous row of threatening carved jaguars. Fragments of marble protrude from every jagged inch of the earth; visitors are bent over collecting them like shells in Florida. After that, the only signs of museum maintenance are the roped-off doorways in the ruins—which indicate that something important lies beyond. Sure enough, one is free to examine startling mosaics that would be safely locked away on mainland sites—Dionysus and his tigers, or blue-bearded Poseidon—but here are left to the sun and the wind.

I climbed the only mountain for a view of the horizon.

Looking across that dark passage of water, I realized the rough boat trip was still with me. It felt like the island of Delos was swaying beneath my feet—like the slow shifting of the unyielding chain that tied the island to the bottom of the sea.

INSIDE THE COLOSSUS

Two days later, ancient tourists were approaching Rhodes—the other unforgettable Aegean highlight—whose harbor was so crowded with masts that it appeared from far out at sea like a swaying field of corn. Its temples were known to contain three thousand works of art worthy of serious attention. But they all paled beside the island's single most famous artifact—the Colossus of Rhodes, which was still accepted as one of the Seven Wonders of the World despite the fact that it had fallen down several centuries earlier. This bronze figure of the sun god Helios had once towered 105 feet high. Although the popular image has the Colossus standing astride the port, one foot planted on either side of the harbor entrance, this would have been impossible for the artist, Chares of Lindos, to cast using the methods available at the time. Instead, Helios was shaped more like a sleek, muscular column: He stood stiffly erect, holding a torch aloft, almost at military attention. Even this posture was not stable enough: the Colossus stood for only half a century. An earthquake in 226 B.C. broke the statue at the knees and sent it crashing to earth on a hillside above the port.

"But even lying on the ground, the Colossus is a marvel," enthuses Pliny the Elder, who climbed over—and inside—the monstrous image in the first century A.D. "Few people can even put their arms around the figure's thumb, and each of its fingers is larger than most statues. Where the limbs have been broken off, enormous cavities yawn, and inside can be seen great masses of rock, which the artists used to steady the figure."

It must have been as awesome a sight as the fallen Talos, the titanic iron warrior that comes to life in the film *Jason and the Argonauts.*

Today, Rhodes is dominated by its impregnable medieval fortifications, erected by the Knights of St. John in the fifteenth century against the Turks; the stone balls projected by enemy catapults lie scattered around the walls like giants' marbles. A new commercial harbor caters to the hydrofoils and yachts that zip back and forth to the Turkish coast. We

*The fallen Colossus of Rhodes, first century A.D.: an artist's impression
from the description of Pliny the Elder.*

found an old hotel almost embedded in the fortifications; the owner
assured us that it had been in continuous operation for one thousand
years. With a little scrambling, I was able to circumnavigate the walls
themselves, making a full circle around to the Mandraki Harbor, the
ancient port. Cobbled roads led back uphill to the Turkish School—an
unassuming nineteenth-century building where scholars guess the
Colossus once stood.

   The eventual fate of history's most famous site-specific sculpture is
surprisingly laced with speculation. According to one Byzantine chron-
icler, the tourist-emperor Hadrian ordered the Colossus to be re-
erected when he visited Rhodes around A.D. 120. He was traveling with
a vast team of engineers and craftsmen, so the plan may well have been
attempted; if it was successful, the statue soon fell down again, since
another earthquake in A.D. 150 devastated the entire town. The only real
certainty is that in A.D. 654, the Colossus was finally broken up by Arab
plunderers and sold as scrap metal. Today, not a footprint remains.

But, as with every great image of antiquity, the specter of the Colossus still has some life in it: In 1970, *The New York Times* reported that city authorities were considering plans to rebuild the entire statue from scratch, as a tourist attraction. Apparently, thousands of people were still coming to Rhodes in the hopes of seeing the Colossus, and were bitterly disappointed to learn that it had disappeared into the melting pot of history.

For reasons of cost, the plan was shelved.

LITTLE CAESARS OF THE CUSTOMS OFFICE

The hydrofoil trip from Rhodes to Marmaris in Turkey took just over an hour. The immigration and customs formalities took six.

Of the two sparring nations, the Greeks were the most difficult: They simply don't want anybody to leave. This should have been flattering, I suppose, but that wasn't quite their intention. Ever since the 1980s, Greek government officials have been peeved that so many travelers—and their dollars—slip away to the cheaper shores of their old enemy, Turkey. They want to make the defection as tedious as possible.

I'd originally scoffed at the warnings: How difficult could it be? So, in the medieval shipyard of Rhodes, we huddled before dawn in a dank stone courtyard as a drizzling rain soaked our luggage. Twenty other abject souls shuffled with us from one unmarked door to another. With no officials around, we formed lines on the basis of rumor alone. One story went around that the hydrofoil was overbooked, another that it was going to be canceled because of the unusually rough seas. Storms crackled in the distance. We all stared at the sky, wondering what our fate would be. The idyllic Aegean holiday was taking something of a final nosedive.

By midmorning, when we finally managed to find a Greek official, he took our passports with practiced disdain. His every glance accused us of cultural betrayal. We were abandoning the West, the EEC, civilization, Christendom—and entering the heathen East. He pored over every page. Compared photos. Pondered stamps. His act was so convincing we were beginning to enjoy it. So he decided to go through our luggage, piece by piece.

Our fellow travelers behind us in line groaned helplessly. We were simply POWs being processed for release, and our captors would take their sweet time about it.

Of course, contrived bureaucratic time-wasting is another of the great perennials of travel. Even here I could draw the ancient parallel.

There may have been no border crossings or highway tolls in the Roman Empire, but when passing from one province to another, there were several layers of nightmarish bureaucracy to contend with. Most ports insisted that passengers obtain an exit pass from the harbormaster, for a fee. The rates were fixed by profession (prostitutes, mysteriously, paid the highest charges). Worse, travelers had to face the imperial customs officers. The Roman system was eerily similar to what we have to endure today. Imperial agents demanded a written *professio* (declaration of their luggage contents) from all transients. *Instrumenta itineris* (materials for the voyage) such as wagons and donkeys were duty-free, as were *instrumenta ad usum proprium* (items for personal use). But anything that had been purchased abroad was liable to tax. Most duties were a modest 2.5 to 5 percent, but luxury items—perfume, gems, spices, silks, eunuchs, dancing girls, and "handsome boys"—attracted a hefty 25 percent. Undeclared items were confiscated; travelers could get them back only by paying double duty.

Ancient accounts of dealing with these self-important autocrats strike a familiar chord. ("We object to customs officials when they finger the insides of our bags," Plutarch forlornly tells his readers, "but they are really only doing their job.") It seems that outwitting them was a sport for well-to-do tourists. Agents were forbidden to physically search married women, a fact that many female travelers used to their advantage; the story goes of one Roman grande dame hiding four hundred pearls in her bosom, causing a standoff when the customs officer noticed her excessive bust and refused to let her pass. The red tape created its own abuses. Travelers with official connections knew how to get around the fees, slipping gems into official correspondence. And on-the-spot bribery was rampant. Some officials in the East even posted a schedule of "gratuities" on the walls of their offices, to avoid awkward misunderstandings.

Just like border officials today, Roman civil servants were chosen for their plodding diligence and blunt lack of imagination. When Oscar Wilde famously told one stiff customs officer that he had nothing to declare but his genius, he was actually preempted by the pagan holy man Apollonius of Tyana in the first century A.D., who inscribed on his written *professio* that he carried with him nothing but "Continence, Justice, Virtue, Self-Control, Valor and Discipline." These were feminine nouns in ancient Greek, so the officer abruptly demanded: "Show me those slaves." Apollonius sanctimoniously remarked that these were noble-women. And he was *their* slave, not the other way around.

One can just imagine the customs officer's disdainful reaction.

INTO THE ARMS OF ALLAH

We plowed into the roughest waters that hydrofoils were legally permit-ted to cruise; one more knot of wind and the trip would have been can-celed. As it was, the vessel was forced to remain in low sluggish mode.

"We cannot fly," mourned the captain, as we rolled up and down the swells.

The vessel was Turkish, a thin shell of a hydrofoil with most of its seats broken or removed. The air of decay didn't help passenger morale. Most of the passengers were sick the moment we left port, but the Turks—the first national characteristic I noticed—were amazingly cheery about it. They would fill their seasickness bags and then wave them gleefully at friends. Those who had bought video cameras merrily taped the others retching; as soon as one fellow recovered, he took the camera to docu-ment the others.

Unhappily, there was no ventilation. It was a rough crossing. Les sto-ically kept her head down, trying not to look, smell, hear, or think.

"The men groaned, the women shrieked, everybody called upon God, cried aloud, remembered their dear ones," reports an ancient Greek aristocrat named Synesius who was caught on an eastern ship in a storm. "Then someone called out that anyone who had any gold should hang it around their neck. This is a time-honored practice: The body of a drowned person must have money on it, so that anyone who finds it won't mind providing a decent funeral."

Finally, through the murky porthole, I saw the coast of Turkey rising from the storm. It wasn't immediately promising. There were sheer cliffs. Gray sea, gray land, gray sky. But a line of blue lay on the hori-zon—a hint of sunny respite.

Sometimes it's good to leave a place on a low note. Things can only improve.

Enough of Greece—bring on the Orient!

Asian Seductions

W<small>HEN WE TOUCHED LAND</small>," says Synesius, echoing the sentiments of many an ancient ship passenger, "we embraced the soil like a long-lost mother."

It wasn't simply relief that filled Roman tourists with elation as they disembarked onto the pine-scented shores of Asia Minor. Like New Orleans, Hawaii, or the French Caribbean today, this province was the ancient world's most alluring case study in cultural fusion. Long before the Roman conquest, waves of Greek colonists had arrived and grafted a Hellenic new world onto the foundation of a dozen Oriental kingdoms; they proceeded to garland the mountainous coast with pearl-white cities, which rose at regular intervals above opalescent harbors. The Pax Romana allowed these busy Asian ports to flourish as never before, blossoming with all the giddy excess of the nouveaux riches: Day and night, their affluent, overdressed citizens teemed along splendid avenues of the latest design—through double-level arcades and fountain-cooled gardens—into sumptuous new temples and academies filled with fine art. To the first tourists, Asia Minor's situation was doubly attractive. Here was an entirely recognizable world, where Greek was spoken and Rome's most civilized traditions were upheld, and yet with hints of the Hittite, Assyrian, and Persian past suffusing the air like unfamiliar spices at a market. (This Greek element would actually last until the early twentieth century, when population exchanges after the demise of the Ottoman Empire purged the coast of their millennial presence.)

Romans ponder a purchase in A Sculpture Gallery *(1874),*
by Sir Lawrence Alma-Tadena.
Wealthy Asia Minor lured many of the best artists in the Empire.

After spending so much time in old Greece—revered, beloved, but sadly impoverished, even a little shabby—the shameless opulence was frankly refreshing. At the port of Halicarnassus, modern Bodrum, travelers had their first taste of its brazen style when they laid eyes on the eponymous Mausoleum—easily the gaudiest of the Seven Wonders, which soared above the coastline like a beached cruise liner. This brilliant white, 140-foot-high, multitiered ziggurat, built as a tomb for King Mausolos by his sister-wife in the third century B.C., deliberately blended Greek artistry with Babylonian ostentation; every inch was crowded with friezes and statues, and at its peak, Mausolos rode a golden chariot toward eternity. To the level-headed Lucian, the result was crass and preposterously vain. "The ugly thing may give the people of Halicarnassus something to show off to tourists," he imagines telling the dead king in the afterlife, "but I can't see what benefit *you* get out of it." Most Romans loved it. Pliny the Elder was openmouthed when he visited in A.D. 75—"even now, the hands of the artists compete with one another"; the engineer Vitruvius wrote an entire book about it. Today, the behemoth has evaporated, leaving only a vague outline of its foundations in the fishing port of Bodrum, a fact that would no doubt have given Lucian some satisfaction.

With the Mausoleum, the tone was set for Asia Minor. Romans worked their way north along the volcanic Aegean coastline, hopping from one dazzling city to the next—Aphrodisias, Knidos, Ephesus, Smyrna, Pergamum—toward the ultimate goal, the ruin of Troy. Most preferred to follow the snaking coastal highways rather than to sail, taking excurisons to the offshore islands en route, since even in the summer season the shrill northern winds could make sea voyages quite terrifying. On this silk highway, many Romans found themselves lingering unexpectedly. It was from conquered Asia Minor, according to the moralists, that the love of luxury was said to have first infiltrated the Empire (not to mention a revered sex manual by Philaenis of Samos, the ancient West's Kama Sutra, now sadly lost)—and the province's subtle Oriental flavors still raised favorite Greco-Roman pleasures to a higher pitch. Its many Xanadus provided the perfect opportunity to pause from the rigors of the road and indulge in some much-needed R and R.

The truth was, Romans felt quite comfortable in this Brave New Greece. The open-minded, can-do, forward-looking atmosphere was a relief after the Old World, whose high culture was monolithic, traditional, and a touch self-righteous. Edifying as cities like Athens were, one felt one had to be on one's best behavior. Asia was far more enter-

taining. The summer weather was invigorating, with sunny days cooled
by gentle sea breezes. The hotels were better, the food finer, the social
intercourse just as cultured and—quite frankly—less pretentious.

BUSING TO BYZANTIUM

"You like to ride the Camel Cock?"

"Excuse me?" Les almost choked on her rose-hip tea.

The agent pointed to a ticket. Kamel Koç, his preferred bus company.

"It is the best. Luxury service. Smooth suspension and rare break-
downs."

Today, Turkey is again one of the great case studies in cultural fusion
between East and West, thanks to the ambitious modernization program
begun by Kemal Atatürk in the 1920s—and just as in Roman times, its
coastline has reasserted its traditional position as the pleasure garden of
the Eastern Med. Travelers have endowed it with a glowing reputation.
Partly because it shares the mythic waters of the Aegean, Turkey is compared again and again to its aloof neighbor Greece and in many tourist
categories is proclaimed the victor. The beaches are more pristine (so the
conventional wisdom goes). The transport system is better. The Turkish
people are friendlier. The food is finer. The ruins are more impressive
(entire cities such as Ephesus, Aphrodisias, and Pergamum have survived
almost intact). The culture is more radiant. And everything—from wine
to taxis to hotels—is about a third the price.

What's more, the Aegean coast here is still traveled more often by land
than sea. Although pleasure boats called *gulets* circle the protected waters
of the Turquoise Coast, Turks generally mistrust the open ocean, operating only an irregular handful of long-distance ferries.

But they *love* highways.

In fact, road worship is a genuine social phenomenon, reminiscent of
the United States in the 1950s. Turkey has yet to produce a Kerouac, but
folk music celebrates the passion with gusto. Steamrollers have created
multilane highways across the hinterland, through mountains, across
deserts, around precipices. They are symbols of a glorious future. To a
Turk—or at least to a Turkish bureaucrat—nothing is more pleasing than
the scent of freshly laid bitumen. Because of the distances and the sheer
number of people involved, the omnibus is the preferred mode of transport—far more popular than rental cars. Turkish bus stations are more
like self-contained cities, all financed by the rabid competition among
the dozens of luxury transport companies.

And the Turkish buses themselves—well, they are to Greyhound as the Concorde is to a B-52.

The Kamel Koç (which I discovered is correctly pronounced Camel Cosh) was indeed a most luxurious service. The bus had two stewards in ties and vests in attendance. They continually offered drinking water, coffee, sweet cakes, and biscuits, with particular solicitude to children and the aged. They even made regular rounds to squirt antiseptic soap on every passenger's hands. When they collected the trash, they wore plastic gloves. It felt like a cross between business class and a mobile hospital.

Through the black-tinted windows, Turkey was flying by, and I tried to catch it. The concrete minarets of Saudi-funded mosques rose like streamlined missiles in the wheat fields, where peasant women carried enormous piles of sticks past young army recruits in oversize khakis. There were glimpses of an Eastern world that looked oddly like Stalinist Russia. Mammoth red flags fluttered in villages, with the crescent and star instead of hammer and sickle. Children in lace-collared uniforms marched along in phalanxes, singing patriotic songs. Portraits of Kemal Atatürk—father of the nation—hung on every wall; bronze statues of him graced every plaza.

But these were distant glimpses. After a few days, it was obvious that this was a deeply schizophrenic place. For most of the time, I couldn't shake the surreal feeling that Turkey was far *less* alien than Greece—and not just because every street sign was in the Latin alphabet rather than the Greek, one result of that all-consuming Westernization program.

Cultural fusion has careened ahead at a pace that even Atatürk couldn't have imagined. We stayed in picturesque fishing villages whose every cove was taken up by yacht marinas full of imported wealth. The loveliest gold-sand beaches stood in the shadow of standard-issue Sheraton hotels, supporting shiny new towns where everyone spoke English and was passionate about 1970s music. There were ATMs at every corner. There were glamorous enclave resorts for foreigners and rich Turks, cut off by barbed wire and guards, with scary corporate names like "Hill-Side Club." There were eco-resorts in the pine forests, where guests could stay in Mongolian yurts and take classes in belly dancing, water colors, and yoga. Plus innumerable guest houses run by sunburned expatriates from Lancashire and Liverpool, including croquet lawns.

What land, friend, is this? You wouldn't know if you were talking to a Turk or a Tory.

It was all perfectly pleasant as a place to soak up the last rays of the season. But here I was, bracing for the Middle Eastern experience, and most of it felt like Southern California.

One aspect of the reputation was certainly correct: Turks regard all the foreign goings-on in their land with an amiability that seems almost Polynesian. Compared to Greeks, with their pushy entrepreneurial spirit that often spills over into rudeness, the Turks were teddy bears—laid-back, placid, almost jellylike; in repose, they smiled contentedly into space. After Greece, where nerves were frayed at the end of summer, it felt like the barometric pressure had suddenly dropped.

With the new, calm vibe, Les was keen to give Turkey's fleshpots a try.

"I think I'm suffering from Stendahl's syndrome," she said, feeling her forehead.

This was a psychological condition she'd once heard about, induced by overexposure to the remote past. Stendahl experienced it in as a tourist in Florence. He'd visited so many churches full of Michelangelos and tombs that one day he started to feel faint and suffer heart palpitations. He finally collapsed, overcome by acute feelings of dread and despair induced by the relentless evidence of human mortality. Basically, he had to stop looking at dead things.

I gleaned that she was feeling worn-out by the steady pace of our journey east. At five months, people in the street recognized that she was pregnant—something of a relief to her, since at the beginning of the trip most strangers assumed she was just overweight. Now she wanted to hole up by the turquoise waters of Turkey and take a deep breath by a crescent beach.

As for me, I could appreciate an Indian summer as much as the next person. Greeks called it "the little summer of Saint Dimitrios"—the sudden two weeks of sunshine in mid-October that fall like a benediction on both sides of the Aegean, before the autumn rains.

But I wasn't about to dilly-dally. Not when there were ruins to behold.

THE FIRST TRAVEL GHETTO

Of all the glittering cities where Roman tourists could bask in neo-Oriental pleasures, none compared with Ephesus, whose porphyry-dappled avenues rose from a harbor many times busier than Piraeus into a wild arena of mountains linked by hefty fortress walls. Tourists rushed to the Temple of Artemis—second of Asia Minor's oversize World Wonders—whose polished walls so brilliantly reflected the vehement sun that guides warned people to avert their eyes in case they should be struck blind. Behind 127 columns, each as thick as a giant redwood, swathed in mysterious clouds of incense, a towering statue of the mother goddess stood with welcoming arms—not the sleek, aerobicized huntress of conventional Greco-Roman legend, but a voluptuous, half-barbaric creation, whose more than twenty milk-filled breasts hung in an enormous cluster from her chest. Teams of eunuch priests prayed at her feet; other male worshipers, who had balked at ritual castration, offered up stone testicles as substitutes for their tender flesh. Guides then led the suitably impressed visitors back out to the courtyard, where Ephesian silversmiths peddled small images of the goddess as souvenirs.

But the real allure of Ephesus was less spiritual. One could wander the Arcadian Way on hot summer nights (this was one of the only cities outside of Rome to invest in street lighting) into a nonstop carnival: "the whole city is full of pipers, and full of effeminate rascals and full of noise," reported a disapproving Apollonius of Tyana. Most notorious were the erotic ballerinas, who prefigured modern belly dancers: Wearing diaphanous robes, they would "gyrate their lascivious loins to a steady beat"—according to Martial—assuming "wanton postures" on the floor while playing tiny cymbals attached to their fingertips. Everything was tolerated in Ephesus—except narrow-minded moralizing. When the hard-line Christian apostle St. Paul denounced their sinful ways in the first century A.D.—and had the temerity to attack the silversmiths' guild for preying on pagan tourists—he provoked a riot. "Great is Artemis of the Ephesians!" bellowed the furious artisans, defending their sacred source of income.

The image of the fertility goddess, breasts cascading down her torso, was ubiquitous; what the Virgin Mary made of it all (she spent much of her life here) is anybody's guess.

Today, Ephesus competes with Pompeii as the ultimate Roman archaeological site.

When its harbor eventually silted up around the sixth century A.D., the city was slowly abandoned; modern archaeologists have been able to expose its broad avenues, gates, libraries, baths, and latrines. As a result, for sheer impact, Ephesus is hard to beat. Its individual structures may not be as iconic as those of Athens, but Ephesus is pure antiquity. There are no layers of subsequent building to blur the angles of the streets or dilute the integrity of its design. It may lack the human detail and vibrant frescoes of Pompeii, but it makes up for the gap with imperial grandeur. The towns of Vesuvius buried by the Bay of Naples were relatively modest, provincial nowheres. Ephesus was a City, home to millionaires, playboys, and wastrels. It was *Broadway:* all singing, all dancing, full of majestic vistas, esplanades that ran for miles, buildings whose facades still rise from the earth like glorious crypts.

Needless to say, I was keen to put in an appearance.

"Even Stendahl wouldn't have missed Ephesus," I assured Les.

A crowded *dolmus,* or local minibus, ferried us from the farming town of Selçuk to the rusted wire fence that marked the perimeter of the site. But once inside, we were as free as any ancient tourist fresh from the highway to stroll through the Hercules Gate. I led us down Marble Street to the restored Library of Celsus—an architecturally unrivaled evocation of ancient times, with its glistening polished columns and serene statues of the goddess of learning. The Temple of Artemis, sadly, has all but disappeared, broken up by Goths and rampaging Christians; a single column marks the site. But along the avenue walls danced tiny carvings of gladiators, pointing the way to the amphitheater, and the remains of the

The highway into Ephesus, leading to the Library of Celsus.

palatial bathhouses. I must have seen dozens of ruined steam rooms and arenas on the trip so far, but only here, in context, did their essential strangeness came to life. Nowhere else is the ancient Roman world so vivid, the intervening centuries so transparent; nowhere in Greece or Italy makes it so shockingly clear that the past *actually happened.* You couldn't just see the ancients enjoying their holiday pleasures; you could hear and smell them.

THE JOY OF STEAM

Baths, wine and sex may ruin our bodies, but they make life worth living.

Roman gravestone

Just after dawn, the melodious bass of a copper gong would resound through the streets of the city, startling pigeons and stirring hungover revelers—a sound, Cicero said, that was sweeter than the voices of all the philosophers in Athens. It marked the opening of the *thermae* (public bathhouses). Turkey, of course, is the perfect place to ponder this key institution: Islamic *hammam*s (steam houses) have carried the tradition, with its three stages of public washing, steaming, and massage intact from antiquity. (In fact, the very name "Turkish bath" was given by British visitors in the sixteenth century, who saw Roman *thermae* still in operation and wrongly assumed they were an Ottoman invention.) Although the *hammam*'s role has been undermined in recent years—modern Turks have developed a passion for private, Western-style bathing—the public versions still thrive in many rural areas (and even worldly Istanbul has sixty-seven of them). Still, it's a far cry from the central role the baths played in daily Roman life. Ancient travelers to any strange city could hardly wait for a visit, setting off with a fresh towel and an oil flask to sample the baths' many delights—physical, mental, and, above all, social.

It was almost impossible *not* to meet people at the baths, since they were often as crowded as public beaches are today. Exercise balls would hit bathers in the head; tempers would flare; bullies lashed out at slaves or other social inferiors. Food vendors bellowed from their own podiums— there were egg sellers, wine vendors, and snack bars that served up cutlets, fried meats, and olives. Professional hair pluckers worked the chambers, as did petty thieves. Curse tablets have been found that condemn these bathhouse felons ("Do not allow sleep or health to him who has done me wrong, whether man or woman, whether slave or

Tepidarium (1881), by Sir Lawrence Alma-Tadena:
A Roman woman unwinds, evidently drained, after a steam bath.

free"). Impoverished nobles scoured the crowds in search of a meal, while the wealthy trawled the steam rooms handing out banquet invitations to potential sexual partners—since lust and bathing often went hand in hand.

Today we tend to assume that modern depictions of ancient Rome as a den of carnality are lurid exaggerations. For the chic upper classes, they aren't. The bulk of Roman citizens may have lived sedate, happily married lives, raised families, and respected the traditional sexual taboos—they never made love in the daylight hours, women covered their breasts even at the height of passion, while it was considered the basest infamy for a man to use his tongue "to give a woman pleasure"—but the fashionable set openly flaunted these restrictions. The libertines of antiquity were not representative of Roman life as a whole, but the titillating visions of Victorian genre painting, the orgies of *I, Claudius,* and even the tedious *Penthouse*-funded *Caligula* are well within the bounds of historical possibility.

Although many baths were same-sex, mixed bathing became common in fashionable circles from the first century A.D.—creating an erotically charged atmosphere more potent than anything so far depicted on the silver screen. Romans always went naked in the heated pools—those who hid themselves were ridiculed. The poet Martial was affronted when one aristocratic young woman he thought had expressed sexual interest in him refused to share a bath; he ponders whether she is trying to hide some dreadful physical defect and finally concludes, charitably enough, that she must be an idiot.

Erotic foreplay continued all the way from the steam rooms to the bar-restaurants attached, where flushed lovers could eye one another over a jug of chilled wine and figs. Private rooms were provided for consummation, decorated with lewd frescoes: The poet Ovid in his *Art of Love* reports the baths as a key trysting place for young romantics, since chaperons could be left outside; they were the scene, says Ulpian, of many an adultery, sometimes between wealthy matrons and their Adonis-like Asian slaves. Special magical spells were devised to incite romance at the baths. (Some were a little bizarre: "To attract a lover at the *thermae:* First, rub a tick from a dead dog on your genitals." Another spell needed to be written in the blood of an ass on a papyrus sheet, which should then be glued onto the vaulted ceiling of the vapor room—"you will marvel at the results," the author promised.) But most respectable couples retired to their own villas to spend the night, leaving the rooms to prostitutes. (As one graffito at Herculaneum boasted: "We, Appelles the Mouse and his brother Dexter, lovingly fucked two women twice.") In an age when homosexuality was socially accepted, at least between adults and teenage boys, male-only baths were more common: One friend of Martial's, Lattara, was always eager to avoid "the baths frequented by the feminine cohorts."

We have a luminous insight into how Romans behaved at the baths, thanks to the fragmentary survival of several Greek-Latin phrase books called *hermeneumata*. Designed for schoolchildren, they would have been of singular use to travelers; many a Roman wanderer must have carried one, to brush up on his more obscure Greek vocabulary on a quiet evening. Like any modern Berlitz guide, the vocabulary lists are complemented by a series of *colloquia* (dialogue scenes) that describe how to behave in certain social situations.

The speaker in one dialogue—transcribed in a rare 1877 French journal—arrives at the *therma* with a sizable party of friends. He rather imperiously chooses an attendant:

Follow us. Yes, you. Look after our clothes carefully, and find us a
place.

Let me have a word with the perfumer. Hello, Julius. Give me
incense and myrrh for twenty people. No, no, best quality. Now, boy,
undo my shoes. Take my clothes. Oil me. All right, let's go in . . .

Tellingly, the dialogue spends more time on the peripheral social event—
ordering a meal at the restaurant—than the actual bathing.

This is my party. Mix wine for us (with water). Let's recline.

To start with, give us beetroot or squash; add some fish sauce to
that. Bring us radishes—a knife—as well as lettuce and cucumber.
We'll have a trotter, blood sausage and a sow's womb. We'll all have
white bread. We'll have pork shoulder and ham and some mustard.

Isn't the fish grilled yet?

Take round some water to rinse peoples' hands. Bring us yogurt, if
you have any, with honey, and some honey pastry [halva]. Cut it into
slices and we can share it out.

Not every dinner was so elegant. Baths were synonymous with
overindulgence in every sense. Juvenal records with disdain how many
fashionable nobles would vomit onto the floor before taking their
meals—an established practice among Roman gourmands, to prepare
the palate. Meals would often end with the diners, exhausted and replete,
simply passing out.

But the vocabulary book ends more politely: "Come on, friends, let's
go out for a walk."

These days, of course, visitors to the baths could also do with a phrase
book. Every time I went and signed up for a massage, I wondered what
the Turkish was for "My spleen is about to burst."

THUMBS-UP FOR DEATH

Next on the list of therapeutic pleasures for a Roman was to catch a
gladiatorial show. Asian Greeks openly welcomed these bloodthirsty
entertainments, while old-world Greeks looked down their noses at
them in favor of athletic competitions. Of course, the displays couldn't

compare with those at the Colosseum—but for provincials, the Ephesians did quite an acceptable job.

Just after dawn, tourists emerged in their finest gowns and colorful togas, then made their way to the amphitheater, taking their time as they wove among the rabble to cast an appreciative eye over the silk costumes of the Asian aristocrats (any day at the arena was as much a fashion event as the Oscars are today). After the sacrifice of animals, the crowds would part and applaud the patron who was putting on the gladiatorial display, who lapped up the adulation. (One mosaic shows a patron crowing: "This is what it is to be rich. This is what it means to be powerful.") The notorious wealth of the Ephesians guaranteed extravagant gestures. The poorer sectors of the audience were pleased to have even their meals provided: in the morning, slaves showered the crowd with figs, dates, nuts, cheeses, and pastries; in the afternoon, the hungry hoped for roasted pheasants or Numidian partridges.

And that was only the beginning . . .

Hollywood's depictions of the Roman games have tended to be solemn, austere, and gruesome, with the focus on single combats, enacted more like modern prizefights. In fact, the events were far more diverse, vulgar, and downright peculiar. A day at the arena was a total pagan entertainment package, segueing from the deadly displays of the gladiators to religious pageantry, sexual titillation, slapstick comedy, and kitschy stage shows. Think of *Gladiator* combined with the Moscow Circus and a pornographic video.

First came the animal parades, the more bizarre the better—three hundred ostriches, say, their feathers tinged with vermilion dye, or performing apes from darkest Africa. The crowds loved animals that had been trained "contrary to nature": wild bulls that would let boys dance on their backs; lions that were as obedient as puppies; elephants that could sit at tables or slowly perform dance steps. Then came the variety skits. There were pantomimes, acrobats, and clowns. The famous erotic dancers would perform in gauzy costumes while perfumes from Arabia were blown over the entire crowd. Stage scenery was prolific and rather gaudy. Enormous props—mountains, lakes, forests—would be raised from underground chambers; the arena re-created in an instant the deserts of Egypt or the jungles of Africa. Live sex acts could then be performed in voluptuous settings.

In the intermissions, while scenes were being changed, condemned men were executed. Many of these murderers, thieves, rapists, and loan defaulters were casually thrown to wild beasts. They might be dropped into cages filled with half-starved lions or poisonous snakes; others were castrated or crucified. One favorite device was the *tunica molesta*: A victim would be dressed in an elaborately embroidered tunic of gold and purple, which suddenly burst into flame, incinerating him. But the crowds craved novelty, and many patrons strained for more imaginative effects. An unlucky victim might be dressed as the hero Orpheus, returning from the underworld to an enchanted forest: Actors dressed as trees, rocks, birds, and animals would all greet him happily, to the soothing strum of harps—until a wild bear would be released, to tear the victim to pieces. Women condemned to death—usually for murder—might be given the role of Europa, who was violated by Zeus as a bull. After the woman's death, the musicians would strike up a light melody, and a more cheerful pantomime might proceed, perhaps involving lovely nymphs lolling by a lake.

And finally, of course, there were the gladiators' fights. These were the main event, the most riveting part of the day, bringing action theater to its highest pitch. The combats were set to music, with flutes and trumpets, horns, even hydraulic organs; more scenery was provided, to evoke great battles of history. Dozens of pairs would be thrown into the arena at one time, and each style of gladiator had partisans in the crowd. Lumbering Samnites, with shields and short swords, were pitted against the naked, agile *retiarii,* with nets and tridents. Men were pitted against panthers. For variety, British war chariots might be let loose, or women dressed as Amazons; for comic relief, dwarves would run among the combatants dressed as Mars and the bloody goddess of bravery, egging them on.

Crowd participation was famously enthusiastic during the blood sports—even among the most compassionate and civilized of Roman writers (St. Augustine himself in his *Confessions* admits to a youthful passion for the games). At every flesh cut, the crowd roared *"Habet!"* (That's got him!). A gladiator who lost his nerve would be driven on by whips and hot irons, while the mob abused him: "Whip him, burn him, kill him! Why is he so afraid of the sword? Why does he die so sullenly?" When a badly wounded gladiator took off his helmet and appealed for mercy, the crowd leaped to its feet and the spectators expressed their opinion: The thumbs-down gesture actually meant that a fighter should be granted life, as did waving a handkerchief; a thumb pointed to the chest meant a man's throat would be slit. Following this, an attendant dressed as Charon, boatman of the underworld, bounded forth with a giant mallet, to administer the coup de grâce; the mangled corpse was finally dragged off by Mercury, through a gateway decorated as the

Pollice Verso (1872), by Jean-Léon Gérôme. A Victorian-era vision of the gladiatorial arena.

entrance to Hades. For the defeated, there was no sympathy: The gladiators were all condemned criminals in any case, and had been sent to the gladiatorial schools only as a delay in their executions. The Roman state was merely demonstrating its invincible power and confirming the social order.

And so the day's entertainment continued, a relentless schedule of gore, sex, comedy, and spectacle. In high summer, the shows went on late into the night, with hundreds of slaves carrying lanterns for illumination. As a final flourish, the patron might have his minions throw lottery-style ivory chits into the crowd, which could be exchanged for prizes of gold, silver, pearls, paintings, tamed beasts, boats—perhaps even a country estate. Among the poor, violent brawls would begin, sometimes fatal. A tourist would be well advised to hire a professional "scrambler" to fling himself into the mêlée and bring back a token or two.

After all, for aristocratic Romans, blood was to be seen, not shed.

THE ROAD TO OBLIVION

As Pompeii is in Italy, Ephesus is Turkey's most popular tourist site—and it's just as full of modern travelers trying to make sense of the ruins. But this time, with my *Crowds are good* mantra, I was well prepared to absorb the national quirks, even when I came across yet another squadron of French matrons in the amphitheater, harmonizing a bloodcurdling round of "Frère Jacques" to test the acoustics. In otherwise silent groves, the laughter of Korean groups would erupt from ancient brothels, sounding like a flock of startled flamingos; their guide had just told them how prostitutes carved their names on walls like calling cards, "with fax number and e-mail." And through a doorway, I overheard three English travelers picking their way over the stones.

"Is this it?" one of them asked excitedly.

"Gotta be."

They promptly dropped their trousers and took photographs of one another's rear ends.

I soon discerned that this odd ritual wasn't just a perverse leftover of British boarding-school life, but a souvenir of the ancient public latrine we were standing in, with its dozens of marble seats—heated in winter by steam pipes—still intact.

A Turkish guard accidentally stumbled onto the scene, carrying two asps he'd just captured, coiled up in a plastic bag. Frowning in confusion, he held up the snakes:

"Danger! Danger!"

St. Paul and the Virgin Mary might still have been a bit appalled by Ephesus.

There was only one problem with the site: The Arcadian Way, the famous boulevard that once led down to the harbor, was, to my disgust, blocked off to the public for new excavations.

But this wasn't the time to comply with archaeological site rules. Fate had clearly decreed that I should walk down the promenade; I knew that I wouldn't be caught. So, while pregnant Les stood guard, I ducked under the barricade chain and strode euphorically forward, along the huge paving stones, past the upright fragments of columns and statues.

I could hardly believe it. Here I was entirely alone, free at last to walk through history.

Vegetation pressed in on the flanks of the boulevard, blocking out everything else; I felt as if I were entering the Time Tunnel. The wind was hot, coming in searing gusts through the dry bushes; it sounded eerily like the squeaking of masts and rigging of the port that had existed at the end of the avenue. The face of Medusa leered at me from a column, eyes rolled back in its head, the mane of poisonous snakes flailing.

I had the sudden conviction that I could just keep walking this road forever and disappear off the other end. Far away, Les was watching me curiously, like a lonely stork. The wind crashed violently, shaking the dry wood, urging me on; lightning crackled on the horizon.

I turned around and rushed back. Whatever was out there remains undisturbed.

But perhaps I'd already gone too far.

In Sickness
and in Health

Allah Akbar, Allah Akb-a-a-a-a-a-r . . .

At 5:30 A.M., in Izmir—known as Smyrna in Roman times—the muezzin call from the mosque next door lets rip, amplified a hundred times by Godzilla-sized loudspeakers. I put in my earplugs, cursing the razor-thin windowpanes.

At 6:00 A.M., the muezzin is replaced by the Turkish national anthem, this time blasted from every rooftop in town. We have the dubious honor of being in Izmir on National Day. The tune will be played every fifteen minutes until midnight. It's a high-pitched, *Teletubbies* version of the Turkish anthem, shrill and distorted, like a twisted Christmas carol chanted by demented elves.

The Grand Zeybek Hotel stretches its musty limbs like a resurrected corpse. Intimate sounds from every bathroom are conducted through to our room via fissures in the hotel's basic structure. Typical noises here— the screech of plumbing, the smash of doors that don't fit their frames, people falling from beds that lack a leg, masonry crashing off walls.

And this is an *expensive* hotel. We're living it up—under three shiny golden stars.

There's no use trying to sleep. I go to the window and look out at the main avenue, where boxlike high-rises extend like filing cabinets, one after another, ad infinitum. Down below, the market vendors are ensconced with their goods. There are mules and potatoes everywhere. The old men are in position in their cafés, practicing their stares; Turkish women shuffle by wearing *I Dream of Jeannie* pantaloons. As far as traditional costumes go, these duds are quite cute. Even grandmothers wear them in girlish shades of pink and lilac.

The sky is dark, just like that day in Ephesus—a thick, impenetrable cloud from the Book of Revelation. But it never rains. Clouds just press down like damp cotton, turning the streets of Izmir—the people's faces, their clothes, their expressions—a uniform charcoal gray.

This is not the Turkey of hippie backpacker legend, full of light and color. In fact, we'd been chilled to the bone ever since the Aegean "turned." Ancient sailors used to observe the skies keenly for this shift in seasons, the moment when summer sank into dark, stormy autumn; the transition to rough weather could happen overnight, canceling long-distance sea voyages until the following spring. Today, Turks take the opposite tack: They go into what seems a collective state of denial, preferring to pretend that summer never really ends. Heating is unheard of. Cold wind blasts into hotel rooms from all directions. Luxuries like blankets are spurned. As for the hot-water systems—they tend not to actually work. In summer, the guests don't *need* hot water. Icy dousings will do.

And so—this felt oddly inevitable—Les was getting sick.

Becoming ill on the road is perhaps the most distressing constant of travel—and in Roman times it seemed to happen more often in Asia Minor, where merchants from the East brought virulent new diseases along with their perfumes and silks. Many highway inns offered medical attention on their lists of hotel services, but wise travelers were leery of village quacks. They carried their own first-aid kits—packets of sea salt, to dissolve in water and apply to infections; bandages made of wool shorn from the soft necks of newborn lambs; aged olive oil, which was considered effective against fevers; and jars of honey, preferably with dead bees floating in the liquid, for health potions. (Mixed with dried garlic, ground thistles, or the ashes of dead birds, honey made a salve for inflammations.)

But if an illness was more serious, professional treatment was required. Luckily, Asia was blessed with the most famous health spas of the Mediterranean world.

ON A MISSION FROM GOD

All through the summer, my stomach was upset, and I was thirsty night and day, and I perspired unspeakably, and my body was weak, so that I needed two or three men to help lift me from my bed when I wanted to get up.

And that was when, in Smyrna, the god told me I should go on another journey . . .

So begins Aelius Aristides in A.D. 165, as he introduces one of the many counterintuitive expeditions taken along this coastline for his health—which only a couple of weeks later I discovered would parallel our own Turkish sojourn in ways too close for comfort.

Aristides was the original celebrity neurotic—an Empire-famous orator who was entirely self-absorbed, outrageously vain, deeply superstitious, and an extreme hypochondriac. Toward the end of his life, he wrote a treatise called *Sacred Teachings,* which chronicles in graphic detail his many physical ailments, real and imagined, and his endless travels through all the curative luxury spas of Asia Minor. The most prestigious of these—in fact, the most magnificent sanitarium in the Roman Empire—was in Pergamum. It dwarfed all the older health resorts of Greece. In a wild mountain setting, it had state-of-the-art thermal baths, a renowned library, a thirty-five-hundred-seat amphitheater, and a sacred fountain whose burbling waters could restore all ills. Like all medical sanctuaries, Pergamum was dedicated to the god of healing, Asclepius "the Savior"—for centuries the main pagan rival to Jesus.

Wealthy patients could spend years in this holy refuge, lounging under shaded colonnades and conversing with other cultured internees while harmless yellow snakes slithered underfoot (the shedding of their skins was a symbol of regeneration for the ancients). Pergamum's refined atmosphere anticipated the Swiss sanitariums of the nineteenth century, where aristocratic English consumptives slowly wasted away alongside fellow aesthetes, comforted by their pages of freshly penned poetry. (In the ancient world, tuberculosis was a major cause of death for the young and affluent—along with the ever-democratic malaria.) But the precinct's serenity was often broken by the ancient world's most knowledgeable health specialists—a dizzying parade of drug vendors, amulet makers, midwives, dietitians, gymnastics trainers, masseurs, surgeons, and astrologers; there were also experts at giving enemas and virtuoso phlebotomists (bloodletters). Not all of the sanctuary's treatments look like quackery today. In the second century, the spa was home to the physician Galen, whose ideas on the four bodily humors would dominate Western medicine until the nineteenth century. Galen's advocacy of regular exercise and his dietary recommendations—lots of fresh fruit and vegetables—seem entirely modern.

But even Galen knew that the best cures were passed down from heaven.

Aristides had avoided earthly physicians ever since, as a young man visiting Rome in A.D. 140, he had come down with a fever. After two days of purges—he was allowed to drink nothing but cucumber juice—he began urinating blood, so the doctors sliced open his torso to release the sickness. ("A pain, numbing and impossible to bear, passed through me," he recalled later, "and everything around was smeared with gore.") For the next twenty-five years, he would be struck down by ailments—abdominal pains, fevers, diarrhea, dyspepsia, constipation, insomnia, fainting fits, respiratory problems, "fiery spasms," and inexplicable swellings. But instead of consulting doctors, Aristides put his faith entirely in "dream visions." These dreams, which came direct from the god Asclepius, were sometimes easy to understand—Plato might appear with specific instructions, for example. Others had to be interpreted. What did it mean for Aristides to dream that he was floating on a raft in the middle of the Red Sea? Or captured by Parthians, who wanted to brand him as a slave? "Induce vomiting, go without bathing, rest," the patient prescribes for himself.

To discern the divine diagnosis, Aristides certainly consulted the famous dream compendium of Artemidorus, which listed common visions—a man feeding cheese to his own penis, say—and interpreted them as allegories. (Not surprisingly, Freud was very taken with Artemidorus, praising him as an early explorer of the unconscious mind. But Freud's prudish German translation left out the account of a man who dreams he is having sex with his mother. According to Artemidorus, the nuances of an incest dream are crucial during an illness. If it involves frontal penetration, it simply predicts that the dreamer will have a falling out with his father. If there is anal penetration, any illness is bound to get worse. But if the mother is *riding* the son—well, a healthy man will live in great ease, but a sick man will always die.)

The god's prescriptions were definitely from the school of tough love. Asclepius regularly told Aristides to drag himself out of his sickbed in the middle of winter, run more than a mile through the forest, and then leap into an ice-encrusted river ("My skin had a rosy hue," he says lightly of the aftereffects). Sometimes small crowds would gather and marvel at the extreme nature of the divine cure—especially one day when Aristides leaped into a river that was in full flood, with branches and debris hurtling dangerously downstream. Once, a sick friend joined him in one of these frozen swims, only to be "seized with convulsions" and nearly die. The variety of other dream-induced cures was dizzying. There were enemas, blood purges, fasts, special diets—barley gruel and lentils seemed to be a celestial favorite—and so much exercise that Aristides wrote an oration, *In Defense of Running,* the first pro-jogging tract in known history. Sometimes he had to smear himself with cold mud; later, he went without bathing "for five consecutive years." To modern readers, the god Asclepius seems hardly short of murderous: He even ordered Aristides to sail across the bay of Smyrna in the middle of a thunderstorm . . .

But very often—and no less arduously—the god advised a road trip. Aristides would wake up from a dream shouting a famous health spa's name—"Aliani!"—and hit the highway.

IN SEARCH OF THE TURKISH DREAM SPA

Ancient soothsayers often blamed a sudden illness on a curse placed by an unknown witch or sorcerer. As for Lesley's Turkish ague, we had a fair idea whom to blame.

A few days earlier, we'd met a Maugham-esque English expatriate named Dunbar, who had set up a pirate yachting fiefdom on the Turkish coast. He'd invited us to his rustic villa for a home-cooked dinner—wild mushrooms, homemade wine, all seductively civilized. Unfortunately, Dunbar was also coming down with a noxious influenza, a brutal Asian strain that was cutting a swath through the local populace. We'd sat with frozen grins as he sneezed into his mushroom cream sauce, wiped his nose with the back of his hand, and continued cooking.

Much later I learned from Les that this vision had sent her into a fatalistic spiral. She wasn't about to refuse the meal and cause a diplomatic incident. She'd fought a lot of germs in the last two months of travel. She couldn't fight any more.

We ate the glutinous pasta.

Late the next day, perched in the Kamel Koç, as the vapor of frozen air-conditioning cascaded like a waterfall over our heads, Les was gritting her teeth and looking ominously pale.

If falling ill in a foreign land is one of those timeless rites of travel, being five months pregnant raises the stakes a little. Now she lay there in Izmir, unable to get clean, unable to get a bath, and unable to eat Turkish food, most of which swims in bright orange oil.

But the solution—Les was convinced—was to just keep moving. Wherever we ended up couldn't be worse than the Grand Zeybeck Hotel, she figured.

Logic might suggest that being sick is hardly the best time to travel. Unfortunately, the ill don't always think clearly; what seems utterly urgent to the feverish mind may later seem entirely addled—and any survey of Aristides' "health tours" certainly bears that out.

The most extraordinary example of Aristides' misguided ventures occurred one summer day in A.D. 165, when Aristides was living in Smyrna (Izmir) and did seem genuinely sick—in fact, he was barely able to move without help. So the god told him to go straight to Pergamum. Fifty miles away. In the middle of a heat wave.

It was noon when Asclepius issued this sadistic instruction and far too hot to travel; modern heat waves in this part of Turkey often hit 110 degrees Fahrenheit—so Aristides decided to send his servants ahead with the luggage. Later, in the relative cool of the afternoon, he was lifted into the back of a covered wagon, where he lay for hours as it swayed across the sun-scorched mountains, eyes drifting in and out of focus, covered in sweat from head to toe. By dusk, he had traveled fourteen miles, as far as the river Hermus, and decided to stop; but to his disgust the inn there was one of the ranker fleapits of the ancient road. Its dark, stifling rooms were a disgrace; he refused to stay, and pushed on into the evening.

At this point, Aristides' feverish behavior becomes truly erratic. He arrives at the next village, but there is no sign of his servants with the luggage. He orders his men to drive on, by torchlight. Around midnight, he's made it to a place called Cyme. The attendants are exhausted, but Aristides maniacally wraps a blanket around his shoulders—the night has become quite cold—and insists on traveling until dawn. As the cock crows, around 4 A.M., the motley, half-frozen entourage trundles into the deserted town of Myrina—forty-two miles from their starting point.

Unfortunately, the inns are all boarded up for the night. His servants start banging on doors, but nobody answers. Finally, Aristides finds the address of an old acquaintance, who lets them in and lights a warming fire. But as the sun begins to rise, Aristides decides—madly—to keep the momentum up. He elects to continue for yet another ten miles, so he can sacrifice at a temple to Apollo, before collapsing nearly dead in the heat.

Aristides did make it to Pergamum the next day, crawling from his wagon to slurp from the holy fountain—and feeling far sicker than when he started.

By the time we reached modern Bergama (Pergamum) ourselves—late, hungry, exhausted, dragging our bags along the concrete mall past one sullen café after another, with no idea where the city center was, let alone a hotel—Les was behaving as erratically as Aristides.

Her needs sounded simple. *A hot shower,* that was all she wanted. She kept repeating it, just in case I missed the point. It was all she needed to avoid her threatening grippe. I could see the vision dancing before her eyes—as therapeutic as the sacred waters of the ancient sanitarium. The problem was that in Turkey, a hot shower seemed just as elusive.

We turned down all the touts at the bus station—cheap places never had systems that worked, so we'd resolved to pay for *class.* But every hotel in Bergama seemed to have some baffling flaw. One stood next to a roaring factory. Another reeked of petroleum. Another was run by a lecher. Another had broken windows. Many proudly advertised hot water—but they couldn't fool the Holmes-like Les, who marched straight into the bathrooms, turned on the faucets, and irrefutably proved otherwise.

There's a strange thing about looking for hotels in unfamiliar cities: If you don't find one quickly, a negative momentum tends to set in. The ancients believed in "unlucky journeys," when a traveler would be caught in the twisted skeins of destiny. Bad luck would pile up—it was even contagious. And that night in Bergama, the skeins seemed to be tightening around our necks.

We finally chose a place that looked vaguely respectable—the carpet wasn't too dank, and, yes, hot water poured from the taps when Les tested them. But a short time later, as I was heading out the door to give the owner our passports, a *Psycho*-pitch scream shot from the bathroom. The moment Les had stepped under the shower, the water turned ice cold. She just stood there under the frozen torrent, finally losing it. The hotel had installed individual electric water heaters to every shower faucet—a diabolical device familiar to anyone who has traveled the Third World, because they give you a short electric shock whenever you touch them—and this one's fuse had just blown.

I found the fuse box outside, turned it back on, but it blew again in another ten seconds.

"This is a conspiracy," Les was muttering incredulously, by now feeling the most violent assaults of Dunbar's bacterial dinner gift.

The owner seemed mystified by Lesley's wrath. He offered to let us use a shower in another room. The same thing happened. He then offered to stay by the fuse box while Les had a shower, flicking the switch every ten seconds to maintain a continuous current.

"We're getting out of here!" Les announced, looking like something out of *Wuthering Heights.* Her hair was dripping wet. It was dark outside.

A cold gale was whipping up. I gently suggested that we wait until tomorrow . . .

Ten minutes later, we were dragging our luggage around the mall again.

Meanwhile, back in A.D. 165—the very night after Aristides arrived at the spa at Pergamum, as he was relaxing in the light-filled sanitarium, he was blessed with another dream.

This time, the god Asclepius himself appeared in all his glory "and ordered me to press on and not to do otherwise. 'For they are in pursuit.' " (One can only imagine the servants' sideways glances as Aristides related this enigmatic vision the next day.) But divine orders were divine orders. The party trundled on, while Aristides became racked by a sore throat, and a sirocco covered them in dust from head to foot. Only after making a sacrifice at an important altar of Zeus did the god allow his patient to stop.

"And after this," sighed Aristides, "my way of life was manifestly more comfortable."

Until the summer of the following year, that is, when Aristides reported: "My sleep became troubled, and I could scarcely digest a thing." Aristides lay down, nodded off, awaited a dream, and—*Cyzicus!*

"I got up and told the servants to pack and to leave immediately."

For Aristides, traveling for his health was a lifelong pursuit. He never found a cure for all his endless coughs and fevers, but he did live to over sixty years of age, two decades longer than the average life expectancy of an aristocrat at the time.

Which I suppose should have been encouraging.

PART SIX

HOMER'S HEROES

Troy:
The Ultimate
Faux-Historical Site

Aᴅᴅɪᴄᴛɪᴠᴇ ᴀs ᴛʜᴇ ʜᴇᴀʟᴛʜ sᴘᴀs and fleshpots of Asia Minor must have been, the ancient travelers never forgot that their sight-seeing grail lay farther to the north, by the gates of the Hellespont (now known as the Dardanelles). Perched above the dark churning waters that narrowly divide Europe from Asia, a quiet hamlet called Novum Ilium—New Troy—was enjoying a lucrative career as the most spurious of Rome's national shrines.

This strategically placed outpost—described by one visitor as a village-city—had raised an enviable tourist franchise on the slippery rubble of myth. It occupied the site of the illustrious Bronze Age Troy, whose ten-year siege and eventual destruction by the Greeks was the stuff of the first and most revered epic in all literature, Homer's *Iliad*. (The date of the war is thought by most archaeologists to be 1260 B.C., although some still don't believe it ever happened.) This literary connection alone would have guaranteed headline billing on the ancient Grand Tour: the name Troy conjured unforgettable images embedded at the core of the classi-cal psyche—of the sublimely beautiful Helen, whose face had launched the proverbial thousand ships; of titanic battles between heroes; of divine interventions on the battlefields by the Olympian gods; and of the wooden horse, devised by Ulysses, which finally proved Troy's tragic undoing.

But for patriotic Romans, the site had an even more potent attraction. The fall of King Priam's citadel was linked in legend to the foundation of Rome itself. It was said that a handful of refugees had escaped their burning city led by a Trojan warrior named Aeneas, and sailed west to Italy; his descendant Romulus had gone on to plant Rome's sacred seed.

This edifying tale had not the slightest basis in fact, but Rome was in need of a foundation saga: a regal Trojan pedigree seemed far more suitable for an Eternal City than the haphazard truth of barefoot shepherds joining forces by the Tiber. Although Aeneas had been revered for centuries, his true celebrity coincided with the birth of the Empire. The first emperor, Augustus, liked to model himself as the New Aeneas, and claimed descent from the Trojan prince; hence his enthusiastic reviews of Virgil's *Aeneid* as the Latin answer to Homer. Lavish Trojan games were celebrated in Rome every year. Above all, special honors were voted for the town of Novum Ilium itself, on the faraway Hellespont: Gifts of money were sent to restore its temples and war graves, while the New Trojans were exempted from paying imperial tribute and taxes. Subsequent emperors followed Augustus' lead. The artistic Nero went so far as to compose his own tortured epic on the city's cataclysm, *The Capture of Troy* (which he allegedly sang, accompanied by the lyre, when Rome burned in A.D. 64).

The imperial passion for all things Trojan filtered down through Roman society. Villas were decorated with statues of the valiant Aeneas fleeing his burning home, carrying his father on his back and leading his young son. Paintings depicted the hero's resolute, noble, very *Roman* face. The Trojan War was a favored topic of refined dinner conversation: Banquets were spent swapping mythological footnotes to the siege, comparing the imagery of Homer to that of Virgil. There were dozens of lyric poems and plays that fleshed out episodes of the war, and even "eyewitness accounts" supposedly written by humble soldiers from Agamemnon's army. These immensely popular literary hoaxes were packaged as unvarnished, off-the-cuff accounts of the military engagements at Troy, without any of the divine appearances of Zeus, Apollo, and Athena that clutter Homer's poem. An imaginative preamble was included to explain each book's discovery: One had supposedly been found by Cretan shepherds when an earthquake opened a soldier's tomb.

With a lifetime of cultural associations behind them, it's hardly surprising that when Romans set out on their Grand Tours, the firm hand of Aeneas led them directly to the gates of New Troy in northwestern Asia Minor—the sightseer's Elysium.

The residents of Novum Ilium must have been thrilled with their luck. The strategic town, which was resettled in the seventh century B.C.,

had for generations enjoyed a modicum of respect from Homer fans—
even moments of glory when world conquerors like Alexander the
Great, Xerxes, and Julius Caesar came to visit—but afterward had always
sunk back into a provincial torpor. When the Roman emperors suddenly began showering the town with gifts, it was like a gift from the
heavens. Basking in a golden beam of prosperity, the dowdy village-city
was spruced up into a showpiece Tidy Town of the Near East. Throughout the first two centuries A.D., the *Who's Who* of Roman VIPs beat a
path to New Troy—everyone from the poet Ovid to Augustus' daughter Julia, the antiquarian Germanicus, and the emperor Hadrian.

But it was the unofficial Roman visitors—those Homer-loving,
genealogy-tracing citizen-tourists—who were the tourist industry's
bread and butter. Like dewy-eyed Irish-Americans visiting the Gaelic
bogs to behold the ancestral hearth, Roman sightseers converged on the
first "roots tours" to behold the land they felt had shaped their lives.

Naturally, the New Trojans were more than happy to oblige. Teams of
professional guides were formed to welcome each arriving vessel in the
port nearby (Philostratus records 150 boats in the second century A.D.,
making it as crowded as the parking lot at Pompeii today). Although it
was perched on a prominent hill, the outpost that Roman tourists were
led to looked nothing at all like a military fortress; there were no signs of
the walls Homer had described as "massive," "steep," and "beetling,"
nor any "topless towers." Instead, New Troy had the restrained, pious
atmosphere of a quaint religious sanctuary, befitting one of the most
sacred shrines of pagan lore. But the Ilians had no shortage of imaginative tricks to bring the words of Homer to life. They had designed an
evocative battlefield tour woven around the tombs of the war dead,
maintained as memorials in pristine glory, and some extraordinary
"props" from the past.

At the town's highest point, in a temple to Athena, patron of ancient
Troy, the fabulous war relics of Homer's heroes were on display. These
mixed the plausible, like the bronze armor warriors had supposedly
worn in battle—Achilles' shield, Ajax's helmet, Hector's sword—with
the decidedly dubious, such as the lyre Paris was said to have strummed
while wooing the delectable Helen. Even more astonishing were the
anvils the god Zeus had used to bind his wife Hera's feet, as a punishment for meddling in the course of the war. Propped up on marble
pedestals were the bones of Homeric warriors—a femur, a shoulder
blade, a molar—three times the size of a normal man's. And while there
were no remains of the famous Trojan Horse to be found, equestrian

graphics were chiseled all over the temple walls—not to mention every other pillar and sanctuary wall in the town. Last but not least, portraits of Rome's founding father, Aeneas, were stamped on the New Trojan coins, making ideal souvenirs.

New Troy had won the scratch-off lottery of history; it would milk Rome for all it was worth.

In the competitive world of modern tourism, Turks have gone one up on the Ilians.

Truva, or Troy, is today widely regarded as one of the Mediterranean world's greatest disappointments; guidebook after guidebook insists that it's not worth the effort to visit. In fact, the ancient ruins are so notoriously abject that desperate locals have built a giant wooden model Trojan Horse—just to give baffled tourists something to photograph.

Film siren Rossana Podesta portrays the faithless Helen in Helen of Troy, *Hollywood's lavish 1956 retelling of Homer's tale.*

Apparently even this wasn't working, but it was irresistible to me.

After all, the mystique of Troy is as potent now as ever—thanks as much to cinematic versions as Homer's thunderous verse. Today, Homer's screed is admired but rarely read; for modern tastes, its 15,600 lines of mythological digressions, genealogy, formulaic combat, and bombastic rhetoric comprise an all but impenetrable quagmire. It's an effort for us to imagine how utterly revered the *Iliad* was in the Roman era, when it was considered the ultimate text, as profound as Scripture and as insightful as Shakespeare. I was carrying an extraordinary new translation by Stanley Lombardo, which was more approachable: His terse, clipped lines made the narrative crackle again, and the heroes' speeches fluid. But even for those who have never read a line of Homer, the stories of the siege remain brilliantly alive, embedded deep in the Western psyche. In the nineteenth century, the quest to discover "lost Troy" became one of the great historical adventure stories of modern times. And the site can grab headlines: the war of words about the factual basis of Homer's account is as emotionally charged as when the redoubtable "father of field archaeology," Heinrich Schliemann, dug his first spade here in the 1870s. And then there are those endless reruns of *Ulysses* and *Helen of Troy,* circa 1956 . . .

How could you be in Turkey and *not* make the pilgrimage to Troy?

"Even the Ruins Are Ruined"

So noted the poet Annaeus Lucanus, who visited the site around A.D. 60, in the reign of Nero, and used his impressions to describe the tour of Julius Caesar.

> He walked around what had once been Troy, now only a name, and looked for traces of the great wall which the god Apollo had built. But he found the hill clothed with thorny scrub and decaying trees, whose aged roots were embedded in the foundations.

The sight-seeing Caesar, in the poem, doesn't pack up and leave in disappointment, or wish he hadn't bothered. To Romans, the disappearance of Troy's famous fortifications was logical and expected—after all, the city had been caught in a "whirlwind of doom," as Aeschylus said in one play, its glories "ground to dust." So the absence of significant ruins actually added an extra poetic dimension to a visit, allowing visitors to muse poignantly on the fragility of human endeavor. Empires pass; fame and memory endure. "Every stone had a name," notes Lucanus, and Caesar's guide sardonically warns him not to tread on Hector's ghost.

This, I had a feeling, was something that modern visitors might need to keep in mind; standard tourist expectations might have to be left by the wayside.

The nearest town for visits to Troy today lies directly above the pebbly shore of the Dardanelles strait. Çanakkale—pronounced *cha-knuckle-ay*—

is yet another of Turkey's mysteriously faceless cities. It exists to the tune of high-pitched drilling, with every street and building in a perpetual state of renovation from earthquake damage. Its fractured hotel balconies provide ringside seats for the parade of supertankers on their way to the Black Sea; down below, car ferries break loose from the Asian shore and plow through the syrupy waters, describing a wide parabola as they defy the powerful current. On both sides of this two-mile-wide passage—one of the great strategic bottlenecks of history—Ottoman fortresses squat like bloated gargoyles. Turkish air force jets regularly buzz overhead, naval recruits fill the streets, and worried neighbors still rattle sabers over Turkey's dominance of crucial oil shipping lanes.

On our visit, the weather remained resolutely English. Day after day, walls of rain and fog advanced and retreated in subtle tactical maneuvers.

Les wasn't getting any healthier in this damp northern climate, but at least she seemed to be enjoying the view, staring in mesmerized prenatal bliss at the eddying currents. As for me, I wandered the sodden streets of the town, meeting up with provincial scholars at the museums, watching Turkish navy drills, returning with lamb-kebab dinners and bottles of Troy Pilsner, the local brew with—of course!—the silhouette of the Trojan Horse on its label.

We'd been trapped in industrial outposts before, caught by bad weather, and accepted our lot; gloomy Çanakkale was almost a welcome punctuation in our regime of constant travel. But then, on the fourth morning, the skies cleared up without warning. It was like the opening credits of *The Simpsons*. By noon, not a cloud was left in the pearly blue sky. Down below, Turks were blinking at the brilliance with the expressions of coal miners emerged from the pit.

I left Les wrapped in a blanket, pondering the dark waters that Lord Byron had swum (tour companies now help swimmers emulate the feat at a mere $550 a pop), and headed out into that "whirlwind of doom," birthplace of Western civilization's most cherished tales.

From Çanakkale bus station, a crowded *dolmus* was carrying cotton farmers into the fields. It already felt like a serious step back in time. The men sat silently in peaked caps and woolen suit jackets; the women's gold teeth sparkled in the sun as they belly-laughed.

I sat with my knees against my chest, watching the driver work his way, cigarette by cigarette, through the pack. He passed me some Turkish delight. ("Turkish Viagra—with cashew flavor.") Outside, it might have been French wine country; the pastures were filled with canary-yellow wildflowers. But inside the bus, this was definitely Asia. Manic music clawed its way out of the radio. Piled boxes full of fish and cheese swayed in the aisles. Now I knew why one of the infatuated British expatriates I'd spoken to down south had compared rural Turkey to Spain fifty years ago. It felt a million miles away from the coast with its English pubs and ATMs.

The driver stopped outside the Helen Restaurant, which was nearly obliterated by plaster sculptures, and directed me down an empty agricultural road. Overhead, a pair of Turkish F-111s shot past like Apollo's silver arrows; they tore open the sky as they broke the sound barrier. Then it was back to millennial silence, broken only by the scuttling of beetles on the stones.

So this was it—the high road to Troy. I couldn't quite believe it. The approach to the most famous city in history—symbol, in a way, of all man's cities—the place where the ancients felt the historical enmity between East and West had begun.

*A re-creation of the Trojan Horse, a desperate ploy
to lure visitors to the site of Troy.*

The entrance to the site was announced by a ranch house, where the guards were sipping tea from tall glasses, too pleased with the weather to bother charging me the entrance fee. I gathered I was the only visitor that afternoon. A shady path wound directly to the main attraction—a wooden horse standing above a trimmed rose garden.

Today's Trojan Horse isn't quite the "steed of monstrous height" sung by the poets; in fact, it's a bit of a dwarf. It had been lacquered with a staunch dark gloss; the mane was trimmed into a brittle Mohawk. You could climb inside its belly and play Ulysses; windows were inserted for a better view of the flowers. The reconstruction wasn't an entirely risible effort, though. After all, even the guidebook writers who cruelly mocked it had included pictures. It filled a need, obviously, as much as ancient Ilium's guides had needed imaginative props like Paris' lyre.

Naturally, I took several photographs.

A rocky path led out to the hill now called Hissarlik—a spearhead of land jutting above an apple-green plain, which runs five miles out to the indigo sea. Only after drinking in the space and light did I realize that there were some archaeological trenches around my feet. A few haphazard mounds of excavated earth rose like refuse heaps. I'd passed through the legendary Scaean gates of Troy—or at least their foundations—and hadn't even noticed.

Yes, it was undeniably a far stretch from the standardized visions of the city's grandeur—not only Homer's grandiose epithets but all those chintzy film versions. In the execrable *Helen of Troy,* for example, the ancient towers look taller than Babylon's; giant gates swing back and forth, while thirty thousand extras and war chariots charge in and out. Kirk Douglas himself had been needed to get past them in *Ulysses.* But the walls of Troy today look like they've been pulverized by a giant hammer. A sailor passing through the Dardanelles would barely glance at this mutilated hillock—an industrial slag heap, perhaps, or an abandoned Turkish mine?

The frustration is that there has never been just one Troy. Archaeologists have actually found *nine* Troys, each built on the ruins of the last (and just to make things even more confusing, there are forty-seven subdivisions, too). The hill is best thought of as a giant chocolate wafer with layer upon layer of Troys inside. The oldest version of the city, called prosaically enough Troy I, dates back five thousand years. The Troy everyone is actually interested in—Heroic Troy, of Homer's poem, which fell around 1260 B.C.—has been identified as Troy VI. The Roman city of Novum Ilium, or New Troy, is the last exposed layer, called Troy IX.

Despite the glut of Troys on the site, there's not really very much left of *any* of them. The city suffered a second devastation at the end of antiquity. Sacked by Goths from beyond the Black Sea, its port silted, the site was abandoned in the sixth century A.D. Earthquakes and floods did the rest, burying the remains for fifteen hundred years. Modern excavations have exposed slivers of one Troy, fragments of another, the rubble of the next. Of course, just like any ancient tourist, I was compelled to seek out the shreds of Homer's version—Troy VI. And there it was—a single exposed corner of the world's most famous fortress wall, angled and steep, just as the poet promised. I stopped, stared, and—pathetic as the fragment was—couldn't help shuddering with amazement. It was no effort at all to imagine that these stones once echoed with the howls of soldiers.

I could taste the sheer anticipation that ancient sightseers felt when standing on this blood-soaked spot. All along their Grand Tour, Romans had been fed a tantalizing diet of Trojan War bric-a-brac. Rhodes had Helen's personal silver cup, fashioned in the shape of one of her perfect breasts; Sparta the egg from which she emerged (she was the daughter of Leda, who had been violated by Zeus in the form of a swan; the giant egg was probably an African ostrich's). A temple in southern Italy displayed the carpentry tools that the Greeks had supposedly used to build the Trojan Horse; cities in Asia proudly showed the papyrus letters of warriors to their loved ones. But nothing could compare to standing on the hallowed turf of Troy itself—or drinking in the famous view of the seashore. By the time of Roman visits, fourteen centuries of silt had already begun to distort the coastline. But, miraculously, everything else about the topography fit the precise descriptions of Homer: the landing cove with its "gaping mouth, enclosed by the jaws of two jutting headlands" (now called Besika Bay); the course of the two rivers, the Simoïs and the Scamander; the locations of the burbling freshwater springs. On clear days, ancient tourists could make out the mountainous island of Samothrace in the distance, from where the god Poseidon, swathed in pale sea mist, had watched the battles.

After dinner on their first evening, the tourists would leave their inns and gaze down upon the moonlit scene, perhaps reciting one of the most beloved passages from Homer, when the Trojan soldiers camped before the foray they hoped would shatter the siege:

> *The Trojans had great notions that night,*
> *Sitting on the bridge of war by their watchfires.*

Stars: crowds of them in the sky, sharp
In the moonglow when the wind falls
And all the cliffs and hills and peaks
Stand out and the air shears down
From heaven, and all the stars are visible
And the watching shepherd smiles.

So the bonfires between the Greek ships
And the banks of the Xanthus, burning
On the plain before Ilion.

Gazing out at that storied scene, I could almost smell the smoke; once again, the past was lurching to life.

THRUST AND PARRY FOR HELEN

The next morning at dawn, the tourists prepared for a sight-seeing routine that was by now almost second nature to them. After a perfunctory breakfast of bread dipped in wine, they sallied forth to meet the Ilian guides, accompanied by servants carrying simple food for lunch— cheese, olives, fruit—a spare cloak in case of rain, and the papyrus guidebook. Many would also have copies of Homer and Virgil—even though educated Romans knew the lines of both by heart. Some had no doubt picked up the pulpy "eyewitness accounts" of Trojan heroes; like war comics, unpoetic, but full of the clash of swordplay and the dust of the plains.

And then they set off down the hill to the world's most famous battlefield.

We can reconstruct the standard format of the tour from such disparate sources as Strabo's *Geography*, Philostratus' biography of Apollonius, Tacitus' description of Germanicus' visit, and accounts of Hadrian's trip in A.D. 120. It began with a visit to the beach where the Greeks' thousand black-hulled ships had made the first recorded amphibious landing. The warriors in boar's-tusk helmets had forced their way onto Asian soil against stiff Trojan resistance; the armada was soon moored by the "gray churning surf," the tents of troops making a miniature city in the grass. As ever, the historical was mixed with the mythological: Roman tourists clamored to see the actual cave where the Trojan prince Paris judged the beauty contest between Hera, Athena, and Aphrodite, starting the goddesses' jealousy that would dog mortals throughout the war, and the exact spot where Zeus, shaped as an eagle, swept down on the handsome Trojan prince Ganymede and carried him off to be his wine bearer in Olympus.

As the tour groups proceeded inland, the landmarks allowed them to relive the story. *Here* was the site where Achilles, the greatest Greek warrior, had argued with commander King Agamemnon, and in his majestic sulk threatened to abandon the campaign. Over *there* was where Achilles' lover, Patroclus, was killed by the Trojans, inspiring Achilles with a new lust for blood. *Here* was where Achilles cornered and slew Hector, the greatest of the Trojan warriors (the *Iliad* actually ends at this point; the rest of the Troy tale is recounted in myriad poems and plays). *This* was where the Wooden Horse was built, *here* it was found by the Trojans. *This* was the spot where the skeptic Laocoön denounced the Horse as a trick—and for his pains was plucked, with his sons, into the sea by a giant serpent. This divine signal convinced the Trojans that the Horse was a genuine gift, convincing them to go on their all-night drunken bender . . .

The conclusion of the tale hardly needs repeating.

Next stop on the tours were the graves of the war dead—not the common foot soldiers, but Homer's heroes. To keep Roman interest at fever pitch, the Ilians made sure there were helpful visual aids: Each tumulus, or funerary mound, was crowned by a fine statue of the character whose bones and ashes lay inside; Ilian priests kept a small fire burning year-round at his feet.

The hands-down favorite, out on the windy Sigeum promontory, was the tomb of Achilles, the Homeric killing machine—invulnerable except for his famous heel. This was the perfect place for Roman tourists' displays of *pietas* (religious piety). They anointed its weathered stones with oil and perfume, garlanded the statue with fragrant flowers, and burned incense at its base. The more sophomoric ran around the tomb three times naked, mimicking Achilles' chase of Hector around Troy's walls (Alexander the Great had repeated the feat). Two miles east, doused by ocean waves at high tide, lay the cairn of Ajax, the Greeks' second-string warrior. This was the scene of one of ancient tourism's most memorable events: around A.D. 120, the burial mound collapsed from erosion and revealed the bones of a powerful giant. Awestruck Ilian priests measured the hero's skeleton at eleven cubits (seventeen feet) high. No less a personage than the emperor Hadrian himself traveled to

New Troy to restore the grave, with all the pomp and ceremony the occasion demanded. He reverently placed the bones in a new marble tomb, kissing and embracing them as he did so.

Again and again, the discovery of "heroes' bones" would prove a tourist boon for Ilium. The most sensational moment came in A.D. 170, when the collapse of a coastal cliff exposed dozens of monstrous skulls and rib cages; sightseers sailed from all over the Aegean to inspect skeletons over thirty feet in length, many purloining them as souvenirs. (In her study, *The First Fossil Hunters,* Adrienne Mayor suggests that they were probably the remains of mastodons from the Pleistocene epoch; to the untrained eye, the skeletons of these giant mammals appear to be enormous human bones. Roman scientists including Pliny the Elder studied them closely, and mourned the fact that mortals were obviously becoming punier with the passage of time.)

After Achilles and Ajax came the Trojan tombs—King Priam was buried there, as was Paris, with his jilted wife. The local favorite was naturally Hector—the noble, doomed family man who gave his life to defend Troy, despite his conviction that Helen and Paris' adultery was wrong. It was the perfect site for soulful musings on filial duty: Many a Roman was moved to record his thoughts, such as Germanicus in A.D. 18, who composed an epigram, "On the Barrow of Hector." Unfortunately, the lines are now lost.

In such an emotionally charged, evocative locale—Troy was more a pagan Jerusalem than a historic Gettysburg—it's hardly surprising that some Roman tourists had visions.

Specters of the heroes might be encountered at night, illuminated by flashes of lightning; even at noon, the clash of arms could be heard as the pair eternally reenacted their famous duel. The statues astride their burial mounds were credited with supernatural powers by local herdsmen. Achilles' image—a dandyish figure, apparently, wearing a fine cloak and earrings—foretold the future: If it was covered with moisture, floods were coming; a layer of dust meant drought; if it was speckled with blood, that meant plague. Hector's statue was sometimes seen to breathe; during Troy's annual athletic games, it perspired in empathy with the competitors. An Assyrian traveler who foolishly insulted Hector's statue was drowned soon afterward in a raging river; eyewitnesses said that an armored man ordered the waters to rise. And shepherds kept their flocks away from the tomb of Ajax: the Greek hero had gone mad at the end of his life and started slaughtering sheep, so it was said that the grass around his grave was poisonous.

Christians accepted that Troy was a powerful node of pagan belief and avoided it on their journeys. If forced to travel nearby, they continually crossed themselves—and as they passed Troy's haunted tombs, they hissed between their teeth to ward off evil spirits.

The ghost tales were fascinating, if a little unnerving, for the Romans. But at least one visitor actively sought out the supernatural: Apollonius of Tyana, the pagan holy man. According to his biography, he took the standard Troy Battlefield Tour in the mid-first century, then at dusk alarmed his followers by announcing that he would spend the night alone at Achilles' tomb:

"O Achilles!" Apollonius chants after dark. "Most of mankind declare that you are dead, but I do not agree with them. If I am correct, then show yourself to me . . .

"Thereupon a minor earthquake shook the area around the tomb, and a man came forth eight foot high, wearing a Thessalian cloak."

Apparently Achilles is far more handsome than his statue suggests, with rippling muscles, long flowing hair, and "the first down of youth" on his cheeks—the contemporary Greek pinup boy. The ghost then grows to twenty feet in height and—in exchange for a promise that Apollonius will travel to his birthplace in Thessaly—allows Apollonius to ask five questions. To modern ears, the queries he chooses are painfully obscure, focusing on the *Iliad*'s finer details: Why does Homer not mention a Greek hero called Palamedes? Was Helen really brought to Troy, or was she hidden in Egypt as some suggest? Is Achilles buried in the way Homer describes? Were there really as many great heroes in the war as Homer says? Yes, answers the ghost—for "at that time excellence flourished all over the earth."

Achilles then vanishes "with a flash of summer lightning" just as dawn is breaking.

If a modern traveler were put in the same position as Apollonius, the first question would be far more basic: Did the Trojan War ever *really* happen?

Nobody in antiquity ever doubted the historical reality of the Trojan War. The opinion that Homer's epic was a fantasy emerged only in the modern era, when travelers battled their way to the Dardanelles and found no trace of the pagan sanctuary—just fields of brushwood crossed by shepherds and camel traders. Romantic visitors grasped at straws. But in the absence of physical evidence, most historians became convinced that the *Iliad* was a beautiful fiction. King Agamemnon, Achilles, Helen, and Hector were fairy-tale figures.

Famously, it was the larger-than-life adventurer Heinrich Schliemann who in the early 1870s argued that not only did Troy exist, it could be found by using the *Iliad* as a guidebook. He identified key passages that corresponded to physically identifiable locations and decided that the undistinguished hill of Hissarlik was really the Homeric site. As a fellow excavator later joked, it was as if Schliemann's tiny wire-rimmed spectacles gave him X-ray vision. The balding, beetlelike German, accompanied by his Greek mail-order bride, proceeded to dig a series of trenches that revealed an ancient fortress, and then a cache of treasure—weapons, diadems, 60 earrings, and no less than 8,750 small gold ornaments (for dramatic effect, Schliemann combined all the objects he'd found over the course of three years into the one "find"—a rampant case of result fudging, but the artifacts themselves were authentic). Schliemann proclaimed the cache to be King Priam's treasure and took photographs of his wife wearing the jewels of Helen.

It seemed as if Schliemann really had found Homer's Troy—until it was proven that the artifacts were around a thousand years too old to correspond to any Bronze Age invasion by Greeks. It was left to another German, Wilhelm Dörpfeld, to solve the riddle in 1894. It was he who proved that there were in fact a smorgasbord of nine different Troys. In his excitement, Schliemann had delved down to Troy II—circa 2500 B.C. Dörpfeld identified the parts of Troy VI we can now see—the imposing, angled bastion that fell within the time frame of Homer's war.

Unfortunately, this in itself did not prove that the Trojan War had ever occurred.

Today, while there is still violent dispute over the historical basis of Homer's war, most archaeologists accept that there is a kernel of truth to the story.

The most thoughtful assessment to date is given by Michael Wood in his book *In Search of the Trojan War*. Although the finer details can never be proven, evidence for some sort of conflict is now considerable. In 1275–60 B.C., a Bronze Age Greek force probably *did* mount an amphibious invasion of Troy and lay siege to its imposing walls. The Greeks' motive may well have been disappointingly unromantic—seizing the trading routes from the Aegean to the Black Sea. And it's certainly not *impossible* that a Spartan woman named Helen was abducted to Troy; the capture of women as prisoners was a common practice in that piratical era. The leader of the Greek alliance may well have been called King

Agamemnon, and given the chaotic relations among cities at that time, he certainly would have spent much energy in controlling his unruly gaggle of self-serving warlords from around Greece.

Even the Trojan Horse—the least plausible but arguably most beloved part of the tale—may be an imaginative reinvention of a real event. One hypothesis explaining the fall of Troy is that an earthquake shattered the impregnable fortress (there is some evidence for this at the site). The horse was sacred to Poseidon, god of the sea and earthquakes, and the triumphant Greek warriors may have left a cult statue of a wooden horse as a thanks offering when they departed.

Homer himself—if he was only one man, and his works aren't a composite of different poets—didn't visit Troy until around 750 B.C., five hundred years after the fact. By then, Greek storytellers had already turned the war into a national epic of gods and heroes.

Whatever the original facts, Troy was rebuilt on Greek mythomania.

The Eternal
Killing Fields

As the return *dolmuş* barreled back through the vegetable patches to Çanakkale, I had to wonder: What was it about the Dardanelles and patriotic myths?

In the Middle Ages, both the British and French royal courts claimed to trace their lineage back to the original Trojan refugees—just as Roman emperors had looked to Aeneas. Then, in the early twentieth century, two even more remote countries proclaimed that they were "born" of a defeat on the Dardanelles. Today, their citizens come in droves to pay homage to the war graves, join battlefield tours, lay wreaths, and pour libations—very much as the Romans did. Their governments fund special commissions to make sure that the war graves are kept intact.

Improbably enough, those distant lands are *Australia* and *New Zealand*.

One spring dawn in 1915, the age-old conflict of East versus West was replayed on a grisly industrialized scale when a huge amphibious force stormed ashore on the peninsula opposite Troy, called Gallipoli. The Allies, led by the British and under the command of the young Winston Churchill, planned in one bold stroke to knock the Ottoman Empire out of World War I; the ANZACs (Australian and New Zealand Army Corps) were chosen as the most expendable shock troops. They were pinned down on the beaches and slaughtered by the thousand before gaining a tenuous fingerhold on the coast, while the Turks settled in to brutal trench warfare—with obscene losses on both sides. The stench of rotting corpses filled the air for miles around (as one observer memorably put it: "The smell of death was tangible . . . and clammy as the membrane of a bat's wing"). Finally, after nine months of carnage, the Allies withdrew.

As one of the most futile campaigns in the most futile of wars, Gallipoli might have sunk into the black hole of history. But for the Australians particularly, the loss of so many young men in the country's first full-scale war—8,587 killed, nearly 20,000 wounded—was a national trauma, a shocking swath of casualties that had torn through the small population. Nationalists hailed Gallipoli as a "baptism of fire." The day of the invasion, April 25, 1915, is still commemorated with undiminished emotion each year in Australia. Every little town has its ANZAC parade. Endless books and newspaper articles annually explore the event. It was the subject of one of Australia's first international hit movies, *Gallipoli,* starring the fresh-faced Mel Gibson.

Thousands of Aussies make the pilgrimage to the battlefield every year—mostly young backpackers, who include Gallipoli in their Grand Tours somewhere between the running of the bulls in Pamplona and Oktoberfest in Munich.

The Turks have certainly buried the hatchet. Dusting the Trojan soil from my boots, I dropped by ANZAC House, the biggest backpacker hotel in Çanakkale and a Middle Eastern shrine to suburban Sydney. In the hostel's café were jars of Vegemite stacked up for the breakfast toast. There were towels emblazoned with koalas pinned to the walls, photos of the Opera House, and football stars. The Turkish desk clerk grunted "G'day, mate" with a pitch-perfect Paul Hogan twang, while in the back room, a TV showed a scratchy video of *Gallipoli* on a perpetual loop: Mel in army fatigues, the Aussie Achilles preparing to die for eternal glory.

"'Ow are yuz?" said a Turkish guy in a Bondi Beach T-shirt (it turned out he'd once run a kebab restaurant in Sydney's Woolloomooloo).

I asked about the battlefield tours they operated every day.

"Too easy, mate. Captain Ali will see you right."

The desk clerk chimed in: "Captain Ali's tops. Used to be a submarine commander in the Turkish navy. Knows everything there is to know about military yarns. Just get here at nine A.M.—*sharp,* eh?"

I paid up with a sinking feeling. Despite the obvious parallel with Roman war buffs visiting Troy, I felt an unexpected resistance to this particular blast from the past.

As it happens, my great-uncle fought in the Gallipoli invasion. He was killed there, at the age of twenty-two. Lesley's grandfather was wounded there.

Perhaps it was impending paternity again, but it all seemed a little too close to home.

BEWARE OF GREEKS CREATING MYTHICAL ARCHETYPES

At 0900 hours precisely, Captain Ali appeared in the doorway of ANZAC House and cast a disapproving eye around the messy dining room. He was short and intense, without an ounce of fat. His silver hair was trim and slicked down. In his peacoat and creased trousers, with a pillbox naval cap that emphasized his large ears, he looked like Starbuck from *Moby Dick*.

Methodically, he checked off his clients from a clipboard, then frowned. Two people were missing—apparently they'd gone to the bathroom.

Captain Ali shook his head at the suggestion of waiting. "We have a ferry to catch," he barked. At 0903, he strode purposefully out into the street, leaving us racing to catch up.

At 0910, he looked at his wristwatch with a weary, knowing smile. The ferry was late, as it always is in Turkey. The two people who went to the bathroom caught up with panicked looks on their faces. They'd learned a valuable lesson: Stragglers will be left behind the lines.

Two hours later, on the opposite shore, Captain Ali was talking about carnage—unimaginable stupidity and waste. He swept his arms dramatically across the stony beach of Anzac Cove, explaining how the Australians had landed at this location by a tragic mistake—following a light buoy that came adrift in the night—only to be trapped in the surf beneath a steep bluff. It was the First World War's version of Omaha Beach, with corpses clogging the waves.

Captain Ali—nobody ever referred to him by any other name, as if he'd been born with the title—was unexpectedly eloquent for a submarine commander: In fact, he was the ultimate military guide, the New New Trojan, who spoke with the mixture of envy and compassion peculiar to officers who have never seen action. He orated with a distant expression, as if he were reliving the battle itself. At the most poignant moments, his eyes welled up with tears. Then he paused, embarrassed by his emotion: "Historical fact! Tell it to your children."

The blueprint of Ali's tour might have been taken from the Romans'. At a small museum, he carefully pointed out the sacred curiosities— skulls with bullets embedded in them, photos of the battle, bayonets, uniforms. Just as ancient temples reverently stored the papyrus correspondence of Trojan veterans, there was a letter from a young Turkish soldier to his mother, describing the beauty of the cornfields and poppies. He was killed—needless to say—two days later. There was a ritualistic element to the displays, as well as to Ali's anecdotes: Their motifs of war must include tales of sensitive youth untimely plucked. Common soldiers must survive against incredible odds. And there must be unexpected humanity among the savagery—assistance of the wounded and informal truces (enemies tossing one another food and drink at festivals, or playing games between the trenches). These are our conventional images of combat, which turn up like some cathartic roster in everything from *All Quiet on the Western Front* to *Full Metal Jacket,* and they all derive from Homer's *Iliad.*

Anzac Cove was the most incongruous place on earth to be talking about slaughter. The day was even more brilliant than when I went to Troy, and we were all lounging about on the downy green grass as if in a picnic scene from Renoir. The golden sun, the lapping waves, the warm sea breeze—it made the idea of Turks killing Aussies more absurd than ever.

Captain Ali turned sternly toward the first cemetery. "Five minutes!" he barked.

After a snack of Vegemite sandwiches, Captain Ali led us into the hills where the most ferocious battles occurred between trenches that were only five yards apart. Whole companies of men were mowed down within seconds of putting their heads above the dirt. For every six feet of soil that each side gained, a thousand lives were lost. The topography of the area seemed to change as bodies were piled into artificial hillsides. Even today, the millions of cartridges and shards of shrapnel turn the soil into a glittering metal mosaic.

At least the commander of the Turkish forces, Mustafa Kemal—later Atatürk, father of the nation—was frank with his troops: "I order you not simply to attack," he told them cheerily, "but to die. And in the time it takes us to die, other troops will arrive to take our places."

"We call this the Hill of Courage," Captain Ali said. "We Turks respect suicidal valor."

The Australians looked at one another uneasily. We weren't so keen on suicidal valor.

At last, we arrived at Lone Pine Cemetery, a lawn surrounded by cenotaphs engraved with thousands of names of the dead. It's a memorial for those without graves.

"Five minutes, ladies and gentlemen!"

The marble panels were blinding in the afternoon sun. There it was: B.J. PERROTTET. 1ST MAY, 1915. AGE 22. I ran my finger over the golden letters, amazed that they had spelled our name right. He'd lasted only six days here in Gallipoli. I thought of a line from the *Iliad,* about a wounded Trojan soldier:

> *[He] breathed out his life stretched on the ground*
> *Like an earthworm in a pool of black blood.*

At first, Lone Pine seemed poles apart from the war memorials of New Troy, so beloved by the Romans. The ancients glorified their individual superheroes and sang the praises of Achilles and Hector; the mass graves of Gallipoli convey the slaughter of humble soldiers, many of whose bodies were never identified. The idea of glorious war has taken a serious battering.

But the final effect of both battlefield tours wasn't so different. No Roman tourist would have left the Dardanelles skipping with joy about the human condition.

Coincidentally, nowhere was this clearer than at the ancient site of Gallipoli itself, which Romans would visit on sailing day trips from Ilium. At the tip of the peninsula—a few miles from where Lone Pine Cemetery stands today—they found the most ambiguous of all ancient war shrines, the tomb of the Greek soldier Protesilaus, first casualty of the Trojan War.

As Homer relates, the gods had decreed that the first Greek soldier to step ashore in Asia would die. In a scene worthy of *Saving Private Ryan,* young Protesilaus decided to sacrifice himself for the cause. He leaped first from the ship—and was immediately speared.

His body was given lavish honors by the Greeks—they certainly respected "suicidal valor." By the Roman era, Protesilaus' ashes were still kept in a small temple on the Gallipoli peninsula, surrounded by divinely blessed elm trees: Every time their leaves reached a height from which the Asian shore was visible, they miraculously withered—reenacting the warrior's sad fate. And ancient tourists could ponder how Protesilaus' decision had had consequences far from the battlefield. Back home in Thessaly, his wife tore her face in grief, and eventually committed suicide; the house they were building together burned; his father went mad.

It was a place that commemorated the hidden cost of heroism.

For all their bluster about glory, the ancients weren't blind to the downside of war. In Homer, death in battle is never a pretty sight. Wounded warriors scream in agony until seized by "hateful darkness"; the prospect of Hades is cold comfort. Even Achilles meditates around the campfire on the futility of the soldier's life. He reappears in the *Odyssey* as a lonely ghost in the underworld, confessing that he would rather be alive as the lowliest slave on a peasant's farm than lord of all the hosts of Hades. In fact, much of the poetic force of the *Iliad* comes from its unflagging reference to the domestic lives soldiers left behind—those distant villages alive with farming, threshing, plowing, goat herding.

Homer's broader message in the *Iliad* is also rather bleak. Troy, symbol of all great cities, was doomed by its own civilized achievements, which made it vulnerable to the rampaging Greeks; any era of peace, by softening its benefactors, contains the seeds of its own demise. Romans readily believed this idea (as indeed do many people today, amid our own span of comfort). They loved to scourge themselves for their love of luxury, and predict their own imminent decline. Troy was the perfect place to meditate on the coming holocaust.

But what did all really matter, the *Iliad* finally asks—the end of one life or an entire culture?

> *Human generations are like leaves in their season.*
> *The wind blows them to the ground, but the tree*
> *Sprouts new ones when spring comes again.*
> *Men too. Their generations come and go.*

It was getting dark when Ali launched into his last, emotional oration:

"My dear ladies and gentlemen. Have many children. They will be the apple of your own parents' eyes, and make them happy."

The backpackers and I don't know quite how to react here at this serene slaughter site; we resist the urge to salute, and quietly applaud.

After drifting back to Çanakkale on the ferry in the starry dusk, I pick up some *kefta* for dinner. The smell of spiced lamb is delicious; fresh olives and basil leaves are on the side.

Les is up in our room, reading. She seems to be feeling a little better, but the urchin has been kicking a lot today. I try to feel him with my hand, usually an absentminded gesture for me.

I'm surprised how emotionally drained I feel. This is all too profound, this life-and-death thing. Way too serious for me.

Under a brilliant full moon, the straits are so calm they seem to have stopped flowing.

The whole city is still under that bright night sky. Even Hector and Achilles must be asleep tonight, dreaming of their distant hearths.

Sailing from Byzantium

IN ANCIENT TIMES, a Roman tourist would have picked up a merchant vessel going from any of a half-dozen busy ports along the Hellespont to Alexandria. So I went back one night to the docks of Istanbul, looking for a ship—any ship—heading south.

Commuter ferries were roaring along the Golden Horn in the dark, their horns echoing like emergency sirens, the brilliant lights of the minarets shimmering in their wake. Fishing skiffs were tied up alongside the dock, their crews grilling sardines on open coals. All along the waterfront, warehouses had been converted into showrooms for rich Russians. Each one was a makeshift Macy's filled with furs and floor tiles, carpets and kitchen sinks, Volvos and frozen meat.

Like any ancient traveler looking for a berth, I climbed the gangplanks of the ocean liners in dock. Some were going to Athens and Cyprus. One to Odessa. None to Egypt.

My fundamental idea on this trip was to use forms of transport equivalent to the Romans'; but thanks to Egypt's political turmoil over the last decade, passenger-ship services had withered and died. I'd been researching this voyage since our arrival in Italy, following up rumors of freight ships that might carry passengers, but I was still no closer to getting a cabin.

Sailors knitted their brows when I persisted: Why would I even *want* to go to Alexandria? And why by sea? It seemed an inexplicable request.

I was starting to wonder if this wasn't some kind of message to call it quits. After Troy—all that mortality stuff—I did have doubts about the wisdom of dragging Les in her fragile state along the gangrenous fringes of the Nile.

I made a list of the pros and cons. On the plus side for Egypt: one of the world's great travel destinations; a warm, dry climate. After all, ancient aristocrats were always being sent there for their health; the young Seneca spent years in Egypt for a respiratory disorder.

On the minus side: overwhelming crowds; pollution; disease; squalor; terrorism.

The next day, I bought two plane tickets. Our only alternative was swimming.

PART SEVEN

ALEXANDRIA
AD AEGYPTUM

Cleopatra's Capital,
"On the Way to Egypt"

What is the city over the mountains
Cracks and reforms and bursts in the violet air
Falling towers
Jerusalem Athens Alexandria
Vienna London
Unreal

　　　　T. S. ELIOT, *The Waste Land*

ON THE ROSTER of civilization's most brilliant and ephemeral creations, ancient Alexandria has always received top billing. The excitement began a full thirty miles out to sea, when lookouts first glimpsed the Pharos—the three-tiered lighthouse, as high as the Statue of Liberty, whose enormous flame glowed in the night like an orange star. As dawn broke, passengers crowded the decks to gape at the limestone structure towering above their ships' masts. The Pharos was the seventh Wonder of the World, the only one with a practical purpose, and ancient souvenirs bearing its likeness have turned up as far away as Afghanistan. Beside the lighthouse, six statues of Ptolemaic kings and queens in pharaonic regalia stood forty feet high; stately palm trees swayed among them, brushing their shoulders like the fans of attentive slaves.

It was an impeccably choreographed introduction to the most ravishing of Rome's possessions—Aegyptus, Egypt. When Alexandria was founded in 331 B.C. by Alexander the Great, the city burst onto the world stage as both Queen of the Mediterranean and Mistress of the Nile; it flowered as the world's capital of science and the luxurious retreat of Cleopatra and Antony during their larger-than-life romance. Now, for those eager ancient sightseers leaning over the bulwarks of their galleys, the port had a new lease on life as the eastern pole of the Roman Empire—the true crossroads of the continents, a clearinghouse for spices, glass, papyrus, and Nubian slaves, as well as for geometrical theorems and astronomical charts. And with over half a million inhabitants,

Alexandria was the only city on earth that could genuinely rival Rome in size, ambition, and grandeur; it made Athens, its intellectual parent, seem like a feeble elder.

Alexandria's contagious energy was felt by new arrivals even before they set foot on shore. The Eastern Harbor had nine miles of bustling docks, and the face of the waterfront rose in a gleaming tidal wave of extravagant architecture—"temples pompous with lofty roofs," as the fourth-century soldier-historian Ammianus Marcellinus reported, each bristling with obelisks and adorned with sphinxes. Enormous freighters loaded grain to feed Rome; African merchants led camel trains through the crowds; snow-white ibis picked their way among the cargoes; the sea itself was sweetened by the effluence of the Nile, the world's greatest river, whose annual rise and fall was regulated by the gods.

Beyond the city gates lay Egypt immemorial, where the most astonishing monuments on earth basked in the haunted desert—the Pyramids, the Sphinx, the Temples of Karnak—all attended by shaven-headed priests, who buried embalmed corpses in the sand and read magical hieroglyphs. This was the true climax of the Roman Grand Tour—an entire alien universe where the fundamental secrets of life and death might be explored. And Alexandria was the spectacular halfway point, a signpost for the tourists' paradise.

The city was properly known as *Alexandria Ad Aegyptum* (Alexandria on the way to Egypt), and at heart it remained an island of Greco-Roman culture on the fringe of Africa. The last dynasty of Pharaohs, the Ptolemies, who had made the city their capital before the Roman conquest in 30 B.C., were actually Greeks, descended from one of Alexander the Great's generals; only Cleopatra, the last queen of Egypt, had even bothered to learn the Egyptian tongue. Under Roman rule, Alexandria's unique isolation became even more rarefied. Here was a city that eagerly practiced every Nilotic superstition, from the worship of the goddess Isis and her lover Osiris to the macabre rite of mummification—and yet where native-born Egyptians from the interior were allowed only as laborers and servants. The first apartheid laws forbade Romans, Greeks, and Egyptians from intermarrying or passing on property. For their part, Egyptians of the era dismissed the alien city of Alexandria as *Ra-qed* (the building site). Its existence was a shallow, transient intrusion on the timeless face of the Nile.

But for ancient tourists, Alexandria was a phenomenon in its own right, a self-contained enclave that was neither Roman, Greek, nor Egyptian—and was utterly, fatally romantic.

Visitors allowed themselves to be swept up in its whirlwind the moment they disembarked—throwing themselves at the mercy of the Alexandrian service industry, itself a bewildering phenomenon where the now-familiar retinue of inns, guides, restaurants, and souvenir shops achieved maximum efficiency. Dazed and confused, new arrivals edged along the Canopic Way—one hundred feet wide, it was the Champs-Élysées of its time—dodging chariots, beggars, and vendors. Many, as the romance novelist Achilles Tatius describes, were simply agog at the splendor, gaping like yokels: "I tried to visit every avenue, but . . . I could not absorb the beauty all at once. Some parts of the city I saw, other parts I missed; some parts I desperately tried to see, but found others I could not pass by. . . . Finally, I cried out in exhaustion, 'Give up, my eyes—we are beaten.' " They followed papyrus guidebooks such as *On Alexandria* by Callixeinus to the tomb of Alexander the Great in the royal cemetery of the Ptolemies, where the world conqueror was embalmed in honey and encased in glass. From there they rushed to the Museion, or House of the Muses, the world's first government-funded research facility, where Archimedes and Euclid had once worked. Its most famous wing was the Great Library of Alexandria, which was built to house every book on earth under one roof—seven hundred thousand volumes. In its luminous reading rooms, dozens of academics muttered away to themselves, creating a din like an angry horde of bees (reading in silence was never the ancient rule).

On the way, Alexandrians were tourist attractions in themselves: They were known to be arrogant, opinionated, fractious, and rambunctious, willing to riot on any pretext. But their work ethic was a revelation— they labored diligently from dawn until dusk, in complete contrast to the lazy, idling citizens of Rome whose bellies were filled on handouts of Nile wheat. "Everyone plies a trade here," marveled one second-century Roman visitor. "Even the gouty, the blind and arthritic."

For a new class of corporate Egyptians, life was for making money— and spending it.

Roman tourists eagerly joined them in the latter. They sampled the city's culinary specialties—lamb kebabs, nicknamed obelisks for their slender skewers, accompanied by a date wine so potent, it was said, that "even the Gods wet themselves in their soft beds when they imbibed"; for dessert, they savored pyramid cakes—rock-hard sesame sweets that threatened to break teeth. Tourists bargained for Egyptian linens—the finest in the known world, these could be sheer to the point of transparency—and scoured the markets for exotic rarities: tortoiseshells from

the Land of the Troglodytes, pepper from Sumatra, shark teeth from the
Red Sea, insects petrified in amber, Persian pearls, Chinese silks (as Aristides said in A.D. 140, the only thing you couldn't purchase in Alexandria
was snow). They visited busy synagogues—a quarter of the population
was Jewish, a far higher percentage than in Rome. And they made sure
to attend a kithara concert, since cosmopolitan Alexandria was the
acknowledged capital of ancient music, where even illiterate shopkeepers could identify a false note.

And if it was less-edifying entertainment you were after, along the
coast to the east lay the resort village of Canopus, whose reputation for
profligacy was second only to Baiae's. Here were the most outrageous
inns and nightclubs of Egypt, devoted to every form of decadent pleasure. Below the windows, drunken revelers would cruise in gondolas
across lotus-strewn canals, competing to sing the loudest; their boats
slipped back and forth beneath the palm trees; guests feasted to the
accompaniment of flutes while almond-eyed dancing girls shimmied and
stripped. The ebony-skinned courtesans of Ethiopia made fashionable
conquests for Romans, commanding high prices. ("Whoever loves
Nigra burns over black coals," read one graffito in Italy. "When I see
Nigra, I gladly eat blackberries.") Some expensive hotel rooms had
peepholes for observing the carnal calisthenics of fellow guests, either by
arrangement or in secret.

As Dio the Golden-Tongued wrote, life in Alexandria was "a continuous revel . . . of dancers, whistlers and murderers."

It was as if travelers today found themselves transported to Weimar
Berlin.

A TRYST AT THE CECIL

It must be admitted that arriving in Alexandria today is not quite the
glamorous experience of antiquity. Like most visitors, we slipped into the
city by the back door, on a vintage bus from the airport, then plunged
with fixed smiles into the surging seas of Third World tourism—dodging
the invigorating cascade of porters grabbing our bags, taxi drivers clutching our shoulders, hotel touts pulling our arms (many of them ingeniously dressed in suits and ties, with fake photo IDs from the Egyptian
Tourist Authority). In a plaza, hundreds of beat-up taxis were being
driven around in a huge corral, kicking up clouds of dust like some aimless demolition derby. At random we hailed a cab whose driver was
named—surprisingly—Ahmed.

After fifteen minutes of haggling, I congratulated myself on my bargaining skills, having beaten Ahmed down from his astronomical starting price to a mere fistful of dollars—until it turned out the destination was only five hundred yards away.

"This is it?" I gaped out at the Cecil Hotel. "You're charging twenty dollars for this?"

"Fifteen percent tip in addition," Ahmed suggested, then offered to take any duty-free liquor instead.

All this, I supposed, dragging the bags into the lobby, was as it should be. Alexandrians had always been notorious for their financial acumen. It was here, after all, that one second-century Roman traveler had so memorably proclaimed: "They worship only one god here—*Cash!*"

I was desperate to set eyes on the most illustrious harbor in the Mediterranean. At last, a pair of salt-splattered louver windows creaked open and I leaned out over Alex's waterfront, breathing in the crisp sea air. There

The Corniche, the celebrated promenade of Alexandria.

was the serpentine arc of the Corniche, the grand boulevard, sweeping into the distance with the purity of line reminiscent of a Matisse. Along its perfect parabola, men in long robes darted in and out of traffic, deftly avoiding buses and horse-drawn carts. At the farthest promontory, almost out to sea, squatted Fort Qait-Bey: This was once the site of the Pharos, the ever-burning lighthouse crowned by Zeus the Savior, greeting all newcomers. The panoramic view was doubly alluring, since modern Alexandria's reputation is no less potent than the ancient city's. Relatively recent visitors such as Flaubert, Gide, Rimbaud, Cavafy, and E. M. Forster immortalized the city's oriental mystique. Most famously, Lawrence Durrell, a resident during World War II, conjured an alluring setting in his *Alexandria Quartet*. His Alex was a steamy, voluptuous, sinister entrepôt, an Arabic version of Shanghai—a "winepress of love," "seductive and divine," with "five races, five languages . . . five fleets, turning through their greasy reflections behind the harbor bar."

By a pleasing historical coincidence, Alexandria's British-era hotels were built above the epicenter of the ancient city—and in an optimistic grab at nostalgia, we'd booked into the most notorious. Wartime headquarters of General Montgomery, scene of adulterous trysts of Durrell's lovers, the Cecil Hotel is actually the most celebrated lodging place in all Egypt, the Raffles of the Near East, and thanks to Egypt's tourist slump it was offering deep, deep discounts. For days, we'd been rubbing our hands in anticipation of faded colonial luxury; I could see us sipping pink gins in walnut-paneled bars under slowly rotating ceiling fans. But it was not to be. Sometime after the Egyptian revolution of 1952, the owners had decided to give the hotel a major face-lift along the lines of a Caribbean bordello. The walls were now coral pink, the picture rail lime, the ceiling lavender. The raffish charm of the Durrell years was buried beneath a half inch of psychedelic paint; the hotel was all but empty.

"It could be worse," Les opined, crawling contentedly into the king-size bed and turning on the TV. It was the first we'd seen in three months. One of the English-language channels was a cable station from Bombay, which showed nothing but cartoons.

Scooby-Dooby-Doo, Where Are You?

Les was entranced.

"Feel like walking to the Pharos?" I asked.

"Maybe tomorrow," she said, grabbing the room-service menu.

I was starting to wonder about Les's dedication to the cause of ancient research.

"What do you think an Egyptian BLT would be like?" she mused.

I slipped downstairs, out through the lobby—where three Iranian women in black chadors were barking orders into cell phones—and into the grassy square.

So this was once the heart of ancient Alexandria, which, according to the drooling account of the first-century philosopher Philo, was then an astonishing sculpture garden, sparkling with precious metals and row after row of royal sphinxes. Our Hotel Cecil, I calculated, was built above the Emporium, a vast warehouse where all those Chinese silks, Indian spices, and Arabian perfumes were first unloaded. Across the plaza, the Metropole Hotel occupied the site of the Caesareum—a temple begun by Cleopatra originally for Mark Antony in the course of their made-for-Hollywood affair (according to Plutarch, the queen was actually rather plain-looking, but she was irresistibly vivacious and intelligent; Antony's handsome looks, meanwhile, were marred by his "wine-puffed cheeks"). And today, instead of the Temple of Poseidon— an early stop for tourists thankful for a safe sea passage—there was a British Airways office. The modern plaza is certainly not without its frayed charm, graced as it is by cafés left over from the 1930s, art deco relics such as the New Imperial and Les Delices, where waxy pastries with fluorescent icing were being served, and men—always men—were lounging in their cane chairs, sipping potent mint teas and puffing on their water pipes, with the inscrutable stares of camels. Dusty palm trees swayed in the square; women in bright scarves scurried by; shoeshine boys brawled for attention; businessmen discussed the latest real estate coups.

It was all perfectly pleasant. But like every visitor to modern Alexandria, I had to get over an initial confusion. At first glance, the city appeared not much more than a vacation spot for middle-class Egyptians. Its historical remains are shockingly paltry. In fact, it seems to have less in the way of Greco-Roman relics than certain museums in the American Midwest.

I had to remind myself that this was an optical illusion. For some years now, archaeologists have learned that much of ancient Alexandria lies farther north—in the middle of that serene empty harbor. Somewhere, below the waterline, scuba divers were salvaging the city's illustrious past, and putting the ancient city back on the world map.

The New Atlantis

UNTIL A FEW YEARS AGO, Alexandria had made quite a career of disillusioning its admirers. Nineteenth-century archaeologists were frankly appalled: They could find no sign of the city's legendary icons—the Pharos, Alexander's tomb, the Museion or Library—only a pair of obelisks from the Caesareum, which were promptly shipped off to London and Manhattan. Cleopatra's capital seemed to have been consumed by an unremarkable provincial port.

"Forget this city," fumed one English excavator in the 1890s, exasperated at his failure to find anything comparable to the Colosseum or the Parthenon. Even Heinrich Schliemann, fresh from Troy, found that his X-ray vision failed him: He gave up on Alex and took a Nile cruise instead. Most scholars followed suit. Apart from a few sporadic digs, archaeology was left in the hands of half-demented amateurs: Searching for Alexander's mausoleum became a fetish in the 1970s, luring American psychics and inspiring local eccentrics to come forward with their secret hunches. One Alexandrian café waiter became a minor celebrity for his persistence, making 322 assorted applications for excavation permits, tunneling with official approval several times, and once being chased off by police for an unauthorized midnight dig in a church courtyard.

Yet, throughout this long night of failed dreams and wild-goose chases, Alexandria never quite shook its mysterious allure. And then, suddenly, in 1994, a young Egyptian documentary maker spotted hieroglyph-covered shapes beneath the water near Fort Qait-Bey. The secret of "missing Alexandria" was about to be solved: Thanks to earth-

*French marine archaeologists recover a statue
in the Eastern Harbor of Alexandria.*

quakes, tidal waves, and erosion, the shoreline of the city had in places been pushed back as much as a hundred yards, so many of the most famous buildings of the ancient waterfront now lay beneath the waves.

The ensuing buzz helped ease the Egyptian navy's ban on scuba diving, in force since World War II. Within a year, a team of French underwater archaeologists was raising boatloads of artifacts from the prodigiously polluted depths. The massive objects beneath Fort Qait-Bey, it was deduced, were actually chunks of the Pharos itself, which scholars had assumed was broken up for building materials by the Arabs in the Middle Ages; the lighthouse had tumbled into the water during an earthquake, along with the three pairs of forty-five-foot-high statues that once ushered galleys into Alexandria. The giant torsos hewn from pink Aswan granite were raised from the waves to international acclaim. But the most famous image, published instantly around the world, portrayed a scuba diver kneeling face-to-face with an intact sphinx on the sandy sea floor. It was like James Bond with his waterproof notepad. Underwater archaeology, and with it Alexandria, came suddenly into pop-academic vogue.

Since then, enough artifacts have been found—a sunken palace that Cleopatra must have lived in, shipwrecked Roman galleys—for the Egyptian government to announce that the Eastern Harbor would become "the world's first underwater archaeological park," open to visitors.

The reality, however, remains charmingly obscure. There are two minor hurdles before a marine park takes off. First, sea breaks must be built to calm the surprisingly rough waters. Second, and far more disturbing, there's the filth factor. The refuse of four million Alexandrians had made the harbor's waters even more rancid than the Bay of Naples— which I knew from experience would make scuba diving a doubtful entertainment.

But for my own purposes, if I was going to get a glimpse of ancient Alexandria, there was no way around it. I would have to seek out *les archéologues sous-marins.*

MERDE, MERDE EVERYWHERE

My aquatic quest began with an improbable stroke of luck.

I'd talked my way into the office of Mr. Ahmed Abd El Fattah, the corpulent and monumentally bureaucratic director-general of Alexandria's Greco-Roman Museum, who presided over a dozen female secretaries from behind his desk like some benevolent pasha—and had just spent an hour being told how impossible it was that I should meet his wet-suited French celebrities.

"But there is no *pleasure* in such a dive!" Mr. El Fattah pleaded for the fifth consecutive time, squeezing the rings on his sausagelike digits. I was sunk in a lounge chair from whose grimy upholstery seeped a millennial mustiness. Above his desk was a map of the harbor, showing intriguing outlines of recent discoveries. The mildewed brown wallpaper and retro office fittings would have suited any Dashiell Hammett private eye.

"The water pollution! We are a poor country. Our sewerage is not treated." Mr. El Fattah sighed wearily. "And the Egyptian navy will be most unwilling—"

Suddenly he reared up from his chair and let out a walrus roar.

"But *quelle coïncidence*! It is the man himself! *Monsieur! Ça va?*"

Bowing at the door was Jean-Yves Empereur, the leading archaeologist in Alexandria, founder of the Centre d'Etudes Alexandrines (CEA). It was Empereur who led the first dives on the fallen Pharos and who is still directing excavations all over the city. A well-dressed, almost foppish figure, he was gadding about town in his trademark silk cravat and Panama hat of the purest white, which framed his cherubic face.

Standing by his side were a French couple. The gentleman, equally dapper and in his early sixties, was the owner of the largest sonar company in the world—he immediately presented me with his business card—and was visiting Alexandria accompanied by his elegant, birdlike wife.

There were warm handshakes all around, and then we sank into the musty lounge chairs, clouds of dust rising visibly. I couldn't believe my luck. I was surrounded by the compatriots of Cousteau, pioneers in this new craze of underwater research—and not surprisingly, the conversation quickly turned around to the pioneer days of diving.

"*Regardez!*" Mr. El Fattah pushed forward a French celebrity magazine. "Bee-bee."

"Ah, Brigitte Bardot!" Monsieur Delauze, the sonar expert, grinned, licking his lips. "I taught her to scuba, you know. When she was eighteen years old . . ."

"In Saint-Tropez?" Mr. El Fattah inquired eagerly.

"Saint-Tropez. In 1952. But she has aged horribly. Her skin is a tragedy."

"Ah, age." Mr. El Fattah shook his head philosophically. "Were you . . . *close?*"

"Not like that! No—she used men up, and discarded them."

"Oh, but Sophia," piped in the wife, "*she* is still beautiful."

"Ah! Sophia Loren! Age has not dulled her charms!"

"Did you see her in Cannes this year?"

The cavalcade of scuba stars went on: Deneuve, Signoret, Aznavour . . . Now *this* was history.

With some regret, I nudged the conversation away from the social side of diving. I was curious as to why underwater archaeology had become the height of academic chic. Though Alexandria was the choicest plum, dives off Greece, Turkey, and Israel were making headlines.

"It is simply a matter of technology." Jean-Yves Empereur grinned angelically at his good fortune. Refinements in the Aqua-Lung since the 1970s had made it simplicity itself to take professional archaeologists and set them to work beneath the waves, he explained—far easier than taking professional divers and training them in the field of archaeological excavation.

"Today, scuba is child's play. All you have to do is remember to breathe!"

But enough of these *petits riens*. Empereur's face grew dark, his jaw set. "Monsieur Ahmed, I have a serious matter to discuss with you."

Mr. El Fattah flinched, and sat back in his armchair; he looked like a
schoolboy bracing for a tongue-lashing. As Empereur coolly listed his
grievances, El Fattah sank deeper into his chair. It seemed there was a
rival French team of underwater archaeologists, and Empereur believed
they were getting special treatment, having their finds cleaned immediately by the Egyptian Antiquities Department, while the CEA had a
two-year backlog of work. In the rarefied world of Alexandrian archaeology, this breach of priority was a serious snub.

"You have the right to be angry!" Mr. El Fattah held his arms over his
head, like a boxer in a defensive crouch.

"We have two *thousand* coins waiting for your people to clean."

"Oh yes, you have the right! *You have the right . . .*"

When Empereur had finished his tirade, Mr. El Fattah hung his head,
chastened, then looked up mischievously. "You must write a letter
explaining your grievances!"

Jean-Yves Empereur groaned quietly.

I soon discovered that it wasn't just technology that had changed the
world of diving since the carefree days of Bardot on the Riviera. It
seems archaeology itself is no longer the gentlemanly science of yore. In
the last couple of years, the two French teams at work in Alexandria have displayed a marked lack of *fraternité*. (One English-speaking
spokesman eloquently described an adversary: "He's a fucking scumbag
and I hope he dies a miserable death.") They have been catfighting from
the start, vying for work permits, international attention, funding—and
now, I gathered, scientific assistance from the Egyptian Antiquities
Department.

"They are like Arab versus Israeli!" Mr. El Fattah whispered to me
after Empereur had left.

I had the distinct impression that he found the idea of a former colonial power at the mercy of the Egyptian Antiquities Department not
altogether unamusing.

When I caught up with Empereur afterward, and delicately raised the
subject of getting a diving permit for myself, he first looked at me as if I
were stark raving mad.

"The Egyptian bureaucracy is quite tiring," he explained patiently.
"Fishermen cannot even cast a line off the waterfront without gaining a
special paper from the navy. Normally, a diving permit would take three
months. With *extreme* diligence."

"Is there somewhere I can start?"

"*Eh, bien*—I will give you an introduction."

ALZHEIMER'S IN THE "CAPITAL
OF MEMORY"

Yes, I was definitely starting to wonder about Les's dedication to the cause of ancient research. Every morning, she'd religiously turn on the TV at 8 A.M. to catch a Japanese cartoon from the 1970s called *Speed Racer.* It was a samurai version of Tintin, with a catchy theme song:

   Go Speed Racer, go Speed Racer, go Speed Racer, GO!

Then she would draw up lists of all the old black-and-white movies showing that day. There was a Bette Davis festival, a *Twilight Zone* festival, even a Monkeys festival. And when she discovered *Mystery Science Theater*—well, Alexandria could hardly compete.

It was beginning to dawn on me that side effect of pregnancy number 245, by month six, was the ability to extract mental stimulation from the most obscure sources. It seemed there was so much going on inside her body, she didn't need to leave the hotel room to be completely engrossed. And after three months of constant change, the streets of Egypt were stimulation overload. I didn't mind. It freed me to race around Alexandria, stalking officials for my diving permit. It was a Sisyphean slog. Egyptian bureaucracy has been monolithic since pharaonic times. With aeons of inertia behind them, not much gets done in Alexandria today. The offices I visited were always dark, verminous refuges hidden at the top of broken stairs. Many were uninhabited. Desks would be piled high with dog-eared papers, half-empty tea glasses, and ashtrays full of cigarette butts—all still mysteriously warm, as if the clerks had run away in a panic when they heard me coming.

But not all was lost. Traipsing from one doorway to another, I was able to construct a mental picture of the spectral city, ancient Alexandria, most of which lay ten yards beneath my feet. In fact, following the geometric street grid of the ancient city planner, Dinocrates of Rhodes, seemed easier than navigating the modern version: Alexandria has never been properly mapped, so even taxi drivers have little idea of street names or building numbers. But somewhere down there, the avenues of ancient Alexandria were all laid out with mathematical precision and alphabetical Greek names. Along those busy promenades everything in the world could be seen, raved a character in a skit by the playwright Herondas: "Money, gymnasia, power, tranquility, sights, philosophers, gold, handsome men, shrines . . . the Museion, wine and *women*—more women I swear than the stars in heaven. And their looks—like the goddesses!"

One modern street that does have a name—Sharia Faroud—lies

directly above the ancient Canopic Way, archaeologists have proved. I followed it past art deco movie houses to a seedy outer slum, where the only one of Roman Alexandria's must-sees is still standing—Pompey's Pillar, a towering column that was actually dedicated to the emperor Diocletian. At a temple here, tourists admired an iron idol of the god Serapis, which was seen to shudder, shake, grind, and finally float in midair (a "pagan miracle" that was later proved by Christian writers to involve an enormous magnet). Along the avenue, where Alexandrian merchants now sell an array of pirated music tapes and Chuck Norris videos, Roman souvenir hunters once sought rarities like Indian medicinal leaves and African jewels. "There were pearls as big as walnuts," raved one satisfied customer in a novel by Heliodorus. "Delicate green emeralds, as shining and smooth as olives; jacinths the color of an orange sea-beach tinged purple by the changing shadows from an over-hanging rock." Ethiopian amethyst was highly prized by the ancients as an "anti-inebriate": Anyone who wore one would stay sober at a symposium, no matter how much he imbibed.

Soon enough, the imaginative trail started to fade and grow cold. Many of the city's icons—Alexander's tomb, the Museion and the Library—have so utterly vanished that archaeologists can only guess at their locations. But in at least one respect, modern and ancient Alexandria are alike: All roads lead back to that brandy-glass harbor, where the blazing Pharos lighthouse once kept the waterfront bathed in its warm orange glow. Today, the causeway to the Pharos island, the Heptastadion, has silted over and grown into a residential neighborhood—archaeologists plan to use seismic instruments to retrace its route. So I strolled along the stolid medieval turrets of Fort Qait-Bey, where chaste Muslim lovers were self-consciously holding hands, and tried to glimpse some of the three thousand giant blocks of the Pharos that lie scattered over five acres offshore, twenty-five feet below the waves. The top tier of the lighthouse was destroyed by an Arab caliph in the seventh century, ending its millennium of continuous service; the rest fell into the harbor after an earthquake in the 1300s.

Now the fragments glimmered below the surface like a jagged limestone reef—and I enviously watched a trio of scuba divers getting ready to survey the hallowed heap firsthand.

If all went according to plan, I would be joining them soon enough.

Bar-Crawling in
the Ruins

A CLERK AT THE NAVAL OFFICE in charge of the harbor had offered me an appointment for the following Monday. This left me the weekend for another key investigation—piecing together the remnants of Alex's fabled nightlife, whose reputation had managed to survive from the Romans' steamy Canopus district through to the seedy fantasies of Lawrence Durrell. I had a feeling that this was not going to be easy. Nothing much seemed to have changed since the 1960s, when a pair of American tourists, having wandered the city clutching his novels in hand, wrote to Durrell demanding a refund for their trip. They found Alexandria to be a neglected provincial hub, bleached of its cosmopolitan decadence by socialism and Islamic law.

Sprawling, yes; den of iniquity, not quite.

But I had faith in the myth. Even though, after dark, Alex still had the defensive, shell-shocked ambience of a city immersed in wartime, the vestiges of the past must be *somewhere* . . .

I slipped out the hotel doors at ten o'clock on Saturday night, as electrical blackouts flickered across garbage-strewn avenues and hotel generators began to fire up—allowing Les to catch *Dive Bomber,* starring Errol Flynn. The dark waterfront was thick with teenagers absently watching the waves. All along the Corniche, café lights flared, died, and flared again.

Feeling like Graham Greene in London during the Blitz, I turned into the back streets and picked my way over broken crates and shattered sidewalks. In squalid little eateries, patrons were idly stabbing at stale-looking parfaits. One popular restaurant was run by an aged bohemian woman who had as a child known the Greek poet Cavafy; she now doled out boarding-school gruel to the sound of scratchy Cole Porter recordings. In the frayed scarlet cavern of the Spitfire Bar—a watering hole for British pilots in World War II—young English teachers were roaring like lager louts fresh from a soccer brawl. The walls were covered with tattered military memorabilia. Photos of Monty hung beside a painting of a feline Arabic princess. An inflatable airplane dangled half collapsed from the ceiling.

My eventual goal was something called Nagy's Havana Bar, an Egyptian speakeasy I'd heard about from an expatriate German hosiery salesman (who said he'd moved to Alex, converted to Islam, and married an Egyptian woman—all to escape "tax problems" back home). He could only give me the vaguest idea of its location, since of course it had no sign or street number. After wandering along the same block five times, I decided on a promising-looking door.

I knocked. A viewing slat cracked open. A pair of watery eyes stared at me blankly.

"Ah . . . Nagy?" I tried.

The door to the Havana Bar creaked open ominously.

Inside, there were four tables in a bare linoleum room, a study in funereal brown, made all the more gloomy by the pallor of twenty-five-watt bulbs. Two Egyptian men looked me up and down, then guiltily returned to their drinks. It might have been Nagy's living room. In fact, I think it was.

I took a stool at the wooden bar and ordered a beer, while Nagy himself polished glasses. He was in his forties, mild-mannered, unflappable—every Western barfly's friend. Only the pink frilly apron distinguished him from a swarthy English publican.

I half expected to see a wartime sign: IDLE TALK COSTS LIVES. To break the silence, I asked Nagy when the bar usually got going. He seemed to think it already had.

"Alexandria is not Paris." He smiled apologetically, then turned on a portable radio to create a little atmosphere. An Arabic elegy tinkled sadly through the room. "So many of our young people move to Cairo. And perhaps why not? It is *Umm Dunnya,* Mother of the World. You can get anything there. But Alexandria's time is coming. You will see."

The two men who were chatting looked up, and one added in French: "Our city has been through some evil days. But the pendulum is swinging back."

It seemed I'd hit a pet subject.

"We were taught in our schools to call the period before Islam Jahiliyah, the Age of Ignorance," the other said, referring to the Arab conquest of Egypt in the seventh century, when Christian Alexandria was regarded as a bastion of foreign pollution. "The armies of the Prophet destroyed all the idols in our city, according to the instructions of the Koran. They tore down the old temples and threw all the beautiful sphinxes into the sea. But today, we are not so harsh. We must teach our children pride in what Alexandria was."

The pair rattled off details of all the underwater discoveries in recent years with obvious excitement. The archaeological triumphs have meant an enormous amount to Alexandrians—after all, it's been thirteen hundred years, give or take, since they were in the world's eye. Now there is a sense that a new golden age is approaching for the city, a dazzling renaissance.

Ahmed and Mohammed—those were their names—were particularly enthusiastic about the upcoming archaeological marine park. They owned two fishing boats, which they were now planning to convert into glass-bottom barges.

The business plan was deliciously simple. A horde of rich European tourists would soon descend on Alexandria, all year round, filling the hotels and restaurants that usually only host summer vacationers from the Egyptian middle class. Local tour-boat operators would shuttle these hordes in groups to the famous sites, across the submerged ruins of ancient palaces, out to the underwater Pharos, back to the newly opened modern library, which has been funded by UNESCO. In the process, *they would all get very rich.*

We clinked glasses at the time-honored dream of Alexandrians.

It was a neat reversal of the usual impact of rediscovered ruins that the ancient Roman tourists, with their vivid sense of the past, would have appreciated.

Since the Romantic era, excavated sites from Pompeii to the Parthenon have inspired ruminations on the vanity of human endeavor. But in Alexandria, every discovery feels like a vindication—proof that memory can actually endure in the face of history's ruthless ebb and flow. The population's vision of ancient glory has survived some desperate troughs: Overshadowed by Cairo after the seventh-century Arab conquest, Alexandria was reduced to the size of a fishing village by the early 1800s; under British rule, it went through a modern cycle of boom and bust as Egypt's cotton capital; finally, since the revolution of 1952, it

was allowed to wither again by nationalists suspicious of its decadent foreign flavor. And yet, Alexandria never entirely abandoned the cosmopolitan, outward-looking spirit it was born with.

Today, the Roman and Greek ghosts have been freed from their
watery graves, helping usher the city into the next phase of its long,
unpredictable life. It's as if some centers of civilization are fated to rein-
vent themselves forever. Whether or not Ahmed, Mohammed, and
Nagy are right in predicting a new golden age for Alex, re-creating its
role as the tourist beacon of the Eastern Mediterranean, the pattern of
human aspirations is certainly resilient.

It's archaeology in reverse: The past is deftly salvaging the ruins of the
present.

Nagy's Havana Bar was like one of the Roman *popinae,* where patrons
quietly sipped wine and nibbled on fried snails and lentil stews (the
gourmands tried barley beer, the favorite drink of Egyptians). If I
wanted to see real Alexandrian nightclubs, the now-voluble Nagy confided, I should head east, far east—out to the seaside suburbs.

"Ask a driver for the Aquarius. That's real Muslim entertainment."

And so I hopped a taxi along the darkened coastline, out past Stanley
Bay—and precisely toward where the Roman red-light district, Canopus, had stood. The car headlights flashed across abandoned colonial
mansions and canals clogged with sunken rowboats—the very same
canals that ancient party kids once rowed in their gondolas, the waters
perfumed with petals. But the seafront, to my relief, was very much alive.
In the strip of hotels along the shoreline, nightclub after nightclub was
filled with immaculately groomed, teetotaling young Egyptians enjoying
their pop music.

This festive corner of antiquity had never truly died, obviously; it was
just a little restricted by Allah. At the Aquarius, I forked over forty dollars for the privilege of sitting in a dark corner of a room filled with
middle-aged Egyptian businessmen, who swigged industrial quantities of
Coca-Cola as a full-bodied belly dancer gyrated up on a stage in a
nylon body stocking. By 2 A.M., the party was in full swing. Three men
hopped-up on Coke were invited up onstage, roaring with laughter,
stealing touches of nylon-covered flesh.

I thought of an inscription that had been found on one Canopic
inn, announcing that it offered all the pleasures of peace rather than
war:

These walls are alive with feasts and young men,
Who listen to sweet flutes instead of bugles;
The blood of beef, not men, reddens the earth;
We wear fine clothes, not armor;
In our hands are goblets, not swords.
All night long we sing our choruses to the Sun-god,
Wine cups in hand, heads wreathed with vines.

And the ancient dancers gyrated their hips and tinkled castanets on their fingers, as travelers drank wine from ivory horns, their faces shining in the light of torches.

THE ALEX AGUE

Despite her days of rest in the Cecil Hotel, Les was feeling worse.

The dreaded Asian influenza had migrated to her lungs; she spent her nights convulsed by racking, tubercular coughs. Pregnant women were forbidden to take antibiotics—at least that was what we'd heard—but now things were looking grim.

Oddly enough, on the ancient Roman tours, if you were going to get sick anywhere, it was better to do it in Africa than in Asia. Pergamum may have been the top sanitarium for *divine* cures, but for anything resembling the empirical science we favor today, the medical academy at Alexandria's Museion had no peer. It was here that student surgeons were first given human bodies to dissect—the corpses of executed criminals who had been administered adder bites, a swift and apparently painless death. And Alexandrian pharmacology was surprisingly advanced. One medical volume from A.D. 65—*Materia Medica,* by Pedanius Dioscorides—methodically listed six hundred herbal cures (although to be truly effective, the leaves had to be picked under specific alignments of the zodiac). Opium was also used here as a painkiller. For bronchitis—Lesley's current ailment—a leaf of the autumn crocus was prescribed.

Unfortunately, I had no idea where to get an autumn crocus in modern Alexandria, so we had opted instead for plenty of warm liquids and bed rest. Now, the prospect of consulting a local doctor was somewhat unnerving.

For advice, I went to the French-run Center of Alexandrian Studies—the modern House of the Muses. It was located at the top of a rickety apartment building whose elevator was filled with the ammoniac reek of stray cats. But once the CEA's doors opened upstairs, the harsh edges of the Third World were replaced by the soft and welcoming light of what, at first glance, could have been the genteel abode of an elderly *grand-mère*. The scent in the air was now of freshly ground French coffee—thus confirming the center's status as a bastion of foreign culture.

I passed through wood-paneled rooms, where crusty international scholars quietly plied their specialized trades—computer graphics programs were rearranging fragments of mosaics, printers whirring out 3-D reconstructions of excavated buildings—until someone found the telephone number of a doctor the French archaeologists all swore by.

"You know, Egyptian medicine is more advanced than you might think," the spokesman said. "The whole Arab world comes here for treatment. And doctors even do house visits."

A few hours later, Dr. Nawal al-Hakim appeared at our doorway—a stately, elderly man, in an impeccably tailored checker suit, wearing a porkpie hat that he never took off. There was something classically Egyptian about his thin frame and purse-lipped authority; I couldn't help thinking of the loyal eunuch adviser to Elizabeth Taylor in *Cleopatra*.

He examined Les, and scribbled the name of an antibiotic called Xanthax.

It sounded like some laboratory-produced killer virus.

"Are you really sure it's safe for pregnant women?" I asked, trying not to sound incredulous. "We'd heard it wasn't . . ."

"These are *special* antibiotics," Dr. al-Hakim said in his hypnotically calm tone. "Perfectly safe. She must take them."

"She must take them," I repeated.

I went down to a hole-in-the-wall pharmacy with the scrap of paper—you couldn't exactly call it a prescription—where a skeletal old man doled out unmarked white pills into an unmarked plastic bag.

At this point, I was starting to feel a little unhinged myself.

TO THE LIGHTHOUSE

While Xanthax was working its magic in Les's blood system, I headed back to the Egyptian navy's barracks to pick up my diving permit. It was a beautiful day; I could just see myself that afternoon, skimming across the hieroglyph-covered bones of the Pharos. Even the recruits at the barbed-wire gates seemed to recognize that my moment had come.

Everything went smoothly. The top naval commissioner of Egypt—well, actually, his secretary—ushered me into a comfortable armchair. He sympathetically listened to my case, told me to fill out three forms, photocopied my passport, and added it to a pile of paperwork four feet high, kept steady by a grimy brick.

"It will be no problem at all!" He grinned, shaking my hand in congratulations for navigating a difficult obstacle course. "Return to me in ninety days."

"Ah," I gurgled, with a fixed smile. "You mean minutes?"

"No." He giggled, as if it were the funniest thing he'd every heard.

I diplomatically pointed out that the diving season ended this very week.

"Quatre-vingt-dix jours." He smiled, pointing to his calendar, in case I hadn't understood.

I took the news quite well, under the circumstances, never once using Steve Martin's immortal phrase "son of a motherless goat." Instead, I had a quiet cup of tea and waxy cake, then headed back to Fort Qait-Bey for one last look at the reflection of that absurdly elusive ruin.

Down by the crashing waterline, I recognized one of the CEA's marine archaeologists—a Welshman named Randall—dragging himself unsteadily out of the waves. Two Egyptian guards with machine guns didn't seem to mind if I went down to the hut to say hello.

I told the dripping Randall about the tragic result of my permit hunt—he wasn't in the least surprised—and asked how the visibility was underwater.

"Mixed," he said tersely, before shakily lighting a cigarette. After a minute of silence, he decided to fill me in on the true situation of Alexandrian scuba.

"You see, diving in Alex, everything depends on the sewage vents. If the wind is blowing the right way, everything is fine. If it's blowing the wrong way . . . well, you're swimming in shit, quite literally. Visibility's about three inches."

I sniffed the breeze; there was definitely a skunky whiff in the air. Perhaps I hadn't missed out on as much as I'd thought.

"I'm off to have a shower," Randall grunted. "In fucking antiseptic."

For ancient Roman tourists too, there came a time when the many pleasures of Alexandria began to wear thin. After the heady regime of intel-

lectual debates and late-night parties, they were psychologically prepared
to leave this cultural oasis and confront Egypt proper.

As for us, after two days on Xanthax, Les's bronchitis magically evaporated.

Her illness had given us the worst misstep of the trip so far. It was an
uncomfortable brush with reality; I hadn't felt any readier to deal with it
than with the imminent result of pregnancy itself. But the trip now had
its own momentum: We agreed to press on to the deserts of the Nile.

As we packed up, I read out potentially useful phrases for her from an
Arabic phrase book:

"Ana mish amrikiyya," I read over and again.

"What does that mean?"

" 'I am not American.' "

PART EIGHT

IN THE REALM OF THE EXOTIC

Magic and Mummification
on the Nile

IF YOU WERE A NAZI WAR CRIMINAL, the Long Bar of Cairo's Windsor Hotel is where you would hang out. The funereal cocoon of scarlet felt and walnut paneling hasn't changed since the 1930s, when it was a British Officers' Club, so customers can still hide in the shadows, studiously avoiding rusty springs in the horsehair-and-leather armchairs, or flicking through fifteen-year-old magazines underneath torn lampshades. Impala heads decompose on the walls alongside antelope-horn chandeliers. Octogenarian bartenders wearing frayed galabia robes and red fezzes eye their customers suspiciously, sometimes incredulously. I started to feel pretty shifty myself, ready to cut a deal in weapons, bootleg penicillin, or hijacked body organs.

My eye was fixed on one wraithlike regular, impeccably dressed in linen suit and tie, who looked like a cross between Klaus Barbie and Nosferatu. He sat in the same corner every night with his bodyguard, always in silence, smoking black cigarettes—more accurately, devouring them. Every time he inhaled, his cheeks disappeared into his jaw, turning his head into a hollow skull. No smoke ever seemed to escape his mouth. His guard—a sweating boulder of flesh—attended to his every need. He lit his cigarettes and mixed his drinks. I imagined him muttering in a Peter Lorre voice: "Can I get you anything, master? Perhaps a little something for myself? You're comfortable I hope?"

It was the perfect base for exploring Egypt and its haunted relics. I took out a map and drew a clean line along the length of the Nile Valley, to our goal—the final frontier.

Of the entire ancient tourist trail, this last section in Egypt is the easiest
to trace. Modern travelers still follow the same logical itinerary as the
Romans along the Nile River—heading south from Alexandria, via
Cairo and the Pyramids, to the deserts hiding the Valley of the Kings.
And nowhere does the aura of the Grand Tour lie so intact as in those
shifting sands. At every stop in Africa, we would be seeking out the same
sun-basted monuments—within the same parched and silent landscape—as the pioneer sightseers did, and with a similar sense of millennial awe. To those first-century A.D. *spectatores,* the Nile's relics already
belonged to a forgotten epoch, standing as aloof and enigmatic as they
are to us today.

The sheer age of Egypt was mind-boggling to Romans. While Greek
aristocrats might trace their lineage back to Hercules or Jason, who lived
long before the Trojan War, the high priests of Thebes cataloged their
ancestors back a further 360 generations—roughly *ten thousand years.* This
was a patriotic exaggeration—dynastic rule began around 3100 B.C.—but
Egypt was accepted as the oldest land on earth, and thus was irresistible
to any inquiring Roman mind. It stood to reason that its deserts hid
chthonic secrets. Egypt's macabre Cult of the Dead revealed familiarity
with the deities of the underworld; the inscrutable, tonsured priests, who
offered their services as guides for affluent Roman visitors, were privy to
the most arcane wisdom of the ages. The greatest astrologers, necro-
mancers, exorcists, and fortune-tellers lived by the Nile, practicing the
infernal arts handed down to them over aeons. Even the hieroglyphs
were regarded as magical riddles, their messages enchantments and spells.

Attracted by this enigmatic world, many doctors, lawyers, philosophers, historians, and antiquarians were among the Roman-era tourists
who descended on Egypt "to investigate in person" the reports they had
read, and often to write their own esoteric treatises on the mysteries of
the Nile. Most of these intellectuals hired their comfortable barges in
Alexandria, replete with cooks, scientists, and professional poets. The
full Nile cruise was expensive, so groups of like-minded tourists often
joined forces—a group of five Neoplatonist philosophers is recorded in
Luxor—taking a month or longer to reach the cataracts at Aswan. A
hearty minority, including the pagan holy man Apollonius of Tyana,
covered the entire distance on camelback: He made his way through the
Nile Valley with a team of scholar friends, crossing the river when nec-
essary by small sailboats—early versions of the felucca—along the way.

All accounts indicate that these first Nile tours were pedantically thor-

Re-creation of a luxury barge on the Nile, for the 1963 film Cleopatra.

ough. "There was not a city, temple or sacred site in Egypt that they passed by without discussion," notes Apollonius' biographer. Aelius Aristides, the sickly orator, took no fewer than four Nile cruises in the mid-second century A.D. to gather information that might shed light on such long-disputed secrets as the source of the Nile and the purpose of the Sphinx. ("I left nothing unexamined, not the Pyramids, the Labyrinth, no temple, no canals, but I got the measurements of some from books where possible, and where they were not readily available, I measured them myself with the assistance of the priests and prophets of each place." Unfortunately, he lost his voluminous notes on his return to Asia Minor.) Every tourist became a fact finder in Egypt. Strabo researched his geography while on a cruise, Pliny the Elder his encyclopedia, Seneca a treatise on religion (published to some acclaim, but now lost). VIPs like Germanicus in A.D. 19 and the tourist-emperor Hadrian a century later were as diligent as any fresh-faced student.

Nobody, it seems, left unsatisfied.

The sheer intensity of the experience made everything that had passed before seem like a dress rehearsal, a preview for the true pageant.

It did not matter that the Egyptian sites were desolate or in decay. Like modern tourists, Romans sought out any image of the pharaonic past—gladly accepted any tawdry vestige of it—and had a soft spot for African kitsch: Floor shows were lapped up, and Romans paid to see priests perform sorcery and parade sacred crocodiles, or peasants run the rapids of the Nile in canoes. Some of these exhibits they found thrilling, some shocking, some simply bemusing. When they wanted to express their approval, tourists engraved graffiti: *Miravi* (I was amazed!) was a popular favorite. (As in: *Ianuarius primipilaris vidi et miravi locum* [I, Januarius, chief centurion, saw this place and was amazed].) One note in the Valley of the Kings echoed the now-famous line of Julius Caesar: "*I looked, I investigated, I arrived, I marveled.*" A woman nearby wrote laconically, *I am from Rome.* Even the first rules for crowd control appeared in graffiti. In one Egyptian sanctuary, a first-century A.D. scrawl read: *No urinating or defecating is permitted at the sacred place.*

And it wasn't just the dead past that Romans loved to observe. Egypt was an upside-down land, the Antipodes of Antiquity, where even the

Romans loved to decorate their villas with images from Egypt,
which represented the ultimate in the exotic.

cycles of nature ran opposite those of the rest of the world. The Nile rose in summer instead of winter without a drop of rain to fill it, and was full of unique fauna from man-eating reptiles to screaming monkeys. The human inhabitants were just as contrary: They worshiped cats and dogs; holy men shaved their heads instead of letting their hair grow; and they practiced circumcision ("preferring to be clean rather than comely," marveled Herodotus, the Greek travel writer of the fifth century B.C., whose account every Roman had read). The land was a cultural time capsule, where peasants sowed the fields just as they had for the Old Kingdom Pharaohs, with a religion as vibrant as it had been when the Pyramids were raised.

Egypt was, in short, the acme of the exotic—and the apogee of the Grand Tour.

On the surface, it seemed a compliment that Romans displayed such an interest in the alien elements of Egyptian civilization: Everywhere else in the Empire, they had reveled in the superiority of the Greco-Roman way. And yet, as they tried to make sense of the Nile's mysteries, the pioneer tourists remained profoundly egocentric. They viewed the land through the distorting prism of their own culture—and as a result, they misinterpreted almost everything.

To explain the obvious antiquity of Egyptian religion, the Romans, like the Greeks before them, deftly inserted their own pantheon. Western scholars like Diodorus decided that the gods of Mount Olympus had first walked the earth in Egypt—and had even ruled there as the first Pharaohs. Thus the Egyptian deity Amun was really the Roman god Jupiter. Osiris, the god who dies and is reborn, was Bacchus by another name. Apollo was worshiped in Egypt as a crow, Diana as a cat, Juno as a cow, Venus as a fish, and Mercury as a bird. The ancient Greek hero Orpheus was believed to have visited the Nile, as had a slew of Homeric characters: Historians identified the caves where Trojans had supposedly been kept as prisoners, and where Helen had rested after her rescue from Troy.

Egyptians happily fueled the disinformation. Guides told tourists that one pyramid was really the tomb of a Greek courtesan, a lover of Aesop. They encouraged the dotty belief that Plato had studied astronomy in Egypt, showing off the mud house in Heliopolis where he supposedly lived for thirteen years, and one of the tombs in the Valley of the Kings as Plato's study. Statues of spurious celebrity visitors like Sophocles were

set up in temples. Some even insisted that Homer was born in Egypt—
the son of a high priest in Thebes.

In fact, the Romans and Greeks were the first "Orientalists," to use
Edward Said's now-famous term: Their *idea* of Egypt was more potent
than the reality itself. Just as the British and French would in the nineteenth century (or, according to Said, all Westerners do today), Romans
viewed "exotic Egypt" through the inverted telescope of their own culture, seeing only what they wanted to see. The final result was to garble
their own observations and create a shadow world where, for example,
any reference to the pharaoh Amenhotep III—sometimes called by his
praenomen Memmonia by Egyptians—was mistaken for Memnon, a
mythical black African prince who Homer said had fought and died at
Troy. For centuries, Romans would make long journeys to behold what
they thought was the hero's giant statue near Thebes.

It is no wonder, then, that Egypt was a beautiful puzzle. Romans
delighted in pondering the obscure and often contradictory data; their
tourist project was to extract honest answers from these wily Egyptian
priests in order to shed light on everything from the birth of the gods to
the celestial order behind life and death.

Feluccas drifting along the Nile today.

And the first stop in this extraordinary quest was the apex of the Nile delta, where the Old Kingdom's greatest monuments, the Pyramids and the Sphinx, along with its twin capitals Memphis and Heliopolis, were clustered within a few miles of one another.

CITY OF THE SUN, CITY OF THE NIGHT

Today, the whole titanic sculpture garden lies within the overwhelming orbit of Cairo.

It was after dark when Les and I first arrived in the Mother of Cities. From a wrought-iron Victorian railway station of World's Fair proportions, our taxi squeezed its way along an urban artery bulging with mosques and thick with billboards, whose Arabic script looked to us like gorgeous doodles. We stared openmouthed at the sheer scale and archaic glamour of the place. Alexandria had been a summer camp compared to Cairo—a conglomeration of twelve million people, less a city than a controlled nuclear explosion. On one side passed an endless medieval cemetery now inhabited by thousands of squatters; on the other, the bazaars of old Cairo, where brilliant silks fluttered like ostrich feathers in the light of kerosene lamps. Somewhere beneath those knotted alleyways was the Roman river port called Babylon, where one of the three imperial legions in Egypt was once based. Modern Cairo swallowed up all evidence of it long ago. In a northern suburb, a single obelisk remains from Heliopolis, the pharaohs' ancient City of the Sun, where the enormous magical bird called the Phoenix rose from its own ashes every 1,461 years. But every other square inch of the metropolis has been concreted over, and is today either bumper-to-bumper with cars or shoulder-to-shoulder with pedestrians.

Eventually, we forced our way into Cairo's throbbing downtown, which has been preserved in aspic since the Depression by politics and poverty. It's a Kafka-esque gallery of old storefronts complete with their original interiors and unchanged fittings like clunky Bakelite telephones and ivory mirror frames. Wrought-iron stoops lead up to Walker Evans soda fountains; police cars have sirens that sound straight out of old Dick Tracy cartoons; the backstreet cafés are crowded with men sucking on hookah pipes as if there's no tomorrow. Perhaps inevitably, we were viewing it all with the eyes of modern Orientalists. The city fulfills a Western nostalgic fantasy of the Middle East. Cairenes don't regard their clothes as vintage or their furnishings as retro chic, and that's one reason why the city seems so exotic to us. Without any effort, it oozes noirish allure.

Even in those first hours, the city convinced me of one thing: Egypt is as overwhelming today as it ever was. In terms of travel experience, it threatens to blot out all that has gone before. It wasn't always pleasant, but you knew you were somewhere amazing. Every sight was a shock. The very air shuddered with energy.

At last, in a dark back lane, when the iron gates of the Windsor Hotel yawned open like a crypt, fantasy and reality became inseparable.

The art nouveau lobby framed a timeworn reception desk, where old postcards were on sale of Arabs sitting on camels; I caught the sweet whiff of rat poison as a cast-iron elevator straight out of *The Third Man* took us up through musty floors whose mahogany walls absorbed light like black marble. Most of the hotel porters wore Western-style tunics still monogrammed with the queen of England's initials, but our floor was being cleaned by a seven-foot-tall Nubian man wearing a long white robe and a dirty turban. His red eyes seemed to glow in the dark and he bared his yellow teeth in a terrifying smile, as we scurried up to the Nazi-era bar.

Yes, this was just the atmosphere that I was looking for.

I didn't *want* to be a modern Orientalist, focusing on a twisted Western reflection of Egypt. But I couldn't resist imagining myself with Boris Karloff.

Interview
with the Mortician

WOULD YOU LIKE TO TOUCH HIM?"

In Room 354, a conservation lab in the darkest recess of Cairo's wonderfully decrepit Museum of Egyptian Antiquities, Nasry Iskander, chief curator of mummies, was peering at me from behind thick spectacles, his rheumy eyes narrowing.

Between us, unswathed on a table, lay the mortal remains of Pharaoh Thutmose III.

I looked around for plastic gloves, but apparently they were unnecessary.

"Go ahead and touch him. . . . *It's quite okay . . .*"

Room 354 was a fair imitation of a mad scientist's laboratory—not at all the antiseptic white cubicle you might expect at such a world-famous institution. Test tubes were scattered all over desks among jars of nameless chemicals, charred Bunsen burners, X-ray machines, scalpels, swabs, great tomes that explained the intricacies of DNA testing, and even inexplicable flashing lights—all the semifictional paraphernalia of things scientific. It all seemed to emphasize the sheer organic reality of the mummy unwrapped on the operating table.

The pharaoh looked like an ebony statue, his skin taut as cured leather across his shallow rib cage, his hands curled up in an arthritic gesture of self-defense. A few wisps of hair still fell across his pate, the timeless brush-over of vain patriarchs. Still, he didn't look bad for thirty-five hundred years old.

Thutmose III—pronounced *thut-moe-suh*—was once the most powerful individual on earth; one historian dubbed him the Napoleon of the East for his brilliant campaigns of conquest, which expanded Egypt's New Kingdom to its greatest territorial extent. King Thutmose died around 1450 B.C., in his late eighties, and was buried in the Valley of the Kings, but his resting place has changed many times. After grave robbers pillaged his sumptuous, cleverly booby-trapped tomb, Egyptian priests secretly reburied him with thirty-nine other royal mummies in a humble cache in Deir al-Bahri. Archaeologists found him there in 1881, and since then, Thutmose was on the road constantly. His corpse made a circuitous journey via Egypt's medical school and university before arriving at its final resting place in Cairo's grand old museum.

And even here, Mr. Iskander was making me an offer I couldn't refuse.

For century after century, nothing has symbolized the exotic mystery of ancient Egypt so completely as the mummy. At the time our Roman tourists were visiting the Nile, the sacred art of embalming the dead was still being practiced—in fact, it was more popular than ever, with many of the Romans and Greeks living in Egypt demanding the full mummy service. After all, who would dare miss the ultimate journey—to the Land of the Dead, where they would be greeted by Lord Osiris and live for eternity in a world that very much resembled this one? The morticians of the Nile worked around the clock preparing clients for their final trip; scribes churned out copies of *The Book of the Dead,* which was basically a Rough Guide to the Underworld, providing handy directions and rote answers to the queries posed by its guardians.

A visit to an Egyptian embalming shop was at the top of any Roman tourist's agenda. The largest and most illustrious lay in Memphis, once the capital of the Old Kingdom Pharaohs, but by the first century A.D. a small town of fifty thousand people, whose majestic avenue of sphinxes lay half-buried in sand. Its mortuaries had the air of vast, efficient factories, turning out dozens of mummies a day. As everywhere in Egypt, embalmers now offered different grades of service, from first class to budget. The cheapest option was little more than desiccation by the dry desert sands, but the deluxe, pharaonic standard procedure took about ten weeks.

Roman sightseers, no doubt holding perfumed handkerchiefs over their noses, would take tours of inspection, where they could view the

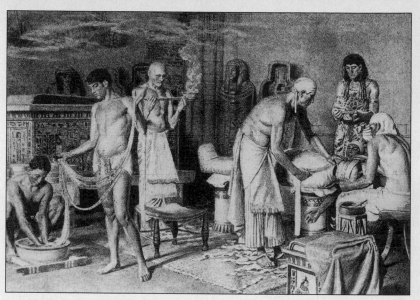

The Embalming Shop, *a nineteenth-century newspaper etching showing the ancient Egyptian practice that has long obsessed Westerners.*

grisly rites they had often read about. They noted how the brain was skillfully removed with a long metal hook through an incision in the nose, and how the intestines were excised and placed in delicately carved alabaster jars. They saw the troughs where the gutted bodies were soaked in natron, which dried and preserved the flesh for forty days and forty nights until it began to resemble cured leather. Finally, they watched as the corpse was soaked in resin, wrapped in bandages, and adorned with jewelry—ready for entombment. Greek and Roman families living in Egypt added a new dimension to this age-old ritual by affixing realistic face portraits onto the finished mummies. Many have survived to the modern day—the so-called Faiyum portraits. Regarded as the finest examples of ancient painting, they now stare back from the grave with a disturbing vivacity. Tourists could then visit the necropolis, or mummy pit—quite a sight with its thousands of corpses laid out in tunnels, complete with feasting halls where relatives would gather to dine with their dear departed.

Today, the Western fascination with mummies has if anything become keener. For almost every visitor to Egypt, the first stop is still an eerie repository of the dead.

MYSTERIES WRAPPED IN ENIGMAS
WRAPPED IN
THREE-THOUSAND-YEAR-OLD BANDAGES

A visit to the Museum of Egyptian Antiquities, where I'd found Nasry Iskander, is suitably skin-crawling. Glowering through black iron gates like the House of Usher, it is the least regenerate of the world's old-school museums; most of its artifacts are still stored in the same wooden display cases built for them a century ago, with the same recondite labels. I strolled through echoing, barrel-vaulted corridors where dozens of mummies in their sarcophagi are stacked along the walls, gathering dust behind glass. Only the Royal Mummy Vault, where the Pharaohs themselves are kept with their queens, has been updated for the twenty-first century. It's a sleek, space-age environment where eleven New Kingdom rulers are maintained in cases of pure nitrogen, like astronauts in deep freeze. Armed guards hush all conversation; lights are dimmed to a minimum, which adds to the morbid effect.

Room 354, where Mr. Iskander works, is where these kings and queens are given their annual physicals. When I dropped by, Thutmose III was about to have a new and malevolent fungal growth excised from his armpit. It didn't look like he approved. His mouth was curled into a furious expression of contempt.

Iskander hovered above the pharaoh's shrunken frame, waving a scalpel protectively.

"Before I started working at the museum, there was no scientific care for these *poor guys!*" he explained, eyes moist with emotion. "The Conservation Department was only looking after parchments and paintings. I was shocked that nobody was giving any attention to Egypt's greatest royalty. The mummies had been very badly treated by their discoverers." In fact, he found most of the pharaonic mummies in the museum's dark basement.

"They were deteriorating," he said, quaking. "They were rotting!"

For a museum scientist, Mr. Iskander is a surprisingly extroverted character, grandfatherly and bespectacled, with the jovial mien of all morticians. His appointment to chief curator was, in a way, hereditary. His uncle was the first Egyptian-born director-general of antiquities; many of his family were chemists. Conservation was a natural career. For forty years he has devoted his life to the Pharaohs, staving off decay from their fragile bodies, setting up the Royal Vault, overseeing the fireproofing, the security, and the humidity, lighting, and temperature controls.

Not surprisingly, Iskander has no time for those Egyptians who argue that displaying the dead is a violation.

"There are *still* those who want to put the Pharaohs back in their original tombs!" He shook his head sadly. "They say it is more *correct* to hide them. But then the mummies would deteriorate very quickly indeed. How can you preserve something locked away in the earth?"

For once, science is in accord with ancient religion: Decay is the ultimate sacrilege.

Obviously, the royal mummies now enjoy care that is meticulous, almost fanatical. And yet, while Iskander was tossing off statistics on the effects of nitrogen gas on cured flesh, I couldn't keep my eyes off King Thutmose III—*just lying there.*

Only four feet tall, with black skin and dry bones. A cotton shroud was swathed across his midriff, but it seemed somehow pornographic having the pharaoh exposed like that.

Iskander caught my expression. He motioned me closer to the body, a little conspiratorially, and shared his excitement at the ancient embalmers' skill.

"*Look.* His fingerprints are perfectly intact."

It was true—they were black enamel swirls. I muttered some words of admiration.

This was when Iskander suggested I give the pharaoh a friendly prod.

It seemed a little against the high-tech conservation spirit—but how could I resist?

Feeling oddly nervous, I put out a finger and ran it along Thutmose's forearm. The skin was hard and cold—beyond leather, it felt like stone. It was unbelievable. Here was an actual pharaoh, a god on earth, who had taken his last breath three and a half millennia ago. And I was as good as shaking hands with him. His teeth now seemed to be bared in a contorted smile of triumph—or was it rage?

One hymn in the ancient Egyptian *Book of the Dead* reads:

Hail Father Osiris! I shall possess my body forever; I shall not be corrupted; I shall not disintegrate! Nor will I fall prey to worms! I exist! I am alive!

Immediately, I felt a wave of guilt. What was I doing? Defiling a corpse?

Back within the gloomy walls of the Windsor Hotel, I washed my hands, still feeling the cold touch of Thutmose III.

The Nubian zombie swept by our door in long flowing robes, flashing his insane grin from the shadows. Throughout the hotel, lead pipes gurgled and groaned. Floorboards squeaked under the tread of visitors. Mirrors shuddered. Ceilings echoed.

Outside, Cairo steamed and boiled, threatening to swallow us in its faceless enormity.

The Deathless
Pyramids

I have seen the Pyramids without you, sweetest brother. I have sadly shed my tears here—that was all I could do for you—and carve this lament as a memorial to my grief.

Graffito at Giza, from Terentia to her
dead brother Terentius Gentianus, c. A.D. 130

LIKE TOURISTS TODAY, the Romans could never say they had visited Egypt until they had beheld the first and most astonishing of the Seven Wonders of the World towering like a trio of icebergs on an undulating ocean of sand.

Under the Empire, the Pyramids were even more majestic than they are now: They were sheathed in white limestone copings, sleek and polished to the apex, that brilliantly reflected the sun's violent rays (these were stripped by Arabs in the Middle Ages to build the mosques of Cairo, leaving the raw steps we see on the Pyramids today). The majority of Roman visitors enjoyed this ultimate Egyptian day-trip on camelback across the dunes—although in summer, when the Nile was in flood, they could sail their barges to the very base of the Giza Plateau (the river's course has since drifted about two miles east). Either way, the experience was breathtaking. It was Egypt's premier event, seared into every visitor's memory.

This did not mean that every visit was particularly pleasant: At the Pyramids, it seemed half of Egypt wanted a piece of the tourist pie. Boys from the nearby village of Busiris offered to scale the Great Pyramid for a few bronze coins. Local vendors clamored for attention, along with a colorful menagerie of nomadic astrologers, portraitists, and sages. Elbowing through the barrage, Roman tourists made their way along a hundred-yard causeway to the funerary temple of the pharaoh, where priest-guides could be hired to impart their learned commentaries.

Finally, they entered the inner sanctum: At that time, a wall ran around the entire base of each pyramid, separating the sacred space of the monument from the mortal world beyond. Here tourists could touch the reflective limestone surface of the structure itself, whose lower portions were covered with hieroglyphs and the carefully composed graffiti of fellow wanderers. In fact, by Roman times, the Great Pyramid had become a vast, open visitors' book, where every tourist could chisel his or her impressions. This was not considered defacement, but a grab at immortality—an effort by visitors to join their own fates to the most enduring of mankind's creations.

The sacred guides of the Giza Plateau were the luckiest in Egypt: They monopolized a site that no foreigner would miss—monuments that simply begged for extravagant explanations—and yet about which almost nothing was known for certain. The Pyramids were already twenty-five hundred years old in the first century A.D., and from all accounts their spiritual role—as mounds from which the mummified Pharaohs' *ka,* or spirit, would rise to the heavens—had been forgotten. Instead, they were regarded simply as insanely extravagant tombs—"a wasteful and foolish display of wealth on the part of the kings," sniffed the supercilious Pliny the Elder. Ancient tourists were far more interested in the practical matters of Egyptian engineering: How were the Pyramids built? How long did it take? How much did it cost? Where was the stone quarried? How was it transported?

Since nobody could contradict them, Giza's guides let their imaginations run wild, glibly repeating the fantasies that Herodotus had been fed, half a millennium before. They explained how each of the three Pyramids extended down under the sands as far as they went up, making them far more enormous than they appeared, and related how the second Pyramid had been financed by the pharaoh's daughter, who set up a brothel with herself as the prize harlot. (This paragon of the ancient sex industry had also demanded that each of her clients donate one cut stone until she gathered enough to make her own mini-pyramid.) And guides helpfully "deciphered" hieroglyphs that conveniently answered the Romans' most common statistical questions: One inscription of Cheops (the Greek name of the builder of the Great Pyramid) said it took 360,000 men twenty years to build, then provided the cost—a bargain at sixteen hundred silver coins. It even supposedly listed the daily food rations of the workers (heavy on garnishes—radishes, onions, and garlic). From here, the tales became increasingly implausible. The smallest Pyramid, guides swore, contained the remains of an illustrious Greek courtesan who jilted the poet Aesop for the pharaoh's love. Strabo was informed that the very pebbles lying at his feet were actually petrified lentils, which were eaten by the pyramid builders. Diodorus overheard guides say that mountains of salt were built up around the Pyramid as giant ramps for moving building blocks to the apex. Nile water was used to melt them away.

Tourists were just as fascinated by the Sphinx, the man-headed lion that had crouched beside the Pyramids, apparently for aeons. The statue was half covered in drifting sand until A.D. 55, when a Roman viceroy named Tiberius Balbillus ordered it cleared to provide a better view for the growing number of visitors. A plaque was laid to commemorate the restoration, which may rank as the first act of field archaeology in history. We can only envy Pliny the Elder, who saw the Sphinx soon afterward. He reports that its fine features included a long ceremonial beard and a cobra rearing from its crown; the face was painted a vivid red-ocher. While Pliny's servants measured the Sphinx, the Egyptian guides showed rare self-restraint by admitting that this was actually *not* the Sphinx

South of the Giza Plateau, the so-called Bent Pyramid at Dahshur,
the only pyramid to survive with a large part of its limestone coating intact.

from Greek mythology. Instead, it was a sun god they called Harmachis. (Today, archaeologists guess that it depicted Pharaoh Chephren as Ra-Horakhty, the sun god in his incarnation as dawn.) Whatever they were told, the Romans were certainly impressed. As one tourist giddily inscribed on the Sphinx's paw:

> *This Sphinx is a wonder—a heavenly vision.*
> *Gaze upon her shape, this sacred apparition.*
> *Her face is holy, a truly divine rendition.*
> *Her body royal and leonine, oh masterful composition!*

Seventeen such inscriptions survive on the Sphinx, but the Pyramids' graffiti disappeared with their limestone copings. An invaluable treasury of heartfelt ancient musings went with them. One of the last to see them with their stone sheaths, the Arab traveler Abd el-Latif in the twelfth century, said the ancient scribbling on the Great Pyramid alone would be enough to fill ten thousand pages. Today, we know of only three examples—including the lament by Terentia to her brother—and these almost by accident, because they were copied down by medieval travelers (one dutifully records the Greek names of the three Pyramids, as explained by guides; another raves that their height "reaches the stars").

And as Roman tourists pondered the magnificent monument field, one last question naturally arose: What, if anything, lay inside?

THE VEIN BENEATH GIZA

By telephone, I pestered the antiquities department for permission to descend to the off-limits "unfinished chamber" of the Great Pyramid. From a reference in Strabo, who visited around A.D. 10, it appears that some ancient tourists actually entered the Great Pyramid via a pivoting slab on its east face and shuffled down a steep passageway to a subterranean room, which was mistakenly assumed to have been the pharaoh's tomb. (The superbly crafted King's Chamber, which is open today to the public, was discovered by Arabs many centuries later—although it had already been pillaged by grave robbers in the Middle Kingdom and sealed up.) Why shouldn't I repeat the experience?

A baffled antiquities secretary said that I should make my way out to Giza, to discuss the matter with the "director of the Pyramids" himself.

And so, like most tourists today, my first glimpse of the world's most famous monuments occurred in the middle of a snail-paced highway called Sharia al-Ahram (Pyramids Road). Cairo's suburban sprawl has extended to the very edge of the Giza Plateau, and this six-lane concrete strip runs right up to the site, beautified on both sides by souvenir shops and four-star hotels. Somehow, thankfully, the sheer incongruity of it all only makes the Pyramids seem more timeless. In fact, nothing that has happened in the last two millennia can really detract from that first approach. Not the disappearance of the Pyramids' shining limestone sheaths (only a fragment at one apex survives), not the hundreds of Bedouin camel drivers digging the whole precinct into a dust bowl, not the multitudes of international visitors clogging the causeways (and this was apparently an all-time low for Egyptian tourism), not even the hundreds of guides who insist they are university professors and launch into spiels lifted straight from Herodotus. The one about the pharaoh's prostitute-daughter always gets a few chuckles.

In fact, the addled commentaries of the guides provided an encouraging continuity: The Pyramids have remained a blank slate for freakish theorists from the West. In the nineteenth century, a British savant named Charles Piazzi Smyth said that the dimensions of the Great Pyramid, if measured in "pyramid inches," was the key to future world history; it proved, among other things, that the British were descended from the Lost Tribe of Israel. The twentieth century gave us Erich Von Däniken's alien ravings, hours of creative TV "documentaries" with names like *Secrets of the Galaxy Revealed,* and the new-age belief that pyramids hold the cosmic key to eternal spiritual peace. The Egyptian authorities have decided to turn a profit from the groups they label Pyramidiots—new-age tourist groups can now hold annual rituals inside the Great Pyramid for a mere five hundred dollars an hour. In fact, the "wasteful and foolish" Pyramids once scoffed at by Pliny have many practical uses today. It was Friday when Les and I made our expedition—the Muslim day of rest—so thousands of Egyptian families were having picnics and playing ball around their base as if this were Central Park. After dark, along with the inevitable sound-and-light shows, the monuments have recently provided the ultimate setting for a rock concert by Sting, a live performance of *Aïda,* an international squash tournament, and a mass wedding of five hundred couples.

The man responsible for managing the cosmic balance between the sublime and the bizarre, Dr. Zahi Hawass, has the coolest business card on earth. It is simplicity itself, framed in gold, embossed with that magisterial title—Director of the Pyramids—and in the corner are two intricately detailed pyramids, along with an oasis and palm tree.

But no sooner had I stepped inside his office, which is perched on the

fringe of the plateau, than Mr. Hawass announced his disapproval of
Giza's whole commercial extravaganza, and in particular what he saw as
the perverse Western fetish for penetrating the monuments. The twenty
grams of salt left by each visitors' breath was causing irreparable damage
to the interior walls.

"My personal opinion? I would close the Pyramids tomorrow. But
the pressure from the government is too great. It is too valuable for
tourism."

As befits Egypt's leading archaeological spokesman, Hawass is a stately,
pharaonic figure, with a helmet of wiry gray hair, a stentorian voice, and
harsh judgments.

"I ask these millions of tourists: Why would you visit the Pyramids
and then destroy them? There are simply too many people. That is why
we are building an IMAX theater, so we can close it. Nobody will go
inside."

"But don't you think people will still want to see for themselves?"

"Why?" Hawass seemed genuinely surprised by the notion. "You go
to New Jersey and see the IMAX theater there. The tourists *love* the
IMAX." He thumped his desk emphatically. "It is *better* than the real
thing! It will *increase* tourism."

I promised I would one day visit New Jersey, but in the meantime I
had an unusual research project involving the off-limits subterranean
chamber.

I pressed forward my own business card—a rather sorry affair compared to Hawass's, I had to admit—but an essential tool, I'd learned, for
any official dealings in Egypt.

To my amazement, Dr. Hawass agreed. And so I set out to "investigate in person" (as the Roman tourist graffiti often announced) "all that
I had read about."

The elegant, silk-veiled guide I was assigned, named Aidya El-Fattah,
took me up to the entrance of the Great Pyramid, sniffed the fetid air, and
gestured down the narrow passageway plunging into murk. There had
been some recent restoration work, apparently; now the air was so
opaque that someone might have been operating a barbecue down below.

"You may continue alone," she said, before turning on her heel. "Me,
I don't like to."

I crept sideways down the first steep steps in a contorted, fetal crouch.
The staircase was lit by the occasional household bulb, which cast a sickly

sepia light across the ominously smooth stone. Soon my thighs were aching and sweat was pouring down my back, while the air became progressively colder and staler as I continued deeper into the solid bedrock of Giza. After about one hundred yards of this tendon-twisting descent, the shaft bottomed out. But the Great Pyramid's secret tunnel continued straight ahead—through a passageway that looked two and a half feet high. This was a tad more claustrophobic than I'd bargained for—I would have to continue on hands and knees. One of the bulbs behind me flickered and died.

I heard a strange drumming in the deathly silence, then realized it was the sound of my blood throbbing in my ears. I was beginning to see spots in the dismal half-light. Fighting a vague panic—was I going to black out?—I tried to regulate my breathing, like a coal miner preserving his air in a collapsed mine shaft. Any Roman tourist who made it down here would have felt even worse, I supposed—the smoke from his guide's torchlight would have filled the tunnel, and the flame would have threatened to flicker out.

Squirming ahead like a worm, I did my best not to think of the 2.3 million stone blocks above my back, each one of which could compress me into a wafer of Egyptian pita. I also tried not to imagine all the folks enjoying their visits to the King's Chamber, where a new Swiss-designed ventilation system had just been installed. The air down here tasted like it hadn't been cleared in forty-five hundred years.

At last I groveled into the rough-hewn chamber—a raw cube of stone, about twenty feet square, not much larger than the interior of a giant sarcophagus. The passage continued for a few yards, to a dead end, designed to confound tomb robbers. There was nothing else there.

I sat at the end of the line, half frozen, sweat slithering like tiny cobras along my limbs. What was wrong with me? I wondered. I didn't usually react quite so skittishly to underground explorations; even rappelling down subterranean waterfalls was less disturbing than this. There was something about Egypt's atmosphere that was making me susceptible to attacks of nerves.

In the deafening silence, I remembered how Dr. Hawass, apropos of nothing, had told me that he wanted all the Royal Mummies reburied in their original tombs.

"How would you feel if in a few thousand years from now you were put on show for a thrill? Even in Victorian England, many thought that the display of our Egyptian dead was wrong. They called it 'morbid and unwholesome.' You have to have respect!"

I'd nodded sympathetically but was thinking of my recent encounter with Thutmose.

Without meaning to, I had tapped into the richest vein of Western superstition about Egypt, which has its roots in the time of those first sightseers.

CURIOSITY KILLED THE OCCULTIST

The depth of Roman superstition has been documented at every stage of the Grand Tour. Obsessed with death and the afterlife, wrestling with metaphysical despair, tormented by the knowledge that they were toys of a capricious fate, educated Romans were already profoundly vulnerable to suggestions of the occult. But touring Egypt—where images of the grave lurked at every corner, and timeless monuments inspired a painful awareness of one's own mortality—raised their neuroses to a pitch of near hysteria.

Most educated travelers actively sought out Egyptian magic. They watched priests perform intricate, age-old rituals that would hold back the forces of chaos, ensure that the Nile kept flowing, that the sun stayed on its course. They bought spell books supposedly written ten thousand years earlier by Hermes Trismegistus, the Egyptian version of the Greek god Hermes. The hieroglyphic originals were highly prized souvenirs, and spurious translations were churned out for the tourist trade—artificially aged in damp sand for added authenticity. At night, in abandoned temples filled with drifting sands, they even paid sorcerers to perform macabre rites. A papyrus in a Parisian archive recounts how the emperor Hadrian himself hired a famous sorcerer named Pachrates to perform in Heliopolis:

> The high priest calmed an hysteric within one hour, made someone sick within two hours, induced a man's death within seven hours, and then sent dreams to the Emperor himself. Thus he proved his reputation as a sorcerer. The Emperor marveled at the high priest and ordered that he should be given double his usual fee.

Pachrates no doubt fit the popular image of an Egyptian magician as a shaven-headed ascetic in white cotton robes, using as a prop the round glass *kondy*, precursor to the crystal ball. Hadrian was seriously ill at the time, and the shadows dancing on the temple carvings, the smell of dust and desert, must have made it a bewildering experience. (Especially the part when a man's death was "induced." Our modern cinema-fed imaginations conjure a trussed-up peasant having the life bled out of him by a secretly administered adder bite.) And less elaborate acts of magic could be seen on every street corner in Egypt, reported the horrified Christian author Origen: "The *magi* drive out demons from men, cure illness with a breath of air, evoke the souls of heroes and conjure visions of rich meals, tables filled with delicacies of all kinds that in reality do not exist."

The ubiquity of the occult was not without its dangers. Travelers ran the risk of enchantment even at barber shops, where Egyptian women might steal locks of their hair for use in curses. Locals were not immune. They were just as wary of strangers, who might perform "erotic magic" on their spouses. (Young married women were often bewitched into "mad passion," apparently, and drugged to forget their behavior afterward.) Unlucky tourists might be charged with sorcery—magic was technically against the law in the Empire, despite being practiced on every corner—and have to defend themselves in court against such suspicious signs as owning a mirror or buying unusual types of fish.

But most worrying for Romans was the conviction that mortals could be punished for dabbling with the infernal forces, which turns up again and again in the many ancient horror stories set in Egypt. There was the tale of Nenefarkaptah, a scholar who tried to find a spell book by the god Thoth, only to end up dead, with his spirit cursed. In an anonymous Roman best-seller, the *Letter of Thessalos,* a medical student from Alexandria in search of infernal secrets narrowly escapes a grisly fate. And in Heliodorus' novel *Ethiopian Tale,* a witch who reanimates her son's corpse is quickly punished by fate: She trips and is impaled on a spear. These tales were so popular that Lucian satirized them in *Lovers of Lies:* His beloved story of a sorcerer's apprentice who gets in over his head animating brooms and pestles was turned into a poem by Goethe and inspired the symphonic work *The Sorceror's Apprentice* by Paul Dukas— which was most memorably acted out by Mickey Mouse in *Fantasia.*

All these strands of ancient superstition have been passed on to us today virtually intact. In Victorian Britain, they became key ingredients of Egyptian gothic horror tales with suggestive titles like *The Mummy's Foot, Some Words with a Mummy,* and *Imprisoned with the Pharaohs.* Hollywood, meanwhile, has preserved the idea of the Pharaoh's Curse, which posits that archaeologists, little better than grave robbers, will die in mysterious circumstances.

Lying in that frozen pit in the Great Pyramid, I started to feel increasingly uneasy. Here we were, about to embark on the most delicate leg of our journey. The talk in Egypt was still of religious extremists targeting foreigners. Reports were maddeningly vague. I tried to remain ironic and bemused by the sediment of guilt I was carrying: Prodding the mummy had been only natural.

But by the time I staggered out of the Great Pyramid on all fours like some beaten vampire cringing from the sun, I had a terrible feeling that our journey was about to spin out of control.

Missives
from the Beyond

THAT NIGHT, back at the Windsor Hotel, I felt an insatiable urge to indulge in that most dangerous of modern travel rituals—calling home to check the telephone messages.

I almost never did this. When visiting places like Samoa and Bolivia, sheer technological backwardness usually helped me maintain a blissful indifference to news from New York. But while we were in Greece, Touch-Tone phones were so easy to find that almost against my will I'd fallen into the habit of checking the messages every couple of weeks. It felt like I was playing Russian roulette—I vaguely expected to be punished for removing myself from real life in such a frivolous fashion—but the ritual had become so ingrained that even now, in low-tech Egypt, I found myself clutching the single antique phone in the Windsor Hotel, at the front desk, swatting away enormous black moths beneath the flickering neon light.

Perhaps I shouldn't have been surprised when, after a string of banal messages, I heard the distraught voice of our downstairs neighbor back in New York:

"Hello, Tony? Lesley? This is Rosanna downstairs. Is anybody up there? There's a waterfall pouring down from your apartment. It's like a rain forest down here. . . ."

It took a few seconds for the meaning of this to sink in. There had been a flood in our apartment. Water pouring through the floor. And the message was *ten days old*?

I could actually have done without this piece of information.

In Roman times, it would take travelers months, sometimes years, to receive news from home. There was no public postal system. The imperial government had its own network of couriers for official correspondence—the *cursus publicus,* whose riders were known to cover 160 miles a day in emergencies—but individual citizens had to come up with their own arrangements. For truly urgent missives, the wealthy would dispatch a slave carrying a letter. But most long-distance correspondence was carried as a favor—by travelers, merchants, sea captains, friends. Romans had to rely on the kindness of strangers to keep communications open.

A letter from Naples to Rome might arrive in less than a week, from Athens to Rome between three to seven weeks. From Asia Minor or Egypt, two to four months. But this was only if the letters were not lost or misdirected.

Most missives were written on papyrus; they were rolled, sealed with wax, and, since they were delivered by hand, very simply addressed: "To Gaius, from his sister Livilla," "To Paulus, from his mother." They were fragile—and perishable. In the damp climate of Europe, few papryuses managed to survive antiquity. But in 1897, British archaeologists began digging in the communal rubbish heaps of an obscure desert town called Oxyrhynchus in Egypt, and found entire caches of Roman-era letters preserved in the sand. The dump has since yielded 70 percent of the surviving private letters from the ancient world. The authors were often from the Roman and Greek classes who lived in this corner of Egypt. But the sentiments they expressed were no doubt typical of all ancient travelers—and are entirely familiar to us today.

The main concern was to let families know that they were well. "Having arrived safely on Italian soil, I felt it essential to let you know that I and all with me are in good health. We had a slow voyage but not an unpleasant one." Another: "Finding someone traveling your way from Cyrene, I wanted to let you know I was safe and sound." Sea travelers reported lucky escapes from storms: "I give grateful thanks to the god Serapis who came to my rescue." The more thoughtful included inexpensive painted portraits of themselves.

Separated lovers conveyed the time-honored messages. "You have said 'Do not forget me.' How can I forget you? I beg you not to be anxious." Another pleads: "Please, please send for me; I will die if I don't see you daily. I wish that I had wings to fly, so that I could be with you now." There were prodigal sons begging their parents for money ("I was ashamed to come home, because I go about in filth"), while other sons demanded news from home ("Dear Mother! If you'd just send a note telling me if you're well or how you are, so I can stop worrying!").

There are touching letters between spouses, as well as less-blissful recriminations: "I'm disgusted at your not coming home," one wife writes to her peripatetic, deadbeat husband. "Here I've steered myself and the child through a time like this, and been driven to the last resort because of the price of food . . . all these crises, and you've sent us nothing!"

One traveling husband wrote a long, affectionate letter to his pregnant wife, then added chillingly, "If the child is a girl, abandon it."

The ancient mail system was slow, painful, unreliable—but it occurred to me in Cairo that it had had one advantage. When Romans went on journeys, they could really *disappear.* Such heady freedom is difficult to imagine in this hypercommunicative world of cell phones, faxes, and e-mail. The high-pitched beep of an answering machine, like the grind of a desktop making an Internet connection, is now one of the familiar background tunes of life.

And as I squeezed the hefty Bakelite receiver to my ear at the Windsor's gloomy desk, the news was not cheery.

"This is Rosanna again. Hello? *Hello?* I guess you guys aren't up there. Ummm . . . It's still pouring water down here. I'm worried the ceiling is going to cave in on me."

That was the last message. Then just a blank and empty silence.

Feeling like a man caught in quicksand, I whipped out my phone card—as indispensable as a passport for today's traveler—and called our other neighbor, who had keys to our apartment.

"Oh, honey, I just don't know what to say." I could vaguely hear the Texas drawl.

This, from Sheryl, meant things had to be pretty awful.

Apparently our new upstairs neighbors had left their sink running when they went away for a weekend. The flow of water into our apartment had been prodigious. The ceiling had indeed collapsed—right over our wardrobe and my writing desk.

"There's a lot of mold now," Sheryl added, warming to her subject. "Your computer's ruined, I guess . . . all your photographs are soaked . . . your printer's full of this dirty white plaster."

Thankfully, we were disconnected.

I went outside for a breath of fresh air, to the alley where men sucked on their gurgling water pipes. Through the smoke I detected the odor of rotting fruit and acrid gasoline fumes—and something else, beyond all of that, which might have been the desert.

It was safe to say that calling had been a mistake. There wasn't a thing we could do about what had happened at home and I wasn't about to abandon the trip now. Still, I decided it was best not to tell Les about it. In her condition, who knew how she'd react? (The nest fouled! With only weeks to go before B-day . . .) I wished I didn't know about it myself.

Outside the café, a skeletal waiter offered me a chair. I remembered him because of his friendly smile—or was it the face of Thutmose bared into a grin?

GREETINGS FROM THE RUE MORGUE

Slinking back up the dark stairs, I knew that there would be no respite from the chaos of Cairo, which was making my thought processes more addled every day. And the very last place to look for solace was in that supposedly sacrosanct traveler's refuge—the hotel room.

We'd stayed at a lot of unusual hostelries on this trip, but none quite compared to the Windsor. The former British Officers' Club had begun its misbegotten career in the hospitality industry fifty years ago, and every room we stayed in (we switched five times) was a miniature housing museum—shredded carpets, mattresses like marble slabs, a clock with no hands, art deco radios emitting tormented squeals. Pulling the old ropes that opened the wooden window blinds was like raising the rigging every morning. At first, all this had seemed perfect. The Windsor had more gritty character than all the other hotels on the trip put together—but it came at an emotional price. Every day there was some new psychodrama that took hours to resolve. Once, Les returned to the room to find the entire toilet bowl shattered by forces unknown. In our new room, the door lock was jammed. Around midnight, the door would slowly swing open.

The owner—a cleft-chinned, debonair Egyptian businessman—overflowed with sympathy when hearing his guests' complaints but had an encyclopedia of excuses.

"The hotel repairman—well, we just had to let him go. I cannot hire any others without references, you understand. This is, however, a very safe hotel."

"Of course." I nodded, and changed to another room—where the antique blinds immediately broke, entombing us in darkness.

While the owner was deeply apologetic, there was nothing he could do.

"They are very old, you understand, our blinds. The only man in Cairo who knows how to repair them—well, he's dead."

"Dead?"

"Dead. Nobody else in Cairo has that particular skill."

"So the blinds are going to stay permanently down? Forever?"

He smiled consolingly. "But surely you're out much of the day?"

It finally occurred to us that, Old World charm or no, the suave hotel owner was running the most lucrative racket in Cairo—and had turned the tables on all us Western Orientalists by deftly milking our fantasies of Egypt. Every Western guidebook in existence had written up the Windsor as *the* place to stay in Cairo—the *atmospheric* option, that is. So the owner had jacked up the prices and then made it his official policy to never lift a finger. Guests could enjoy the old furnishings and priceless ambience of colonial decay—why make repairs? He didn't have to. There was a steady supply of travelers who would spend a few sleepless nights and then leave, exhausted. If guests complained, he cheerfully shuffled them about from room to room, until they got the message.

The trouble was, we refused to take the hint. It became a point of honor not to be defeated by the nonchalant owner, to crack his smug exterior.

It was admittedly a masochistic approach. If it wasn't the hot water giving out, it was the elevator jamming or the lights blowing or the laundry disappearing or the demonic Nubian attendant spying on Les from the darkness, baring his broken teeth in what seemed an ever more menacing grin. Even breakfast was exhausting—the room, putrid from moldy air-conditioning, was serviced by a waiter who looked permanently terrified by the constant confrontations with guests over the week-old bread and milk that smelled of fish.

Nauseating, yes. But we weren't going to be defeated. There was too much to do near Cairo—too many amazing sites beloved by the Romans. We were caught like flies in the city's orbit.

VIP Seeks
Crocodile God

Even before Rome conquered Egypt, its celebrities were receiving five-star treatment in parts of the Nile Valley. From a papryus to the chief official of the Faiyum, 112 B.C.:

> Lucius Memmius is sailing from Alexandria to your district, Faiyum Oasis, to see the sights. He is a Roman Senator, a man of importance and honor. Receive him in the most lavish style, and make sure that lodgings are prepared for him, as well as landing facilities. . . . You should provide furniture at his lodging places, the finest treats for feeding to the Crocodile God, and materials for sacrifice at the Labyrinth. Do everything in your power to please him; make your best effort.

Under the Empire, the attention given to Roman VIPs was more solicitous still. Germanicus was a high-profile example in A.D. 19; the emperor Hadrian in A.D. 130; Septimius Severus sixty years after that. This top brass followed the same route as average tourists, but in far more regal style. Their barges glittered with the most exquisite luxuries; they were met by local dignitaries for lavish feasts, and escorted in large groups to the great sites. In the case of the emperors, construction of facilities for their comfort, such as new bathhouses and palaces, commenced years before their arrival.

But for every foreign sightseer, from humble antiquarian to semidivine ruler, the verdant Faiyum, just south of the Nile delta, was the next stop after the Pyramids. Thanks to an intricate irrigation system built in the time of the Pharaohs, the Faiyum was the ultimate Egyptian oasis, a lotus flowering in the desert, with two world-famous sites: the enormous Labyrinth, which was thought to be the prototype for the Minotaur's lair in Crete, and Crocodilopolis—which, as the name suggests, was devoted to the worship of crocodiles.

Crocodili Nilotici were regarded as the most bizarre of Egypt's many divine creatures. In antiquity, specimens were regularly recorded at lengths of thirty feet; today they have been hunted to the verge of extinction along the Nile and rarely reach ten feet. Ancient novelists loved to describe the creatures' hideous and scaly skin, lashing tails, claws, and monstrous spines. "When a crocodile yawns," says Achilles Tatius, "it is all mouth"—with exactly 365 teeth, naturalists believed, miraculously matching the number of days in the year.

In Crocodilopolis, a temple had been built beside a lake, where dozens of these reptiles were kept in a private zoo. All were tame, and so well trained that priests could summon them by name. The largest and fattest specimen was worshiped as the incarnation of crocodile god Sobek himself. Like other lucky holy animals in Egypt—the Apis bull in Memphis, the sacred lion at Leontopolis, the sacred goat at Mendes, the sacred ibis of Hermopolis—the crocodile god was maintained in the sort of extravagant luxury that the majority of Egyptians could only dream of. Sobek was provided with sumptuous quarters, where he was given fine food on golden platters, slept on a silk-sheeted mattress, and was washed and perfumed by a retinue of personal attendants. And when he died, the corpse was mummified and taken on a splendid funerary boat to a private necropolis, where he was buried with full ceremonial honors.

But in order to support his standard of living, Sobek, like other sacred animals, was expected to perform in public. The hand-feeding of the crocodile god was one of the great floor shows of antiquity—and as regular as dolphin shows in Florida today.

Every morning, tourists came to the lakeside temple bearing culinary treats for the divinity. Strabo says he brought meat, pastries, and honeyed wine—an inappropriate diet for a reptile, but not, presumably, for a god. At the priests' command, Sobek waddled along the bank before a crowd of admirers. His short legs glittered with golden bracelets, his tail with bands of jewels. A team of burly sacristans then pried open the beast's powerful jaws, while another tossed the meat and pastries into his mouth and squirted in the wine (the crocodile's sharp claws had been filed blunt as a precaution). They then hand-polished the reptile god's sharp teeth.

The flow of tourists was so steady that Sobek's diet verged on force-feeding. Strabo records that he had just seen the ritual "when another foreigner arrived, carrying an offering of fruit. The priests took the food, went around the lake in a run, took hold of the animal, and in the same manner fed it the offering."

These animal displays were immensely popular with visitors throughout Roman Egypt. In Memphis, priests were obliged to put a peephole in the Apis bull's stable, so that tourists could watch him even outside the specified exercise times. His every movement was considered: Germanicus fell into a profound depression when the Apis bull refused to eat his offering (it foretold his imminent death). To others, all this zoolatry was comical. "*Qualia demens Aegyptos portenta colat?*" scoffed Juvenal. (Who knows what monsters crazy Egypt worships?)

This didn't slow the flow of gawpers. Whatever else, Crocodilopolis was a spectacle, and even the most doubting tourists—especially VIPs—diplomatically suspended their disbelief. Afterward, they followed the Egyptian faithful and purchased a mummified baby crocodile for burial as a sacrificial offering. The demand for these and other embalmed animals reached its height in the early Roman Empire. Archaeologists have found some four *million* ibis buried in jars during that period in Saqqara alone; elsewhere, cats, falcons, and monkeys were similarly processed. Egypt's "sacred livestock farms" (as one historian dubbed them) were as efficient as Perdue chicken facilities today. But the local priests were not above a good swindle: Many sealed jars found at Saqqara were actually empty. In the Faiyum, supposedly mummified baby crocodiles were in fact wooden dolls wrapped in bandages. Others contained only a bone or an egg.

THE OASIS OF LOST SOULS

For some reason, more than many other sites on the Grand Tour, I couldn't wait to see what remained of the Faiyum oasis. Perhaps it had to do with grade-B horror movies I watched as a kid: The crocodile cult seems like the ancient building block for such Hollywood depictions of savage rites as the *Cobra Woman* and *King Kong*. Sadly, visiting the Faiyum seemed quite complicated. It's only sixty miles from Cairo—but it lies at the fringe of religious extremists' strongholds. Due to the endless vague reports of recent activity, tourists were said to need official permission for the pilgrimage. This wasn't really true, but every taxi driver in Cairo seemed to believe it. "No foreigner should make such a journey," one intoned to me glumly, casting his eyes to the heavens. The Faiyum sounded more tantalizing than ever.

The bureaucrats at the Egyptian Travel Ministry were slightly embarrassed by all this. "You don't need permission to travel in Egypt," they informed me, smiling. "Everything is perfectly safe, the situation quite under control." They would even provide me with a VIP escort.

This was fine by me; I assumed the high-level status would grease the wheels of travel. A woman named Sehed would pick me up the next day at 9 A.M.

Not long after noon, a minibus pulled up in front of the hotel. A short, elfin Egyptian woman in a brilliant yellow scarf was sitting there with a driver and two "trainee guides"—young Muslim girls in Technicolor scarves.

"You are the VIP?" Sehed asked me suspiciously.

"That's me."

"Do you have the permission?" she asked gravely.

"I don't need permission! And the sites down there all close at four P.M."

Time was running out, but we would make it to the remains of Crocodilopolis if we hurried.

Before long, we were tearing down the southern highway by the Nile, through a baleful desert wasteland littered with rusting jeeps and oil drums that had been beaten by the sun into abstract sculptures. Above the blistering horizon of dunes, the tip of a pyramid would occasionally emerge. (Despite Giza's notoriety, there are actually a total of 107 pyramids scattered along the west bank of the Nile. Most have now eroded into mud formations strangely resembling the mesas of Monument Valley, but one—the so-called Bent Pyramid—still has a decent segment of its original limestone coping. It's the only pyramid that still gleams and shimmers in the desert sun, as it did for the Romans—looking, in fact, as if it were lit from within.)

And then, in the blink of an eye, the color scheme changed from postnuclear brown to English green. The Faiyum oasis was still an Oz-like refuge from the desert: Its roads were lined with robust palms, fields glowed with grass. In the irrigation canals, waterwheels were churning. The lake and marshes may no longer contain crocodiles, but Sobek had still blessed the land.

At around one-thirty, well within schedule, we roared confidently into Faiyum City—and, to my horror, straight into a government complex.

"We must greet the governor before we can do anything," Sehed whispered.

"For permission?"

"No, no." She laughed nervously. "You don't need permission to travel in Egypt. He would simply like to greet you. You are a VIP. It's a simple formality."

In a rambling office building that had the air of an abandoned school-house, the governor was holding court, flanked by two armed body-guards. I already knew that Egypt was a land of old men presiding from behind huge desks, but Mr. Ahmed was truly a king among bureaucrats. He reminded me of Toad in *The Wind in the Willows*—bald and round, with greenish skin, and amphibian lips fixed in a smirk. There were mysterious dollops of white cream all over his face, and as he dispensed the usual VIP pleasantries—"Where are you from? How do you like Egypt?"—he kept his left palm clamped over one eye, his elbow point-ing directly at me. It was a little disconcerting. Mr. Ahmed talked to everyone like that, swiveling his elbow from one person to the next, like a periscope.

"You must stay for tea," he announced.

I stood up and began to make my heartfelt apologies.

"You *must*!" he repeated. "It is a tradition in Egypt."

Sehed squirmed nervously. For the next hour, Mr. Ahmed demon-strated his importance by idly talking to his lackeys in Arabic, ignoring me completely while I sipped the sugary brew. The whole picture sup-ported one fact: *Nobody* comes to the Faiyum anymore, for any reason. Mr. Ahmed had nothing better to do. Having a VIP in his clutches was his dream come true.

The next time I stood up to leave, the governor clutched my arm with his free hand, the other still clamped to his eye. It was time for me to inspect his homemade Museum of the Faiyum, whose exhibits had been put together by local schoolchildren. These included colored-pencil drawings of the local river levels; a fish tank in which two Nile perch floated, semidecomposed; and an enormous drawing of a mos-quito. "We are the only place in Egypt where malaria is endemic!" he beamed, apparently proud of Faiyum's one claim to fame.

"To the Labyrinth!" I exclaimed brightly, looking for fellow enthusi-asts.

I made it out the door, but it was obvious that the VIP treatment was far from over. A small crowd had gathered around the minivan. The gov-ernor had arranged more special companions for my visit. There was a "local expert" to complement Sehed—a certain Mr. Ibrahim. And no fewer than three armed policemen were coming with us, one in the car with me, the other two following in a jeep, all touting machine guns. It was a presidential cavalcade.

After an eternity of handshaking and backslapping, we sauntered off. Mr. Ibrahim, exuding the indolent charm of a Vegas nightclub host, lit a cigarette inside our tiny van, then began his guided tour of the Faiyum by pointing out the window at objects of interest.

"Chicken farm . . . village . . . chicken farm . . . school . . . palm trees . . ."

"Thanks," I muttered, sinking into my seat. "It's okay. Really."

But Mr. Ibrahim wouldn't be silenced. His voice was like a saw cutting metal, squeaking relentlessly into my brain.

"Village . . . village . . . *town*. Different to village. It has more buildings."

I peered at Mr. Ibrahim. Was he serious? Or was this some new and insidious torture?

"School . . . chicken farm . . . *grass*. Maybe you know grass?"

I closed my eyes, trying to block out Mr. Ibrahim's high-pitched monologue, wondering if Thutmose had had anything to do with this.

At the Labyrinth of Hawara, six soldiers with carbines stood at the gate, which looked like it guarded an empty pasture. It took some time to convince them that they should keep the site open past 4 P.M., even though I was the first visitor in months.

"Twenty pounds?" I looked at the ticket. "I thought I was a VIP?"

Sehed shrugged indifferently. I paid up, but said I was going to view the Labyrinth without my retinue. Mr. Ibrahim looked wounded and doe-eyed, but I heartlessly strode away—followed at a discreet distance by two policemen.

Ancient tourists loved the Labyrinth, which they thought was a prototype for the Cretan version stalked by the Minotaur (today we know it was actually the mortuary temple of Pharaoh Amenemhet III, built so that he could be worshiped in the afterlife). It was by all accounts a mind-boggling creation, with reputedly three thousand chambers, all linked together in a maze of Escher-like dizziness. The guides at Hawara did a roaring trade, since tourists could not explore the site alone without getting lost. Pliny the Elder agreed with Herodotus' verdict that the Labyrinth was actually more impressive than the Pyramids. In the first century A.D., Romans could share the Greek writer's excitement. "We

saw the upper chambers, and they surpass all the other works of man.
The endless passageways in and out of rooms, and the detours this way
and that way through the courtyards, produce wonder after wonder. You
move from courtyard to chamber, from chamber to gallery, then into different chambers from the galleries, then different courtyards from the
chambers. . . ."

I felt lost just reading his description.

Now, as I looked around, there was nothing left of the Labyrinth but
a mound of dark rubble, which sat like an enormous cowpat on the
fields. Archaeologists have identified its foundations, but the rest was pillaged for building materials.

"Next site," I said to Sehed.

Mr. Ibrahim brightened up as we drove away.

"Bullock . . . palm tree . . . canal," he noted cheerily, pointing out
the window.

What was once the center of Crocodilopolis is now known as Kiman
Faris (Horseman's Mounds)—a paddock the size of a football field,
fenced off by corrugated iron on the northern fringe of Faiyum City.
Mr. Ibrahim undid the rusty padlock and we went inside. The soil was a
sandy conglomerate of ancient pottery; you couldn't pick up a handful
without encountering sharp chunks that Strabo or Pliny might have
touched. At the center sat a round stone fountain base, which seemed to
be decorated with some sort of carved reptiles. This may—*possibly*—have
been where the crocodile god Sobek was fed by performing priests, his
jeweled tail swaying with carnal pleasure. After all—if not here, where?

Mr. Ibrahim and Sehed were standing by the modest relic apologetically; the trainee guides and policemen were watching from the minivan
in glum silence.

"The archaeologists came here a long time ago," Mr. Ibrahim
squeaked, peering up at the sky. "There is some discussion of their
return."

I started to feel a little bad for them. It wasn't their fault that so little
was left. Then Mr. Ibrahim whacked his forehead in the cartoon gesture
of a man having a brainstorm.

"The crocodile cult! Then I will take you to Qasr Qaroun!"

It seemed impossible. How could it be that Mr. Ibrahim knew anything about anything at all? But he swore it was the finest site in
Faiyum—all the locals knew about it. Strange that my guidebook didn't

mention it—but if there was a significant ruin, I had to see it. It might even redeem this fiasco of a day.

"To Qasr Qaroun!" I said hopefully, gathering my entourage.

And an hour later, we were stumbling across sand dunes of purest white toward what appeared to be an entire ruined city. The setting sun was casting long shadows across a column-lined avenue to a hulking temple. In the Roman era, a lake had lapped right up to its gates, but over the last thousand years it receded and disappeared. Now, the edifice was guarded by two elderly Bedouins living in a tent. They waved us over for a glass of black tea—adding five spoonfuls of sugar to every cup—and showed off their rifles. The problem was that they had been given no ammunition, they said. I promised to pass on their complaint to the governor.

At last, we went over to the temple, which had began to flame orange in the sunset. Gusts of wind brought mournful sighs from the desert.

Through its entrance, I could see, was a large chamber. Mr. Ibrahim motioned me inside. A pair of dark wings flapped suddenly in the ceiling. Another doorway, half blocked by rubble, led into darkness beyond. A green lizard stared at me, then sidled into a crack.

Mr. Ibrahim handed me a torch and nodded for me to continue. For a second I wondered if they had decided to exterminate their irritating VIP.

"Are you coming?" I asked Mr. Ibrahim, feeling a new sense of camaraderie.

He furrowed his brow. "You can go," he muttered. "I have done it."

I squeezed through the doorway, flashing my light at every slithering and rustling thing I heard. Dozens of bats hung quivering above, like ripe leathery fruit ready to drop. This chamber led to another room, then another. The walls were tattooed with hieroglyphs—including an outline of Sobek, the crocodile god. He had the body of a man, the head of a reptile. He was in full stride across the desert, arms angled up like a power walker.

I flashed my torch ahead. I could see more rooms, more corridors, more stairs, more lizards, more bats. For a horrible second, I thought I was lost. Later, I learned that nineteenth-century European travelers mistook this complex for the famous Labyrinth, riding nine hours across the desert to visit it. As I flashed my torch furiously over three identical doorways, I remembered the words of Strabo on the maze of Hawara: "No stranger can find his way either into any court or out of it without an Egyptian guide."

Then I heard the cadences of Mr. Ibrahim echoing through the door to my left—"Mr. Tony . . . Mr. Tony, don't go too far."

I couldn't have been happier to hear that rasping voice; it was more soothing than Pavarotti's.

"*Definitely* the sacred crocodiles were fed there," Mr. Ibrahim assured me, as we hurtled back across the darkening desert, toward the electric glow of Faiyum City.

"I'm sure you're right," I said to my new best friend.

Mr. Ibrahim smiled contentedly, then looked out at the highway and continued his professional commentary.

"Canal . . . cemetery . . . petrol station . . . village . . ."

ESCAPE FROM THE DELTA

Shaking the sand from my shoes back at the Windsor Hotel, I found Les in the Nazi bar, trying to avoid the stares of the usual suspects. She said that something strange had happened in our room and she chose not to stay there. When I went in, my suitcase was open on the bed, half full of water. Beside it was a bar of soap embedded with *tiny iron filings.* It was like a clue to some Hercule Poirot mystery.

The dapper owner nodded as sympathetically as ever. "The cleaner on your floor—the Nubian man? He's quite retarded, you know. We're Copts, and these poor fellows are sent to us by the church.

"In fact, you've probably already noticed how many of our cleaners are—*not quite right,*" the owner went on. "Abdul's been with us for thirty years. *Severely* retarded."

So *that* was why he bared his yellow teeth so maniacally whenever we passed. He was actually only trying to be friendly.

"We also have a block booking of the hotel tomorrow. Three Belgian soccer teams . . ."

The owner smiled serenely, with a look that said: Now are you going to leave?

I nodded serenely, thinking: I have nothing against the Belgians. But we leave tomorrow.

Loving Middle Egypt

For reasons of security, the authorities want tourists to use only specially designated A/C trains between Cairo and Upper Egypt, so railway clerks have been instructed not to sell tickets for other trains. . . .
However, wagon-lits are also shot at quite often, so are probably best avoided.

The Rough Guide to Egypt

ANCIENT ROMANS were able to travel the entire distance from Alexandria to Aswan by barge along the Nile. This charming tradition, revived by the colonial British, lasted until the mid-1990s, when Middle Egypt became a stronghold of terrorist groups. Killing tourists was a highly efficient way of devastating the Egyptian economy. After riverboats were sprayed with machine-gun fire and attacks on foreigners occurred at more isolated ruins, boat companies canceled services that covered the length of the Nile Valley. We would be able to cruise only the final stretch.

And yet, through thick and thin, the train services from Cairo to Luxor (Roman Thebes) have been kept intact—despite the fact that these are also shot at on a semiregular basis. The Egyptian army has taken measures to protect the railway. Soldiers regularly scorch the fields near the tracks, so snipers cannot hide. And tourists are put in special cars with their own armed guards—despite the rather obvious drawback of making them easy targets.

"Oh, no," Sehed had laughed indulgently, when I politely inquired if we were likely to be butchered on the train. "The Luxor service is very safe now. And most interesting."

I didn't know whether to believe her or the guidebooks with their dire warnings. It wouldn't do to have Les dodging bullets. But if the train trip really *was* safe, I thought, then it was the obvious way to reach Luxor—indeed, the closest way to follow the ancient Roman tourist trail, absorbing the mythic landscape of the Nile Valley.

"One hundred percent safe!" Sehed reiterated, shaking her head at the folly of the question. Then she added—"But you're taking the *day* train, of course?"

Strangely, Les acknowledged the historical logic of following the Nile by land—and agreed that it would be far more entertaining than an hour on Egypt Air. The train might not be quite the Orient Express, but perhaps it had the raffish charm of British colonial rail. This position she maintained until we got on board. The first-class car was a splintery wooden hull, with hard seats and cracked opaque windows. The air-conditioning was an icy blast on our heads. The single toilet was blocked by a towering pyramid of excreta—and we hadn't even left the station yet.

A seedy character slumped in a corner, wearing gray pajamas that exposed his stomach, turned out to be the steward. It wasn't his job to clean the toilets, he told her.

"I'd hate to see what second class looks like," Les said sweetly.

The steward looked perplexed. "Why did you not *fly* to Luxor?"

We looked around and saw only three other passengers who'd made the same irrational decision. There was a French backpacking couple who had, like us, thought they might enjoy *la romance du Nil*—fellow fools for Orientalism. At the far end of the car was a minor Egyptian official, sitting next to the plainclothes armed guard. This twitching protector had one pistol in a shoulder holster, another poking out of the back pocket of his pants, as if he was just hoping someone would make a grab for it.

As the train creaked out of the Cairo station, the steward came by with a hot tea service. The French girl thought this was *charmant* until he dropped a scalding glass into her lap. A slight smile crossed his lips. When the same accident nearly happened to Les, I realized that our twisted Jeeves was getting some kind of kick out of it. Western women traveling in Muslim countries enjoy a perplexing range of encounters with some of the local men, from acts of childish perversion to aggressive groping and spitting. This was a new twist. Every time he staggered by, juggling the kettle in one hand, cups in the other, the prospect of third-degree burns loomed.

In contrast to all this, the view outside the train could not have been dreamier. We were rattling through the antique picture-postcard fantasy of the Nile. Fellahin (farm laborers) were driving bullocks through the green fields. Women in colored veils were drawing water from narrow canals. Almost nothing from the last two centuries dated the scene.

I kicked back to enjoy the pageant—five hundred miles of solitude, ten hours to Luxor.

Sixteen hours later, we were trundling through the moonless night, wearing four layers of clothing, as well as gloves and hats, to ward off an arctic combination of air-conditioning and frozen desert air that was blasting through cracks in the floor.

Outside, villages were speeding past in dim, icy flashes. I had been mildly unsettled to learn that, due to delays, we wouldn't make it through the Qena bend in daylight. This hook in the Nile, just before Luxor, was where most extremist attacks on trains had occurred in the past—usually after dark. Our carriage was lit up like a birthday cake. I kept imagining our clearly silhouetted heads from the vantage point of a sharpshooter out there in the dark, dressed like an extra from *Lawrence of Arabia* and getting ready for a bloodbath. I'd also just discovered that, by absurd mischance, this was November 16—the anniversary of the Hatshepsut massacre in 1997, which had occurred near Luxor. The French couple was surprisingly familiar with the grisly details: How the assassins had hidden themselves above the temple ruins to rain down an initial spray of gunfire. How they then spent a leisurely hour hunting down tourists who were hiding within the enormous building complex, killing them in cold blood. Fifty-eight people died that day. I hoped the extremists had no commemorative plans.

By the time we were at the outskirts of Luxor, nothing had happened, and I was smiling indulgently at my temerity. There were only a dozen miles to go. Even the security guard was starting to doze off beside the snoring bureaucrat, eyelids drooping, arms crossed.

And then: *Crack!*

The window behind us shattered. The Frenchwoman let out a scream and made a dive for the aisle. I grabbed Les by the shoulders and pulled her down to the floor.

Crack! A second window exploded into white.

The security guard took out his pistol and waved it in the air. He ran forward in a crouch, more Maxwell Smart than 007. The bureaucrat was awake, eyes wide with fear.

The train trundled on. We held our breath. It was silent.

After what seemed an eternity, the potbellied conductor walked hesitantly to the window. He pushed at the splinter-proof glass, to examine the jagged holes.

"Village boys," he snorted. "Not bullets. Rocks."

The security guard put his pistol back in his holster and laughed. "Boys!" He shook his head at us on the floor, as if he'd never had any doubt.

"They can throw very hard," the Frenchwoman muttered.

The bodyguard roared with laughter. "You thought it was bullets!"

He went back down to the bureaucrat, to tell him about our mistake. They quivered with hilarity, a little too loudly.

We all sat down again, pensively waiting out the last few minutes of the ride.

"You know, Tone," Les confided, "I'm not sure I need all this. I just want a relaxing time from now on. A quiet sort of trip."

The Frenchwoman looked at her pityingly. "I think you are in the wrong country."

As we pulled into the platform, I gazed out at a mob of expectant faces—there must have been a hundred hotel and taxi touts standing outside the train, waiting for us four foreigners. Pickings were slim these days.

A sign in Arabic and English was lit up above the poised crowd:

SMILE, YOU ARE IN LUXOR

The Dark Side
of the Nile

TEN DAYS' SAIL FROM THE PYRAMIDS, Roman tourists woke to the cries of boatmen casting ropes at Thebes, present-day Luxor. At last! This was Egypt's most affecting altar to lost glory. Around 1500 B.C., as capital of the New Kingdom Pharaohs, Thebes had presided over an empire that stretched across North Africa and the Near East. Its ascendancy lasted five hundred years, with conquerors like Ramses II (today popularly thought to be the Pharaoh of Exodus) presiding in palaces of such megalomaniacal grandeur that a mere glimpse persuaded enemy ambassadors to surrender. Then came the long decline. By the first century A.D., when the pioneer tourists were arriving, Egypt's pride was an isolated field of ruins, with only five thousand inhabitants farming the narrow green fringe of the Nile. But even in its twilight, the relics dwarfed anything the Romans or Greeks had ever created. Alexander the Great's generals had renamed it Diospolis, the City of Zeus, but the name did not stick: It was still the "hundred-gated Thebes" that Homer had praised as the most magnificent city on earth. (Today's name, Luxor, comes from the medieval Arabic *El-Uqsur,* for palaces or castles.)

Upon their arrival, ancient tourists were unfazed by the scenes of desert squalor. They eagerly followed their guides ashore from the dusty river docks, through humble villages squatting in the husk of the Pharaohs' capital. (The basic rural cottage design—mud-brick walls, with cone-shaped roofs to house pigeons and an oven in the courtyard to incubate the eggs with camel dung—is still in use today.) These modest realities of provincial Egypt were forgotten once the visitors reached a ceremonial avenue lined with ram-headed sphinxes. For a mile and a half the path continued through irrigated gardens, with lotus flowers floating artfully in delicate ponds, although Roman sightseers barely noticed the greenery. The whole horizon was obliterated by the monstrous Temples of Karnak—House of all the Gods, "most esteemed of places," and the most ostentatious building project ever conceived by man.

Karnak's central precinct alone covered one hundred acres; for an indication of its profligate, overblown grandiosity, its Temple of Amun was nearly twenty times the size of the Parthenon. In every direction, a perspective of columns and chambers stretched to infinity. The main vestibule—the Great Hypostyle Hall—seemed to have been designed to accommodate Titans: The sprawling complex was far larger than Egyptian priests could properly maintain, and vast areas of it had been abandoned to nature; sand dunes drifted among the pillars of once-great temples; flocks of doves settled in the ceilings. As the sun beat mercilessly down, tourists strolled past Brobdingnagian courts, colossi, obelisks, sacred lakes, and giant scarabs until their heads swam. Roman viceroys had installed statues of the emperors in Karnak to continue the pharaonic tradition of the divine-ruler cult, but they would have appeared sorry figures in that playground of giants—the tallest reaching only to the knees of a statue of Ramses.

Incised on every wall were reliefs celebrating the wars of pouting Pharaohs—all brilliantly painted, unlike their bare monochrome state today—and Roman tourists hired elderly priests to translate the hieroglyphs. Germanicus in A.D. 19 was told that Ramses II had fielded an army of seven hundred thousand men—more than five times the number of troops available to the Roman Empire—and exacted a far greater tribute in the form of grain, ivory, and spices. It must have been an unimaginative Roman whose assumptions about his Eternal City were not shaken by Karnak.

At the end of the visit, the priests solemnly gestured across to the west bank of the river. The desolate Theban Hills, where the sun set, was the Land of the Dead, they intoned.

By now the Roman tourists were prepared to believe almost anything. All of Egypt had been shamelessly ghoulish, but here the stark desert landscape set their overstimulated imaginations aflame. These blistering hills really did seem like the gateway to the beyond, stalked as they were by the jackal-headed god Set, Egyptian prince of the underworld; his evil minions, the hyenas, could be heard laughing at night, while by day vultures circled overhead, feeding on carrion. Remote valleys hid tombs riddled with spells, and whole armies of mummies would be revealed in passing sand drifts. Beggars in the street sold amulets of unspeakable age, stolen from defiled graves, laden with the curses of those doomed never to reach the afterlife.

Roman tourists could hardly wait to see it all for themselves.

HOLIDAY IN HADES

We were alive in Luxor, ancient Thebes. Les was safely sleeping off her terrors, but I couldn't settle. All night long, it had been raining hieroglyphs in my dreams; at 4 A.M., I woke with a start and went out to the hotel balcony.

Luxor was improbably calm. Even the Nile seemed to be dozing: From time to time, its mirror-flat surface was disturbed by shudders of movement, unexplained ripples like the quivering of snakes beneath the water. And there on the western riverbank—referred to by Egyptians now simply as *min Gharb* (the other side)—a fine mist was circling the stalks of palm trees. The crumbling Theban Hills, which had so enthralled and disturbed ancient visitors, were glowing beneath the morning stars in lurid shades of violet and scarlet.

Although Luxor has always been one of Egypt's top tourist draws—the Victorian British sightseers always flocked here—its modern fate began one November morning in 1922 when Howard Carter pushed a candle into an underground chamber and muttered, "I see things—wonderful things." The discovery of Tutankhamen, the only pharaoh whose tomb was intact, still rates as the single most famous archaeological find in history. Not only did Carter become as well known as Valentino, Luxor was rocketed back into the touristic empyrean, just as it had been in the days of the Romans (the day is celebrated as a holiday in Luxor every year, with parades and street parties). The consequences have also passed into legend. While visiting the freshly opened tomb, Carter's patron, Lord Carnarvon, was bitten on the cheek by a mosquito; he contracted a mysterious disease and died in Cairo soon afterward. At the moment he expired, the lights in the hospital blacked out; in faraway Scotland, the lord's favorite dog let out a howl and fell dead. The world was transfixed by the palpable evidence of the Pharaoh's Curse, and although most members of the 1922 team, including Carter himself, lived to ripe old ages, the myth was unshakable.

As the base for visits to the Valley of the Kings, Luxor is now devoted to tourism—with all the unsettling social distortions this brings. Every

morning, a hurricane blast of activity clogs the riverfront with tour
buses and felucca touts and *calesh* (carriage) drivers and sunken-eyed
children peddling cat statues in alabaster, asking ten dollars, then five,
then one, as foreigners pass. And the ancient Cult of the Dead still turns
a tidy profit: a spanking new Museum of Mummification has been
opened, along with the attached Anubis Café (a bravura act to name a
restaurant after the god who "fed on decay"—but they do a delicious
pizza *napolitana*).

Thus far, our visit to Luxor had not been a raging success. After the
heart-stopping train trip, Lesley had gotten food poisoning in the hotel
restaurant. The next afternoon, we were stuck in the elevator for half
an hour—the resulting phobia seems even more extreme for pregnant
women. Les was starting to feel personally victimized by the genial
incompetence that is Egypt's trademark. I still hadn't told her about the
disaster of our apartment in New York. But I had a plan for our trip
across the Nile that at least might fix the bad luck.

It was time to work on our own low-grade Pharaoh's Curse.

On the predawn local ferry, women in black veils nursed children with
terrible rashes, making Les even paler than usual. As the boat pulled into
the west bank, I scanned a row of black taxis. Only one driver was
awake—a one-eyed man named Gagarg.

By way of introduction, Gagarg said he was descended from a distinguished family of grave robbers—a far more honorable trade, it was
implied, than driving a taxi, and certainly more profitable. In ancient
Egyptian times, it had been a dangerous career: The penalty was to be
impaled through the anus. But by the Roman era, tomb robbing was a
thriving cottage industry, filtering a steady flow of antiquities through
the Theban markets to tourists.

"And how are you, my friends?" Gagarg asked, as we rattled along.
"You like Luxor?"

"It's a little exhausting," I said, in an ill-advised moment of honesty.
We had been barked at by souvenir vendors for eight solid hours the day
before. "Everyone's very persistent."

Gagarg surveyed me sardonically in the rearview mirror with his one
gimlet eye.

"This is a problem, yes. Soon you will be able to leave, and forget all
of this in Luxor."

Just what we needed. A driver with a sense of postcolonial politics.

The Colossi of Memnon, which once "sang" to Roman tourists.

Suddenly, up ahead, sitting incongruously in a field by the side of the road, perched a pair of enthroned pharaonic statues, each the size of a six-story tenement.

"Stop—Gagarg. *Stop!*"

"You will not go to the Valley of the Kings?" He pointed off to the barren mountains a few miles farther west, rising through the morning mist.

"Just one minute . . ."

We clambered out of the taxi and proceeded to inspect the statues' three-yard-long feet. Sure enough, among the centuries of graffiti were strings of Latin epigrams and Greek poems, all written with the same motivation as modern tourist scribble. Nestled in among the *Daryl Jones, Christmas 1811* and *Ich bin ein Berliner* were notes from the likes of Lucius Charisius and Falernus, "professor and poet." Today, the colossi sit in a recess, while once they were visible for miles around. But they still have a potent aura of majesty, if not of magic.

To the Romans, these statues marked the single most important tourist site in Egypt—perhaps in their entire world. They were believed to be of Memnon, that mythical Ethiopian demigod who died in the

Trojan War. And these "Colossi of Memnon" were far more than inert sentinels of the Nile: They were imbued with tangible evidence of the divine on earth.

THE SINGING STONE

It was a pagan miracle more reliable than any weeping Madonna today and tourists traveled across the Mediterranean to witness it.

Judging from the many travelers' accounts, a heterogeneous band of spectators would gather here in the darkness before dawn—wandering scholars, lady poets, army officers from the legion at Thebes—all wrapping their cloaks tightly about them in the brisk desert air. The features of the twin statues were finer than today, but the right-hand colossus had been broken at the hips; the top half lay embedded in the sand, so that by torchlight the small audience could inspect its glassy-eyed, impassively handsome face. There would have been hushed whispers of anticipation as the sun pierced the horizon and its light started to creep along the

Ancient tourist graffiti on the leg of one colossus.

rugged Theban Hills behind. As the golden light settled upon the statues, Egyptian priests offered a sacrifice at an altar before their feet. At
last, as the broken statue began to glow in the full blast of the sun, it let
out a high-pitched cry—like the melodious twang of a harp string, Pausanias the guidebook writer said.

It was Memnon calling out a greeting to his mother, the Dawn.

Although today we might suspect charlatan priests at work, the expla-
nation for the singing statue was almost certainly natural. Memnon's
performing career began in 27 B.C., when an earthquake broke the statue
in two. Historians speculate that air must have been trapped inside the
broken figure, which expanded in the warm morning sun and escaped
through a crack—creating the distinctive alto wail. Some said it sounded
like a copper vessel being struck, others a mournful human sigh. Strabo,
who heard Memnon in 25 B.C., was skeptical ("It was like a gentle banging," he reported, "but I could not tell whether it came from the statue
itself or was made by one of the hangers-on around the base"). His
doubts were drowned out, as the ancients fell over one another in praising the enchanted colossi. The art critic Callistratus wrote that Ethio-
pean artists had magically mingled the hero's pain with the inert rock.

Here the most highbrow Romans felt an insuperable desire to express
their delight in graffiti—usually in verse, and often in the complicated,
archaic meter of Homer (one reason why tourists often brought professional poets with them on their journeys). Since carving long poems was
hot work, Egyptians provided stonecutters for the service. A certain
Falernus, a professor, raved:

> At the sight of his mother, the saffron-robed dawn,
> He utters a sound that flows more sweetly than ever did mortal song.

Modern critics have unkindly dismissed the Romans' hundred-odd
poetic efforts as doggerel, and certainly they do seem rather stiff and
formal:

> O Memnon! Your voice still booms,
> Though your body was broken by enemies.
> The Viceroy Mettius Rufus witnessed the event.
> This verse was written by the poet Paeon.

One Roman viceroy started out in leaden Latin and switched to
creaking Greek:

I, Titus Petronius Secundus, Governor of Egypt, on the day before the Ides of March, in the 16th consulship of the Emperor Domitian [that is, March 14, A.D. 92], heard Memnon at the first hour after dawn and honor him with the following Greek verse:

> Lord Memnon! whose majestic spirit remains in this place—
> You sang loud and clear when struck by Apollo's burning rays!

We can also gather from the scrawl that Egypt's Old Faithful sometimes let his fans down. When Hadrian visited in A.D. 130, Memnon embarrassingly failed to perform. Deeply disturbed by the silence—*had the gods turned their back on him?*—the emperor retired in a sulk. His wife, Sabina, attended the next day, and heard Memnon sing on cue. She persuaded her husband to make another visit, and to everyone's evident relief, the statue obliged.

"Lord Hadrian himself loudly greeted Memnon," the poetess Julia Balbilla recorded, evidently to assuage the emperor's battered ego, "and it was clear to all that the Gods love him."

In the end, the singing statue was a victim of its own success. In 199 B.C., another touring emperor, Septimius Severus, heard the divine performance and was so impressed that he ordered Memnon to be repaired as a gesture of homage. The last Roman graffito on the statue is dated A.D. 205—the year that Roman army engineers replaced the enormous torso with cranes.

The peculiar natural accident that had trapped air within the colossus was removed. Memnon was struck dumb, and has remained silent to this day.

As we watched the golden sun on Memnon's sunken chest, Gagarg surveyed us carefully from above, as if we were dangerous extremists. I felt a little sorry for Amenhotep III, Egypt's ruler of the fourteenth century B.C., whose statues these originally were. Today, the pair are still universally referred to as the Colossi of Memnon—memorials more to the Roman tourists with their bizarre pseudomythic rituals than to the dead pharaoh.

"Mister!" Gagarg finally yelled down, his patience exhausted. "Why are you here? There is nothing at this place."

"Five minutes."

"What about your poor lady wife? You must go to the Valley of the Kings. Tutankhamen's tomb is a wonderful thing. There you will embrace the real history!"

So as not to torment Gagarg any further, we climbed into the back of his jalopy and charged into the heart of the Theban Hills.

SPELUNKERS OF THE SECRET TOMBS

After the colossus's song, at a nearby temple of Memnon—now called the Ramesseum—the more energetic Roman tourists would hire guides, mules, and drivers from local villagers, along with torches and ropes, then set off riding the mules along a narrow trail into the bleak mountains. With the sun high in the sky, it was a decidedly uncomfortable couple of hours; the landscape was pitiless, scorched, and searingly hot. But finally, the group would descend into a bright sandy valley, honeycombed with crevices that would reveal the entrances to caves.

This was the Valley of the Kings, riddled with sixty-two New Kingdom Pharaohs' tombs—then referred to by their Greek name, *syringes* (pipes). In Roman times, only ten were open for viewing—grave robbers had sealed up the others after they'd finished with them—and of those ten, only one was considered a must-see: that of Pharaoh Ramses VI, which, because of its unusually lavish decoration, was believed to be (surprise!) the tomb of Memnon himself.

The entrance to what archaeologists now call KV9 was piled with rubble; tourists had to squeeze into a cold, dismal chamber, where guides would pass them resin torches. But as they penetrated the darkness, those flickering lights revealed a fantastic scene: Every inch of the tomb's walls exploded with hieroglyphs and hallucinogenic murals—fire-breathing snakes, kings in flaming chariots, ram-headed beetles being pulled in boats—which the Egyptian guides fancifully related to episodes in King Memnon's short and tragic life. (Today we know they were texts to assist in the pharaoh's passage to the afterlife—the *Book of Gates, Book of the Caverns, Book of Day and Night*). Many tourists stayed within sight of the entrance, but the iron-nerved continued through nine chambers in all to view the giant black sarcophagus of the hero, now empty inside the cool heart of the mountain.

Thunderstruck, tourists knew exactly what they had to do: They pulled out a stylus and ink and jotted a few thoughts on the plaster.

Today—luckily for Lesley's aggrieved lower spine—visitors to the Valley of the Kings can dispense with the mule ride; instead, little red kiddies' trains shuttle from the parking lot to the gates. But inside the Valley, the site is as intimidating as ever. Soaring cliffs concentrate the sun; fine dust eddies in the bone-dry wind; concrete slabs over the tomb entrances make it look like a missile silo in the Nevada desert. At 10 A.M., it was 100 degrees and rising fast.

"And now is winter!"—Gagarg patted my shoulder consolingly— perhaps the same bemused remark as locals have made for two thousand years.

KV9 wasn't hard to find; its cold interior was instantly refreshing. Glass plates now protect the brilliant murals—the tomb has suffered many indignities, including a roof cave-in—as well as the exuberant scrawl in Latin and Greek, which is now considered as historically valuable as the images they originally defaced.

Etching into plaster or scribbling with a stylus (tourists evidently carried black, brown, green, and red ink) was easy, spontaneous—and the results surprisingly durable. Precisely 2,105 pieces of ancient graffiti survive in the Valley of the Kings, nearly half of them on the walls of "Memnon's tomb." They are cataloged in musty French volumes from the 1840s and have been subject to endless scholarly analyses, interpretation, statistical assessment, and literary review in obscure modern Ph.D. theses. The result is a unique window on ancient tourist culture—far more lively than the formulaic paeans on the Colossi of Memnon.

"I was amazed!" was (of course) the perennial favorite—in fact, the vacationing centurion Januarius repeated the phrase in four different chambers, signing also for his wife and daughters. "I was *more than amazed!*" wrote one visitor, a master of one-upmanship. But a certain Ephiphanius, perhaps exhausted by the searing heat, was morose: "The only amazing thing here is the size of the tomb."

Apart from such conventional declarations—"Those who have not seen this tomb have seen nothing; happy are those who have"—Roman travelers liked to leave a little information about themselves. Like many a backpacker today, they bragged of their past journeys. "I, Antonius, son of Theodorus . . . who have long resided in Rome and gazed on the marvels there, have seen them here too." A certain Isodorius slips in that he has studied in Athens. Many visitors give their professions; as would be expected, there are a large number of erudite professionals—doctors, orators, judges, as well as "Amsouphis, Magician," who signed the walls nine times. A lawyer named Bourichios had evidently hoped to crack the mystery of the hieroglyphs: "My visit to Egypt is over, and I curse myself for failing to decipher these messages." Another visitor responded: "You are too harsh on yourself, Bourichios!" A couple of

Greek ditties are repeated on different tombs. "Horus, son of Zeus, help me return home safe and sound," goes one. The other: "These pipes carved in rock are works of astounding horror." They may well have been jingles suggested by the guides.

The author Plutarch deplored all tourist graffiti as mindless. "Rarely is there anything constructive or charming in their scribbling," he lamented, "just nonsense like 'So-and-so asks for blessed remembrance for so-and-so.' " This is probably a little unfair. The casual and unpremeditated scribbles in the Valley of the Kings had a vaguely metaphysical purpose. No less than the Pharaohs themselves, tourists wanted to join themselves to eternity: "Whoever erases this writing shall have his own name extinguished for ever and ever," one graffito threatens. Or, from an Egyptian sanctuary to Pan: "A dead man is revived when his name is pronounced."

While the ancient celebrity of "Memnon's tomb" may seem a whimsical footnote to world history, it did have one long-standing consequence: The very rubble from KV9's original entrance, scrambled over by tourists for century after century, accidentally helped obscure the entrance of a certain boy-pharaoh's tomb directly beneath, preserving it for posterity.

Today, Tutankhamen has replaced Memnon as the West's top Egyptian celebrity; his tomb draws endless battalions of visitors, despite being one of the least artistically impressive in the Valley. Tut is also the only pharaoh to have actually been *reburied* in modern times. He was put back inside his less valuable outer sarcophagus and returned to the Valley by Howard Carter—supposedly as a gesture of respect. There it still sits, in a cozy vestibule. But Carter's pious gesture was a red herring. A reexamination of the mummy in the 1970s found that his team had physically broken up the resin-saturated corpse in order to separate it from the exquisite innermost coffin, which now sits in Cairo's Museum of Antiquities. Investigators were also shocked to find that King Tut was missing his, ah, *member*—apparently "souvenired" by someone on Carter's team.

I thought this made my prodding of Thutmose III seem pretty tame.

CONVERSATION WITH A PHARAOH

Tame—and yet, still discomforting. Especially for a lapsed Catholic. One who was heatstruck in the desert, staggering from one tomb to the next.

Sacrilege is sacrilege, I had to admit. There aren't *degrees* of defiling of the dead. I had succumbed to base curiosity. And Les, too, was paying the price.

The disaster in our apartment in New York—I'd heard about it *the very next night.* The mad trip to the Faiyum. The terrifying train ride. Les getting food poisoning, then trapped in an elevator. What if something *serious* happened? I was as bad as those maniacally superstitious Romans, both fascinated and unnerved by the dark forces of Egypt.

"I've got to sit down," Les was saying. I took her to a rest area, where benches and mineral water were provided for collapsing Westerners.

"There's just one more tomb I've got to visit," I explained.

Les groaned quietly.

At the very farthest recess of the Valley, rarely visited by modern visitors, concealed in its own private wadi, was KV34—the tomb of Thutmose III.

I climbed up a metal ladder, then down steep stairs. The ruthless old general made sure his was one of the best-defended resting places in the Valley—booby traps included a collapsing floor that sent thieves plunging onto sharpened stakes. With the cautious tread of the guilty, I crossed the same dark pit, and moved through dimly lit chambers whose walls, dancing with hieroglyphs, curled through the rock like a beckoning, arthritic finger. I arrived in the final hall. At the far end, a huge stone sarcophagus squatted as immovable as any altar. I was alone, except for one guard in pale robes and turban, who eyed me eagerly. He was ready to launch into the usual incoherent spiel and touch me for baksheesh, but I avoided eye contact and went straight to the dark stone crypt, original resting place of the pharaoh's remains.

Feeling decidedly foolish, I put my hands on the broad rim.

What on earth was I doing? The guard shook his head, warning me away, so I dug out some Egyptian pounds. He withdrew with a knowing nod, as if he'd seen this sort of thing before.

I put one leg over, then the other, and slowly lay down in the sarcophagus. The stone on my back was as cold as the mummy's fossilized arm back in Cairo.

This can't hurt, I reminded myself. I closed my eyes. And apologized to Thutmose. In case this seemed a little pathetic to the Napoleon of the East, I offered to make more-tangible amends. *A dead man is revived when his name is pronounced.* I promised to one day tell the story of prodding his corpse, and subsequently make his name live on.

I opened my eyes. Two Swiss tourists clutching their *Guides Routardes* were staring down at me as if I were a dangerous lunatic. I didn't care: Perhaps it was my first twinge of paternal responsibility, acting like a superstitious idiot in Egypt. And the most embarrassing thing was—*I felt better.* I realized that if the positions had been reversed—if I were a decrepit mummy, and the general had stumbled upon *me*—he would hardly feel guilty about some serious prodding. In fact, he would probably have broken off my member and made it into a key ring.

Divine River Cruising

THE STRETCH OF THE NILE from Luxor to Aswan happens to be the most majestic in Egypt. With every mile, the raw ocher bluffs of the Valley press ever closer to the riverbank, until they rear above the palm trees like enormous dykes holding back the golden desert sands. By pleasant coincidence, it's also the only section of the ancient Roman journey that travelers can actually repeat by water these days. Since the river cruise is still regarded as the quintessential Egyptian travel ritual, the docks of Luxor are clogged with every class of riverboat, stacked sideways in threes and fours. It may be an abbreviated taste of the once-epic Nile trip—it's a modest three-day hop to Aswan—but the mythic reputation is simply inescapable.

At last, we would be cruising the River of Life—in the Romans' favored mode of transport, if not quite their standard of comfort.

Ever since 48 B.C., when Cleopatra cruised with Julius Caesar in the royal barge of the Ptolemies, floating pleasure palaces had been an Egyptian specialty. According to a meticulous description provided by the author Athenaeus, Cleopatra's version was a three-hundred-foot catamaran. The cedarwood decks were designed like a covered pedestrian arcade, with gilded archways, ivory statues, and shrines to Aphrodite, along with a "secret grotto" for romantic encounters. There were four dining rooms—one on the roof for alfresco dining on warm nights—and a master bedroom with twenty beds.

The vessels in use by ordinary Roman tourists may have fallen short of that semi-divine standard, but judging from the lack of complaints in literature, they were very pleasant nonetheless. Sheltered from the sun by lilac canopies, lounging on their pillows with a beaker of wine, passengers watched scenes from the Nilotic mosaics popular in Roman villas come alive before their eyes. Magical animals such as hippopotamuses wallowed among the reeds. Hunters went by in canoes. Sandstone temples rose like fortresses above the palms—each with its own small army of priests, its own schools, libraries, and lodgings. In this fantastic landscape, travelers composed literary homages to the divine Nile. The novelist Achilles Tatius raved, describing its water as a godly nectar, sweeter than wine, and more transparent than any glass.

"Is there anything not marvelous in that river?" asked the orator Aristides. "Its entire length is a gallery of wonders. No tributaries feed it— the rocks all around are splitting with the desert's dryness, and the mountains are almost bursting into flame. And yet, the volume of its flow could fill every lake and every gulf. . . . It is like a single spring for the whole land of Egypt."

Egyptian priests were invited on board to give lectures on the greatest geographical issue of ancient times: the source of the Nile. Did it flow into Africa from the river Oceanus that encircled the earth? Or did it burble directly from the ground? And how did it flood like clockwork every year, without any rains? Experts reviewed standard theories— Egyptian, Persian, and Greek—which were drawn not from science but from literary sources. Itinerant ivory traders knew that the Nile's tributaries were filled by springtime rains in the mountains to the south (in modern Uganda). But the reports of these rustics were dismissed out of hand by all respected ancient thinkers: Any idiot could see that the sun's heat actually *increased* the farther south one traveled, singeing men's skin to the color of ash, so these verdant mountains could not exist. The ancients actually *preferred* the Nile's source to be unknowable for mortals. The river's annual rhythm was proof of the divine order of the cosmos.

AGAINST THE FLOW

Les found us a luxury barge from the Oberoi Hotel group, evocatively named the *Oberoi III*. Like every Nile cruiser today, it resembled a floating brick—no prow or stern, just a solid rectangle of tourist accommodation that made the boat easy to dock.

This was the *Oberoi III*'s maiden voyage, and the cabins smelled of fresh paint and sawed wood, a definite improvement on the overpowering odor of beer-sodden carpet that most of the older riverboats exuded.

Our interior designer had favored lime green with lashings of chrome, although the pink linoleum evoked the subtler tones of rose marble beloved by the ancients.

"We have three staff members for every passenger," boasted the steward, Mr. Kamahl. "And we are the only boat on the Nile that has *two bathrooms* for every cabin."

Like every cruise boat, the *Oberoi III* had a pool on the roof, surrounded by plastic lawn. Egyptian boat owners are under no illusions: The first priority for foreigners on a Nile cruise is to soak up the winter sun. So we joined a bevy of escapees from Toronto, loud, cheery, and permanently drunk, who basked like sea lions on the glittering green grass, while thin tuxedoed waiters hovered at our elbows. At first we felt like neocolonial swine. But relaxing in the warm glow of Africa, with the cliffs of the Nile drifting indifferently by, we soon got used to it.

River trips are inherently passive experiences, and often excruciatingly dull. But here in intense, desperate Egypt, the *Oberoi III* was a godsend. We were both exhausted—exhausted and sated.

Stendahl's syndrome had hit with a vengeance: Even I couldn't absorb any more ancient ruins. The leviathan temples with their vacant-eyed statues had all started to blur. The stylistic repetition had a numbing effect. And I *definitely* couldn't listen to another Egyptian myth. Hearing about all those deities—some diligent modern scholar had counted 641, beetle-headed, roach-winged, croc-tailed—was like listening to someone else's fantastic dreams. They went in one ear and out the other.

So we decided to skip a few land visits. All we wanted to do was wallow in the pool and stare at the riverbank. I felt a little ashamed of this philistine behavior, until I read that Julius Caesar and Cleopatra had enjoyed the same sort of trip. Caesar was exhausted after his years of battle. Cleopatra was heavily pregnant with his son. Of course, Julius had just conquered the entire known world. But apart from that minor detail, the parallel seemed fairly apt.

Whenever the Canadians grew too voluble, I retreated to the cabin to read about one of the more disastrous Nile river trips in history—Hadrian's melancholy cruise in A.D. 130. By all accounts, the imperial barge was a floating den of carnal intrigue. Although he had invited his wife, Sabina, the aging emperor focused his affections entirely on his boy favorite, Antinous, whose striking good looks have been compared to a "melancholy Apollo." The disgruntled empress, for her part, found solace with her own special companion, Julia Balbilla, who wrote erotic verse in the style of Sappho of Lesbos. The atmosphere as they sailed through Egypt became increasingly tense.

When the young Antinous was discovered floating dead in the reeds of the Nile, it appeared to be an accidental drowning. But rumors began to fly around the Empire. Had the emperor's lover been murdered by Sabina—or even, at Hadrian's own behest, been sacrificed by the priests of Egypt? It was well known that magicians could extend one man's life by substituting another to die in his place, and the emperor was deathly ill.

Modern historians have suggested suicide. Anyone who drowned in the Nile, according to Egyptians, achieved immortality with Lord Osiris. For Antinous, this may have seemed an appealing option on a vacation that was going horribly awry. It appears that Hadrian wanted to keep their romance going as Antinous grew into his adult years—which for conservative Greeks was considered a shameful and degrading situation. Affected by the imagery of death that barraged him from all sides on the trip, he may have chosen to slip quietly into the Nile as the only honorable course, incidentally gaining minor divinity for himself and the foretold new lease on life for his ailing lover.

The End of the World
As They Knew It

A STONE PYLON covered with worn hieroglyphs announced the final stop for Nile River traffic.

Aswan—then known as Syene—was a true frontier town, the ancient equivalent of a Foreign Legion outpost, blessed with one of the most enchanted natural settings in Egypt. It was located by the Elephantine, a beautiful stone outcrop that looked like the smoothly rounded flanks of a pachyderm. The high desert here seemed not quite of this earth—as if it were closer to the gods, suffused with a heavenly light—and all the exoticism of Egypt was distilled in its sandy streets. Snake charmers performed with defanged cobras; camel trains bore perfumes from Arabia; ebony-skinned courtesans mingled in bars with off-duty centurions. Here on the Tropic of Cancer, natural wonders unfolded every summer equinox, when the sun shone directly overhead and obelisks cast no shadow. (In the third century B.C., the Greek scientist Eratosthenes had used this fact to prove that the world was round: By comparing the lengths of shadows at the summer equinox in Alexandria, he calculated by trigonometry the circumference of the planet, and was accurate to within fifty miles.)

Aswan was also the scene for the Grand Tour's last rite—the day-trip to the island of Philae.

On this tiny splinter of land in the middle of the Nile, the Egyptian service industry provided Romans with a rounded touristic package that made a deeply satisfying end to the trans-Mediterranean odyssey. On the spiritual plane, the island was sacred to Isis, most popular of Egyptian deities (her maternal qualities would one day be co-opted by Christians for the Virgin Mary); her bunkerlike shrine attracted fifty thousand pilgrims a year. On the terrestrial, it marked the symbolic end of the Roman Empire. Legions patrolled a buffer zone for another seventy-five miles, but Philae was accepted as the outer limit of control—and geographical knowledge. (Only one Roman expedition that we know of was sent into Africa's interior: Around A.D. 60, Nero ordered a force of legionnaires to follow the Nile on foot. The soldiers penetrated into modern-day Sudan, but were nearly lost in torpid, labyrinthine marshes. The philosopher Seneca met two of the surviving centurions in Rome and learned about their privations. No European explorer would match their feat until the nineteenth century.)

But far more exciting than any of this was Egypt's most eccentric tourist show. Philae lay above the first cataract of the Nile, a set of surging rapids roaring violently in the desert. Teams of local boatmen would shoot the white water in papyrus-reed canoes, to the delight of Roman spectators who gathered on the island's edge for panoramic views. Even

Philae: the sacred island of Isis, the last stop of the Grand Tour of Antiquity.

the hypochondriacal Aristides took boyish pleasure in making these canoe displays the climax of his A.D. 160 Egyptian tour:

> Although I was in poor condition due to ill health, I asked the garrison commander of Syene [Aswan] to give me a light boat so that I could visit the Cataracts . . . and join the local boatmen's mysterious spectacle. The commander was amazed at my intention, and did his best to dissuade me: He said that it was very difficult, and that he was not brave enough to try it himself. But when he saw he could not dissuade me, he agreed to help. I sailed up stream. First . . . I watched the local boatmen riding the rapids. And then I decided to board a skiff myself, and try sailing around—not only to go over the rapids, but to explore the whole area. . . .

Most Romans shared the garrison commander's caution, since it was widely believed that going too close to the Nile's waterfalls would deafen those unaccustomed to their din.

The sense of emotional closure all this inspired in travelers is suggested by the graffiti at Philae, which are filled with homesickness and longing for family:

> *I, Demetrius, have traveled the length of fruit-blessed Nile,*
> *And now I bow before Isis, the all-powerful one,*
> *To beg her sacred protection for those dear to me—*
> *All my children, my brothers, my sisters and friends.*

Romans, of course, would also have paid particular attention to their sacrifices, since Isis was Egypt's protector of sailors. It was a long way home—and every mile of it by water.

"So this is it," Les said, easing herself into the shade of a column. "We made it."

There we were, standing on that holy teardrop of an island. Today, Philae is still the last stop on most Egyptian journeys—the government does not allow land travel farther south except via armed convoy. It's crawling with Egyptian soldiers in black berets who cradle machine guns and keep an eye out for extremists from the Sudan. But as I strained to feel the emotional parallel—some sense of triumphant arrival—I found myself failing miserably.

Partly it was the knowledge that we were standing on *virtual* Philae. The island today is actually a superb fake. In the 1970s, when it became clear that the original outpost was about to be submerged beneath a lake created by the Aswan High Dam, UNESCO arranged for Philae's temples to be cut into giant Lego blocks and rebuilt on another island, Agilika. On the face of it, the landscapers had done a sterling job. The arches and palm trees look as carefully arranged as a Japanese garden, with every view framed by purifying blue water.

But there was something missing—something indefinable. I knelt down and picked up a handful of soil, rubbed it around in my palm like Russell Crowe before a fight.

"This is it," Les repeated from the shadows. "Right?"

I tossed down the handful of earth and watched some scuttling scorpions. Maybe the journey was technically over—but I demanded *closure*.

THE LAST RITE (OF PASSAGE)

[In my dream] a bolt of lightning darted from the sky and skimmed the edge of my head so closely that I was surprised my hair had not been set on fire. But the fact that I had been hit on the right side of the head instead of the left was explained to me as a good omen.

This dream, in addition to many others, was interpreted to foretell . . . my need to stop traveling.

ARISTIDES, The Sacred Discourses

Lesley took the news about our flooded apartment very well, all things considered. It was, however, time to go back and repair the hearth. Enough was enough: She wanted to sleep in our own bed, feel winter, cook her own meals. On the face of it, I agreed. The sheer irreversibility of what was happening was hard for me to deny. Les was nearly seven months pregnant now. I didn't see how she could get any bigger without bursting. Soon airlines wouldn't even let her fly. But I found myself coming up with excuses to delay.

Why not enjoy a little of Aswan's unearthly beauty? After all, we'd found a stunning room in the New Cataract Hotel—up on the fiftieth floor. Built for Russian dam engineers in the 1960s, its balconies surveyed the entire landscape, with its bloodred cliffs, the Nile shimmering like black opal, and the sails of feluccas fluttering across the horizon like flakes of white gold. Up there, it felt like you could see the curvature of the earth itself. Lesley preferred to spend her time plotting to steal hotel dinnerware. She's not usually the type to pilfer towels or bathrobes, but these were kitsch classics, like old cruise-ship treasures with ancient Egyptian motifs—and the hotel was getting rid of them, waiters had told her, in favor of generic new china. Every day, Les managed to slip some crockery into her luggage, saving it from the dustbin of history. I suppose it was the closest she could get to nesting on the Egyptian frontier.

But I knew that homesickness was finally getting to her when she suggested we attend a Thanksgiving dinner at the Old Cataract Hotel—the snobbish colonial dowager of Aswan.

Thanksgiving? Of course! Anything, I reasoned, a little madly, to postpone the inevitable.

The meal, as I recall it, had the rhythm of a nightmare.

Pulling out our best clothes—the only ones that hadn't been shredded by months of travel—we made our way along the plush carpeted hallways, where rows of tuxedoed staff were standing at military attention, and into a cavernous dining room, whose gloomy belfry and faded Arabic symbols would have graced the lair of Bluebeard. For their cross-cultural feast, the management had arranged ten tables in an open circle, so that diners sat staring at one another like members of a Masonic sect. I had the feeling sailors get when stepping onto a blighted ship, but when I half rose from the table, waiters huddled around in a scrum. They had few enough customers. None would escape.

"Relax," Les whispered, with a bravura flourish. "It will be an experience."

And the dinner was, in its way, unforgettable, starting with the palate-cleansing mouthfuls of Nilotic wine, whose distinctive bouquet has earned it the affectionate nickname the Mummy's Armpit among travelers. Egyptian cuisine is one of the finest and most varied in the world, but the interpretation of Thanksgiving inexplicably focused on roast English lamb, whose pearly flesh was hidden by a stiff carapace of congealed gravy. In fact, each dish had the appearance of PVC-molded props used in window displays of lesser Chinese restaurants.

"I'm not sure I should eat this," Les whispered, as her fork stood upright in mint jelly.

Afterward, we shuffled out of the restaurant, flanked by waiters like prison guards.

For Les, this was the last straw—for the night, and perhaps for the trip. She headed back to our haven on the fiftieth floor of the New

Cataract, while I slunk off to the Old Cataract bar, feeling vaguely desperate.

This was where I recognized one of the liveried waiters.

I'd met Mahmoud a few days earlier. He was one of the Egyptian hipsters who loitered around the floating cafés by the Nile, brokering Aswan's commercial deals, from taxi rides to modest quantities of mindbending substances. Out of the blue, he had invited me to the wedding of "a close friend" out in one of the desert villages—it was hard to establish quite where.

Somewhere in Nubia.

This had sounded like an unusually bad idea, even to me. Assuming there really was a wedding, and this wasn't some rudimentary Sudanese kidnap plan, I didn't want to be an intruder on some private event—or worse, part of a segregated viewing party like the tour groups that congregate in the back rows of Harlem religious services every Sunday. But Mahmoud assured me that Nubian village weddings weren't like that. They were open-door festivals, and all comers were welcome.

It would be a prodigious event—a unique spectacle—a climactic extravaganza. For a moment, I had started to imagine this as a direct link to the religious festivals of the ancient Egyptians, full of music and dancing, barley beer and swirling silks.

"You will be *a valued guest,*" Mahmoud stressed. "There will be four or five strangers, who will receive hospitality, as Allah commands. My friend would be honored."

It started about ten o'clock Thursday night—Thanksgiving. I said we'd think about it.

"You'd have to be nuts," Les had opined matter-of-factly back at the hotel. "The guy looks like a hyena. They'll ransom us and then throw our limbs in the Nile."

"Sure," I said vaguely. "I probably won't go."

No more had been said about the wedding. Now here was Mahmoud in the Old Cataract bar, decked out in his night-job gear—delighted to repeat the dubious invitation. It was already 11 P.M.—he was about to drive out to the wedding—and he considered it an undeniable Act of Fate that I had wandered into his ken.

I had to agree. Without hesitation, I bounded back up to our room to tell Les about my brilliant new plan. I suspected it was slightly insane, but responsible life was closing in all around. This might be my last chance to behave disgracefully for some time.

"Oh, go to your Nubian wedding." Les sighed with some resignation. As I went off to find Mahmoud, she looked as if she were saying farewell to me for the last time.

"What's the telephone number out in Nubia? Just in case I go into labor early?"

TONY AND TINA'S NUBIAN WEDDING

Theon, son of Origenes, invites you to the wedding of his sister tomorrow, Tubi 9, at the 8th hour.

Papyrus invitation, Oxyrhynchus, second century A.D.

Ritual gatherings have been sight-seeing treats from the dawn of tourism. In the remoter parts of Roman Egypt, a festival of some nature occurred nearly every second day of the calendar. Each Nile village was holy to a slew of gods, whose feast days had to be observed. Effigies were paraded in boats along the river as crowds sang hymns on shore; sacred offerings were tossed into the current by chanting priests, to be carried away in a cloud of palm fronds. There were religious festivals dictated by the cycles of the Nile—one when the river would begin to rise in June; another when it overflowed its banks; and yet another, at the crest of the flood in late summer, when Nilometers were ceremonially read. There were celebrations for the accession of a new emperor, his birthday, his death (and any other event he deemed worthy). And finally, woven among all these holy days, were the innumerable family festivals. Weddings were the most lavish of all. Cattle were slaughtered, wine flowed with honey. At night, the houses were garlanded with lamps, which sparkled in the dark like swarms of fireflies. There was music, dancing, banqueting, and much lascivious behavior.

As I dashed back through the suddenly inspiring décor of the Old Cataract, I considered: How could I *not* go to a Nubian wedding?

Mahmoud was already drunk when I climbed into his dying Buick. We careened into the darkness of a dirt desert highway, camels and wooden carts flashing in the weak beam of one headlight. Skeletal shepherds spat oaths at us as we passed; mud-brick houses disappeared in clouds of dust; chickens ran maniacally back and forth in our wake. Mahmoud had one ring-covered hand on the wheel, the other on a bottle, from which he swigged at every lurch in the road.

"I thought Muslims didn't drink." I grimaced, clutching the dashboard for support. Mahmoud's eyes bulged; he was wearing a scarf
around his head, like a pirate.

"We are Nubians first, Muslims second! And tonight is a joyous night.
A night of enormous happiness. Allah will make *concessions*."

The Buick's engine finally spluttered and expired in the barren back
street of a village. Pulsing in the distance, I could hear anarchic and
incomprehensible music.

"We go," grunted Mahmoud.

We trudged through a maze of sandy alleyways toward the hysterical
noise. I tried to memorize a few distinguishing landmarks, but I saw
none. Just low mud houses in the moonlight, the occasional kerosene
lamp surrounded by moths the size of pigeons, and ragged children
watching from broken doorways. I thought of Les back in the four-star
hotel. This was all too *Sheltering Sky*.

Finally, the alleyways opened out into a huge courtyard—and there
really was a wedding.

At one end of the yard, rising up a dirt mound like an amphitheater,
endless rows of wooden benches were filled with Nubian men in colored
robes—hundreds of them, all sitting patiently. A few were drinking.
Most were passing around enormous joints like Havana cigars. At the
opposite end, a wooden stage had been set up for six musicians. Distorted Arabic pop music was being blasted on electric guitars and a
keyboard through speakers the size of pyramid blocks. An entire constel-
lation of floodlights blazed from every corner, powered by generators
whose engines roared like lions from the darkness. Despite the cacophony, nobody in that somnolent sea of males was reacting in the slightest
to the rhythms.

"Where are the women?" I shouted the obvious question to Mahmoud.

"We are very early," he replied, shrugging.

Well, this was no fake tourist show, I had to admit; in fact, as the only
foreigner, I began to feel a little self-conscious.

"Are you sure nobody minds me being here?"

"On the contrary! You are a valued guest."

As if to confirm this improbable notion, the groom himself suddenly
materialized at my side. He reminded me of a Nubian version of John
Belushi—roly-poly, bald, and with a vibrant pink cummerbund around
his waist. His wide glassy eyes suggested that he had been partying for
some time already. We shook hands, went through the formalities, with
Mahmoud translating. The village women, he shook his head dismis-

sively, were with the bride, henna-ing her hair (she was fifteen; the groom fifty). They would be along later—to spoil the fun, I gathered.

"In the meantime, we will take tea," Mahmoud announced, and lurched off.

On a balcony overlooking the scene, the hot libations were being served in slender glasses that included shots of an evil-smelling whiskey. Men piled in, sitting on one another's laps, stroking thighs affectionately. The groom pulled out yet another monstrous joint, this one as fat as a bratwurst. The whiskey seared my throat, tearing off taste buds like sulfuric acid. Down in the courtyard shadows, you could see men leaning against the walls, quietly retching. Mahmoud pointed to one poor devil on his knees.

"Egyptian liquor!" He chuckled.

My liver was still trying to process the Mummy's Armpit wine from dinner. No wonder the Prophet banned alcohol in the Koran.

Two hours later, I was down in the courtyard, still wondering when the ceremony was going to start. The band was playing as maniacally as ever; the guitarists must have been rubbing their fingertips raw on the chords. But there was no sign of a bride.

It was slowly dawning on me that this Nubian wedding was going to be an all-night event. Mahmoud finally confessed that this stellar insight was quite true. In fact, he explained, tonight was merely the preliminary round in a festival that would continue nonstop for three full days. This was a little inconvenient, since I had no way of getting back to Aswan.

Noticing my restlessness, the groom came up to us and began stroking my hand consolingly. I grinned at him like an idiot, wondering what was going on.

Mahmoud pointed at the stage. "The groom wants to dance with you."

I grinned even harder, until Mahmoud repeated the suggestion.

"Very hospitable," I gurgled. "But another night."

Mahmoud's smile faded, as he pointed at the stage more insistently. The groom squeezed my hand more warmly. I gently withdrew it.

"Please explain. I've hurt my knee badly and can't dance. A tragic disappointment."

Mahmoud looked grave. "You must! You are *a valued guest!*"

It occurred to me that he might be serious.

"The groom will be very offended." Mahmoud pushed me slightly.

My hesitation was beginning to penetrate the fog behind the groom's eyes. It was threatening to cast a shadow over the happiest event of his life. I was grasping about for some other excuse when he took me by both hands and squeezed imploringly.

Moving like an astronaut in deep space, I followed the bouncing ball up the steps and onto the brilliantly floodlit stage. We were the only ones up there, and the expanse seemed enormous. The music ratcheted up another jagged level to complete distortion.

The groom began to click his knees together, his eyes rolling back in his head ecstatically.

I was frozen like a deer in headlights. Nubian dancing seemed to consist of wiggling knees together energetically while keeping the arms stiff and outstretched—Zorba the Greek from the waist up, funky chicken below. I couldn't discern any beat in the music—nothing resembling a melody—and I knew I would only look even more ridiculous if I attempted to imitate his steps. So I slowly started dancing Western style, trying to imagine that the frenzied band was playing mangled REM numbers—very, very mangled.

As I gyrated my leaden limbs, I glanced furtively up to the balconies, expecting to see an arena exploding with amusement or derision. But the men in fluorescent robes were still just sitting on each other's laps, staring at me without the slightest expression.

The floodlights behind the crowd made everyone look like a black cardboard cutout. It was a moment frozen in time, and the groom and I seemed to be the only ones moving.

I looked out at those still silhouettes and thought: We really should get back to New York.

Epilogue:
Domus, *Sweet* Domus

Homer was quite right to say that Ulysses was wise and prudent because he had traveled so widely and come to know many different peoples. As for myself, my adventures as an ass enormously enlarged my experience, even if they have not taught me wisdom.

APULEIUS, The Golden Ass

These days, when I emerge from the subway at Grand Central Terminal, I always admire the enormous statue of wing-footed Mercury taking flight before I continue on to the giant fluted columns of the New York Public Library. Like Alexandria's eponymous institute, the library contains within its moldy stacks virtually every book ever written—those 1877 French academic journals and 1844 collections of Pyramid graffiti, and 1911 editions of German scholars. In the cavernous reading room, where images of the gods flit across the remote ceiling, I can watch the snow driving down from leaden clouds, and ponder the hot dome of blue above the Parthenon, or Thebes, or Troy.

It seems like a dream, our Grand Tour, as journeys are supposed to when you return—but then again, with only two hours' sleep a night, so do many things, now.

Needless to say, we made it back to Manhattan in one piece. After all those ancient ruins, we were finally able to behold the spectacular ruin of our apartment. It could have been worse, although I wasn't about to imagine how. The goddess Juno had kept her part of the bargain we'd made back in Rome: She'd gotten us safely to Egypt and home. Now, like Aristides dedicating a speech to Apollo, I was bound to complete an opus for her.

Those next few weeks vanished in a blur. Les went into prenatal overdrive: All that pent-up nesting instinct came out in one white-hot burst of energy, which she spent redesigning the apartment for an extra tenant. I'd come home and find her sawing lumber. It was exhausting to watch.

The last lick of paint went up one frozen winter's afternoon. On cue, Les nudged me awake at four o'clock the next morning.

For the whole time we were away, I'd never quite believed that the impending birth was actually going to occur. Then again, if they're honest about it, I don't think many men really do. We're sitting on the sidelines. It's easy to stay detached.

There's a lot of catching up to do, and it all happens in one explosive episode.

That frozen morning, Les and I made the epic voyage up First Avenue—four eternal blocks, which felt like they took longer than from Rome to the Nile. Then it was the basic human story—the most common event in the world, although it feels pretty unique to everyone involved. I suppose that's when I finally got the point. No matter how many people are doing it, no two experiences are ever *quite* the same.

One journey was over. Another had just begun, with a piercing squeal.

And by the way, the delivery was a Caesarean.

Antonius V.S.L.M.
New York A.D. 2001

ACKNOWLEDGMENTS

This book could never have been written without the assistance of dozens of people. I would particularly like to thank Brian Turner, the dean of eccentric travelers, for introducing me to pagan tourism; my agent, Elizabeth Sheinkman, who saw the potential; my editor at Random House, Susanna Porter, and her assistant, Matthew Thornton, who knocked the magnum opus into shape; fellow travelers Tom Clines, Sean Doyle, and Joseph Lennon; the hundreds, if not thousands, of historians who have labored mightily on their specialized and profoundly obscure academic texts, often without thanks or recognition; the Writers Room in downtown Manhattan, the true descendant of Alexandria's Museion, a sacred refuge where authors can meet, write, and muse; and Henry Perrottet, for unwittingly setting the whole thing off. And, of course, Lesley Thelander, who was always game on the road, and willing to edit each and every monstrous draft. All of the best jokes in the book are hers.

APPENDIX I: TIMELINE

Early Antiquity: B.C.

c. 2500: Great Pyramid of Egypt completed (zenith of the Old Kingdom).

1504–1450: Pharaoh Thutmose III extends Egyptian Empire to greatest extent (zenith of the New Kingdom).

1500–1100: Rise of Bronze Age cultures on mainland Greece.

1184: Traditional date of the fall of Troy; according to legend, the Trojan prince Aeneas escapes and sails to Italy, where he dreams of a "second Troy."

1100: Jason and the Argonauts sail on a voyage of discovery to the Black Sea.

753: Traditional date for foundation of Rome by Romulus. (Romans are hardworking, thrifty peasants ruled by a series of kings.)

800–550: Age of Greek colonization in the Mediterranean; settlements in Italy around the Bay of Naples and Sicily.

510: Last king of Rome ousted by an aristocratic coup, replaced by rule of Senate and two annually elected consuls. Roman Republic begins.

490–479: Wars between Persians and Greeks; Persians decisively defeated at Salamis.

480–430: Golden Age of Athenian democracy; cultural flowering under leadership of Pericles, including building of the Parthenon. (Rome at this stage is still a shabby outpost by the Tiber.)

431–404: Peloponnesian Wars: Sparta breaks Athenian domination of Aegean.

399: Suicide of Socrates in Athens; his student Plato goes on to found the Academy.

336–323: Alexander the Great creates a vast eastern empire, extending from Greece to Egypt and the frontiers of India.

The Rise of Rome

275: Roman conquest of Italy completed; Rome emerges as a world force.
264–202: Punic Wars; Rome defeats Carthage and begins imperial expansion.
146: Destruction of Corinth confirms Roman conquest of Greece.
80–30: Period of civil wars racks Rome. Major figures such as Julius Caesar, Pompey, Cicero strut the world scene.
44: Caesar murdered in Rome after five years as "dictator for life." Civil wars recommence.
31: Caesar's heir, Octavian, defeats Mark Antony and Cleopatra at battle of Actium and emerges as undisputed ruler of Rome. The lovers commit suicide in Alexandria the following year.

30 B.C.–C. A.D. 200: Heyday of the Roman Empire; Golden Age of Ancient Tourism

27 B.C.: Octavian changes his name to Augustus ("revered") and becomes *Princeps* (First Citizen)—the first Roman emperor.
27 B.C.–A.D. 14: Rule of Augustus. Order and prosperity restored to the Mediterranean; city of Rome beautified; golden age of Roman literature.
Approx 7–2 B.C.: Unveiling of Agrippa's Map.
A.D. 14–37: Tiberius rules as emperor.
37–41: Caligula.
41–54: Claudius.
54–68: Nero.
66–67: Nero's tour of Greece.
69–79: Vespasian.
98–117: Trajan increases Roman Empire to its largest extent. Silver age of literature begins. The next nine decades are the high-water mark of Roman stability.
117–138: Hadrian.
161–180: Marcus Aurelius.
192: Emperor Commodus, gladiator and tyrant, assassinated.

Decline and Fall of the Western Empire

193–211: Septimius Severus takes power after civil wars. Cracks begin to appear in the Pax Romana.

248: Rome celebrates one thousandth anniversary; increasing anarchy and barbarian invasions prompt "third century crisis."

253–69: Goths in the Aegean.

330: Emperor Constantine, a Christian, moves capital of the Empire east to Constantinople (modern-day Istanbul).

410: Rome sacked by Vandals; disintegration of Western Empire. As Byzantium, Constantinople dominates the Eastern Mediterranean for another millennium.

APPENDIX II:
WHO'S WHO IN
THE ANCIENT WORLD

Achilles—The greatest of the Greek heroes in the Trojan War; a nearly invincible killing machine whose rage at being slighted is the subject of the *Iliad*.

Agamemnon—King of Mycenae, leader of the Greeks in the Trojan War; on his return, murdered by his wife and her lover.

Agrippa, Marcus (64–14 B.C.)—Lifelong friend and right-hand man of Augustus (the pair met as students in Athens); initiator of research on the great world map erected in the Vipsania Colonnade. Agrippa was a brilliant naval tactician—Augustus owed his victory over Antony and Cleopatra at Actium to him—and one of the great polymaths of the ancient world. He took a leading role in the urban revitalization of Rome, donating artworks and creating sumptuous public buildings. He never lived to see his famous wall map and commentary; work was completed after his death by Augustus.

Ajax—Greek hero in the Trojan War, immensely strong but rather doltish and emotionally fragile; when the dead Achilles' armor was given to Ulysses, he went mad with anger, attacked local sheep, and then committed suicide.

Ammianus Marcellinus (c. A.D. 330–395)—The last great Latin historian. Traveled widely around the Mediterranean—and, as part of the personal staff to an army general, saw service on many fronts against the invading barbarians. His writings provide vivid descriptions of imperial cities before the fifth-century devastation.

Annaeus Lucanus (Lucan) (A.D. 39–65)—Roman poet, bosom buddy of Nero, best known for an epic about the Civil War, *Pharsalia*. Implicated in a palace conspiracy against the emperor, he was forced to commit suicide by opening his veins.

Apollonius of Tyana (C. A.D. 20–100?)—A famous holy man, the pagan version of St. Paul, Apollonius was a prophet and philosopher who traveled around the known world (apparently even spending time in India). We know about him mostly through a later biography by Philostratus—which, although fictionalized, reveals many naturalistic details, assumptions, and biases of the age.

Apuleius (A.D. 125–c. 180)—A writer from an aristocratic North African family who traveled extensively as a young man before living in Rome and Athens (he was famously charged with performing magic on a widow who married him in Oea). His wonderful comic tale *The Golden Ass* (also known as *Metamorphoses*), in which the narrator is turned by witchcraft into an ass, is the only Latin novel that survives in its entirety.

Aristides (A.D. 117–c. 185)—Brilliant orator and essayist from Asia Minor, whose illness-plagued life did not stop him from traveling the world by land and sea (he went to Rome on several occasions, journeyed around Greece, and said that he sailed along the Nile four times). His dream diary, the *Sacred Discourses*, is a unique ancient document, whose intimacy prefigures the *Confessions* of St. Augustine ("the fullest first-hand report of personal religious experiences which has come down to us from any pagan writer," according to *The Oxford Classical Dictionary*). It also provides a marvelously eccentric travel journal.

Augustine, St. (A.D. 354–430)—Christian bishop who documented his conversion from a lusty pagan youth to righteousness in his autobiographical masterpiece, *Confessions;* lived to see the sack of Rome, provoking his meditation *City of God.*

Augustus (63 B.C.–A.D. 14)—The first emperor of Rome, who presided over the creation of a framework that would last for three centuries. As the grand-nephew, adopted son, and heir of Julius Caesar, he triumphed in the wars against Mark Antony and Cleopatra (commentators often contrasted Antony's hedonism with Augustus' cold austerity). After securing his power in Rome, he ruled for over forty years, and so had the unique opportunity to imprint his political design and secure the Pax Romana.

Aurelius, Marcus (A.D. 121–180)—Roman emperor A.D. 161–180. Perhaps the most admired by posterity of all Roman leaders, as the ultimate philosopher-ruler. Although he led troops against the first great barbarian invasions across the Danube, he loved the life of the mind: His Stoic reflections on human life, *The Meditations*, is still read.

Caesar (100–44 B.C.)—One of the most charismatic and appealing figures of all classical history, Gaius Julius Caesar was the only Roman who could truly compare in stature with Alexander the Great. After a profligate youth, he entered politics and military life, becoming an invincible tactician. In 49 B.C., he emerged as victor of the ongoing civil wars, but his judgment failed him when he took the title "dictator for life" in Rome and began to plan his own deification; his autocratic behavior led to his murder by Brutus et al.

Caligula (A.D. 12–41)—The third Roman emperor, who, after a promising start, began to show signs of insanity, believing himself to be a divine ruler along Egyptian pharaonic lines (incidents of incest and murder are memorably portrayed by John Hurt in the BBC series *I, Claudius*). His travels as a child with his father, Germanicus, may have inspired later plans to put his own head on the statue of Zeus in Olympia and the Sphinx in Egypt. Assassinated by his own palace guards, to few tears.

Cicero (106–43 B.C.)—The ultimate Latin orator, whose astonishing speeches were studied by generations of Roman schoolchildren (as were his private letters, which were copied by his Jeeves-like secretary for posthumous publication).

Claudius (10 B.C.–A.D. 54)—The fourth Roman emperor, immortalized by Robert Graves in his historical novels *I, Claudius* and *Claudius the God*. Lame, stuttering, and reclusive, he found himself proclaimed emperor after Caligula's murder; surprising many, he went on to rule wisely, and to conquer Britain for the Empire.

Cleopatra VII (69–30 B.C.)—Last of the Ptolemies, the Greek-speaking Pharaohs of Egypt. Much maligned by Roman historians as the "monstrous" femme fatale who seduced both Julius Caesar and Mark Antony, Cleopatra was a brilliant diplomat whose aim was to keep Egypt from direct Roman rule. Her greatest gamble, to ally herself with her lover Mark Antony against Octavian, failed—leading to her suicide (the use of a snake may be apocryphal, but has the ring of truth: The cobra was the royal serpent, whose venom was said to guarantee immortality).

Demosthenes (384–322 B.C.)—Greatest orator of classical Athens.

Dionysius "Periegetes" (c. A.D. 90–150?)—Dionysius "the guide," author of a pseudo-epic poem, the *Geographical Description of the Inhabited World,* covers the three continents in 1,185 hexameters.

Galen (A.D. 129–c. 200)—The greatest physician of the early Empire, who developed the idea of the four bodily humors that would dominate Western medicine until the 1800s. Considered eccentric by many for his advocacy of exercise and a vegetarian diet, he wrote three million words on treatments (including an index called *On the Order of His Own Books*). Started his career tending wounded gladiators in Asia Minor, ended it as court physician in Rome to the emperor Marcus Aurelius himself.

Germanicus (16 B.C.–A.D. 19)—Immensely popular young prince groomed for the imperial succession by Augustus. After military successes on the Rhine, he toured the eastern Empire as consul—assiduously taking in every tourist sight from Olympia to the Pyramids—only to contract a mysterious disease in Syria. His death shocked Romans and provoked widespread suspicion that he was murdered in a palace intrigue.

Hadrian (A.D. 76–138)—Roman emperor A.D. 117–38. Remembered as one of the greatest of the "good" emperors, Hadrian was immensely cultured— a daunting philosopher, an accomplished mathematician and musician, a committed Hellenophile, and an inveterate traveler. As ruler, he spent little time in Rome, preferring to set off on long tours of the eastern Empire, largely following the route set by Germanicus.

Hector—The greatest of the Trojan warriors, a family man who opposed the war with the Greeks but took the field out of filial duty. Killed by Achilles in the *Iliad*.

Heliodorus (third century A.D.?)—Syrian Greek novelist; author of *Aethiopica* (*Ethiopian Tales*), an exotic romance considered a classic of the genre. Plenty of pirates, deserts, magic, and gore. One plot element, of a philter that induces deathlike symptoms, was picked up by Shakespeare for *Romeo and Juliet*.

Herodotus (fifth century B.C.)—"Father of history." A Greek from Halicarnassus (Bodrum in modern Turkey) who wrote the first narrative history. The vivid firsthand reports of his journeys to Egypt, around Asia Minor and Greece also qualify him as "the first travel writer"—although many of his anecdotes are subject to exaggeration, they still make a great read, and his account remains a unique source, particularly for life in Egypt.

Homer (eighth century B.C.)—Author of the epics *Iliad* and *Odyssey*—at least according to ancient tradition. Nothing reliable is known about his life. Some modern scholars have suggested the poems were written by different oral bards, or that "Homer" was a composite of several men. But the changes between the poems could easily have occurred in one lifetime, so most experts now agree they were the work of one individual.

Horace (65–8 B.C.)—One of the great poets of the Augustan Age. Remembered for his witty *Satires,* Horace was (according to Suetonius) short, fat, and "immoderately lustful"—lining his bedroom with mirrors to entertain innumerable prostitutes. A part of the clique of writers fostered by Gaius Maecenas—Augustus' cultural talent scout—he was provided with money and a farm in the Sabine Hills where he could write and meditate.

Jason (twelfth century B.C.?)—Leader of the Argonauts in their voyage to find the golden fleece. The mythological version was probably based on a historical figure who led a journey into the Black Sea—the first recorded voyage of exploration.

Julia (39 B.C.–A.D. 14)—The only daughter of the emperor Augustus, and one of the great bon vivants of Roman history. She was witty, learned, charming—and famously promiscuous. When a friend expressed amazement that despite innumerable lovers, all her children looked like her husband, Marcus Agrippa, Julia confided her secret: "I never take on a passenger unless the ship's hold is full." Her father exiled her for adultery.

Juvenal—(A.D. 60–130?) An acerbic satirist whose indignant poetic attacks on the depravity of Roman life rank as the first great rants in Western literature; modern authors as diverse as Sam Johnson, Céline, and George Orwell have cited him as an influence. Little is known of his actual life. If the references in his own work are to be believed, he was an impoverished aristocrat who had traveled to Egypt.

Livy (59 B.C.–A.D. 17)—Magisterial Roman historian of the Augustan Age.

Lucian (A.D. 120–195?)—One of the great literary figures of the second century A.D., Lucian was born in an obscure Syrian town but became a master of the Greek language. He made his name as a traveling orator and lecturer around the Mediterranean before settling in Athens around A.D. 165 and devoting himself to writing skeptical social satires and scabrous fantasies, which would one day influence Swift, Voltaire, and Verne (the adventures of Baron Munchausen were virtually plagiarized from Lucian's "science fiction" works). Appears to have died in Egypt.

Lycurgus (eighth century B.C.?)—According to tradition, the founder of Sparta's militaristic social order.

Martial (A.D. 38–101)—Prodigiously productive Roman poet of the silver age. Born in Spain, he came to Rome in his mid-twenties to "make it" as a writer, falling in with the fashionable authors and patrons of the day; his comic take on life in the imperial capital (particularly the petty humiliations of dependence on wealthy benefactors) would eventually become a key part of the mythology of the city.

Nero (A.D. 37–68)—Fifth emperor of Rome. Although deranged—he murdered his mother and kicked one of his pregnant wives to death—he initiated many projects that were visionary for the time. Mocked by Roman aristocrats for his love of poetry and the lyre, and devotion to Greek culture—rumor had it he sang his epic poem about Troy's fall during the Great Fire of A.D. 64—Nero remained popular with the masses to the end. In a palace coup, he was found hiding in a slave's house: His final words were "What an artist dies with me!" Vividly portrayed by Peter Ustinov in the film *Quo Vadis.*

Ovid (43 B.C.–A.D. 17)—Roman poet best remembered for his erotic tour de force, *The Art of Love,* and the epic *Metamophoses.* Despite his popularity, he was exiled in A.D. 8 by Augustus for a mysterious "error"—possibly a scandal involving the imperial family. The punishment was pointedly cruel: Rome's most urbane poet ended his days in a bleak and rustic village on the Black Sea, at the farthest fringe of the Empire.

Paris—Trojan prince who eloped with the lovely Spartan queen Helen, starting the great war with the Greeks.

Pausanias (A.D. 100–180?)—Author of the only ancient guidebook that survives intact, the *Description of Greece.* Pausanias was in many ways the consummate ancient tourist—an aristocrat born in Asia Minor, refined, erudite, and rather nitpicking. In his youth, he evidently completed the Mediterranean Grand Tour, taking in all the famous sights from Rome to Egypt, but Greece was his forte. He appears to have spent thirty years researching his guide. Like other guidebook writers of that era, Pausanias wrote not for profit but as a scholarly exercise, to share his arcane learning with sophisticated peers.

Pericles (c. 495–429 B.C.)—Athenian politician who led the city during its democratic golden age; initiated many of the most famous building projects, including the Parthenon.

Petronius (c. A.D. 20–66)—Author of the lusty Latin novel *Satyricon* (which survives only in fragmentary form, and was turned into a surreal, disjointed film by Federico Fellini). A senator who became one of the emperor Nero's confidants—and the ultimate arbiter on matters of taste and style—he was implicated in a court conspiracy (probably wrongly) and forced to commit suicide. Despite his debauched and self-indulgent life, he was praised for the dignity in the way he met his death.

Phidias (c. 485–425 B.C.)—Greatest Athenian sculptor, creator of two vast images of Athena on the Acropolis, and the statue of Zeus at Olympia, one of the Seven Wonders of the World.

Philostratus (c. A.D. 180–245)—Author of the *Life of Apollonius of Tyana,* as well as works on Trojan heroes and their cults.

Plato (c. 429–347 B.C.)—One of the greatest Athenian philosophers, student of Socrates, founder of the Academy, author of works at the very basis of the Western tradition—as well as the describer of Atlantis.

Pliny the Elder (A.D. 23–79)—A passionate observer of the world around him, Pliny's thirty-seven-volume encyclopedia, *The Natural History,* is a great, inchoate, and vaguely maddening mass of barely digested data on everything from artworks to minerals, where details often obscure the most exciting material. As a naval admiral in the Bay of Naples, Pliny's curiosity got the better of him during the A.D. 79 eruption of Vesuvius; he landed at Stabiae, became overcome by poisonous gases, and died soon afterward.

Pliny the Younger (A.D. 61–112)—Nephew of Pliny the Elder, prominent literary figure of the Roman silver age. Best known for his books of carefully composed letters, which set out to depict the social conditions of his times.

Plutarch (c. A.D. 45–125)—The most humane of ancient writers, author of the *Parallel Lives,* comparing Greek and Roman celebrities like Caesar and Alexander. A philosopher who had studied in Athens, he lectured in Rome and Egypt, served as a priest at Delphi, then settled down to write in the modest Greek provincial town of Chaeronea. The popularity of his biographies has never waned, from the Middle Ages to modern times.

Praxiteles (fourth century B.C.)—Athenian sculptor who created (among other master works) the *Aphrodite of Knidos,* modeled on his mistress, the courtesan Phryne.

Propertius (c. 50–2 B.C.)—Roman love poet best known for his celebration of his mistress Cynthia. Her rejection sent him on a tour of Greece.

Seneca (A.D. 1–65)—Roman Stoic philosopher who became tutor of the young Nero, and eventually his victim; he was one of many former friends that the emperor accused of treason and forced to commit suicide. His noble death was modeled on Socrates'. Prolific author of ethical treatises, poetry, literary letters, and tragic plays.

Septimius Severus (A.D. 145–211)—Emperor from 193 to 211 A.D., almost as peripatetic as Hadrian. As an overzealous tourist in Egypt, he ordered the broken Colossus of Memnon to be repaired—ending its "miraculous" song forever.

Sophocles (fifth century B.C.)—Greek tragic playwright.

Statius (c. A.D. 50–96)—Poet born in Naples, achieved fame in Rome, returned to Naples in middle age. A passionate Hellenophile and fan of Greek poetry competitions.

Strabo (c. 64 B.C.–A.D. 24)—Author of the seventeen-volume *Geography,* an invaluable source for how the ancients perceived their world. Born in Asia Minor as a Roman citizen, he traveled extensively around the Mediterranean, studying in Rome, exploring Greece, and cruising the Nile. May have retired to Naples.

Suetonius (c. A.D. 70–130)—Latin biographer, whose *Lives of the Caesars* collates almost every possible rumor into a marvelously scandalous account.

Tacitus (c. A.D. 56–120)—Greatest Roman historian of the early Empire, and one of the finest of all Latin prose stylists. Friend of Pliny the Younger, Martial, et al.

Thucydides (c. 460–400 B.C.)—Revered Greek author of the *History of the Peloponnesian War.*

Tiberius (42 B.C.–A.D. 37)—Second Roman emperor (A.D. 14–37), unpopular for his dour and reclusive nature. In A.D. 27, he retired to the island of Capri, governing the Empire from afar; rumors of his vice-ridden exile quickly proliferated.

Trajan (A.D. 53–117)—Roman emperor A.D. 98–117. Remembered as one of the finest rulers, a career army officer whose reign marked the greatest expansion of Rome's domain (in the east, he reached the Persian Gulf, but the gains were soon abandoned).

Varro (116–27 B.C.)—The most accomplished of Roman antiquarians, who wrote two vast works on the artifacts of Rome, human and divine (now lost).

Virgil (70–19 B.C.)—The most illustrious Latin poet of the Augustan Age, author of the *Aeneid,* an epic poem designed to rival Homer's *Iliad* and *Odyssey.* Virgil was born near Mantua, lived near Rome, studied in Greece, and worked in Naples. He went on a three-year fact-finding trip to Asia Minor and Greece, but contracted a fever overseas and died.

APPENDIX III: SOURCES

Although this is a popular rather than scholarly account, I have made every effort to ensure that my reconstruction of the ancient world is historically accurate.

My research was built on the two fundamental works about Roman tourism. The first was the German historian Ludwig Friedländer's obscure but brilliantly vivid classic *Darstllungen aus der Sittengeschichte Roms,* translated in 1913 as *Roman Life and Manners Under the Early Empire* (London: Routledge and Sons); I found a rare leather-bound copy in the New York Public Library, although every time I turned one of the dusty pages, it almost snapped like a wafer. The second invaluable foundation was Lionel Casson's *Travel in the Ancient World* (London: Allen and Unwin, 1974); the chapters on the Pax Romana remain the finest—and wittiest—modern account of the tourist landscape in the imperial era. Indeed, without the groundbreaking work of Casson's oeuvre, which covers ancient sea travel, trade, communications, and exploration, this book could not have been written.

For my reconstruction of Agrippa's Map, I relied on the unique work of three historians: O.A.W. Dilke (*Greek and Roman Maps* [London: Thames and Hudson, 1985], and his chapters in *The History of Cartography,* vol. 1, J. B. Hartley and David Woodward, eds. [Chicago: University of Chicago Press, 1987]); Claude Nicolet (*Space, Geography and Politics in the Early Roman Empire* [Ann Arbor: University of Michigan Press, 1991]); and R. Moynihan ("Geographical Mythology and Roman Imperial Ideology" in *The Age of Augustus,* Rolf Winkes, ed. [Providence, R.I.: Brown University, 1985]). Moynihan's assessment of the Map's size seems to me the most accurate; given the two decades it took to complete, it seems probable that the mural employed all the lavish artistry at the emperor's command. (Sadly, Agrippa did not live to see his masterwork finished.)

No Roman-era world maps have survived, but reconstructions have been made from the many literary geographies of the era. I chose to reproduce at the beginning of this book the aesthetically pleasing reconstruction of Dionysius Periegetes' vision of the world (reproduced from E. H. Bunbury, *A History of Ancient Geography* [London, 1879]) above some of the more angular and clumsy versions of Agrippa's Map, because ancient sources repeatedly refer to the world as oval and shaped smoothly, "like a sling bullet."

As for the Roman road map known as the Peutinger Table, a fine reproduction was released by Italian academics (*La Tabula Peutingeriana* [Bologna: Edison, 1978]); it is available for inspection in the Map Room of the New York Public Library.

For Latin and Greek texts, I relied on the following stellar editions: Apuleius, *The Golden Ass,* translated by Robert Graves (Noonday Press, 1998); Aristides, *The Complete Works,* translated by Charles A. Behr (Leiden, Brill, 1981); Heliodorus, *An Ethiopian Romance,* translated by Moses Hadas (University of Pennsylvania Press, 1999); Juvenal, *The Sixteen Satires,* translated by Peter Green (Penguin, 1967); Lucian, *Works,* translated by A. M. Harmon (Loeb Classical Library, Harvard University Press, 1913); Petronius, *The Satyricon,* translated by J. P. Sullivan (Penguin, 1965); Philostratus, *The Life of Apollonius of Tyana,* translated by F. C. Conybeare (Loeb Classical Library, 1912); Tacitus, *The Annals of Imperial Rome,* translated by Michael Grant (Penguin, 1956). The Martial poem quoted in the Naples chapter is slightly adapted from Garrett Fagan's use in his excellent book on the Greco-Roman baths, cited below. For many of the more obscure references to ancient inn signs, graffiti, and the like, I have often deferred to the musical ear of the maestro, Lionel Casson. Of the dozens of translations of Homer's *Illiad,* I have relied on my personal favorite, by Stanley Lombardo (Hachett Publishing, 2000). The most appealing translation of the *Description of Greece* by Pausanias is still the Victorian-era six-volume set by Sir James Frazer (Biblo and Tannen, 1965); the erudite and arcane commentary is extraordinary in itself. The traveler might well prefer the more concise, two-volume translation by Peter Levi (Penguin, 1971).

There has been a profusion of academic works on the history of tourism in recent years; the most stimulating is *Voyages and Visions: Towards a Cultural History of Travel,* edited by Jas Elsner and Joan-Pau Rubies (London: Reaktion Books, 1999), which explores the conflicting traditions of Western tourism.

Academic works on Imperial Rome today tend to be extremely specific; in piecing together a synthesis of the ancient world, I consulted innumerable books.

A partial bibliography follows.

Alcock, S. *Graecia Capta: The Landscapes of Roman Greece*. Cambridge, U.K.: Cambridge University Press, 1993.

Arafat, K. W. *Pausanias' Greece*. Cambridge, U.K.: Cambridge University Press, 1996.

Birley, A. R. *Hadrian: The Restless Emperor*. New York: Routledge, 1997.

————. *Septimius Severus: The African Emperor*. London: Eyre and Spottiswoode, 1971.

Bowersock, G. W. *Augustus and the Greek World*. Oxford: Clarendon, 1965.

Carcopino, Jerome. *Daily Life in Ancient Rome*. New Haven, Conn.: Yale University Press, 1968.

Casson, Lionel. *The Ancient Mariners: Seafarers and Sea Fighters of the Mediterranean*. Princeton, N.J.: Princeton University Press, 1991.

————. *Everyday Life in Ancient Rome*. Baltimore: Johns Hopkins University Press, 1999.

————. *Ships and Seafaring in Ancient Times*. London: British Museum Press, 1994.

Chauveau, M. *Egypt in the Age of Cleopatra*. Ithaca, N.Y.: Cornell University Press, 2000.

D'Arms, John. *Romans on the Bay of Naples*. Cambridge, Mass.: Harvard University Press, 1980.

Dalby, Andrew. *Siren Feasts: A History of Food and Gastronomy in Greece*. New York: Routledge, 1996.

Dalby, Andrew, and Sally Grainger. *The Classical Cookbook*. Los Angeles: Getty Museum, 1996.

Daly, L. W. "Roman Study Abroad." *American Journal of Philology* 71 (1950), pp. 40–58.

Davidson, James. *Courtesans and Fishcakes: Consuming Passions of Classical Athens*. New York: Thomas Dunne, 1997.

Edelstein, Emma J. and Ludwig. *Asclepius: Collection and Interpretation of the Testimonies*. Baltimore: Johns Hopkins University Press, 1998.

Edwards, Catharine. *Writing Rome: Textual Approaches to the City*. Cambridge, U.K.: Cambridge University Press, 1996.

Empereur, Jean-Yves. *Alexandria Rediscovered*. New York: George Brazillier Publishers, 1998.

Fagan, G. *Bathing in Public in the Roman World*. Ann Arbor: University of Michigan Press, 1999.

Favro, Diane. *The Urban Image of Augustan Rome*. Cambridge, U.K.: Cambridge University Press, 1996.

Fear, A. T. "The Dancing Girls of Cadiz," *Greece and Rome* 39 (1991).

Finley, M. I., and H. W. Pleket. *The Olympic Games: The First Thousand Years*. London: Chatto and Windus, 1976.

Fortemeyer, Victoria. "Tourism in Graeco-Roman Egypt," Ph.D. dissertation, Princeton University, 1989.

Graf, Fritz. *Magic in the Ancient World,* Cambridge, Mass.: Harvard University Press, 1999.

Greaves, Denise. "Dionysius Periegetes and the Hellenistic Poetic and Geographical Traditions," Ph.D. dissertation, Stanford University, 1994.

Hall, Sir Peter. *Cities in Civilization.* New York: Pantheon, 1998.

Hamblin, Dora, and Mary Jane Grunsfeld. *The Appian Way: A Journey.* New York: Random House, 1974.

Hornblower, Simon, and Antony Spawforth (eds.). *The Oxford Classical Dictionary.* 3rd ed. New York: Oxford University Press, 1996.

Hurwit, Jeffrey M. *The Athenian Acropolis: History, Mythology and Archaeology from the Neolithic Era to the Present.* Cambridge, U.K.: Cambridge University Press, 1999.

Kaimio, J. *The Romans and the Greek Language.* Helsinki: Societas Scientiarum Fennica, 1979.

Kyle, Donald. *Spectacles of Death in Ancient Rome.* New York: Routledge, 1998.

Liversidge, Michael, and Catherine Edwards. *Imagining Rome: British Artists and Rome in the Nineteenth Century.* Bristol: Bristol City Museum, 1996.

MacCannell, Dean. *The Tourist: A New Theory of the Leisure Class.* Berkeley: University of California Press, 1999.

Paget, R. F. *In the Footsteps of Orpheus.* London: Hale, 1967.

Parke, H. W. *Sibyls and Sibylline Prophecy.* New York: Routledge, 1988.

Potter, D. *Prophecy and History in the Crisis of the Roman Empire.* New York: Oxford University Press, 1990.

Romm, James S. *The Edges of the Earth in Ancient Thought.* Princeton, N.J.: Princeton University Press, 1992.

Said, Edward. *Orientalism.* London: Penguin, 1995.

Schobel, Heinz. *The Ancient Olympic Games.* Princeton, N.J.: Van Nostrand, 1966.

Swain, Simon. *Hellenism and Empire.* New York: Oxford University Press, 1996.

Toner, J. P. *Leisure and Ancient Rome.* Cambridge, Mass.: Polity, 1995.

Von Martels, Z. (ed.). *Travel Fact and Travel Fiction.* New York: E. J. Brills, 1994.

Walker, Susan (ed.). *Ancient Faces: Mummy Portraits from Roman Egypt.* New York: Metropolitan Museum of Art, 2000.

Warmington, B. H. *Nero, Reality and Legend.* London: Chatto and Windus, 1969.

Wishart, David. *Germanicus.* London: Scepter, 1997.

Wood, Michael. *In Search of the Trojan War.* Berkeley: University of California Press, 1998.

INDEX

Note: Page numbers in *italics* refer to illustrations.

PERMISSIONS

Grateful acknowledgment is made to the following for permission to use illustrative material.

Frontispiece and title page, and p. 133: courtesy of Austrian National Library, Vienna; pp. 43, 52, 59, 87, 110, 117, 120, 145, 167, 173, 216, 244, 269, 292, 294, 305, 335, 336, and 349: courtesy of the author; p. 2: from Edward Herbert Bunbury, *A History of Ancient Geography Amongst Greeks and Romans from the Earliest Ages till the Fall of the Roman Empire,* vol. 2, London, 1883; p. 9: Phil Woods, Apa Photo Library, London; p. 16: courtesy of the Metropolitan Museum of Art: left (young man), gift of the Egyptian Research Account and the British School of Archaeology, 1912 11.139 (detail), and right (young woman), Rogers Fund, 1909 09.181.6; p. 18: courtesy of the Montreal Museum of Fine Arts, purchase, Horsley and Annie Townsend Bequest; pp. 29, 49, 66, 194, 240, and 291: courtesy of Photofest; p. 77: courtesy of the Philadelphia Museum of Art, George W. Ekins Collection; p. 122: courtesy of the Metropolitan Museum of Art, purchase, 1890, Levi Hale Willard Bequest 90.35.3; p. 153: courtesy Guildhall Art Gallery, Corporation of London; p. 205: drawing © Lesley Thelander; p. 210: courtesy of the Hood Museum of Art, Dartmouth College, Hanover, New Hampshire, gift of Arthur M. Leow, Class of 1912A; p. 218: courtesy of the Board of Trustees of the National Museums and Galleries on Merseyside (Lady Lever Art Gallery, Port Sunlight); p. 223: courtesy of Collection of Phoenix Art Museum, Museum Purchase; p. 273: courtesy of Discovery Channel; p. 299: AKG Photo Library, London.